COLLEGE STUDENTS: THE EVOLVING NATURE OF RESEARCH

Edited by
Frances K. Stage
Guadalupe L. Anaya
John P. Bean
Don Hossler
George D. Kuh

Series Editor:
Barbara Townsend

ASHE READER SERIES

SIMON & SCHUSTER CUSTOM PUBLISHING

10 9 8 7 6 5 4 3 2 1

ISBN 0–536–59088–5
BA 0170

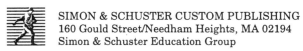
SIMON & SCHUSTER CUSTOM PUBLISHING
160 Gould Street/Needham Heights, MA 02194
Simon & Schuster Education Group

COPYRIGHT ACKNOWLEDGMENTS

Contents

PART III   THE DEVELOPMENTAL EXPERIENCE

PART IV   SUMMARY AND REFLECTIONS

Acknowledgments

We would like to thank Flo Hamrick, doctoral candidate, for very helpful suggestions on an earlier draft of our introductory chapter and help in gathering materials for this volume. We would also like to thank Barbara Townsend, Memphis State University, the editor of the ASHE Reader series, and Kathleen Kourian, Senior Editor, Simon and Schuster, for their support, suggestions, and encouragement throughout. In addition, we are grateful to colleagues who assisted in the selection of the readings included in this volume: Marilyn Amey, University of Kansas; Sandy Astin, UCLA; Alberto F. Cabrera, Arizona State University-West; Harold Cheatham, Pennsylvania State University; Nancy Evans, Pennsylvania State University; James Hearn, University of Georgia; Sylvia Hurtado, UCLA; Patricia King, Bowling Green State University; Kathleen Manning, University of Vermont; Amaury Nora, University of Illinois-Chicago; Ernest Pascarella, University of Illinois-Chicago; John H. Schuh, Wichita State University; Daryl Smith, Claremont Graduate School; Daniel Solorzano, UCLA; Patrick Terenzini, Pennsylvania State University; Melvin Terrell, Northeastern Illinois University; Caroline Turner, University of Minnesota; Lee Upcraft, Pennsylvania State University; and Elizabeth J. Whitt, University of Illinois-Chicago.

The ASHE Reader Series

The ASHE Reader Series presents a collection of high quality readers on topics of sweeping interest in today's higher education scene. The books are designed to be used as supplementary text material in courses in the field of higher education or as reference. They reflect the collective ideas of those who teach in particular areas.

NEW! TEACHING AND LEARNING IN THE COLLEGE CLASSROOM
Edited by Kenneth A. Feldman and Michael B. Paulsen

A comprehensive review of classic and recent research in the area, TEACHING AND LEARNING IN THE COLLEGE CLASSROOM addresses issues from diverse theoretical and philosophical perspectives. Each section includes quantitative and qualitative research, a separate introductory essay, research reports, literature reviews, theoretical essays, and practitioner-oriented articles. It emphasizes teacher-student and student-student interaction. It considers multicultural and gender issues and contains practical teaching strategies based on research.

Paperbound 704 pages ISBN 0-536-58535-0

NEW! ASSESSMENT AND PROGRAM EVALUATION
Edited by Joan S. Stark and Alice Thomas

This reader effectively provides the broad perspective necessary for the study of assessment by consolidating articles from a wide range of sources, some not easily obtained. By addressing such topics as the historical and philosophical context and ethical issues, this volume will help readers develop the necessary assessment skills, attitudes and knowledge to conduct and supervise studies and program reviews or to be informed clients inside or outside the academic environment.

Paperbound 832 pages ISBN 0-536-58586-5

COMMUNITY COLLEGES
Edited by James L. Ratcliff

This updated edition includes new information on the diversity of the student population and features a special focus on community college scholarship and faculty renewal. It will give you and your students a review of the current community college systems in American history, philosophy, and purpose: organization, administration, and finance; programs and services; students; professional staff; and the social role.

Paperbound 503 pages ISBN 0-536-58571-7

QUALITATIVE RESEARCH IN HIGHER EDUCATION:
Experiencing Alternative Perspectives and Approaches

Edited by Clifton E. Conrad, Anna Neuman, Jennifer Grant Haworth, and Patricia Scott

Designed to help students and teachers prepare for, enter into, participate in, reflect on, and give voice to the experience of doing qualitative research. Organized around six topics: Explicating Frames of Reference, Approaching Inquiry, Doing Fieldwork, Interacting with Self and Other, Creating a Text, Reading a Text.

Paperbound 600 pages ISBN 0-536-58417-0

WOMEN IN HIGHER EDUCATION: A Feminist Perspective

Edited by Judith Glazer, Estela Bensimon, and Barbara Townsend

Essays representing the best of feminist scholarship in the field of higher education on four main themes: Theoretical and Research Perspectives, Context Historical, Social, and Professional, Institutional, Women in Academe: As Student, Faculty, Administrators, and Trustees, and The Transformation of Knowledge: Circular Change and Feminist Pedagogy.

Paperbound 600 pages ISBN 0-536-58351-0

FOUNDATIONS OF AMERICAN HIGHER EDUCATION

Edited by James L. Bess

A comprehensive introduction to the basics of American higher education—45 articles by some of today's most respected leaders in the field, in six parts: The Scope of Higher Education in American Society, The Participants, The Conduct of Education and Research, The Management of the College or University, Innovation, Change, and the Future, The Study and Practice of Higher Education Administration.

Paperbound 772 pages ISBN 0-536-58013-8

THE HISTORY OF HIGHER EDUCATION

Edited by Lester E. Goodchild and Harold S. Wechsler

Included are an introductory essay on American higher education historiography; introductory overviews of each of the five chronological periods of higher education; in-depth scholarly analyses from journal articles, book chapters, and essays; and the use of primary readings to capture the flavor and meaning of important issues for each period.

Paperbound 675 pages ISBN 0-536-57566-5

ORGANIZATION AND GOVERNANCE IN HIGHER EDUCATION, Fourth Edition

Edited by Marvin W. Peterson, with Associate Editors Ellen E. Chaffee and Theodore H. White

The selections not only reflect the changing views of colleges and universities as organizations, but also highlight the areas of literature applied to higher education that need to be addressed. The text is divided into three parts: Organization Theory and Models, Governance and Management Processes, and Leadership Perspectives.

Paperbound 475 pages ISBN 0-536-57981-4

FINANCE IN HIGHER EDUCATION

Edited by Dave Breneman, Larry L. Leslie and Richard E. Anderson

> Practical and theoretical, the selections look at the financial management of colleges and universities, higher education economies, and federal and state policies, and represent a number of divergent perspectives and opinions.

> Paperbound 450 pages ISBN 0-536-58352-8

UPCOMING TITLES IN THE SERIES:
MINORITIES IN HIGHER EDUCATION: A HISTORY

Edited by Caroline Turner, Mildred Garcia, Laura Rendón, and Amaury Nora

ISBN 0-536-59003-6

FACULTY AND FACULTY ISSUES IN COLLEGES AND UNIVERSITIES

Edited by Dorothy E. Finnegan, David Webster, and Zelda F. Gamson

To Order:

To order copies of these titles for your class, please contact your campus bookstore and provide them with the quantity and ISBN. You can receive a complimentary desk copy with an order of 10 or more copies.

To order copies for yourself, simply call Simon & Schuster Custom Publishing at 800-428-4466 (or 617-455-7000 in Massachusetts and Canada) from 8:30 to 5:00 EST.

A Transformational View of College Student Research

FRANCES K. STAGE AND GUADALUPE ANAYA

Research on the college student experience has been conducted since at least 1900. The methodological evolution of that research has been discussed extensively (Attinasi & Nora, 1990; Feldman & Newcomb, 1969; 1994; Pascarella & Terenzini, 1991). Currently sophisticated models simulate college outcome processes and complex theories describe the epistemological, moral, and emotional development of college students. Indeed Pascarella and Terenzini's (1991) review of the literature, *How College Affects Students*, contained nearly 3000 entries on college student research. We have, so to speak, an "embarrassment of riches" in terms of the volume of research that exists. However, we can speak confidently of only a few conclusions. For example, the research tells us that college outcomes for students who are not part of the elite still lag behind outcomes for those who are. Research also tells us that African-American college students, in general, are far more comfortable in the historically black college environment than at predominantly white institutions. Additionally, research tells us that women college students, in contrast to men, experience reductions in academic self esteem during the college years, unless they attend a women only college. Perhaps we can think of a few other 'truths', the point is, our knowledge about college students is incomplete and the applications of this knowledge apparently have little effect on practice (Conrad, 1989; Keller, 1985). Research does not tell us much that has made an appreciable difference in changing these realities.

While these gaps in our understanding of college students might be viewed as depressing or discouraging by some, they can also be viewed as opportunities to reinvent ourselves and our craft. We view the research process as dynamic and evolving. As in biological evolution, the earliest, sometimes faltering, sometimes eloquent attempts to explain the college students' realities as important as any of the hundreds of attempts generated currently.

In this volume, we hope to highlight the latest in college student research in an effort to inspire both future researchers and future administrators. For the researchers, we hope these exemplars will generate new questions and suggest new ways to address old questions. For administrators, we hope to inspire new ways of conceptualizing solutions to campus problems and to empower them to ask even more difficult questions of the research community. We envision a future where researchers and practitioners draw closely together and inform one another as they go about their respective businesses. To this end we have included articles from several genres: 1) works that might be characterized as summarizations of traditional college student research, 2) works that are transformational, particularly those focusing on populations that are just now beginning to receive attention in college student research, and 3) works that critique the status quo in college student research and challenge us to reexamine our ways of viewing the research enterprise. The two latter types of articles, we argue, are necessary given changing demographics. The volume begins to address a host of questions posed by thousands of individuals seeking an understanding of our college students. This introduction and the readings are part of set of building blocks for a research future that is dynamic and evolving. In this introduction we hope to set the stage for the volume by presenting a template against which to view college student research. All of us, new scholars as well as seasoned researchers, are poised at a transition point. The purpose of this introductory chapter is to discuss the alternate and emerging, as opposed to conventional, perspectives. We call these perspectives transformational. But first, we juxtapose today's reality and the history of college student research.

A Current Reality

Much existing research on college students emulates previous research and describes current conditions on college campuses reinforcing our existing knowledge base. Researchers find that variables measuring family educational level, social status, gender, race, and ethnicity continue to exert strong influence whether modeling choice and predisposition to attend college (Hamrick & Hossler, in press; Hossler, Braxton & Coopersmith, 1989), math/science major choice (Maple & Stage, 1991; Oakes, 1990), persistence (Stage, 1989), or status attainment after graduation (Smart & Pascarella, 1986). With our accumulated wealth of research, we have not yet learned how to equalize the opportunities that college presents. In other words, we are good at documenting and observing factors and effects, but not as good at proffering advice that helps change the status quo.

The changing socio-economic conditions and demographics of our country will continue to be felt on our college campuses. More than half the college going population has been women since 1980 (Sagaria, 1988). An ever increasing wave of students of color is projected to be the norm for the next thirty to fifty years (at which time people of color will comprise the numerical majority in our society). These groups, women, the poor, and those of color have often been relegated to the fringes of the academy, but they have not ceased to examine their human experiences. The disenfranchised have often attempted to communicate to others "the experiences which divide us . . . to examine the incidents of intolerance, prejudice and denial of differences . . . to explore the causes and sources of, and solutions to these divisions" (Moraga & Anzaldua, 1981), in essence to present perspective on their lives. To understand the new American college students we must continue to unearth and to examine the perspectives of our new students. The information and knowledge that we have is of limited relevance for the current college population. As things stand currently, we know little about the development and experiences of most of our college students.

The changing face of American college students is demonstrated clearly by the figures in Table l. In 1966 White students made up 90.7% of the college population and Women comprised only 44.4%. The proportion of Women reached a peak by 1980 at over 51%. Latinos were not counted until the changes made in the 1970 census forms. However, Native Americans, African-Americans, and Asian-Americans were being counted and in 1966 they made up 0.6%, 5.0%, and 0.7% of the student population, respectively. The Higher Education Act of 1965 (Title IV, subpart 4), made it possible for larger numbers of students of color to attend college, particularly those who were first generation college students and from low-income families. Thus, by 1975 the proportion of African-American students reached its peak at 9.2%. The proportion of Asian-American students has increased slowly but continuously and continues to do so well into this decade. Unfortunately, the proportion of Native-Americans (below 1 %) and of Latina/o (approximately 1.5%) students has not changed appreciably.

The new profile of America's college students propels us toward different perspectives.

Background

Until approximately fifteen years ago, most college student research resembled current medical research, largely the study of white males (Goodman, 1990). Much of this research was completed in elite institutions (e.g., Abel, 1966; Chickering, 1984; Iffert, 1958; Kamens, 1974; Rootman, 1972; Spady, 1971). This early descriptive and correlational research shaped models of college student development and causal models of student outcomes and are the bases of much of what we know

Table 1
Enrollment Patterns for First-time Full-time Freshmen.*

	1966	1970	1975	1980	1985	1989	1994
White	90.7	89.2	86.5	86.0	86.2	84.3	81.5
African-American	5.0	6.0	9.0	9.2	9.1	9.2	10.0
Asian-American	0.7	1.1	1.5	1.4	2.0	2.9	4.2
Chicano/Mexican-American	—	—	1.7	2.1	1.2	1.4	2.3
Native-American	0.6	0.8	0.9	0.8	1.0	0.9	1.1
Puerto Rican	—	—	0.7	0.9	0.6	0.8	0.7
Women	44.4**	45.2	46.8	51.5	51.8	53.79	53.58
18 yrs. or younger	81.7	77.1	77.4	75.3	74.7	74.5	68.8

*Source: American Council on Education (1966, 1970, 1975, 1980, 1985, 1989, & 1990). *The American Freshman.* UCLA: Higher Education Research Institute. Cooperative Institutional Research Program.
**ibid., 1967.

about today's college student. Gaps in our knowledge about students stemmed from a set of common research practices in education and psychology in particular, and in the social sciences in general. For example, psychologists commonly assumed the universality of their theories. That is, they generated theories based on observations of human behavior and development of a limited sample, often White middle or upper class males. They proclaimed that their data or theory applied to all human beings regardless of gender, culture, race, or national identity. In fact the research reported in American Psychological Association journals has recently been characterized as research on human behavior conducted with White subjects (Graham, 1992). From this point of reference, researchers often proceed to study the 'other': people of color, women, the disenfranchised. Thus everyone's life is then examined in a comparative framework with the norms based on samples of White middle class subjects (most often males). Naturally, diverse persons and diverse experiences often appear as other than 'normal'.

A second major contributor to our lack of knowledge is the failure of social scientists to examine socio-cultural factors (Betancourt & Lopez, 1993; Garza & Lipton, 1982, Hernandez, 1970). Social science and education research has indeed set out to account for socio-cultural differences but has summarily failed to do so. Basically racial or cultural factors that are typically included in sets of independent variables generally go no further than identifying membership in a particular racial or cultural group. Thus, the data can only point to relationships between these group characteristics and social or educational factors. We are able to say only, for example, that race is associated with a particular variable(s) or outcome(s) but mere association is insufficient to our understanding of why the association exists. This invariably leads to a dangerous simplification of the pictures we paint about individuals. In the end we are still unable to explain the observed differences associated with culture or with race.

The research problems discussed above permeate our curriculum and continue to spill over into educational research and our knowledge base on college students. Let us provide two simple examples, the first from our personal experience with curriculum. While pursuing doctorate degrees we studied the history of higher education text, Brubacher and Rudy (1976). Of over 500 pages only five were devoted to women's colleges and coeducation. The history of traditionally black institutions was covered in a few sentences. Eight years later, while preparing to teach higher education courses, we learned the history of women in higher education from historians Horowitz (1986) and Solomon (1985). As a second example, a simple review of the subject indices of major volumes on colleges students, provides a poignant example of the source of our problems in understanding students of color.

The problems with our knowledge base and with the current research are in part due to the absence of research that includes diverse college student groups. A small but significant body of work does exist but, in the academic marketplace of salience and citation, many of these works are undervalued. In fact, it is not difficult to apprehend the actual status of the research on diverse college student groups because such research is unfamiliar to most of us and therefore underutilized by both researchers and practitioners. Early works provided descriptive background on women (e.g., Blandin, 1909; Olin 1909; Starrett, 1896; Talbot, 1936) that was similar to research on white men conducted during the same period. And just 35 years ago Greenleaf (1952), Komarovsky (1953), Mueller (1954), and Noble (1956) all conducted studies focusing specifically on women and their issues. Similarly, Scales' (1960) study of African American college student retention and other studies (Allman, 1960; Gaier & Watts, 1969; Hare, 1965; Hope, 1961; Pitman, 1960; Roth, 1961) focusing on African American students during that time period, remain uncited in subsequent literature reviews.

Today one can find a sparse but continuous stream of research on women college students (e.g., Belenky, Clinchy, Goldberger & Tarule, 1986; Gilligan, 1982; Komarovsky, 1985; Sagaria, 1988), on African American students [e.g., Allen, Epps & Haniff, 1991; Altbach and Lomotey, 1991; D'Augelli & Hershberger, 1993; Hood, 1992; Fleming, 1984; Kobrak, 1992; Nyankori, 1991; Robinson, 1990; Sedlacek, 1987; Washington & Newman, 1991] and on Latina/o students (e.g. Aguirre, & Martinez, 1993; Duran, 1983; Lopez, Madrid-Barela, & Macias, 1976; and Olivas, 1986). However, a much larger lacuna exists in the research on students who are Native-American, low SES, gay-lesbian-bisexual (Evans, & Wall, 1991) and others who, for reasons of physical characteristics or culture, might be disenfranchised by the dominant culture. Until recently, however, these works seemed to have small informational and methodological impact on the field of higher education and the study of college students.

A Perspective on Research

To define transformational research, we paraphrase Delgado (1984), Harding (1987) and Townsend (1992) and borrow from the work of Banks (1993). Transformational research may be characterized by the following features: 1) all students' experiences are viewed as source and subject of pertinent facts, priorities, and research problems, 2) the resulting research is to provide useful and helpful explanations of these problems, and 3) the researcher is neither objective nor distanced from those who are the focus of the research but is "in the same critical plane" (p. 11). In fact the lack of "empathy, and inability to share the values, desires, and perspectives" (Delgado, 1984) of the group being studied can sometimes be a major source of problems for the researcher both practically and interpretively.

Scholarly views of college students' experiences can be classified in a way that loosely resembles an evolution gradually leading to transformational perspectives. Most research on college students can be classified according to one of the following: 1) students' experiences (often elite males) are generalizable to all other students' experiences, 2) gender, ethnicity, and socioeconomic status are used as explanatory variables, 3) alternative models based on early models are created, 3B) models are created based on knowledge gained within transformational perspectives, 4) individual students' experiences are described and valued in their own right, and 5) social issues are addressed within the context of research (See Table 2).

We call the first three views conventional perspectives. They constitute necessary steps in a progression of awareness within a society that initially valued understanding of primarily the elite male experience partly because that was who college students used to be. Within these earlier perspectives researchers often ignored the possibility of differences among students. Research conducted within later perspectives seeks to understand such differences.

Perspective 3B is located between the conventional and transformative perspectives. It represents a link between the two; models created here are based on knowledge generated in perspectives 4 and 5. Additionally, using different methods and assumptions, builds on the techniques and rich history of college student research. Ideally, it represents the cyclical nature of knowledge accumulation as researchers learn from and inform all perspectives. The final two perspectives are necessary and mutually supportive of one another in attempts to describe and transform the status quo.

Table 2
Research Perspectives on Student's College Experiences

Conventional

1. Student's experiences (often elite males) are generalizable to all other students' experiences.

2. Gender, ethnicity, and socioeconomic status are used as explanatory variables or separate analyses are conducted for each group.

3. Alternative models based on early models are created.

— — — — — — — — — — — — — — — — — —

Transformational

3B. Models are created based on knowledge gathered within the transformational perseptives.

4. Individual students' experiences are described and valued in their own right.

5. Social issues are addressed within the research context.

These perspectives can be used as a framework to describe an evolution in the study of the college student and to influence research of the future the topic of the next section.

Research on Student Outcomes and Development

Students' experiences (often elite males) are generalizable to all other students' experiences. Much of today's research on college student outcomes is heavily influenced by causal modeling structures presented in the 1970s (Bean, 1980; Spady, 1971; Tinto, 1975) and tested in the eighties. For the most part, these models were based on research conducted prior to 1975. Frequently, studies of college students cited as foundations for these models, were actually studies of men and usually at relatively elite institutions. For example, Pervin and Rubin (1967) studied men at Princeton University and Rootman (1972) conducted studies at the United States Coast Guard Academy. The influential Spady (1971) work, precursor to the Tinto model, examined experiences of students at the University of Chicago of whom 62% were men; the percentage of ethnic minorities was not reported but was likely very low. Spady included a measure (not unusual for the time) "religious-ethnic origin (Jewish, Gentile, and other)" (p. 41).

Similarly, foundational research for student development theories were based on studies of males most often attending elite universities (Kohlberg, 1972; Perry, 1970). As college students became increasingly female, knowledge of men's college experience was extrapolated by researchers to women without questioning its relevance. For the most part, this work represents the first perspective, that students' experiences (often elite males) are generalizable to all students. As colleges became increasingly diverse, that information was often applied to other students as well.

Gender, ethnicity, and socioeconomic status are used as explanatory variables or separate analyses are conducted for each group. Some researchers recognized that theories and knowledge derived from these early studies did not always match other students' experiences. Gender, ethnicity, and socioeconomic status were then frequently added as explanatory variables. These studies included a wide range of research on college students. This perspective initially included comparisons of mean scores of men and women or of ethnic minority and majority students. Correlations of gender, ethnicity, and SES with outcomes began to be included in studies. Such studies were able to demonstrate that significant differences in college student experiences across various groups existed, but lacked the robustness to account for observed differences.

Alternative models based on earlier models are created. The third perspective represents a transition to transformational perspectives on college student research. Research of this type also employed regression and structural models to simulate educational processes separately for varying groups of students (Pascarella & Terenzini, 1979; Stage, 1989). This line of research is characterized in general by a dualist perspective that demonstrates women's, ethnic minorities' and other diverse students' experiences as discrepant from original theories. The models and assumptions from the earlier perspectives became the bases for comparison. Unsurprisingly this research, based on models from the first two perspectives, resulted in discrepancies when analyzed separately for nonmainstream groups of students. Typically, even when sample sizes were similar, fewer explanatory variables were significant and percentages of explained variance were low when compared mainstream groups (Maple & Stage, 1991). In others words, the models poorly explained educational processes for nonmainstream groups of students; something was missing.

In a further iteration of this stage researchers also attempted to create alternative models relying extensively on what was known about mainstream models and combining that with other kinds of literature on nonmainstream students (Bean & Metzner, 1985; Chacon, Cohen & Strover, 1986). The more skilled researchers became at codifying and describing what they knew, the more they realized how little we knew about many students (Stage, 1990, 1994). Addressing the scarcity of information on minority students after reviewing thousands of articles, Pascarella and Terenzini (1991) declare "Certainly more research is needed to clarify the nature of the college experience and its effects on cognitive and social change among nonwhite students." (p. 644) This dissatisfaction with conventional research conducted within these perspectives sometimes leads to research employing differing ways of gathering information.

Researchers are currently moving from these earlier, narrow views in their models and gradually considering ever-widening ways of describing and analyzing relationships. As we begin to incorporate new knowledge generated by transformational perspectives on research, researchers in the third perspective form a nexus between the conventional and the transformational.

Models are created based on knowledge gathered within transformational perspectives. This perspective is very similar to the perspective three above but it is accompanied by a realization of the limitations of research generated previously. It incorporates an openness to research from all sources as a basis for model generation and analysis. Numerically a gap exists between the volume of research conducted within the first three perspectives and information generated through later perspectives.

The need for work conducted from the constructivist and critical perspectives described below however, does not completely eclipse the need for knowledge generated through quantitative analyses. In the past decade we have seen an increase in data bases that for the first time provide information about large numbers of those who are not the elite. Those data bases have not been used productively. By focusing on particular, homogeneous population groups, such as women who are first generation college attenders, we can provide broad, general descriptions of particular types of experiences. Quantitative analyses of factors related to academic success, development and other achievements for groups of interest here, while informed by constructivist and critical research, could also generate information that can form the basis of further constructivist and critical work. This perspective forms an important link in the cycle of knowledge generation.

Individual students' experiences are described and valued in their own right. The fourth perspective seeks to understand all students' experiences. The researcher recognizes an inherent "theoretical bias" in attempts to describe all students' realities under the influence of theoretical descriptions of elite men's realities. This perspective means recognizing assumptions and discussing them as part of describing others' realities. (Friere, 1985; Lincoln, 1989; Tappan & Brown, 1992). Within this perspective the researcher recognizes the impossibility of producing objective, value-free facts (Lather, 1986). Christ (1987) and Novak (1965) call this way of conducting research assuming an "intelligent subjectivity." The researcher recognizes herself or himself and his or her own assumptions and sees changes in self and assumptions as a result of the research. Ramirez's (1977) and Gilligan's (1982, 1987) work represent examples of this perspective. Research on moral development indicated that women's moral development lagged behind that of men. Recognizing the discrepancies between the implications of moral development theory and research and the women she studied, Gilligan (1982) crafted a study to describe women's moral development based on women's perspectives of their own experiences. The work resulted in a new characterization of moral development more relevant to many women than traditional descriptions. For American social scientists "membership in a minority group has been regarded not as a potential source of multicultural functioning but as a developmental disadvantage" Ramirez (1977). However, Ramirez examined life histories of Chicano college students and documented the development of bicultural perspectives, values, behaviors, as well as a synthesis of elements from two cultures into a unique bicultural mode. Biculturalism has been successfully incorporated in numerous lines of research by a cadre of Latina/o social scientists. It recasts the experiences of Latina/os in the United States (as well as those of other minorities) in a non-comparative framework.

By focusing on individual students and their experiences, we are able to identify and amplify pertinent cultural and psychological factors (communication, interaction, values, behaviors, traditions). Otherwise all we have to work with are global descriptors of groups of individuals that fail to capture the specific elements of social, cultural or racial sources of influence on human behavior. Betancourt and Lopez (1993) suggest that qualitative researchers go beyond the study of cultural differences and move on to the task of identifying "specific aspects of culture and related variables that are thought to influence behavior." Both quantitative and qualitative research are poised to begin identifying and measuring directly the psychological, cultural and socioeconomic elements that are believed to be associated with the phenomena being researched. In this way we can begin to amass data that will allow us to differentiate between truly universal human processes and those that are generally bound by gender, culture, and by socioeconomic status.

This research perspective is closely linked with the final, critical perspective that seeks to transform. Without adequate and accurate descriptions of the experiences of people of color, women, and the poor the questions formulated in the following perspective would be ill-conceived and based on assumption.

Social issues are addressed within the context of research. The final classification, the critical perspective (Bruner, 1986; Gage, 1989; Giroux, 1990), represents a shift from a probabilistic or descriptive base to one seeking a transformation of realities. This perspective is characterized by a focus on the future. The researcher holding this perspective uses knowledge generated from previously described perspectives to craft questions focused on future possibilities. Perhaps this interaction can be compared to the transition from realist and impressionist art of the late 19th century to the post-impressionists of the early twentieth century. Realists and impressionists (e.g. Thomas Eakins, Harriet Hosmer, Edmonia Lewis, Berthe Morisot, and Auguste Rodin) sought to present the world as they perceived it. Their clarity of presentation or description, if you will, formed the basis for the more daring post-impressionist artists of the early twentieth century (e.g. Paul Klee, Henry Moore, Georgia O'Keefe, Constance Richardson, and Marguerite Zorach). These artists reflected their visions or "realities" through components of everyday life in their art in a way that transformed aspects of culture—media, advertising, architecture (Janson, 1969; Tufts, 1987; Varnedoe & Gopnik, 1990).

Similarly, the critical researcher reflects results of previous research based on constructions of realities in new questions to be asked and sees herself or himself as an agent of institutional transformation. The fourth and fifth perspectives are mutually dependent and mutually shaping; new realities require new descriptions.

New Perspectives on the College Student

In our own view of the transformational perspective, we borrow Harding's (1987) description of the feminist perspective, and view individuals as the source and subject of research problems, seek useful answers to useful questions, and do not distance ourselves, but seek to understand culturally, those whom we study.

It is not difficult to envision the types of questions that might be asked from transformational perspectives. Christ (1987) asserted that engaging in feminist scholarship requires a paradigm shift that begins with "the assumption that all women (and non-elite men) are as intelligent and as valuable as elite men . . ." (p. 53). The following questions, generated from the results of mostly conventional research, provide the kindling for a new research agenda. Why do women typically fare badly in the math/science pipeline? What is the African American student experience on the predominantly white campus? What cultural or institutional structures, programs, or policies inhibit the educational progress of students of color? Is a student's race, class, or gender the central factor in influencing his or her college experience? Is it as important to educate a border-line first generation college attender as it is to educate a merit scholar? If so, then why do we do such a good job with the latter and know little about educating the former? How does the educational experience for a woman attending a coeducational college differ from the experience of a woman attending a women's college? Why are graduate fellowships based on standardized test scores that have been shown to be unpredictive of women's and minorities successes in graduate school? How do we empower women and minority students in classrooms and institutions dominated by alien assumptions? These questions give rise to the kinds of research that is characteristic of a critical perspective on college students.

A Closing Note

In a short story writing class offered by a university continuing education department and taught by a highly successful author, the instructor kept telling the aspiring writers that their stories told "too much of the known and too little of the imagined." The comment has relevance for much of the literature in higher education. After nearly a century's study of college students, much of what we read today is already known; we have read it before. And little of what we read can get us to what we imagine, a higher educational system that is truly the great equalizer, one that is as negotiable for the non-elite as it is for the elite. By taking a new perspective, one that asks questions focusing on future possibilities, perhaps we can help the higher education system move toward that which we hold as ideal.

References

Abel, W. H. (1966). Attrition and the student who is certain. *Personnel and Guidance Journal*, 44, 1042–1045.

Aguirre, A., Jr. & Martinez, R. O. (1993). *Chicanos in higher education: issues and dilemmas for the 21st century*. ERIC Clearinghouse on Higher Education, the George Washington University in cooperation with ASHE, Association for the Study of Higher Education. Washington, D.C.: George Washington University.

Allen, W. R, Epps, E. G. & Haniff, N. Z., editors (1991). *College in black and white: African American students in predominantly white and in historically Black public universities*. Albany, N.Y.: State University of New York Press.

Allman, R. A., (1960). An evaluation of the goals of higher education by 294 college seniors of Alabama. *The Journal of Negro Education*, 29(2), 198–203.

Altbach, P. G. & Lomotey, K., editors (1991). *The Racial crisis in American higher education*. Albany: State University of New York Press.

Anzaldua, G. (1987). *La conciencia de la mestiza: Toward a new consciousness. Borderlands-La frontera: the new mestiza?* San Francisco: Aunt Lute Books.

Astin, A. W. (1968). Undergraduate achievement and institutional "excellence." *Science*, 161, 661–668.

Attinasi, L. & Nora, A. (1990). Combining qualitative and quantitative modes of college student research. Paper presented at the annual meeting of the Association for the Study of Higher Education.

Banks, J. (1993). The canon debate, knowledge construction, and multicultural education. *Educational Researcher, 22*(5), 4–14.

Bean, J. P. (1980). Dropouts and turnover: The synthesis and test of a causal model of student attrition. *Research in Higher Education, 12*(2), 155–187.

Bean, J. P. & Metzner, B. S. (1985). A conceptual model of nontraditional undergraduate student attrition. *Review of Educational Research, 55*, 485–539.

Belenky, M. F., Clinchy, B. M., Goldberger, N. R., & Tarule, J. M. (1986). *Women's Ways of Knowing: The Development of Self, Voice, and Mind.* New York: Basic Books.

Betancourt, H. & Lopez, R. S. (1993). "The study of culture, ethnicity, and race in American psychology". *American Psychologist*, Vol. 48, No. 6, 629–637.

Blandin, I. M. (1909). *History of Higher Education of Women in the South Prior to 1870.* New York: Neale.

Brubacher, J. S. & Rudy, W. (1976). *Higher Education in Transition: A History of American Colleges and Universities, 1636-1976.* New York: Harper & Row.

Bruner, J. (1986). *Actual minds, possible worlds.* Cambridge, MA: Harvard University Press.

Chacon, M. A., Cohen, E.G., & Strover, S. (1986). Chicanas and Chicanos: Barriers to Progress in Higher Education. In M. Olivas (Ed.) *Latino College Students.* New York: Teacher's College Press.

Chickering, A. (1984). *Education and Identity.* San Francisco: Jossey-Bass.

Christ, C. P. (1987). Toward a paradigm shift in the academy and in religious studies. In C. Farnham (ed.) *The Impact of Feminist Research in the Academy.* Bloomington: Indiana University Press.

Conrad, C.F. (1989). Meditations of the ideology of inquiry in higher education: Exposition, critique, and conjecture. *The Review of Higher Education, 12*(3), 199–220.

D'Augelli, A. R., & Hershberger, S . L. (1993). African American undergraduates on a predominantly White campus: Academic factors, social networks, and campus climate. *The Journal of Negro Education, 62*(1), 67–81.

Delgado, R. (1984) The imperial scholar: Reflections on a review of civil rights literature. *University of Pennsylvania Law Review.* Vol. 132, No. 56, 561–578.

Duran, R. P. (1983). *Hispanics' education and background: predictors of college achievement.* New York: College Entrance Examination Board

Evans, N. & Wall, V. A. (eds.) (1991). *Beyond tolerance: Gay, lesbians and bisexuals on campus.* Alexandria, VA: American College Personnel Association.

Feldman, K. & Newcomb, T. (1969). *The Impact of College on Students.* San Francisco: Jossey-Bass.

Feldman, K. & Newcomb, T. (1969). *The Impact of College on Students.* New Brunswick: Transaction Publishers.

Fox-Keller, E. (1990). Personal remarks. Indiana University, Bloomington, March 29.

Fox-Keller, E. (1985). *Reflections on Gender and Science.* New Haven, CT: Yale University Press .

Fleming, J. (1984). *Blacks in College.* San Francisco: Jossey-Bass.

Friere, P. (1985). *The Politics of Education: Culture, Power and Liberation.* Boston: Bergin & Garvey.

Gage, N. L. (1989). "The Paradigm Wars and Their Aftermath: A 'Historical' Sketch of Research on Teaching Since 1989." *Educational Researcher 18* (October 1989): 4–10.

Gaier, E. L. & Watts, W. A. (1969). Current attitudes and socialization patterns of White and Negro students entering college. *The Journal of Negro Education, 38*(4), 342–350.

Garza, R. T. & Lipton, J. P. (1982). Theoretical perspectives on Chicano personality development. *Hispanic Journal of Social Sciences.* Vol. 4, No. 4, 407–432.

Gilligan, C. (1987). Remapping development: The power of divergent data. In C. Farnham (ed.) *The Impact of Feminist Research in the Academy.* Bloomington: Indiana University Press.

Gilligan C. (1982). *In a different voice: Psychological theory and women's development.* Cambridge: Harvard University Press.

Giroux, H. A. (1990). Liberal arts education and the struggle for public life: Dreaming about democracy. *South Atlantic Quarterly, 89*(1), 113–138.

Goodman, E. (1990). Beware of research involving only white male rats. *The Herald-Times,* June 22, A8.

Graham, S. (1992). Most of the subjects were White and middle class: Trends in published research on African Americans in selected APA journals, 1970–1989. *American Psychologist, 47,* 629–639.

Grant, C. A. & Sleeter, C. E. (1986). Race, class, and gender in educational research: An argument for integrative analysis. *Review of Educational Research, 56*(2), 195–211.

Greenleaf, E. A. (1952). A Comparison of Women at Indiana University Majoring in Three Different Colleges. Doctoral Dissertation. Bloomington: Indiana University.

Hamrick, F. & Hossler, D. (in press). The use of diverse information-gathering techniques in the postsecondary decision-making process. *The Review of Higher Education.*

Harding, S. (1987). *Feminism and methodology: Social science issues.* Bloomington: Indiana University Press.

Hare, N. (1965). Conflicting racial orientation of Negro college students and professors. *The Journal of Negro Education, 34*(4), 431–434.

Hernandez, D. (1970). "Mexican American challenge to a sacred cow". Chicano Studies Center, Monograph No. 1. Aztlan Publications, University of California, Los Angeles.

Hood, D. W. (1992). Academic and noncognitive factors affecting the retention of Black men at a predominantly White university. *The Journal of Negro Education, 61*(1), 12–23.

Hope II, J. (1961). The Negro college, student protest and the future. *The Journal of Negro Education, 30*(4), 368–376.

Horowitz, H. L. (1986). *Alma Mater: Design and Experience in the Women's Colleges from Their Nineteenth Century Beginnings to the 1930s.* Boston, Beacon Press.

Hossler, D., Braxton, J. & Coopersmith, G. (1989).

Iffert, R. (1958). *Retention and Withdrawal of College Students.* Washington, D.C.: United States Department of Health, Education, and Welfare.

Janson, H. W. (1969). *History of Art: A Survey of the Major Visual Arts from the Dawn of History to the Present Day.* Englewood Cliffs, NJ: Prentice Hall.

Kamens, D. (1974). Colleges and elite formation: The case of prestigious American colleges. *Sociology of Education, 47,* 354–78.

Keller, G. (1985). Trees without fruit: The problem with research about higher education. *Change,* (1), 7–11.

Kobrak, P. (1992). Black student retention in predominantly White regional universities: The politics of faculty involvement. *The Journal of Negro Education, 61*(4), 509–530.

Kohlberg, L. (1972). A cognitive developmental approach to moral education. *Humanist, 6,* 13–16.

Komarovsky, M. (1953). *Women in the Modern World: Their Education and Their Dilemmas.* New York: Irvington.

Komarovsky, M. (1985). *Women in College: Shaping New Feminine Identities.* New York: Basic Books.

Lather, P. (1986). Research as praxis. *Harvard Educational Review, 56*(3), 257–277.

Lincoln, Y. S. (1989). Trouble in the land: The paradigm revolution in the academic disciplines. In J. Smart (ed.), *Higher Education: Handbook of Theory and Research. Volume V*. NY: Agathon Press.

Lincoln, Y. S. & Guba, E.G. (1985). *Naturalistic Inquiry*. Beverly Hills: Sage.

Lopez, R. W., Madrid-Barela, A., & R. F. Macias (1976). Chicanos in higher education, status and issues. Chicano Studies Center publications: monograph; no. 7. Los Angeles: University of California, Los Angeles.

Maple, S. A. & Stage, F. K. (1991). Influences on the choice of math/science major by gender and ethnicity. *American Educational Research Journal, 28*(1), 37–60.

Moraga, C. & Anzaldua, G. (1981). *This bridge called my back*. New York: Women of Color Press.

Mueller, K. H. (1954). Educating Women for a Changing World. Minneapolis: University of Minnesota Press.

Noble, J. L. (1956). *The Negro Woman's College Education*. New York: Teacher's College, Columbia University.

Noddings, N. (1990). Feminist critiques in the professions. In C. Cazden, *Review of Research in Education. No. 16*. Washington, D.C.: American Educational Research Association.

Novak, M. (1965). *Belief and Unbelief*. New York: New American Library.

Nyankori, J. C. (1991). Postsecondary enrollment patterns after court ordered desegregation: The case of South Carolina. *The Journal of Negro Education, 60*(4), 602–611.

Oakes, J. (1990). Opportunities, achievement, and choice: Women and minority students in science and mathematics. In C. Cazden, *Review of Research in Education No. 16*. Washington, D.C.: American Educational Research Association.

Offen, K. (1988). Defining feminism: A comparative historical approach. *Signs, 14*(1), 119–157.

Olin, H.R. (1909). The Women of a State University: An Illustration of the Workings of Coeducation in the Middle West. New York: Putnam.

Olivas, M. (1986). *Latino College Students*. New York: Teacher's College Press.

Pascarella, E. T. & Terenzini, P. T. (1979). Interaction effects in Spady's and Tinto's conceptual models of college dropout. *Sociology of Education, 52*, 197–210.

Pascarella, E. & Terenzini, P. (1991). *How college affects students: Findings and insights from twenty years of research*. San Francisco: Jossey Bass.

Perry, W. G. (1970). *Forms of Intellectual and Ethical Development in the College Years*. New York: Holt, Rinehart, and Winston.

Pervin, L. A. & Rubin, D. B. (1967). Student dissatisfaction with college and the college dropout: A transactional approach. *The Journal of Social Psychology, 72*, 285–295.

Pittman, J. A. (1960). A study of the academic achievement of 415 college students in relation to remedial courses taken. *The Journal of Negro Education, 29*(4), 426–437.

Ramirez, M. III (1977). "Recognizing and understanding diversity: multiculturalism and the Chicano movement in psychology".

Robinson, T. (1990). Understanding the gap between entry and exit: A cohort analysis of African American students' persistence. *The Journal of Negro Education, 59*(2), 207–218.

Rootman, I. (1972). Voluntary withdrawal from a total adult socializing organization: A model. *Sociology of Education, 45*, 258–270.

Roth, R. M. (1961). The adjustment of Negro college students at Hampton Institute. *The Journal of Negro Education, 30*(1), 72–74.

Sagaria, M. D. (ed.) (1988). *Empowering women: Leadership development strategies on campus.* New Directions for Student Services, No. 44. San Francisco: Jossey-Bass.

Scales, E. E. (1960). A study of college student retention and withdrawal. *The Journal of Negro Education, 29*(4), 438–444.

Sedlacek, W. E. (1987). "Black students on White campuses: 20 years of research." *Journal of College Student Personnel.* Nov., pp, 287–298.

Smart, J. C. & Pascarella, E. T. (1986). Socioeconomic Achievements of former college students. *The Journal of Higher Education, 57*(5), 529–549.

Solomon, B. M. (1985). *In the Company of Educated Women: Women and Higher Education in America.* New Haven, CT: Yale University Press.

Spady, W. G. (1971). Dropouts from higher education: Toward an empirical model. *Interchange, 2*(3), 38–62.

Stage, F. K. (1989). Motivation, Academic and Social Integration, and the Early Dropout. *American Educational Research Journal 26* (Winter 1989).

Stage, F. K. (1990). Research on college students: Commonality, difference, and direction. *The Review of Higher Education, 13*(3), 249–258.

Stage, F. K. (1994). Chanting the names of the ancestors. *Educational Researcher, 22*(6), 22–24.

Starrett, H. E. (1896). *After College What? For Girls.* New York: Crowell.

Talbot, M. (1936). *More than Lore: Reminiscences of Marion Talbot, Dean of Women, the University of Chicago, 1892–1925.* Chicago: The University of Chicago Press.

Tappan, M. & Brown, L. (1992). Hermeneutics and developmental psychology: Toward an ethic of interpretation. In W. Kurtines, M. Azmitia, & J. Gewirtz (Eds.), *The role of values in psychology and human development* (pp. 105–130). New York: John Wiley & Sons.

Tinto, V. (1975). Dropout from higher education: A theoretical synthesis of recent research. *Review of Educational Research, 45*(4), 89–125.

Townsend, B. K. (1992). Feminist scholarship and the study of women in higher education. *Initiatives, 55*(1), 1–9.

Tufts, E. (1987). *American Women Artists 1839/1930.* Museum Catalogue, The National Museum of Women in the Arts, Washington, D.C.

Varnedoe, K. & Gopnik, A. (1990). *High and Low: Modern Art and Popular Culture.* Exhibition Catalogue, Museum of Modern Art, New York. Willis.

Washington, V., & Newman, J. (1991). Setting our own agenda: Exploring the meaning of gender disparities among Blacks in higher education. *The Journal of Negro Education, 60*(1), 19–35.

Overview of the Readings

The nature of American higher education has been such that movement toward an increasingly diverse student body has been characteristic rather than unusual. For example, early planned changes in the American system were implemented with the establishment of institutions of higher learning for women and later for African-Americans. In this century the G.I. Bill and the 1968 Higher Education Act served as instruments of planned national change. However, the changes that were predicted in the late 70s and early 80s, changes that are now taking place, are not planned or intended changes. They are the result of natural demographic trends and of economic and technological activity. The face of the American college student has changed considerably in the last ten years. In compiling this reader the transformation of the college student body was foremost in our minds. Capturing the nature of change while it is in process is a difficult task. One can never be sure one has focused on the appropriate or enduring aspects of the evolving profile. Certainly all is not changing and appropriately we must rely on tried and tested knowledge in studying college students as well. Thus, our goal has been to include material representative of an established perspective on college students as well as that reflecting emerging perspectives that resonate with the voices of our fastest growing constituencies. In keeping with our earlier assertion, that all perspectives inform all other perspectives, we have included research from a variety of perspectives in the reader.

This reader consists of four sections laid out in the sequence of the college-going experience. The first section in the chronology includes a profile of college-bound students, examinations of the college choice and college transition processes, and includes a 'template' for studying college students. The second and third sections focus on the impact of the college environment and on student development, respectively. The last section includes a summary of twenty-five years of research, and two critiques of the literature and research on college students.

Finally, we were unable to include all the readings that we thought were important to developing a knowledge base on college students. Therefore, we have included a short list of readings that faculty and students might find useful as they delve more deeply into some of these topics.

PART I
GETTING TO COLLEGE

Introduction

The section on students' transitions to college begins by providing pertinent demographic information, a review of the research on the college choice and college transition processes, and concludes with a 'template' for studying college students. Typically the questions we have asked about college students have been of the 'who, what, where' nature. Rarely do we ask "how". This set of articles addresses both types of questions. Astone and Nunez-Wormack give us a crisp and concise picture of the diverse pools of potential college students. In -their article, "Demographics and diversity: What colleges should know", they sketch the population trends, socioeconomnic status, and geographic distribution of the African-American, Latino, Native-American, and Asian and Pacific Islander communities. They also outline the educational profile of students of color beginning with their high school completion rates, participation rates in the major segments of the higher education system, as well as undergraduate and graduate attainment rates.

The "how" questions are addressed in two articles; one is representative of the conventional research perspective and the other is representative of research that begins to bridge towards transformational perspectives. The research reviewed in "Understanding student college choice" by Hossler, Braxton, and Coopersmith is conventional research on the student college choice process. The authors underscore the importance and utility of employing a variety of research methods to the questions we ask about college students. More importantly, they present three conceptual approaches to the college choice process.

Terenzini, Rendon, Upcraft, Millar, Allison, Gregg, and Jalomo report in their methodology section that the sample for their study is not representative of the college going population. Significantly, they obtained samples "of students with characteristics generally typical of the overall entering student population" at each of four institutions. Thus, the proportion of women and students of color in the sample reflects their participation rates at their respective colleges. The study includes focus groups which simulated the reality of the collegiate environment. This approach acknowledges the differences in the experiences and the realities of different groups of students. As such we consider this piece an example of research linking the conventional and transformational research perspectives as discussed in our introductory chapter.

Finally, Astin presents a simple yet versatile conceptual model in his chapter "Studying college impact". The quintessence of his work is the I-E-O model, input-environment-outcomes model (student characteristics, college environments, and developmental outcomes). The basic elements of the model are readily recognized by social science and education researchers. The model emphasizes the interactional nature of the individual and the environment. Astin presents a straightforward approach to identifying and measuring student characteristics, collegiate experiences, and developmental outcomes. This template can guide us as we formulate our questions about colleges students, as we peruse and critique the existing literature, or as we design our own studies.

Population Trends, Socioeconomic Status, and Geographic Distribution

B. Astone and E. Nunez-Wormack

During the past 20 years, the proportion of minorities in the general population has increased so sharply as to "ensure future changes in the population balance between Anglo-Americans and minorities" (*Oxford Analytica* 1986, p. 35). This change is largely the result of two factors: immigration and higher birthrates. Immigration is higher than at any time since before 1920 (Robey 1985).

> American immigration continues to flow at a rate unknown elsewhere in the world. The U.S., with 5 percent of the world's population, takes about 50 percent of its international migrants, not counting refugees (Oxford Analytica 1986, p. 20).

Because most immigrants who have arrived in the United States since 1970 (77 percent by the end of the 1970s) have been people of color (*Oxford Analytica* 1986, p. 21), immigration is a significant factor in the discussion of minorities in higher education. Immigration is changing the racial fabric of the United States. In the 1950s, about 50 percent of U.S. immigrants came from Europe. During the 1970s, only 18 percent came from Europe, while more than 33 percent came from Asia and 30 percent from Latin American countries (Robey 1985). Immigration phenomena vary for the two groups relevant to this review, Asians/Pacific Islanders and Hispanics.

Birthrates within the African-American and Hispanic populations are higher than in the white community. A summary of the size of population groups by race and ethnicity in 1980 and projected into 1990 and 2000 appears in table 1, indicating the growth expected in the minority populations. By 2000, racial and ethnic minorities will make up nearly 30 percent of the U.S. population.

Table 1
U.S. Population by Race and Ethnicity (Percent)

	1980	1990	2000
		Projected	
Total Population (Millions)	226.5	250.4	268.3
Hispanics	6.4%	7.9%	11.7%
African-Americans	11.7	12.5	13.4
Asians/Pacific Islanders	1.5	2.6	3.7
American Indians/Native Alaskans	0.6	*	*
Whites	80.1	76.2	73.2

Figures for 1980 for whites arrived at by subtracting "other races"; projections for 1990 and 2000 for whites arrived at by subtracting "Spanish origin." Columns of projected figures include estimates from different sources and do not total 100.
* = Not available.
Sources: Hsai and Hirano-Nakanishi 1989; Mingle 1987; U.S. Bureau of the Census 1980a, 1980b, 1980c.

The general decline in the number of school-age children that is expected to continue through the middle of this decade is not evenly reflected in all parts of the country. Because regional demographics vary, national figures can often mask major differences in states. From 1970 to 1980, public school enrollments decreased 13 percent nationwide. But in 12 Sunbelt states, enrollments increased, while many Frostbelt states decreased up to 25 percent (Hodgkinson 1983, 1986).

The high-growth states are also those with the lowest levels of high school retention: To a significant extent, students in these states are poor, handicapped, and of minority backgrounds, and speak limited English (Hodgkinson 1986). In other words, those states with the higher rates of high school retention will continue to experience diminishing numbers of students, while the states with the poorest records—those with high numbers of minorities, including students whose English is limited—will see bigger and bigger class sizes (see table 2).

Table 2
Projected Population of 18- to 24-year-olds (000s)

Region	1990	2000
New England	1,369	1,185
Mideast	4,391	3,829
Southeast	6,344	6,238
Great Lakes	4,362	3,852
Plains	1,748	1,681
Southwest	2,672	2,814
Rocky Mountains	781	858
Far West	4,080	4,325

Source: American Council on Education 1989.

Regardless of student population, however, differential fertility ensures that the proportion of minority students in U.S. elementary schools will continue to grow. By the mid-1980s "each of our 24 largest city school systems [had] a 'minority majority,' [and about] 27 percent of all public school students in the U.S. [came from racial and ethnic] minorities" (Hodgkinson 1986, p. 9).

The socioeconomic status of minorities in the United States is substantially lower than that of whites, as measured by several different factors. Median family income (discussed in detail for each ethnic group later in the section) is significantly lower for African-Americans and Hispanics, and the percentage of families living in poverty is several times higher. Families headed by a single female are three times more likely to live in poverty than are all families, and many more African-American and Hispanic families are headed by women alone. The most powerful statistic of all, however—and the one that perhaps has the greatest import for educators—is that *the single largest group of poor people in the United States is children.* Nearly 20 percent of all American children live below the poverty level (see figure 1): 14 percent of white children, 36 percent of Hispanic children, and 43 percent of African-American children (U.S. Bureau of the Census 1990c). Yet poverty rates decrease dramatically as years of school completed increase. The poverty rate in 1989 was nearly 20 percent for householders who had not completed high school, less than 9 percent for high school graduates without college, and under 4 percent for those with one or more years of college (U.S. Bureau of the Census 1990c).

Reporting on data from the early part of the 1980s, analysts have indicated two major trends affecting the geographic distribution of U.S. population in the 1990s: (1) the move away from the Northeast and North Central states to the South and the West; and (2) the move away from city centers to outer suburban and rural areas. In 1980, "for the first time in the history of the republic, the geographical center of the population crossed the Mississippi" (Oxford Analytica 1986, p. 42). This new migration notwithstanding, the East remains our most densely populated area: 80 percent of the U.S. population resides in the eastern half of the country (Hodgkinson 1986).

Figure 1
Percent of Children in Poverty in 1989, by Racial and Ethnic Group

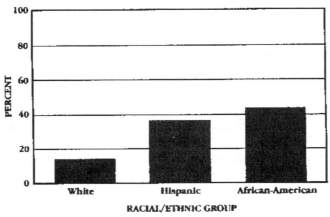

Source: U.S. Bureau of the Census 1990c.

The African-American Community

- African-Americans represent an increasing proportion of the population, but unemployment is higher for this group, especially among youth, than for any other group.

- Well over half of African-American children live with their mothers only, and 54 percent of families headed by African-American women with children under 18 years old live below the poverty level.

- Over half of all African-Americans lived in the South in 1980, and 81 percent lived in metropolitan areas.

Population trends. Although the fertility rate for African Americans has fallen since the 1950s (*Oxford Analytica* 1986), it remains higher than that of the white community, and, as a group, African-Americans represent an increasing proportion of the population. In 1980, the total fertility rate (TFR) for African-Americans was 2.3, compared to 1.7 for whites. (A sustained TFR of about 2.1 is necessary to replace population. U.S. TFR has been below this level since 1971.) Though the number of African-Americans is increasing, circumstances deleterious to their greater social mobility continue to plague them.

Socioeconomic status. In 1989, median income was lower and unemployment was higher among African-Americans than for whites, Asians, or Hispanics (see figure 2). Median family income for African-Americans was $20,200, compared to $34,200 overall (U.S. Bureau of the Census 1990a), and unemployment was 11.4 percent, more than twice that of the total population (U.S. Dept. of Labor 1990a). Despite the gains made by some, African-Americans as a group are more likely to be unemployed today than a generation ago (Robey 1985). The unemployment gap between African-American youths and white youths was more than 20 percentage points in 1983, when nearly 50 percent of African-Americans between 16 and 19 years of age were unemployed. Considering that this age group accounts for a larger portion of the total African-American population than white youths do of the white population, the evident effect is that much more sobering (Robey 1985). Thirty percent of African-American families lived in poverty in 1989 (U.S. Bureau of the Census 1990c).

In terms of its relation to socioeconomic status and ultimately to educational opportunity, one of the most compelling realities affecting African-Americans is the fact that so many families—

Figure 2
Median Family Income in 1989, by Racial and Ethnic Group

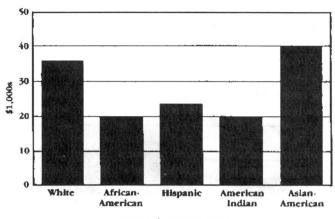

Source: U.S. Bureau of the Census 1990c.

more than three times as many African-American (44 percent) as white (13 percent)—are headed solely by women (U.S. Bureau of the Census 1990c). (The majority of African-American children—58 percent in 1984—live with their mother only [Robey 1985].) Because women continue to earn less than men do and single-parent families are more likely to live in poverty, the prevalence of this circumstance has devastating implications. In 1989, 54 percent of families headed by African-American women with children under 18 years old had incomes below the poverty level (U.S. Bureau of the Census 1990c) (see also figure 3).

Geographic distribution. For African-Americans, migration stems from the South, and their movement out of the South continued in increasing numbers until the 1970s. By the end of that decade, African-Americans started to move back to the South again, perhaps because of changing attitudes there after the Civil Rights movement and perhaps because of the general population shift to the South and West (Robey 1985). Of the nearly 26.5 million African-Americans counted in the 1980 Census, 53 percent lived in the South, 20 percent lived in the North central states, 18.2 percent lived in the Northeast, and 8.7 percent lived in the West.

African-Americans have traditionally lived either in the rural South or in large city centers. Along with the trend for the general population, the number of African-Americans living in the inner cities declined somewhat (from 60 percent to 58 percent) between 1970 and 1980, and those living in city suburbs increased 43 percent. African-Americans are not moving as far away as whites, who are going to the outer suburbs and small towns, but they are settling in the "low-income inner suburbs" (Robey 1985, p. 149). Consequently, African-Americans are becoming a larger portion not only of central city residents but also of metropolitan residents. Eighty-one percent of African-Americans make their home in the metropolis. In many major cities, such as Washington, D.C., Atlanta, Detroit, Baltimore, Memphis, and St. Louis, they are or soon will be a majority.

The Hispanic Community

- In the past decade, the number of Hispanics has increased dramatically in the United States; by 2000, they are expected to constitute nearly 12 percent of the population.

- The socioeconomic characteristics of Chicanos, Puerto Ricans, Cubans, and Central and South Americans vary substantially, and these differences are reflected in the

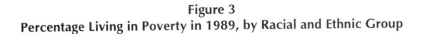

Figure 3
Percentage Living in Poverty in 1989, by Racial and Ethnic Group

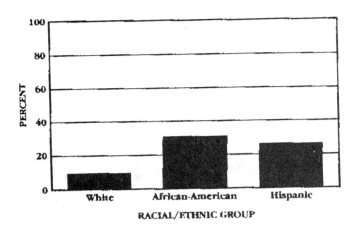

Source: U.S. Bureau of the Census 1990c.

degree of social integration and participation of each group in American society. Among Hispanics, Puerto Ricans have the lowest and Cuban-Americans the highest median incomes.

- Because of migration patterns, more Puerto Rican families are headed by women in the United States than are other Hispanic families, and the median income for these families is considerably lower than for families headed by women generally.

- Of Hispanic women heading households with children under 18 years old, 58 percent live below the poverty level.

- Hispanics reside mainly in cities and cluster regionally according to nationality: Most Mexican-Americans live in California and Texas, the majority of Cubans live in Florida, and Puerto Ricans live mainly in New York.

Population trends. Although the 1990 Census provides a breakdown of Hispanic subgroups, previous data collections do not. Until this time, the prevailing form of reference has therefore been to the Hispanic population in the aggregate. Between 1980 and 1988, the Hispanic population increased 34 percent, compared to 7 percent for non-Hispanics. About half of this growth resulted from natural increase (*Oxford Analytica* 1986). According to U.S. data, a 38 percent difference in births per 1,000 women exists between Hispanic (94 per 1,000) and non-Hispanic (68 per 1,000) women (U.S. Bureau of the Census 1989). 'The age of the average Hispanic female is almost a decade younger than her white counterpart. With no increase in the fertility rate, Hispanics will increase their numbers of young Hispanic females" (Hodgkinson 1986, p. 9).

The remaining increase in the Hispanic population is the result of immigration. It is projected that "immigration and high Hispanic fertility will change America's racial and cultural composition, putting white non-Hispanics in a minority in some states early in the next century" (*Oxford Analytica* 1986, pp. 11–12). Population projections indicate a yearly growth rate of 4.7 percent, declining to 3.5 percent, resulting primarily at first from immigration and then from natural increase. Based on these rates, it is projected that the Hispanic population will exceed the African-American population in the early part of the next century (Oxford Analytica 1986, p. 37).

The major Hispanic subgroups include Chicanos (67 percent), Puerto Ricans (12.7 percent, not including the 1.5 million Puerto Ricans living in Puerto Rico), Central and South Americans (11.5

percent), and Cubans (5.3 percent). The remainder of the Hispanic population was counted in the 1980 Census as "other Hispanic." In terms of factors as significant as economic status, ability to speak English, family life, and demographic characteristics, the people of these four groups differ substantially. Although not much disaggregated data exist regarding Hispanics, some facts are available. The median age, for example, varies according to subgroup: For Mexican-Americans it is 21.9 years, compared to 30 years for Americans in general. More than one-third of both Mexican-Americans and Puerto Ricans are under age 15, compared to one-fourth of all Americans. This fact is significant because Mexican-Americans have a higher fertility rate than Hispanics in general. Cuban-Americans, on the other hand, have a median age of 38, and only 16 percent are under age 15, while 12 percent are 65 or older (U.S. Bureau of the Census 1980a).

Socioeconomic status. Because of different migration patterns, the family structure of Puerto Ricans varies from that of other Hispanics. More Puerto Rican women find work and reside in the United States than do men: 35 percent of all Puerto Rican families in the United States are maintained solely by women, compared to 15 percent of Cuban and 16 percent of Chicano families (Robey 1985). In 1989, 23 percent of all Hispanic families were headed solely by women. Of those with children under 18 years old, 58 percent lived below the poverty level.

The median family income for Hispanics in 1989 was much lower than for all U.S. families— $23,400, compared to $34,200 (U.S. Bureau of the Census 1990a). Income varied significantly, however, depending on Hispanic subgroup. Figures for one year earlier, 1988, indicate that median income for Cubans was $26,900, for Central and South Americans $23,700, for Mexican-Americans $21,000, and for Puerto Ricans $19,000 (U.S. Bureau of the Census 1990a). Unemployment rates corresponded, in that Puerto Ricans and Chicanos were unemployed at the highest rates (9.1 and 8.5, respectively, in 1989), while the Cuban and Central and South American rates were closer to 6 percent. These figures compare to 5.3 percent for the total U.S. population (U.S. Dept. of Labor 1990a). The percentages of families living below the poverty level also varied, although all were higher than for the general population: 31 percent of Puerto Ricans, 24 percent of Mexican-Americans and 16 percent of Cubans and Central and South Americans lived in poverty in 1989, compared to 12.8 percent of all Americans (U.S. Bureau of the Census 1990b).

Geographic distribution. Even more than African-Americans, Hispanics live in cities, but the number of cities in which they are concentrated is fewer because they also congregate according to ethnic origin. California, Texas, and New York alone are home to 60 percent of the nation's Hispanic population. Three out of four Mexican-Americans live in California or Texas, 50 percent of Puerto Ricans live in New York (43 percent in New York City), and two out of three Cubans live in Florida (over 50 percent in the Miami metropolitan area). On the other hand, in much of the country Hispanics are rare: In 34 states, Hispanics make up less than 2 percent of the population. In major cities like Miami, Los Angeles, San Antonio, and New York, Hispanics make up, if not a majority, then a significant portion of the population. Metropolitan areas like Chicago, Houston, and San Francisco-Oakland count 350,000 to 600,000 Hispanics. In seven other metropolitan areas, Hispanics number at least 250,000 (Robey 1985).

The Asian and Pacific Islander Communities

- By 1990, the largest Asian and Pacific Island subgroups were expected to be, in order, Filipinos, Chinese, and Southeast Asians.

- Although Asian-Americans are considered middle class in general, the socioeconomic status of the many Asian subpopulations actually varies enormously: Southeast Asians, the third largest group, averaged 50 percent living at poverty level in 1980, and 35 percent of all those in poverty were Vietnamese.

- The majority of Asian Americans reside in the West, but large portions of some subpopulations are concentrated in other regions of the country, such as the Northeast and the Southeast. Almost all Asian-Americans live in metropolitan areas.

Population trends. From 1971 to 1980, Asian immigration totaled about 1.6 million, and from 1981 to 1988, 1.75 million (Hsia and Hirano-Nakanishi 1989). During the 1980s, Asians were the largest group of immigrants: A greater number of Asian immigrants came to the United States during the 1980s than were counted in the 1970 Census. These figures do not include over 500,000 refugees from Southeast Asia but do include Asian Indian immigrants, who previously had not been included in the Asian category. In the 1980 Census, 62 percent of U.S. Asians reported they were born elsewhere; their differing countries of origin are changing the face of the Asian-American community. Within the Asian population, the Chinese constituted 23.4 percent in 1980, followed by Filipinos (22.6 percent) and Japanese (20.7 percent). Koreans made up 10.3 percent of all Asians (U.S. Bureau of the Census 1980b). By 1990, however, Filipinos were projected to be the largest Asian-American group, followed by Chinese and Southeast Asians, who were expected to number more than 1 million (Hsia and Hirano-Nakanishi 1989). The Pacific Islander population is about 7 percent of the Asian and Pacific Islander group, and over two-thirds come from Hawaii. The median age for both Asian-Americans (28.8) and Pacific Islanders (23.1) is younger than for all Americans (30).

Socioeconomic status. The median family income of Asians and Pacific Islanders was $40,400, compared with the national median of $34,200 (U.S. Bureau of the Census 1990a). More detailed data are not available for 1989, but factors reported in 1982 based on the 1980 Census reveal that while income was higher among Asian-Americans than for the general population ($22,700 compared to $19,900), the proportion of families with three or more workers was also higher, 17 percent compared to 13 percent (U.S. Bureau of the Census 1980b). In 1980, vast differences also existed in socioeconomic status in the Asian/Pacific Island community. More than one third of those in poverty (35 percent) were Vietnamese; in fact, Southeast Asians as a group averaged over 50 percent living at poverty level. For Samoans, the rate was also high, 29.5 per cent. These figures compare to 7 percent for the Japanese and Filipinos (U.S. Bureau of the Census 1980b).

Geographic distribution. Similar to the other minorities described thus far, Asian-Americans cluster in urban areas and are about equally divided between central cities and their suburbs (U.S. Bureau of the Census 1980b). And, like Hispanics, Asians and Pacific Islanders congregate according to their ethnicity. Data from the 1980 Census indicate that over 80 percent of Japanese, 69 percent of Filipinos, and 53 percent of Chinese lived in the West and that proportionately more Asian Indians (34 percent) and Chinese (27 percent) lived in the Northeast than Asian-Americans in general (17 percent). Southeast Asians are found mostly in Texas, Louisiana, Northern Virginia, and California, where two-thirds live (Robey 1985).

For Asian-Americans as a group, 56 percent live in the West. California (35 percent), Hawaii (19 percent), and New York (9 percent) contain 60 percent of Asian-Americans. Illinois, New Jersey, Texas, and Washington have Asian-American populations of 100,000 or more.

The American Indian Community

- The American Indian community is comparatively young and has more children than Americans in general.

- The large majority of American Indians do not live on reservations; in fact, most live in urban areas.

- While about half of all American Indians live in the West, every state contains American Indian communities. Many American Indians also live in the South and Midwest.

- Median income of American Indians is comparable to that of African-Americans and most Hispanics, which is about 40 percent less than the median income for whites.

- Compared to Americans in general, more than twice as many American Indians lived below the poverty level in 1980.

Population trends. The 1980 Census counted 1.4 million American Indians, about 0.5 percent of the overall population. The American Indian population is young, with 44 percent under 20 years of age, compared to 32 percent of Americans as a whole. Only 8 percent were 60 years or older, which is half the proportion for all Americans. The median age of American Indians was 22.9 years in 1980, considerably younger than the U.S. median age (30). At the same time, American Indians have higher fertility rates than the national norm. In 1980, about two thirds of all American Indian families had children under 18, compared to one-half of U.S. families in general (U.S. Bureau of the Census 1980c).

About 500 American Indian tribes and bands were identified in the 1980 Census; about 90 percent of them, however, had populations of less than 10,000. The tribes with the largest populations (from about 160,000 to 235,000) were the Cherokee and Navajo, which together accounted for 27 percent of the entire Indian population. Other larger tribes included the Sioux (5 percent), Chippewa (5 percent), and Choctaw (4 percent) (U.S. Bureau of the Census 1980c).

Socioeconomic status. Median family income in 1989 for American Indians was much lower than for the nation as a whole, $20,000 compared to the U.S. median of $34,200 (U.S. Bureau of the Census 1990a). Like the case of Asian-Americans, the most recent detailed information available regarding American Indians is based on the 1980 Census. About one-fourth of all Indian families were maintained by women alone, and their median income in 1980 was $7,200, about 72 percent of the median for all American families headed by women ($9,960). The proportion of American Indians living below the official poverty level in 1980 was more than twice as high as that of the general population, about 28 percent of all American Indians compared to 12 percent of Americans in general (U.S. Bureau of the Census 1980c).

Geographic distribution. One-third of the American Indian population live on reservations (25 percent) and in the historic areas of Oklahoma (former reservations without established boundaries) (9 percent). While American Indians live in every state in the country, they are largely concentrated in the West, where almost 50 percent live in California, Oklahoma, Arizona, and New Mexico. The North Central region of the country is home to another nearly 20 percent. Of the 75 percent of Indians who live off the reservations, over 50 percent live in urban areas. Of the 10 states with the largest Indian population, only Michigan, North Carolina, and New York are east of the Mississippi River. About 27 percent of the American Indian population is in the South, 18 percent in the Midwest, and 6 percent in the Northeast (U.S. Bureau of the Census 1980c).

The Educational Profile of Ethnic and Racial Minorities. At virtually all transition points along the education continuum, disproportionately large numbers of minorities are lost—at completion of high school, entry to college, completion of college, entry to graduate or professional school, and completion of graduate or professional school (Astin et al. 1982). This reality, within the context of the changing demographics of the country, poses a singular challenge to education.

The size of the cohort of high school graduates will continue to decline until 1998 (Hodgkinson 1983) as a result of the decline in birthrates after 1964 in the white middle class. Higher birthrates among minorities, however, have meant that minority populations will continue to make up an increasing proportion of college-age, if not college-ready, students. Further, the shrinking size of the college-age population is not uniform across the country. As a result of immigration and migration, the birthrate is rising in the Sunbelt states while declining in the North, indicating that higher education enrollments will continue to expand in one part of the country as they constrict in the other.

Most of the disparities in education affect all the ethnic and racial minority groups in general. Because disparities could be more or less severe for each group at different levels of education, however, it is useful to consider the participation and completion statistics for each group, organized by level of education rather than by racial and ethnic group. The following sections therefore discuss the rate of participation and completion for African-Americans, Hispanics, Asian-Americans, and American Indians (where available) relative to the rate for nonminorities for each educational level from high school through graduation from four-year college. Where available, trends in the rate at which each group obtains baccalaureate and advanced degrees and educational statistics comparing the public and private sectors are discussed.

High School Completion

Each minority group exhibits important variations in high school completion rates compared to the white population. Hundreds of tables have been compiled on topics ranging from demographics to economic and enrollment trends to institutional finance and student aid (see, e.g., American Council on Education 1989). U.S. Census data on high school completion rates from 1974 to 1986 tell a discouraging story. After 12 years, and with almost as many setbacks as gains, high school completion rates for Hispanics and African Americans are still much lower than the rate for the majority, especially when they are measured for students 18 and 19 years old. In this category, the difference in high school completion between African Americans and whites is more than 11 percentage points (76.6 percent for whites and 65 percent for African-Americans) and between Hispanics and whites is almost 22 points (only 54.7 percent of Hispanics). By age 24, when 85.4 percent of whites have completed high school, the gap narrows to about 4 points difference between whites and African-Americans, but between Hispanics and whites it increases to almost 24 points, for only 61.6 percent of Hispanics in this age group have completed school (American Council on Education 1989).

In the two years after 1986, high school completion decreased for both groups (Carter and Wilson 1989). In 1988, African-Americans aged 18 to 24 completed high school at a rate of 75.1 percent (82.3 percent for whites), compared to 76.4 percent two years earlier. Despite the continuing disparity, however, until 1987 the high school completion rate for African-Americans was improving slowly but steadily. For Hispanics, the number of high school dropouts is disconcerting. In 1988, only 55.2 percent of 18- to 24-year-olds had finished high school, 4.7 percent fewer than in 1986 (see figure 4). Although rates have fluctuated, reaching a high of 62.8 in 1985, the most recent (1988) high school dropout rate for Hispanics is even lower than it was in 1976. The real school dropout rate for Hispanics is much higher than has been calculated, however, as a large number of Hispanic children never reach ninth grade and are therefore not counted in the high school attrition statistics (Fernandez 1989).

For American Indians, dropping out of high school is also a serious problem. The dropout rate for American Indians—35.5 percent—is similar to that for African-Americans. While American Indians represent 3.1 percent of all dropouts, they account for only 0.9 percent of all elementary and secondary students. Most American Indian students (82 percent) attend state-run public schools, while 11 percent are in schools funded by the Bureau of Indian Affairs and 7 percent attend private (many of them missionary) schools near reservations (O'Brien 1990).

Contrary to the situation for American Indians, Hispanics, and African-Americans, when viewed as a single group, Asian-Americans stay in school: In the 1990 High School and Beyond (HS&B) survey, the Asian-American group had the lowest high school dropout rate, the highest grade point averages (GPAs), the largest percentage of high school graduates who went directly to college, and the highest persistence rate at two-year colleges of any group, including whites (Hsia and Hirano-Nakanishi 1989). These achievements have been attributed to, among other things, a shared value among Asian-Americans in general of education, which is associated with status and respect and has long been considered a vehicle for social mobility (Hsia and Hirano-Nakanishi 1989). The sample used in the HS&B survey, however, did not allow for analysis by subgroups. Any differences among the various populations, therefore, would not be evident. While Pacific Islanders are frequently grouped together with Asians, some researchers maintain that their (Pacific Islander) situation in higher education is closer to that of other minorities (Bagasao 1989).

Other literature refers to state reports that Asian immigrants and refugees, especially those in the lower socioeconomic strata, are burdened by culture shock, limited English, and, in some cases, "a high incidence of violence and prejudice directed against [them]" (Tokuyama 1989, p. 69). Southeast Asians are reported to be falling into the at-risk category, with many not completing high school (Tokuyama 1989).[1]

Figure 4
High School Completion Rate for 18- to 24-year-olds, 1976 versus 1988

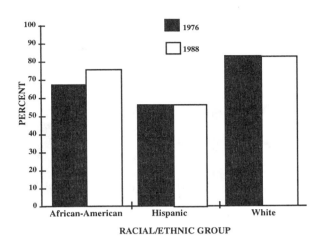

Source: American Council on Education 1989.

Undergraduate Participation

In absolute numbers, data from the National Center for Education Statistics indicate increases in 1988 college enrollment over 1976 for every ethnic and racial category. Nationally, college enrollment increased 13 percent for whites, 9 percent for African-Americans, 77 percent for Hispanics, 151 percent for Asian-Americans, and 22 percent for American Indians. More minorities are going to college, especially Asian-Americans and Hispanics. But given the variation in factors like population growth, the size of different age groups, and high school completion rates from one group to another, interpreting the significance of these numbers is complex.

For example, over the same 12-year period, the number of 18- to 24-year-old whites decreased 8 percent while high school completion rates remained the same. Yet, despite the smaller population, college participation increased 5 percentage points (see figure 5). Among African-Americans, however, the population in this age group increased 7.6 percent, high school graduation almost 8 percent. But out of this bigger population, a greater percentage of whom were high school graduates, a smaller proportion (5 percentage points fewer) enrolled in college. Among Hispanics, the same phenomenon is even more pronounced. The 18- to 24-year-old population increased fully 70 percent while high school completion stayed the same. Yet the percentage enrolling in college of this much bigger population, consisting of the same proportion of high school graduates, also decreased 5 percentage points (Carter and Wilson 1989). While the overall increases in the number of minorities enrolled in college reflect important advances, they must be considered in light of the changes in demographics. These data concerning the same 12-year period seem to indicate that the number of 18- to 24-year-old African-Americans and Hispanics enrolling in college has increased. The number who do *not* enroll has increased even more, however.

The college-going rate of young minority men in particular has dropped significantly in recent years. College enrollments among 18- to 24-year-old white men have increased 14 percentage points since 1976, to a little over 39 percent, but among African-American men in the same age group, they decreased more than 10 percentage points, to 25 percent. Among Hispanic men, almost 31 percent of 18- to 24-year-olds were enrolled in college in 1988, down more than 8 percentage points from 12 years earlier (Carter and Wilson 1989).

Figure 5
College Enrollment for 18- to 24-year-olds, 1976 versus 1988

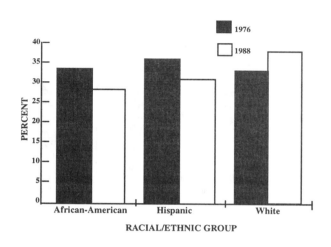

Source: American Council on Education 1989.

The difference in college participation between men and women varies for different populations. Historically, more Hispanic women graduate from high school than men. A smaller percentage, however, enroll in college. The gap between men and women within the 18- to 24-year old group in the 12 years from 1976 to 1988 has closed from a difference of almost 7 percentage points to about 1 point, but not because a greater proportion of women in this age group enrolled in college; it is the result instead of the relative decrease for men in the same age group (Carter and Wilson 1989). In absolute numbers of Hispanics enrolled in college, however, including *all* age groups, the number of Hispanic women grew 112 percent, compared to 48 percent for Hispanic men over the 12-year period (U.S. Dept. of Education 1989, updated 1990).

In the African-American community, the situation is a little different, but the general outcome in terms of gains for young women is the same. In the 18- to 24-year-old group, although a larger percentage of African-American women traditionally graduate from high school, 12 years ago a larger percentage of male high school graduates went to college than female high school graduates. This situation is now reversed: More African-American 18- to 24-year-old women enrolled in college in 1988 than men. The reversal, however, is the result of the precipitous drop in male enrollments rather than of any increase in the proportion of female enrollments. In fact, a smaller proportion of women in this age group enrolled in 1988 than in 1976 (Carter and Wilson 1989).

Two-year Institutions. For all the minority groups and for whites, the proportion of two-year enrollments has increased in the past 10 years (U.S. Dept. of Education 1989, updated 1990). In the 10 years between 1976 and 1986, participation of African-Americans in two-year institutions decreased from 11 percent to 10 percent. For American Indians and Native Alaskans, enrollments remained virtually unchanged, at 1 percent. Hispanic participation increased somewhat, from 5.4 percent to 7.2 percent, and markedly for Asian-Americans, from 2 percent to 4 percent (U.S. Dept. of Education 1984, 1989, updated 1990).

In terms of proportional representation, it is clear that minorities are heavily concentrated in two-year schools. Of all Hispanic and American Indian students in college, the absolute majority are enrolled in community colleges. American Indians have the largest concentration of all minority groups, 56.6 percent, and Hispanics are similarly represented, at 54.8 percent (Taylor 1983). Compared to the enrollment at two-year schools for white students (36 percent), African-

Americans (43.1 percent) and Asian-Americans (42 percent) are also disproportionately represented (U.S. Dept. of Education 1984).

Data from 1984 providing a breakdown of minority participation by full-time versus part-time attendance indicate that two-year institutions have a larger part-time population than full-time population: For Hispanics, Asian-Americans, and American Indians, about two students attend part time for every one who attends full time, which is also the case for whites. For African-Americans, the difference is somewhat smaller, 58 percent part time and 42 percent full time (U.S. Dept. of Education 1984).

Four-year institutions. In four-year colleges, where participation of African-Americans has always been disproportionately low relative to the size of that population overall, participation also decreased over the same 10-year period, from 8.5 percent to 7.9 percent. Hispanic participation increased from 2.4 percent to 3.6 percent but remains significantly underrepresentative, as does participation of American Indians and Native Alaskans in four-year institutions, which remained unchanged at 0.5 percent (U.S. Dept. of Education 1989, updated 1990).

Of students attending college, a larger proportion of Asian-Americans (58.5 percent) and African-Americans (56.9 percent) attended four-year colleges in 1986. These percentages, however, are down 1.6 percent for both groups from 10 years earlier. A smaller proportion of Hispanic (45.2 percent) and American Indian and Native Alaskans (43.3 percent) attended four-year colleges. Among whites, attendance at four-year institutions was 63.9 percent of the college-going population (U.S. Dept. of Education 1989, updated 1990).

College completion in four-year institutions. The college completion rate at the bachelor's level varies enormously, depending on race and ethnicity. According to a 1986 study of 12,000 students, after six years of college, Hispanic students graduated at a rate of 20.4 percent and African-Americans at 23.9 percent, compared to Asian-Americans at 41.5 percent and whites at 43.9 percent. That is, African-Americans and Hispanics in four-year colleges and universities earned degrees after six years at about half the rate of white and Asian American students (Porter 1989).[2]

Baccalaureate and Advanced Degrees Obtained

Minorities as a group obtained more degrees at all levels in 1987 than they did in 1976, but when the data are examined according to subgroup, certain distinctions emerge. Hispanics, Asian-Americans, and American Indians made gains at all levels, and women made considerably more gains than men. But African-Americans, most particularly the men, lost ground: Fewer African-American men obtained degrees at any level in 1987 than in 1976 (Carter and Wilson 1989). From 1976 to 1987, the number of African-Americans earning bachelor's degrees fell 4.3 percent overall but 12.2 percent for men; the number of master's degrees decreased by 31.8 percent but by 34 percent for men. The number of Ph.D.s also declined 22.1 percent from 1978 to 1988, with a 46.7 percent drop among the men. While African-American women did obtain more degrees at the bachelor's, doctorate, and first professional levels, the number of master's degrees dropped 30 percent among African-American women between 1976 and 1987 (Carter and Wilson 1989).

While Hispanics are still seriously underrepresented among those receiving degrees—the percentage of Hispanic undergraduates (5.3 percent) is almost twice the percentage of those obtaining degrees (2.7 percent)—the number of degrees conferred to Hispanics over the period from 1976 to 1987 increased significantly (50.3 percent at the bachelor's level and 32.9 percent at the master's level); 52.8 percent more women and 16.1 percent more men earned a degree. For all degrees in this group, the percentage increases occurred largely among women; however, so few women earned advanced degrees in 1976 that even large increases result in relatively low numbers. For example, from 1978 to 1988, 25.6 percent more Hispanics earned doctorate degrees, 75 percent more women and 1.3 percent more men. In actual numbers, however, 273 doctorates were awarded to women, 321 to men. First professional degrees increased by 90.1 percent for Hispanics, for a total of 2,051 degrees; 748 were awarded to women (a 356 percent increase over 11 years earlier), 1,303 to men (42.4 percent more than in 1976).

The sharpest increases were among Asian-Americans, and, in keeping with the trend, women made the greatest advances. Between 1976 and 1987, bachelor's degrees awarded to this group increased 191.4 percent (215.3 percent among women), master's degrees 118.8 percent (121.1 percent for women); doctorates increased 56.9 percent between 1978 and 1988 (93 percent among women), and first professional degrees increased 24.9 percent (306.2 percent for women).

For American Indians in the same 11-year period, the number of degrees granted to women also increased to a great extent. Bachelor's degrees decreased 5 percent among men but increased 36.1 percent among women, master's degrees increased 21.3 percent among men and 65.9 percent among women, doctorates increased 51 percent for men and 42 percent for women, and first professional degrees increased 12.9 percent for men but 365.4 percent for women. In this group, however, the number of advanced degrees awarded is extremely small. In 1988, 93 doctorates were awarded to American Indians.

Public Sector versus Private Sector

Private institutions continue to have more success in retaining and graduating students than do public institutions, but a recent report from the National Institute of Independent Colleges and Universities (Porter 1989) indicates that for African-American and Hispanic students, the advantage of the independent sector is not really much greater. In that study, the completion rate after six years at private institutions for African-Americans and Hispanics was approximately 30 percent, about half the rate for whites and Asian-Americans and only a few percentage points better than the completion rate for African Americans and Hispanics at public institutions after the same period of time.

The proportion of white students in private institutions is greater than in public ones, although the figure has been slowly decreasing in recent years. In 1986, white students accounted for 81.3 percent of students at private institutions, compared to 78.8 percent at public colleges and universities, about 3 percentage points lower in each sector from 10 years earlier. The difference has been made up by increased enrollments, especially in public institutions of Asian-Americans, Hispanics, and nonresident aliens. African-American participation actually decreased in both private and public colleges since 1976. Proportionately, African-Americans make up the same part of the student population, within 0.1 percent, in both the public and private sectors. Their representation in the public sector, however, decreased 0.9 percent from 1976 to 1988. Hispanic enrollment in private institutions increased from 2 to 3.2 percent between 1976 and 1988 and from 3.9 to 5.8 percent in public colleges. Asian-Americans made up 1.4 percent of private school students in 1976 and 3.2 percent in 1988 but increased from 1.9 to 4 percent of students in public institutions. American Indians and Native Alaskans accounted 0.4 percent of private and 0.8 percent of public students in each year, with no change in either sector in 12 years.

Summary

Disparities persist in high school completion rates between whites on the one hand and African-Americans, Hispanics, and American Indians on the other. While the gap has been narrowing for African-Americans, African-American high school completion rates have decreased in the past two years. The high school completion rate for Hispanics fluctuates almost from year to year. In the 12 years from 1976 to 1988, Hispanics made only small gains and frequent losses. The 1988 rate was slightly lower than that for 1986, and in 1988, close to half of Hispanic 18- to 24-year-olds did not have a high school diploma. The high school attrition rate is as high for American Indians as for African-Americans. The overwhelming majority of American Indians attend state-run public schools. As a group, Asian-Americans complete high school at a higher rate than whites. Large subgroups of the Asian-American community, however, especially Southeast Asians and Filipinos, do not fit the educational profile of other Asian subgroups.

While a growing proportion of white high school graduates goes on to college, the proportion of African American and Hispanic high school graduates who go to college is shrinking. In 1988, the gap was even wider than it was 12 years earlier. Hispanic college enrollment has increased

77 percent overall since 1976, 112 percent among women. Neither Hispanic nor African-American 18- to 24-year-old women are making real gains in college participation, however. Proportionally, fewer of these women attended college in 1988 than in 1976.

The college-going segment of 18- to 24-year-old African-American and Hispanic men has been declining seriously: Only 25 percent of African-American men and 31 percent of Hispanic men enrolled in college in 1988, compared to 39 percent of white men in that age group. This difference is 14 percentage points greater for African-Americans and 8 percentage points greater for Hispanics than in 1976. Compared to whites, a much greater number of all minority groups attend community colleges as opposed to four-year colleges.

According to a recent study, only about half the number of Hispanics and African-Americans earned bachelor's degrees after six years than did whites or Asian-Americans. Contrary to the gains made by Hispanics, Asians, and American Indians in obtaining degrees at all levels, fewer African-Americans obtained degrees in 1987 than they did in 1976. Hispanic, Asian-American, and American Indian women have made great gains since 1976 in obtaining all levels of degrees, from bachelor's through first professional. The actual numbers, however, remain very low. African-American women have made some gains in doctorates and first professional degrees since 1976 but only a very modest gain (1.7 percent) in baccalaureate degrees; the number of master's degrees obtained by African-American women dropped considerably.

Private colleges and universities retain and graduate more students in general than public institutions. African-Americans and Hispanics in private colleges and universities benefit only slightly from the advantage of the private institutions in this regard. The completion rate at private institutions for these two groups is only a few percentage points higher than the completion rate for the same groups at public colleges and universities. The proportional representation of American Indians and Native Alaskans did not increase in public or private colleges in the 12 years from 1976 to 1988.

Notes

1. Not all of the 20 or more ethnicities that comprise the Asian and Pacific Island community have had the same experiences in the United States, nor do they share the same degree of educational attainment. For example, the percent of 25-year-olds with a high school or college education was higher for five of the six Asian groups counted in the 1980 Census than for the average U.S. population, with the exception of the Vietnamese. Consequently, although aggregate figures provide an important overview of trends for Asians and Pacific Islanders as a whole, the gross numbers can obscure a less optimistic reality for certain subgroups, especially Filipinos, Southeast Asians, and other refugee groups.

2. It is also interesting to note that only a small portion of all students (a little more than 15 percent) graduated after four years, although this figure was about 12 points higher for students in the private sector (Porter 1989).

Understanding Student College Choice

DON HOSSLER, JOHN BRAXTON,
AND GEORGIA COOPERSMITH

Increased Interest In Student College Choice

During the past three decades, a diverse set of demographic and public policy issues have fueled increased interest in student college choice. These issues include the emergence of the federal government as a significant source of student financial aid, the declining pool of high school graduates, and past declines in the postsecondary participation rates of black high school students. As a result of these trends, federal, state, and institutional policy-makers, as well as social science researchers, have become interested in understanding the factors that shape the decision to attend a postsecondary educational institution (PEI).

Public policy-makers at the state and federal level have a vested interest in understanding the factors that influence aggregate student enrollments. Both federal and state policy-makers use postsecondary participation rates as indices of economic competitiveness as well as overall quality of life. Although the relationship between education and economic competitiveness and quality of life is multivariate, the commonly held belief is that increased levels of education at the state level improve the quality of life for citizens and attract more business and industry.

As the result of increased state and federal investments in student financial aid, state and federal policy-makers can use research on student college choice to more effectively target financial aid dollars. In some states, policy-makers are also committed to maintaining vitality in both the public and private sectors of postsecondary education. A better understanding of student college choice can provide appropriate incentives to help achieve this goal.

Perspectives on Student College Choice

Conceptual approaches to describing the college choice process are found in three categories of models which specify factors leading to college choice as well as the relationship among the factors: econometric, sociological, and combined (Jackson, 1982). Within each of these three categories, various conceptual approaches or models have also been developed and will be reviewed.

Econometric Models

Two strands of econometric models of college choice are present in the literature. One strand seeks to predict enrollments with institutions, states, and the nation as the units of analysis, while the other strand focuses on the individual student as a unit of analysis (Fuller, Manski, and Wise, 1982). To be conceptually consistent with the definition of student college choice used in this chapter, only those econometric models which seek to estimate the choice process of the individual student will receive attention. Within the strand of econometric literature, which focuses on the choices of individual students, two types of choices are modeled. One type of choice is between enrollment in a PEI or the pursuit of a noncollege alternative such as the military or a job (Kohn, Manski, and Mundel, 1976; Bishop, 1977; Fuller, Manski, and Wise, 1982; Manski and Wise, 1983; Nolfi, 1978), while the choice of a particular PEI from a set of PEIs is the second type of choice process (Radner and Miller, 1970; Kohn et al., 1976; R. Chapman, 1979).

Regardless of the type of choice addressed by the various models, all the models reviewed postulate a weighing of various factors to make a choice. To elaborate, an individual student will select a particular PEI if the perceived benefits of attendance outweigh the perceived benefits of attendance at other PEIs or a noncollege alternative. In other words, the individual student strives to maximize the expected utility of the choice to be made. This formulation specifies the relationships among the factors in each of the models presented. Although the type of choice and the specific factors posited to be influential may differ across the various econometric models, underlying formulations concerning the relationships among factors are the same.

College or Noncollege Choice

Five models have been advanced to describe factors posited to be influential in the process of choice between college attendance or a noncollege alternative (Kohn et al., 1976; Bishop, 1977; Nolfi, 1978; Fuller et al., 1982; Manski and Wise, 1983). Such models have also been termed *college-going models* (Kohn et al., 1976).

Expected costs are factors common to all of the college-going models. Expected costs include tuition, net tuition (tuition minus financial aid), room and board, and various living expenses. Earnings forgone due to college attendance are additional expected costs included in models advanced by Bishop (1977) and Fuller et al., (1982) .

Future earnings expected either from college attendance (Bishop, 1977; Fuller et al., 1982) or from a noncollege alternative (Bishop, 1977; Nolfi, 1978) are additional economic factors. According to Fuller et al., (1982), expected or future earnings from college attendance are estimated by students through the value expected to accrue from receipt of a college degree. Various student background characteristics are factors also predicted to influence college-going behavior (Kohn et al., 1976; Bishop, 1977; Nolfi, 1978). Such family background characteristics as parental educational level (Kohn et al., 1976; Bishop, 1977), parental level of income (Kohn et al., 1976; Bishop, 1977; Nolfi, 1978), number of siblings, and parental occupation (Bishop, 1977) are among the student background characteristics included in some of these econometric models (Kohn et al., 1976; Bishop, 1977; Nolfi, 1978).

High school characteristics such as the proportion of graduates going to college or some other PEI (Nolfi et al., 1978) and high school quality (Bishop, 1977) are also factors predicted to affect college-going behavior. Aspirations of neighborhood peers are an additional factor identified (Bishop, 1977).

College characteristics are also assumed to affect college-going choice. The underlying assumption behind the inclusion of college characteristics in this type of college choice model is that individual students will make a choice between attending a PEI or a non-PEI based on the maximum utility or benefit received from the "most attractive" college available to the individual student (Kohn et al., 1976). Both Bishop (1977) and Kohn et al., (1976) include college characteristics in their models of college-going behavior.

Among the college characteristics adduced as influential in determining the maximum utility of the "most attractive" college available to the student are admissions standards (Bishop, 1977), the average ability of students attending the college, educational expenditures, breadth of institutional offerings, and the quality of campus life (Kohn et al., 1976).

Choice Among Colleges

The term *choice among colleges* refers to the selection of a particular college from a set of alternative colleges from which an individual student has received offerings of admission. Kohn et al., (1976) refer to this process as "college choice." Three econometric models of college choice will be discussed in this chapter subsection (Radner and Miller, 1970; Kohn et al., 1976; R. Chapman, 1979).

Like the models of college-going behavior, each of the three models of college choice also identifies costs as factors which influence the choice of one PEI over a set of alternative PEIs. Costs are influential in that students compare PEIs in their set of choices on the basis of their costs and perceived benefits (Kohn et al., 1976). Out-of-pocket expenses to attend different PEIs are one cost factor (Radner and Miller, 1970; R. Chapman, 1979), while tuition costs and net tuition for all possible PEIs are another factor considered to influence the selection process (Kohn et al., 1976). A ratio of college costs to parental income is an additional factor identified (Radner and Miller, 1970). This ratio suggests that if costs for attendance exceed parental discretionary income for a given PEI, then the probability of selecting that particular PEI decreases.

Such student background characteristics as parental income and student academic ability are also posited as factors in the college choice process (Radner and Miller, 1970; Kohn et al., 1976). Presumably such factors enter into the weighting process for alternative PEIs.

College characteristics are understandably included as factors effecting the choice of a PEI. The admission selectivity of a given PEI is identified by Radner and Miller (1970) and by Kohn et al., (1976) as an indicator of college quality, while academic reputation has been suggested by R. Chapman (1979). Quality dimensions are posited as significant, as students would prefer to attend a higher quality college (Kohn et al., 1976). However, at the same time, students would also prefer not to attend a PEI where average student ability is considerably higher than their own. Thus, this factor is accounted for by two of the econometric models of college choice (R. Chapman, 1979; Kohn, Manski, and Mundel, 1976).

In addition to admissions selectivity, the same array of college characteristics identified as important in the college-going model advanced by Kohn et al., (1976) is also postulated to be influential in their econometric model of college choice. Moreover, a range of college attributes such as the size/graduate orientation, masculinity/technical orientation, ruralness, fine arts orientation, and liberalness are also suggested as factors of importance in the college choice process by R. Chapman (1979).

Sociological Models

Sociological models of college choice have focused on the identification and interrelationship of factors which influence aspirations for college attendance. Aspirations for college are of interest to sociologists, as aspirations are an integral element in the status attainment process. The status attainment process is concerned with the role played by various factors in the allocation of individual positions or occupations of varying degrees of prestige or status (Sewell and Shah, 1978). Within this allocative process, the role of education is of central importance.

The derivative model of status attainment was developed by Blau and Duncan (1967). In this model, family socioeconomic background and student academic ability are predicted to have a joint positive effect on aspirations for college. Parental encouragement (Sewell and Shah, 1978) and the influence of significant others and high school academic performance (Sewell, Haller, and Portes, 1969; Sewell and Hauser, 1975) were factors subsequently added as refinements to the basic model. Significant others are the students' parents, teachers, and peers.

The influence of significant others and academic performance represent a linkage of social-psychological mechanisms with status attainment (Sewell et al., 1969). To elaborate, mental ability is assumed to affect academic performance in high school. High school performance and family socioeconomic status exert positive influences on the perceptions of significant others concerning the focal student. Aspirations for college are, in turn, affected by the influence of significant others. Significant others such as parents, teachers and friends influence student aspirations either as models or through the behavioral expectations they communicate.

Combined Models

Although both status-attainment and econometric models have focused on student decision-making in regard to college selection, neither of these conceptual approaches has provided satisfactory explanations of the *process* of college choice. Renewed interest in the subject has caused scholars to look again at both areas from an applied-research tradition in order to better understand consumer decision-making and recruitment efforts (Hanson and Litten, 1982). The new models, by extricating and combining the most powerful indicators in the decision-making process from previous models, provide a conceptual framework that hopes to predict the effects of policy-making interventions. These combined models, as befitting the longitudinal nature of the college choice process, are presented as sequential and as stages in the decision-making process. Institutional and market research have also made their contribution to the combined models by identifying the difference between student *perceptions* of institutional characteristics and objective institutional indicators and by showing the impact of institutional actions on college choice (i.e., recruitment, financial aid, and admissions activities).

Market research has studied the relationship between the type of student and the category of institution to which he or she applied (Zemsky and Oedel, 1983). Demographics, geographic origins, socioeconomic backgrounds, aptitude, and student interests have been analyzed in order to build a profile of the characteristics of students entering individual institutions. Looking for patterns, market research has found a homogeneity that seemingly cuts across all other variables: that is, the personal characteristics of the student—religious and political preferences, levels of sophistication and readiness for college—relate significantly to the existing student body of the college in which she or he enrolls (Clark et al., 1972; Zemsky and Oedel, 1983). From an institutional perspective, the choice process can be likened to a funnel, with a broad pool of prospective students at the top and a narrow pool of students who choose to enroll at the bottom (Litten, 1982).

As in the college-going models advanced by Kohn et al., (1976), Radner and Miller (1970), and R. Chapman (1979), market research indicates that students seek their set of colleges based on their perception of the college community; that is, they seek a college that most closely fits their social preference. These perspectives may be unrealistic. According to R. Chapman (1979), college-bound high school seniors, regardless of the institution they expect to attend, share a highly stereotyped, idealized image of college life, an image that may not be representative of any actual institution. Market research has identified the duality of a college market and the relationship between the structure of student choice and the structure of institutional comparisons—the forces shaping college-bound students' decisions and the institutional consequences of those decisions (Zemsky and Oedel, 1983, p. 25). As market research has shown, the importance of institutional identity in the college choice process, and these intervening variables, along with those from the status attainment and econometric models, has been incorporated in the combined models now examined.

Figure 1
Causal diagram for school process model

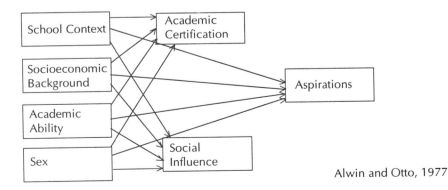

Alwin and Otto, 1977

The major distinction between the combined models and those of status attainment and econometric conceptualizations is that the combined models attempt to identify those factors affecting the decision-making process from a policy analysis perspective; that is, the models attempt to describe the various economic and social forces that affect decision making in order to find opportunities for intervention in the student college choice process. These forces include (1) constraints upon the decision that the researcher and policy-maker should be made aware of and (2) institutional activities that can be undertaken to achieve desired results (beneficial interventions). Because combined models approach the conceptual framework of college choice as applied research and therefore offer opportunities for intervention, they can be more useful to public and institutional policy analysts than could the earlier status-attainment and econometric models.

Two general categories of combined models have been proposed: a three-stage model (Hossler and Gallagher, 1987; Jackson, 1982; Hanson and Litten, 1982) and a multistage model that generally comprises between five and seven stages (Litten, 1982; Kotler, 1976; R. Chapman, 1984).[1] A careful study of both categories reveals much overlap and general consensus (Figure 2). In fact, the three-stage model can be viewed as a simplified, "collapsed" version of the other. Differences between the models lie in the description of the intervening variables and in how they define constraining and institution activity.

The elements of a causal model will be used to provide the framework for a comparative discussion of the combined models of college choice. Intervening variables are those between the independent and dependent variable arranged in stages (or in the terminology of behavioral science, they are the intermediant variables of a cause-and-effect sequence). The two types of variables alluded to are (1) constant variables, which include influential factors effecting the process over which the student has no control, and (2) adjunct variables, which consist of auxiliary action taken by the institution that can beneficially affect the outcome of the decision-making process. These combined models are in agreement in regard to the descriptors that make up the independent variables of the model, although a variety of terms are used to describe the characteristics that cause an individual to consider postsecondary education as a viable alternative following graduation from high school. These include "college aspirations" (Hanson and Litten, 1981: Jackson, 1982; Litten, 1982), which is the referent used to describe the desire to attend. The terminology's source comes out of the literature on status attainment and includes factors such as socioeconomic status, aptitude, high school performance, gender, and family background. *Predisposition* (Hossler and Gallagher, 1987) and *general expectations* (D. Chapman, 1981) are also terms that have been used to describe the same set of individual factors.

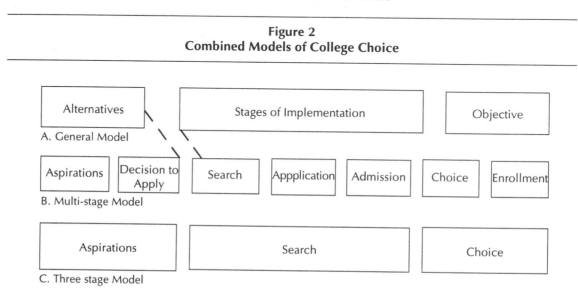

Figure 2
Combined Models of College Choice

Kotler (1976) proposed seven stages of the college choice process in his market research theory: (1) decision to attend, (2) information seeking and receiving, (3) specific college inquiries, (4) applications, (5) admission, (6) college choice, and (7) registration. These stages have been retained in subsequent combined models, although most often several of these individual actions have been incorporated into broader categorical stages. Kotler's model correctly identifies many activities of the college selection process. It also reflects his market research orientation. For instance, by separating "information seeking" from "specific college inquiries," Kotler offers institutions an additional opportunity for interaction. In a later publication, Kotler and Fox (1985) propose that in the information seeking stage, people often form images of schools based on inaccurate or limited information. The image formed affects the student's choice of colleges to which he or she will make specific inquiries. Thus, the image of the college, realistic or not, has a strong influence on the later stages of selection.

D. Chapman (1981) proposed a model of college choice that attempts to identify important variables and influences affecting student college choice. Unlike the other combined models, Chapman's model does not comprise a series of behavioral stages. Rather, it shows the interrelationship of student characteristics with external forces that result in individual expectations of college life. As such, it may not be as useful for devising intervention strategies, but its clear description of influential factors helps to identify important variables.

The model includes SES, aptitude, level of educational aspiration, and high school performance under the general category of student characteristics. D. Chapman states that students not only enter PEIs at different rates due to their socioeconomic status, they also distribute themselves differently across various types of PEIs. Because many PEIs publish test scores and class rank of their entering class, students self-select colleges prior to application based upon their own assessment of aptitude, as indicated by high school performance (Chapman, 1981, p. 483). Student aspirations include both an estimate of their "prospects" and an expression of their hopes and desires for the future. Under the general heading of external influence, Chapman has included as subcategories significant persons, fixed college characteristics, and college communication efforts.

Research has shown that parents exert the most influence on college choice and that other significant influences can include counselors, peers, teachers, and college admissions officers. Fixed college characteristics are those that help to define the institution such as costs, campus environment, location, and program offerings. Together, these create the institutional image. Even though these characteristics are open to change, the image may remain fixed with students and counselors for a long period of time (ibid, p. 476). The market approach to college admissions believes that institutions can promote an image through their recruitment materials and thereby exert desirable influence on a targeted student population. College communication efforts are described as written publications and recruitment materials. The broad categories of student characteristics and external influences shape the individual's expectations of college life, which in turn influence that student's choice of colleges.

The variables that make up the student characteristics (SES, aptitude, level of aspiration, high school performance) have been described in full in the discussion of status attainment and need not be gone into again.

If the purpose of Chapman's model is to identify the variables important to college choice, Jackson's model (1982) is intended to test the strength of the relationships between variables in order to identify the most effective areas of intervention. Jackson proposes a three-phase model of college choice and describes these phases as (1) preference, (2) exclusion, and (3) evaluation. From the status attainment models, Jackson draws individual characteristics that result in educational and occupational aspirations which result in student preferences for postsecondary education. According to Jackson, the strongest correlate of student aspiration is high school achievement, which is affected by other variables. Next in strength is context, which includes peers, neighborhood, and school. The third correlate of student aspiration is family background. High school aspiration reflects not only a preference for certain options but also the perception of access and availability of certain options.

Jackson's analysis of econometric models suggests that alternatives (PEIs) are initially excluded because of geographic, economic, and academic considerations that act as constraints when they interact with student characteristics. Whereas most PEIs are appropriate for most students, it is the consideration of basic cost, programs and requirements, and location that creates a real difference. Location can add to basic expense when the costs of travel, residence, and out-of-state tuition are considered. Secondly, students don't have access to complete information on all possible college options, and they proceed in the choice process with only partial information. Students also come with their own exclusion criteria that are based on their expectations of financial resources and future economic performance. These conscientiously act as constraints on college choice, causing students to limit their range of options. Thus Jackson describes the processes of phase 2 as the exclusion phase.

The final phase includes the student's evaluation of options, the translation of his or her preferences into a rating scheme, the selection of a choice set, and ultimately, the decision to enroll in a particular college. Although the rating scheme by which students evaluate their choices is not well understood, Jackson contends that family background, academic experience, location, and college costs are most important to this model of student choice. Recruitment information, college characteristics, and job benefits are ranked as having moderate effects college choice. In this model, social context can claim only a weak effect.

In summary, Jackson ranks the effects of different variables found in the general three-stage model of student college choice in order to inform the design of enrollment strategies. This model is presented as a means for evaluating enrollment tactics.

Both Chapman and Jackson present a generalized model of the influence of college choice and their relationship to the outcomes of institutional policymaking in general terms. Litten (1982), Hanson and Litten (1982). R. Chapman (1984) and Hossler and Gallagher (1987), on the other hand, have attempted to create models that show how the *process* of college choice is undertaken and how it is different for different people. The most effective marketing strategies address the needs of different target populations in specific ways, and therefore a model of college choice that takes into account how the college selection process is different for various groups provides important information for enrollment strategists (Litten, 1982). These multistep, combined models take into account the personal and family background and characteristics that have been borrowed from the status attainment models. Hanson and Litten's (1981) model was used to distinguish how the college selection process is different for men and for women. It also distinguishes between the parallel activities related to the application for college admission and application for financial aid (p. 74). In this model, the six steps of the admission process—(1) desire to attend, (2) decision to attend, (3) investigation of institutions, (4) application for admission, (5) admission, and (6) enrollment—have been organized as three stages (see figure 3).

Figure 3
College-Attendance and College Selection Process

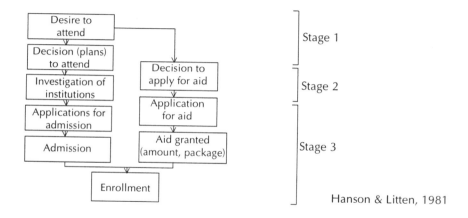

Hanson & Litten, 1981

Stage 1 incorporates the desire and decision to attend. The fact of gender is included as one of the predictors of college aspirations in the sociological models and is emphasized as a controlling variable in the Hanson and Litten model. Variables of self-esteem and self-assessment are seen as differing for men and women, thereby affecting educational aspirations (men have tended to be more self-confident). Stage 2 is described as the investigation stage, and parental influence, geographical location, financial considerations, and college environment have been shown to affect women more than men. Women have been more likely to apply for early decision and to apply earlier in general than men, a difference found later in Stage 3.

Litten later expands this model, drawing upon Chapman's broader, structural model. The "Expanded Model of the College Selection Process" (Litten, 1982, p. 388) draws upon variables from the status-attainment and econometric conceptual approaches. The social attributes of the high school, student performance as indicated by class rank, and high school curriculum are shown to affect student aspirations to attend or not to attend. Likewise, SES and personal attributes—such as academic ability, self-image, and the nature of the economic, political, and cultural environment—are all shown to affect the student's predisposition to attend. At the information-gathering stage, the influence of significant others (parents, peers, close friends) is influential. From market theory, variables of college action (recruitment, policies, publications, media) are demonstrated to have an effect on application. Finally, the college's action to grant or not to grant admission also influences the decision to enroll. Research applied to this model indicated that the timing of steps in the selection process is closely tied in to parental education, especially as it relates to how information on colleges is obtained. By drawing a line around the entire decision-making process, Litten's model illustrates that the control variables have a probable point of principle impact but that they continue to exert influence throughout the process. By developing an awareness of the individual differences in timing, policy-makers may be able to approach targeted groups with information appropriate to their different timetables (Litten, 1982).

R. Chapman (1984) proposes a five-stage theory of how students select a college and adds to the literature by further clarifying the basic terminology used to describe the various behavioral stages. In Chapman's model, the first stage is identified as "Presearch" behavior and is described as that period of time when a student first recognized "the possible need and desirability of a college education." This terminology is close enough to the "college aspirations" or "predisposition stage" of other models to be used interchangeably. By Chapman's definition, the second stage, "Search," is characterized by the active acquisition of alternative variables that characterize colleges, such as cost, quality of life, and academic programs. The search phase concludes when the student decides upon a set of colleges. The set is comprised of the colleges to which applications will be submitted and reveals a process of self-selection. Research has shown that students apply to those colleges they are likely to be admitted to: likewise, we must assume that the colleges in this set are at least minimally acceptable to them (R. Chapman, 1984). At the application decision, however (stage three), the possibility of financial aid is still an unknown but will effect the next stage, the choice decision. Choice is the decision to select one of several colleges to which the student has been admitted. It is at this point that actual, rather than perceived, college characteristics become of primary importance, along with the factors of financial aid. As with all other models, Chapman's model of the college choice process ends with matriculation, the actual action of enrolling in a college.

The conceptual models of college choice identify significant variables and show the sequence of the decision-making process. Of special interest to researchers and policy-makers are the control variables consisting of constraints (environmental factors or characteristics of the population) and adjuncts (auxiliary actions taken by policy-makers to enhance the process, such as pricing, programming, and recruitment materials). The concept of constraints comes from the economic models, which indicated that students first exclude and then evaluate alternatives. Econometric theory has also been used to predict the impact of change in public policy toward financial aid. Research on the relationship of financial aid and college choice has demonstrated that aid has a significant impact on college attendance and choice of college (R. Chapman, 1979; Fields and LeMay, 1973; Litten, 1986). Likewise, the perception of the out-of-pocket cost of attending a particular institution affects the selection decision (Kohn et al., 1976; Bishop, 1977; Nolfi, 1978; Fuller et al., 1982; Manski and Wise, 1983; Litten, 1986). The importance of identifying constraints, therefore, is that they are variables over which public and institutional policy-makers can exert some control. The combined models of college choice provide useful information for the development of enrollment tactics. By describing the relative strength of different variables, the models also provide the means whereby strategies can be evaluated for projected efficiency and effectiveness.

These three conceptual approaches can also be compared on the range of variables included and on their explanatory power. The combined models are the most inclusive of the three approaches, as a wide range of variables is predicted to influence the college choice process. Moreover, the combined models incorporate more than a single stage of the choice process. The econometric models also include a number of variables of presumed influence and focus on one of two stages in the choice process: college-going and choice behavior. The sociological models, however, include a limited number of variables and focus on only the aspiration stage of the choice process.

When the approaches are compared on their explanatory power, the combined models appear to be limited. Although the models of this category posit relationships between various variables, few assumptions and concepts which seek to explicate the linkages between influential variables are advanced, and those that are have not been investigated. While the econometric models offer the option of maximum utility of the perceived benefits of one choice alternative over another, assumptions and linking concepts among variables are also lacking. The sociological models not only provide several alternative perspectives on the mechanisms for the development of aspirations of college choice but also move beyond statements of relationships to the advancement of assumptions and concepts which seek to explain these relationships. Thus, the sociological models appear to have the most explanatory power of the three conceptual approaches to the study of college choice.

Given these assessments, we suggest a need for further development of the econometric and the combined models of the college choice process. Such development should focus on enhancing the explanatory power of these conceptual approaches. However, as the combined models appear to be the most inclusive in terms of the stages and factors included, this category of approaches is perhaps the best candidate for further theoretical development. Specific suggestions for such theoretical development are subsequently discussed in this chapter.

A Review of Research on Student College Choice

In addition to the theoretical work that provides a conceptual framework for this chapter, there are numerous studies that have examined various aspects of student college choice. The foci of these studies include the postsecondary aspirations of high school graduating classes, the relationship between high school guidance counseling and postsecondary plans, the impact of financial aid on postsecondary attendance rates, and institutional studies that attempt to determine which factors affect the decision to attend a specific PEI.

For this review, the three-stage model of student college choice proposed by Hossler and Gallagher (1987) will be used as the conceptual framework for organizing empirical investigations of college choice. Although, this model does not capture the complexities of the choice process that are present, for instance, in the model of Kotler (1985), it includes the major stages of the choice process. In addition, this model combines most of the variables found in both econometric and sociological models of student college choice. The model also suggests that institutional variables have an impact on student college choice. By employing a three-stage model, it is possible to bring some order to a diverse, and sometimes chaotic, set of empirical investigations. By employing a theoretical model to organize and review existing research on student college choice, it is possible to conduct a systematic analysis of methodological questions and theory development in the next section of this chapter. The model of Hossler and Gallagher (1987) is based on the work of R. Chapman (1984), Jackson (1982), and Litten (1982). This model of student college choice includes the following stages:

1. Predisposition—The "developmental phase in which students determine whether or not they would like to continue their formal education beyond high school."

2. Search—Searching for the attributes and values which characterize postsecondary educational alternatives as well as learning about and identifying the right attributes to consider.

3. Choice—Formulating a choice (or application set) and deciding which institution to attend. (Hossler and Gallagher, 1987, p. 211)

In this chapter, each stage is examined separately and related research is reviewed. Although this approach integrates and extends our knowledge of student college choice, such an endeavor is not without conceptual and methodological problems.

A review of the research on student college choice quickly reveals that it has not been based upon a common set of theoretical assumptions. Most of the existing research has not been conceptualized in such a way that these studies can easily be categorized into the three-stage model that has been outlined. Many of the investigations, while grounded in concrete practical problems, lack any guiding theoretical constructs. As a result, many studies are based upon a unique set of assumptions. There is great variance in the survey instruments or interview protocols and the results of these college choice studies.

To clarify relationships among variables, available evidence has been carefully reviewed. In addition, causal ordering has been reported whenever such findings were available. Out of necessity, the format of the examination of each stage of student college choice is different. Because there are so many investigations which have examined the correlates of postsecondary enrollment and the demand for higher education, much is known about the factors that influence the predisposition stage of student college choice. The *correlates* of predisposition, as well as some of the *process characteristics* (timing, variability among different students, etc.) of predisposition can be discussed in detail.

Conversely, the search stage has received little attention. Little is known about how students go about collecting and evaluating information about PEIs before they select the institutions to which to apply. Therefore, the discussion of search in this chapter is limited to an examination of the process characteristics (timing and information sources).

The third stage, choice, has received considerable attention from individual institutions. These institutions have studied the correlates of choice in order to understand why students select one PEI over another. It is more difficult to arrive at generalizations similar to those arrived at when examining predisposition. Nevertheless, more is known about the choice stage than is known about the search stage.

Predisposition

During the predisposition phase of student college choice, students arrive at a tentative conclusion to continue, or not continue, their formal education after high school graduation. Since few studies of student college choice have been conducted using a college choice model, the predisposition section of this chapter draws primarily upon research that has examined correlates of postsecondary participation. From the perspective of a college choice model, studies that examine such variables as the relationship between SES, or levels of parental encouragement, and postsecondary enrollment provide insights into the factors that influence whether or not a student will attend a PEI. The array of variables that have been found to be correlated with a predisposition toward postsecondary attendance include:

1. Family socioeconomic status is positively associated with postsecondary participation (Corrazini et al., 1972; Ekstrom, 1985: Elsworth et al., 1982; Gilmour et al., 1978; Hause, 1969; Jackson, 1978; Manski and Wise, 1983; Perlman, 1973; Sewell et al., 1972; Sewell and Hauser, 1975; Tuttle, 1981; Yang, 1981).

2. Student academic ability and achievement are positively associated with postsecondary participation (Bishop, 1977; Carpenter and Fleishman, 1987; Hause,

1969; Jackson, 1986; Manski and Wise, 1983; Sewell and Hauser, 1975; Tillery, 1973; Tuttle, 1981; Yang, 1981).

3. Race and ethnicity are associated with postsecondary participation. Caucasians and Asians are more likely to participate, black and Hispanic students are less likely to participate (Hossler, 1984; Litten, 1982; Manski and Wise, 1983; Tuttle, 1981).

4. Gender has little impact on postsecondary participation (Carpenter and Fleishman, 1987; Elsworth, 1982; Hossler and Stage, 1987; Marini and Greenberger, 1978; Stage and Hossler, 1988).

5. Parental levels of education are positively associated with postsecondary participation (Carpenter and Fleishman, 1987; Gilmour et al., 1978; Hossler and Stage, 1988; Jackson, 1986; Solmon and Taubman, 1973; Trent and Medsker, 1967; Tuttle, 1981; Yang, 1981).

6. Family residence—urban or rural location—has differential effects on postsecondary participation (Anderson et al., 1972; Dahl, 1982; Lam and Hoffman, 1979).

7. Parental encouragement and support for postsecondary education are positively associated with postsecondary participation (Carpenter and Fleishman, 1987: Conklin and Dailey, 1981; Ekstrom, 1985; Gilmour et al., 1978; Hossler and Stage, 1988: *Parents, Programs and Pennsylvania Student Plans*, 1984: Russell, 1980).

8. Peer encouragement and support are positively associated with postsecondary participation (Carpenter and Fleishman, 1987; Coleman, 1966; Falsey and Heyns, 1984; Jackson, 1986; Russell, 1980; Tillery. 1973).

9. Encouragement from high school counselors and teachers are positively associated with postsecondary participation (Ekstrom, 1985; Falsey and Heyns, 1984; Tillery, 1973; *Parents Programs and Pennsylvania Student Plans* 1984).

10. Student educational aspirations and career plans are positively associated with postsecondary participation (Carpenter and Fleishman, 1987; Dahl, 1982; Gilmour et al., 1978; Hilton, 1982; Jackson, 1978; *Parents Programs and Pennsylvania Student Plans*, 1984; Peters, 1977; Trent and Medsker, 1968).

11. The quality of the high school and the academic track the student is enrolled during high school are positively associated with postsecondary participation (Alexander et al, 1978; Elsworth, 1982; Harnqvist, 1978; Falsey and Heyns, 1984; Kolstad, 1979; *Parents Programs and Pennsylvania Student Plans*, 1984; Peters, 1977).

12. The labor market and increased rates of return[2] are positively associated with postsecondary participation (Adkins, 1975; Bishop, 1977; Campbell and Siegel, 1967; Chressanthis, 1986; Corrazini et al., 1972; Dresch and Waldenberg, 1978; Jackson, 1978; Mattila, 1982).

Although each of these variables has been correlated with a predisposition toward enrollment in a PEI, the strength of the association between these variables and predisposition is not consistent across all studies.

Socioeconomic Status

SES is positively associated with a predisposition to attend a PEI. A consistently positive relationship has been found between SES and postsecondary participation rates (Alexander et al., 1978; Corrazini et al., 1972; Ekstrom, 1985; Elsworth et al., 1982; Gilmour et al., 1978; Hause, 1969; Jackson, 1978; Perlman, 1973; Sewell et al., 1972; Tuttle, 1981; Yang, 1981). Elsworth et al. (1982) found that SES explained 9.3% of the variance in postsecondary participation rates among youth in Australia (p. 71). Tuttle (1981) reported that SES accounted for 6.8% of the explained variance in his study of students from the 1980 High School and beyond study (HSB). The nature of the relationship between SES and prediction, however, is not specified in all of these studies. In addition, there is some evidence that the impact of SES on predisposition may be different for men and women (Marini and Greenberger, 1978; Stage and Hossler, 1988). In a multivariate analysis of the correlates of postsecondary participation in Australia, Ekstrom (1985) concluded that SES (along with sex, age, and home location) explained most of the variance in participation rates. Gilmour et al. (1978), in a qualitative study of the postsecondary plans of high school seniors in Pennsylvania, reported that as the family income and educational level of parents increased, students started to think about their postsecondary plans earlier.

Not all studies, however, have found SES to play an important role in explaining postsecondary participation rates. Jackson (1986) conducted a comparison of the postsecondary participation rates from the National Longitudinal Study of 1972 (NLS) and the 1980 HSB. Using multiple-regression techniques, he found that SES, while significant, explained only 3.0% of the variance in postsecondary participation rates in the NLS sample and 4.4% of the variance in the HSB sample (Jackson 1986, p. 18). Yang (1981), in a longitudinal study of 1,714 high school seniors that employed multiple-regression techniques, found that SES did not add to the amount of explained variance when parental educational background and parental encouragement were also considered. Similarly, Leslie et al. (1977), in a study of 1,000 high school seniors in Pennsylvania that employed qualitative interview techniques and multiple-regression analysis, found that SES did not have a major impact on student plans to attend a PEI.

Despite the findings of Jackson (1986), Yang (1981), and Leslie et al. (1977), when causal modeling techniques are utilized SES does have a significant, although indirect effect on postsecondary participation. Manski and Wise (1983) used conditional logic analysis to examine the college choice decisions of 23,000 high school students who participated in the National Longitudinal Study of 1972. Their results indicated that SES was associated with the likelihood of postsecondary enrollment (or predisposition), but the effect was not strong. In a path-analytic study, Tuttle (1981), using HSB data, found that SES had an indirect effect through student ability/achievement on the predisposition stage. Tuttle's results suggest that although SES may not directly influence predisposition, SES does directly influence student achievement in high school, which in turn does exert a positive influence upon the predisposition stage. Similarly, Carpenter and Fleishman (1987) employed path analysis to study student college choice in Australia and reported that the effect of SES was indirect. The effects of SES on the predisposition of these students were mediated through parental encouragement and explained 15% of the variance in parental encouragement for college attendance (p. 94). In support of an indirect effect of SES on predisposition in a LISREL path-analytic study of the postsecondary aspirations of 2,495 high school juniors in Pennsylvania, Marini and Greenberger (1978) found that SES explained 8.9% more of the variance in ambition for boys. Conversely, SES explained 12.2% more of the variance in academic achievement for girls (p. 73).

A review of the findings suggests that SES does have an impact on predisposition; however, the impact may not be direct. Rather, SES has a positive effect upon the academic success of students, their educational aspirations, and the educational expectations they perceive that others have for them.

Student Ability

Trent and Medsker (1967) stated that "There is some question as to whether socioeconomic status or ability has the greater influence on the decision to attend college" (p. 3). Like SES, the empirical evidence supports the assertion that student ability is positively correlated with a predisposition toward postsecondary education (Bishop, 1977; Carpenter and Fleishman, 1987; Hause, 1969; Jackson, 1978, 1986; Manski and Wise, 1983; Mare, 1980; Peters, 1977; Rumberger, 1982; Tillery, 1973; Tuttle, 1981; Yang, 1981). While Elsworth (1982) did not find that ability added to the amount of variance explained by his path model, this is the only study reviewed that included a measure of ability or achievement and did not find a significant relationship between ability/ achievement and a predisposition toward postsecondary education. Manski and Wise (1983) found that high school GPA and SAT scores were the best predictors of who applied to college. In another analysis of NLS data, Peters (1977) concluded that high-ability high school students are eight times more likely to go to college than low-ability students (p. 9). Tillery (1973) reported similar findings. Jackson (1978) analyzed data from the National Longitudinal Study of 1972. He investigated the impact of financial aid on college choice using discriminant analysis. He found that academic standing improved his ability to predict college enrollment by 12% (p. 568). In a later comparative analysis of NLS and HSB data, Jackson (1986) reported that academic test scores explained 6.4% of the variance in postsecondary participation rates for the NLS sample and 8.1% of the variance for the HSB sample. Grades explained 4.2% of the variance in postsecondary participation rates for the NLS sample and 7.9% of the variance for the HSB sample (p. 18). Yang (1981), using multiple regression, also found that high school grades explained 15% of the variance in postsecondary aspirations and 12% of the variance in the actual attendance rates of high school students (p. 13).

Further support for the contribution of ability/academic achievement comes from Carpenter and Fleishman (1987) in their path-analytic study of Australian high school students. They found that academic achievement and ability had a direct effect on postsecondary participation. In addition they noted that achievement interacts with students' self-assessments of their postsecondary potential. They did not find a one-to-one correspondence between ability/achievement and postsecondary participation, however, because some students do not assess themselves realistically. In another path analysis that used HSB data, Tuttle (1981) found that grades explained 6.3% of the variance in the predisposition toward postsecondary education (p. 12). In a LISREL path-analytic study, Hossler and Stage (1988) also found that student ability was a good predictor of postsecondary aspirations.

The cumulative weight of the findings in these studies reviewed indicates that student ability and student achievement have a significant and direct impact upon the predisposition of high school students toward a postsecondary education. As ability and academic achievement rise, students are more likely to aspire to attend a PEI and they are more likely to follow through on their plans.

Ethnicity

Historically, black students and other minorities were less likely to attend a PEI (Hossler, 1984). Enrollment trends among minority students rose sharply, however, during the 1970s. Between 1966 and 1977 the numbers of black students enrolled in postsecondary education tripled (*Chronicle of Higher Education,* 1978). Through 1986, participation rates slowly declined; however, in 1986 the black student enrollments started to increase (Evangelauf, 1988, p. A33). Such trends make it difficult to anticipate the impact of race on the predisposition phase of college choice. The inclusion of studies that were conducted when the postsecondary participation rates of minority students was higher, or lower, would be misleading since the factors that influenced the participation rates of minority students have changed. In an attempt to try to capture the current impact of race on predisposition, this review has been limited to a sample of recent investigations.

Ekstrom (1985), in an analysis of HSB data, reported that the impact of race upon postsecondary participation rates disappeared when SES was controlled. Tuttle (1981) found similar results; he found that when SES was controlled, minority students of average ability had a 6% higher probability of attendance (p. 13). Manski and Wise (1983), using NLS data, found similar patterns among black students, as did Jackson (1986), who used both NLS and HSB data sets. Hossler and Stage (1987), in a descriptive study of the postsecondary plans of Indiana ninth-grade students, found that ninth-grade minority students reported thinking more about postsecondary education than white students; however, white students were 4% more likely to indicate that they planned to attend a PEI (p. 10).

Similarly, Brown (1982), who compared NLS and HSB data, arrived at some disturbing findings. He found that the numbers of black students aspiring to attend two- and four-year PEIs had increased between the 1972 NLS study and the 1980 HSB study. From an equity perspective, this suggests that although more black students are aspiring to attend PEIs, fewer are actually attending. Attempts to determine the impact of race on predisposition are like tracking a moving target. At the moment, current evidence suggests that any correlation between race and predisposition is the result of other background variables, such as SES, which may be associated with race. Nevertheless, the declining rates of postsecondary participation of black students, when viewed with the knowledge that black students may have higher aspiration rates, give reason to be concerned about access and choice for black students.

Gender

College enrollment patterns for women, like those for minority students, have been in a period of transition. While women have historically been underrepresented in PEIs, there are now more women than men enrolled (*Update*, 1986). The findings from recent studies on the role of gender in aspirations for postsecondary participation are contradictory. Two studies (Hossler and Stage, 1987; Stage and Hossler, 1988) used correlational statistics and LISREL path-analytic techniques to examine the postsecondary aspirations of ninth-grade students in Indiana. They found that women thought more about going to a PEI but received less family support. Carpenter and Fleishman (1987) and Elsworth (1982), who conducted their studies in Australia, found that gender had no impact on postsecondary aspirations and participation. In fact, Tuttle (1981) deleted gender from his path model because it was not significant in the correlation matrix. Based upon these findings the role of gender on predisposition is uncertain. While some evidence suggests that women may receive less encouragement to attend a PEI, the large increase in enrollment rates among women would suggest that gender no longer plays a major role in the predisposition stage of student college choice.

Parental Educational Levels

Several studies have found a relationship between the level of parental education and predisposition (Carpenter and Fleishman, 1987; Gilmour et al., 1978; Hossler and Stage, 1987, 1988; Jackson, 1986; Manski and Wise, 1983; Solmon and Taubman, 1973; Trent and Medsker, 1967; Stage and Hossler, 1988; Tuttle, 1981; Yang, 1981). Carpenter and Fleishman (1987) found a strong relationship between the father's education and postsecondary enrollment. In his study of SES and HSB participants, Jackson (1986) concluded that each year of parental education increased the likelihood of the student attending a PEI by 6% (p. 13).

Yang (1981) followed 1,714 rural high school seniors during their senior year of high school and their first year in college. Using qualitative data and multivariate analysis his results revealed that the father's education exerted a stronger influence than the mother's upon the aspiration levels of the students, but the mother's education exerted more influence on actual attendance rates. Gilmour et al. (1978) reported that students with parents who had a college education started thinking earlier about continuing their education after high school. Tuttle (1981), however, using path analysis to study HSB data, found it parental education was not significant in the correlation matrix and therefore deleted it from his path model.

In two separate analyses of a sample of Indiana high school students, employing LISREL, Hossler and Stage (1988) and Stage and Hossler (1988) looked at the effects of parental education upon the postsecondary plans of Indiana ninth-graders. The first study (Hossler and Stage, 1988) found that the combined level of parents' education had a positive indirect and direct effect on students' educational plans. Parents' education explained 43.5% of the variance in the amount of parental encouragement that parents gave students to attend a PEI (an indirect effect), and in addition, parental education directly explained 9.5% of the variance in students' educational aspirations (p. 7). The second study (Stage and Hossler, 1988) indicated that the mother's level of education had a positive indirect effect upon the educational plans of both male and female students (mediated through parental encouragement), while the father's level of education had both a positive direct and indirect effect upon the postsecondary educational plans of male and female students (total effect was 7.0% for females and 7.6% for males (pp. 20, 21)). In addition, Hossler and Stage (1988) found that the level of parental education was the best predictor of the parents' educational expectations for their children as well as the best predictor of the students'

GPAs (explained 34.7% of the variance, p. 7). These findings are similar to those of Manski and Wise (1983), who compared the application probabilities of students whose parents had less than a high school education with those of students whose parents had a college degree or more. Across income levels ranging from $6,000 to $18,000, they found that in most income brackets, students who had parents with a college education more than doubled the probability that they would apply for college (p. 88).

Overall, the evidence suggests that the level of parental education exerts a strong influence upon predisposition toward postsecondary education, more than either SES or student ability.

Family Residence Characteristics

There is some empirical evidence to support the assertion that the location of family residence affects postsecondary participation rates (Anderson et al., 1972; Astin and others, 1980; Dahl, 1982; Lam and Hoffman, 1979; Willingham, 1970). These studies of family residence typically focus upon the impact of living in an urban or rural location, and whether nearness to a PEI influences postsecondary participation rates. Anderson et al. (1972) used multiple-regression techniques to analyze SCOPE data (which included postsecondary participation rates from four states). They found that the relationship between distance and college attendance was complex and varied in different states and for students of different ability levels. Generally, students who lived within twenty miles of a PEI were more likely to enroll. The variance in the effects of PEI distance from home ranged from a low of no effect on high-ability men from Illinois to an increase in college-going rates of 22% for low-ability men in Illinois (p. 249). The amount of variance explained by nearness to a PEI was small. Astin and others (1980) and Willingham (1970) reported similar findings.

Anderson et al. (1972) also found that students who lived in urban areas were more likely to attend a PEI. More recently, Dahl (1982), employing discriminant analysis in a longitudinal study of Kentucky high school seniors noted that students who resided in urban areas were more likely to enroll in a PEI. Another study employing discriminant analysis (Lam and Hoffman, 1979), conducted at a single Canadian university, reported that students who lived in rural areas were less likely to enroll in a PEI.

Although the effects of residence characteristics were significant in each of these studies, they did not have a strong or even moderate effect upon a predisposition toward postsecondary education. When ability and SES were controlled, the effects of residence characteristics diminished.

Parental Encouragement

Investigations of student college choice have consistently found that the amount of parental encouragement and support for postsecondary education is related to the likelihood of attendance (Carpenter and Fleishman, 1987; Conklin and Dailey, 1981; Ekstrom, 1985; Gilmour et al., 1978; Hossler and Stage, 1988; Murphy, 1981; *Parents, Programs and Pennsylvania Student Plans*, 1984; Russell, 1980; Stage and Hossler, 1988; Soper, 1971; Tillery, 1973). Several descriptive studies have reported a significant positive relationship between parental expectations and the educational aspirations of high school students (Ekstrom, 1985; *Parents, Programs and Pennsylvania Student Plans*, 1984; Russell, 1980; Soper, 1971; Tillery, 1973). Murphy (1981), in a descriptive study of high school seniors and parents, noted that 42.6% of all students and 50% of all parents said that the idea of attending a PEI was first initiated by parents (p. 143). Hossler and Stage (1988), in their LISREL path model, found that parental encouragement for their students explained 18.2% of the variance in the postsecondary plans of Indiana ninth-graders and exerted the largest direct effect on students' plans.

Carpenter and Fleishman (1987) found that parental expectations did not directly influence the postsecondary enrollment decision. Parental expectations, however, did influence student's perceptions of subjective norms (perceptions of what students believed others thought they should do), which in turn were strongly related to postsecondary enrollment. Furthermore these authors' results demonstrated that as the level of parental encouragement increases, student achievement also increases. Conklin and Dailey (1981) used multiple-regression techniques to analyze data gathered from a longitudinal study of high school students from their sophomore to senior year. The sample included 2,700 students in southern New York State. They also found that as the level of parental encouragement increased, students were more likely to attend four-year PEIs and more selective PEIs. Sewell and Shah (1978) made an even stronger case for the importance of parental encouragement. Using data from NLS, they found that the amount of parental encouragement explained 37% of the variance in postsecondary aspirations (p. 12). Parental encouragement explained more of the variance than any other variable, including SES and student ability.

When these findings are considered in total, parental encouragement appears to play an important role in the predisposition phase. Parental level of education, combined with parental educational aspirations for their children, may be the best predictors of student postsecondary plans. Carpenter and Fleishman's (1987) finding—that as parental encouragement rises, so does student achievement—also raised possibilities of a reciprocal relationship between parental encouragement, achievement, and predisposition. That is, as students perform better in school, parents provide more encouragement, which in turn provides further motivation for students to further improve their performance.

Peer Support and Encouragement

In addition to parental encouragement, researchers have found a relationship between predisposition toward postsecondary education and the level of support and encouragement of peers (Carpenter and Fleishman, 1987; Coleman, 1966; Falsey and Heyns, 1984; Jackson, 1986; Russell, 1980; Tillery, 1973). Falsey and Heyns (1984) asserted that one of the outcomes of attending private schools is that students establish friendship patterns that result in more contact with students planning to attend PEIs. For students attending private schools, these patterns increase the likelihood that they will attend college. In a study of 13,000 high school students in Manitoba that did not use inferential statistics, Russell (1980) reported that the postsecondary aspirations of friends were cited as one of the most influential factors in determining students' postsecondary plans. Coleman (1966) and Tillery (1973) described similar findings. In his comparison of the NLS and HSB samples, Jackson (1986) found that the presence of college-going peers produced one of the strongest correlations when he attempted to isolate the most important determinants of postsecondary enrollment. Hossler and Stage (1987), however, employed correlational statistics to examine the relationship among postsecondary plans of Indiana ninth-graders and their peers. They found that those students who were not planning to attend a PEI more frequently consulted their peers. This may suggest that students who are not planning to attend college may be more likely to be influenced by their peers than those students who are planning to go to college. The results from these studies suggest that peers also influence the predisposition phase of student college choice. In total, however, the evidence indicates that peer support and encouragement are not strongly associated with predisposition.

Encouragement from High School Counselors and Teachers

Boyer's recent book, *College: The Undergraduate Experience* (1986), asserted that high school counselors and teachers need to work more with high school students so that the student college choice process will be more informed. Some empirical investigations have examined the influence of encouragement from high school counselors and teachers on predisposition (Ekstrom, 1985; Falsey and Heyns, 1984; Lewis and Morrison, 1975; Tillery, 1973; *Parents, Programs and Pennsylvania Student Plans*, 1984). These investigations indicate that counselors and teachers have little impact on the postsecondary aspirations of students (Lewis and Morrison, 1975; Tillery, 1973; *Parents, Programs and Pennsylvania Student Plans*, 1984). Ekstrom (1985), Hossler and Stage (1987), and Lewis and Morrison (1975) did find that low-income and minority students were more likely to consult with counselors. Even among minority students, however, the actual percentage of students that relied on counselors was far below 50% (Hossler and Stage, 1987; Lewis and Morrison, 1975). These findings suggest that counselors and teachers have very little influence upon the predisposition stage of most high school students.

Student Career Plans and Aspirations

Research on the predisposition stage of student college choice indicates that the educational goals and career aspirations of high school students are positively related to enrollment in a PEI (Carpenter and Fleishman, 1987; Dahl, 1982; Gilmour et al., 1978; Hilton, 1982; Jackson, 1978; *Parents, Programs and Pennsylvania Student Plans,* 1984; Peters, 1977; Trent and Medsker, 1968). Several studies reported that over 80% of all high school students who indicate that they plan to enroll in a PEI follow through on their plans (Dahl, 1982; Hilton, 1982; Peters, 1977; Trent and Medsker, 1967). However, when causal models are developed, it appears that student aspirations are influenced by SES. Student ability/achievement, and parental expectations (Carpenter and Fleishman, 1987; Corazzini et al., 1972; Hossler and Stage, 1988). Thus, while student aspirations may be a good predictor of student outcomes, aspirations may simply reflect the effects of other variables.

School Quality and Academic Track

In addition to all of the variables examined thus far, some investigators have also concluded that the quality of the high school and placement in an academic track influence predisposition (Alexander, 1978; Elsworth, 1982; Falsey and Heyns, 1984; Kolstad, 1979; *Parents Programs and Pennsylvania Student Plans* 1984; Peters, 1977). The effects of school quality, however, are contradictory. Alexander (1978), Elsworth (1982) and Falsey and Heyns (1984) reported evidence suggesting that high school quality does effect predisposition. Elsworth's study (1982), however, was conducted in Australia and may not be generalizable to the United States. Falsey and Heyns's (1984) study focused upon the student outcomes of attending private high schools. Their findings may not be generalizable to all types of high schools. Alexander's (1978) study found that the social status of the high school was correlated with attendance at a PEI. Kolstad (1979), however, used multiple-regression analysis with a sample drawn from NLS and concluded that when SES and other background characteristics are held constant, high school quality is only weakly correlated with enrollment in PEIs.

With respect to the high school curriculum, research suggests that being in an academic track has an impact on the predisposition phase (Jackson, 1986; Kolstad, 1979; *Parents, Programs and Pennsylvania Student Plans,* 1984; Peters, 1977). The Pennsylvania study, in fact, found that high school track was a better predictor of attendance in a PEI than grades. Similarly, Jackson (1986) found strong zero-order correlations between academic track and postsecondary enrollment. Kolstad (1979), however, reported that academic track did not exert much influence on postsecondary participation when background characteristics were controlled. Unfortunately, there were no path analytic models to indicate whether other variables have causal links with academic track. It appears that a student's academic track is correlated with the predisposition phase of student college choice, but the precise nature of the relationship between academic track and the decision to attend a PEI cannot be specified. Causal models, however, might be expected to show that SES, ability, and parental encouragement exert a strong influence upon the academic track that students are enrolled in during high school.

Effects of the Rate of Return and Labor Market

Economists as well as education researchers have also investigated the relationship between (1) the labor market, (2) the rate of return, and (3) postsecondary enrollments (Adkins, 1975; Bishop, 1977; Campbell and Siegel, 1967; Chressanthis, 1986; Corazzini et al., 1972; Dresch and Waldenberg, 1978; Jackson, 1978; Mattila, 1982). The questions driving these investigations are:

1. Do the employment opportunities for graduates of PEIs have any impact on decisions to go to a PEI? When the number of jobs for graduates of PEIs decline do postsecondary enrollments decline? When the number of jobs increases, do postsecondary enrollments increase?

2. Are students' decisions to continue their education beyond high school influenced by their perceptions of the rate of return?

In the aggregate, the answer is that the predisposition phase of college choice is not greatly influenced by either labor market activities or the rate of return. Adkins (1975), after comparing postsecondary enrollment trends since the Great Depression to trends in the labor market, stated that the postsecondary enrollments have increased steadily despite shifting trends in the labor market. Corazzini et al. (1972) concluded that during periods of high unemployment students are more likely to attend a PEI rather than be unemployed. Chressanthis (1986) and Hossler (1984) observed the same trend during the recession of the late 1970s.

Changes in the rate of return also have little effect on the predisposition phase of college choice. Despite the well-documented decline in the rate of return during the 1970s (Bird, 1975; Dresch and Waldenberg, 1978; Freeman, 1976), aggregate postsecondary enrollments continued to increase. Mattila (1982) found that enrollment rates among men during the 1970s declined, and he attributed this to changes in draft laws and the declining rate of return. However, Bishop (1977) and Campbell and Siegel (1967) attempted to measure the effects of rate of return on the demand for higher education. Both studies concluded that high school students were either unaware of shifts in the rate of return or discounted future rates of return at such high levels that it had no effect on their postsecondary educational plans. The results of these econometric studies indicate that although some subpopulations of high school students (e.g., males) may be more responsive to economic inducements, in the aggregate, these inducements have little or on impact on the predisposition phase of most high school students.

This review of the correlates of the predisposition indicates that a number of factors influence the predisposition stage of student college choice. Table I summarizes the strength of the association between these factors and a positive predisposition toward postsecondary education.

Process Characteristics of Predisposition

In addition to the correlates of the predisposition stage, several process characteristics are also involved in the development of a predisposition toward postsecondary education. Gilmour et al.

Table 1
The Correlates of Predisposition

Variable	Strength of Association
Ability/achievement	Strong
Academic track	Strong
Parental levels of education	Strong
Parental encouragement	Strong
Student aspirations	Strong
Peer encouragement	Moderate
Ethnicity	Weak
Family residence	Weak
Gender	Weak
High school counselors and teachers	Weak
Labor market and rate of return	Weak
SES	Weak
School quality	Weak

(1978) concluded that the decision to attend a PEI is closely intertwined with the career-decision-making process. The two processes take place simultaneously. A predisposition toward postsecondary education is an evolving process that proceeds at differential rates for different students. Gilmour et al. (1978) noted that the sharpness, or certainty, of students' postsecondary plans varied greatly among students at the same grade level. For example, when studying two students at the same grade level, one student reported that she wanted to be a premed student at Duke or Stanford, the other student planned to go to a college to be "something better."

These distinctions in the certainty of students' plans are further demonstrated in Ekstrom's (1985) results. Among the students in the HSB study, 41% reported that they decided to attend a PEI by the sixth grade, 53% had decided by the eighth grade, and 61% had decided by the ninth grade (p. 15). Stewart et al. (1987), in a retrospective study conducted at Michigan State University, found that 80% of the students had made the decision to attend a PEI by the end of their junior year in high school (p. 13). Parrish (1979) investigated the postsecondary plans of high school juniors in one high school and reported that 59.8% of the students planned to attend a postsecondary institution and that 22.3% were undecided (p. 3).

Hossler and Stage (1987) found that although nearly 72% of the Indiana ninth-graders in their sample planned to attend a college or vocational institution (p. 8), few ninth-graders had thought beyond the predisposition phase. The ninth-grade questionnaire included a set of questions that asked them to indicate how far they wanted to travel to go to college, the size of the institution they wanted to attend, and whether they wanted to commute or live in campus housing. Most of the respondents were undecided. Students with parents who had more education or who were from high-SES families were more likely to have made some decision about these campus attributes, but over 50% of these students were also undecided (p. 18).

Jackson (1982) observed that the decision to consider attending a PEI was not final. He found that some students who initially planned to attend a PEI eventually decided not to continue their education after high school. The findings from this research review indicate that parents and peers provide information and counseling for students and help shape the predisposition stage. By the end of the junior year in high school, if not sooner, most students have formed their predisposition toward postsecondary education. During the predisposition stage, however, most students think of attending a PEI in global terms and lack specificity in their plans. Table 2 outlines the key process characteristics of the predisposition stage.

Search

Because so little attention has been given to the search stage of student college choice, the format of this section differs from that of the predisposition stage. Rather than a detailed review of the correlates of the search stage, this section concentrates on a discussion of the process characteristics of this stage.

Planning

The junior year of high school is an eventful year for students in the college choice process. Most students have reached closure on the predisposition stage during the junior year and enter the search stage. Gilmour et al. (1978), in their study of high school students in six Pittsburgh high

Table 2
The Process Characteristics of Predisposition

Duration	Early childhood to the 9th–10th grades
Related factors	Closely related to development of career plans
Specificity of plans	Vague, only certain they want to attend a PEI
Important influences	Parents

schools, found that 72% of the students in their sample developed a list of PEIs during their junior year (p. 15. Stewart et al. (1987) also found that 80% of the students who attended Michigan State University started investigating their postsecondary options during their junior year (p. 14).

Gilmour et al. (1978) also discovered that taking the PSAT often precipitated the development of a list of potential PEIs. During the early phase of the search process the list of PEIs included 3–6 institutions (p. 15). Gilmour et al.'s findings suggest that the search process nears completion by the summer of the junior year. They reported that during that summer, most students narrowed their list to 2–4 PEIs (p. 17). However, data collected by Lewis and Morrison (1975), a series of interviews with high school seniors throughout their senior year in high school, indicated that for many students the search stage continued into the senior year. By October of their senior year, students reported that only 50% of the PEIs that they ultimately considered had been added to their list of potential schools. By the end of January, students had dropped 50% of the PEIs which they were considering sending applications. The average number of schools considered by students before they began to eliminate institutions was 9.3; as students continued to evaluate institutions, 5.7 was the average number schools dropped from consideration (p. 17).

Approximately 90% of all PEIs that were considered had been added by February (p. 12). In total, it appears that the junior year and the first months of senior year in high school are the time frame during which most students move from the search stage to the choice stage of student college choice.

Information Sources

As the search stage started, Gilmour et al. reported that most students had only a casual awareness of PEIs. Some of the first sources they consulted were college guidebooks such as *Peterson's Guide*. Cibik (1982), in a study of high school seniors at a single high school, found that most students first learned of PEIs from friends (50.6%), a personal campus visit (12.7%), or campus publications (11.7%) (p. 101). Tierney (1980b) reported that low-SES students have fewer information sources than high-SES students. This seems to be indirectly supported by Ekstrom (1985), who noted differences in whom students consult when selecting a curriculum in high school. She found that students in general and vocational tracks are more likely only to talk to friends when selecting courses. Students in the college preparatory curriculum consult more sources such as parents, counselors, and friends. Litten (1982) has suggested that low-SES students are less likely to have college-educated parents as well as fewer contacts with well-educated role models. As a result these students are more likely to have access to less information about postsecondary education.

Cibik (1982, p. 100) also asked the high school students in her sample to identify their informational needs. Their information needs were:

Academic quality, 67.6%
Cost, 63.2%
Career availability, 55.4%
Qualification criteria for aid, 55.4%
Helpfulness and instructors, 50.2%

Lewis and Morrison (1975) found that the most frequently used sources of information were (in rank order) catalogs, campus visits, guidance counselors, students already enrolled in college, and admissions officers.

Although many observers have suggested that students are not well informed at any point of the college choice process (Jackson, 1982; Lewis and Morrison, 1975; Litten, 1982), the search stage can be characterized as an active, rather than passive, process. Lewis and Morrison (1975) reported that the search activities most frequently engaged in by high school seniors included (1) writing away for a catalog, (2) campus visits and interviews, (3) talking to guidance counselors, (4) using catalogs available in high schools, and (5) talking to students already in college. The two most frequent activities required students to initiate activities as opposed to using sources of convenience or passively waiting for information to come to them. Caution must be exercised in interpreting these results, however, because this study was conducted before the widespread use of mail marketing techniques (which are possible through the sales of prospective students' names by The College Board, American College Testing, and other organizations). The use of mail marketing techniques may have made the search process more passive.

Limits on Search

During the search stage students establish limits on the process. Gilmour et al. (1978) observed that most of the students in their sample first established geographical and cost limits; then they determined which institutions offered programs of interest to them. Tierney (1980a) and Astin and others (1980), using larger data sets, also found that geography and cost are important considerations during the search stage.

Table 3 presents the key characteristics of the search stage of student college choice.

In total, little information is available about the search stage, and a number of questions remain. Other than the PSAT, are there other key events that influence the search stage? For students who are planning to enter a vocational institution or a two-year college, and who are less likely to take the PSAT, are there any key external events that affect the search stage? Little is known about how students discover the range of PEIs. How do students learn the names of institutions in order to decide which ones to consider? Do PEIs play any role in the search stage? Could they play any role in the search stage? Could state and federal agencies intervene by disseminating more information about financial aid or postsecondary educational opportunities? Although Gilmour et al . (1978), Lewis and Morrison (1975), and Cibik (1982) have suggested that college guides and institutional information are used during the search stage, caution should be exercised in interpreting these findings. Johnson and D. Chapman (1979) reported that many of the written materials PEIs use are above the reading level of most high school students. In addition, D. Chapman (1981) noted that students use most written material from PEIs to confirm decisions they have already made. If this is the case, how do students go about evaluating a range of PEIs?

Questions of equity and access are also important questions during the search stage. Ekstrom (1985), Gilmour et al. (1978) and Tierney (1980b) indicated that low-SES students, as well as students enrolled in vocational and general tracks, have fewer sources of information about PEIs. Miller (1983), in an examination of how PEIs use college SEARCH mailings,[3] reported that many colleges exclude students who reside in low-income zip code areas. This may further exacerbate the lack of information available to low-income students. Although researchers can speculate about the relationships between student characteristics and the search stage, investigations of the search stage are few. Multivariate studies of the search stage could greatly enhance our understanding of this important stage of student college choice.

Choice

Although the search stage of student college choice has not received a great deal of attention, the choice stage has attracted considerable attention. This stage includes (1) the selection of an application set of institutions, that is, the identification of the PEIs students actually apply to, as

Table 3
The Process Characteristics of Search

Duration	9th–10th grades to fall of senior year
Nature of search behavior	Active, student-initiated
Information sources	Friends, campus visits, campus publications
Most important concerns	Institutional quality, degrees lead to careers, faculty

well as (2) the final matriculation decision. The research literature on the choice stage is dominated by single-institution studies, conducted either at individual high schools or individual PEIs. These studies typically examine the factors that influenced a student's decision to enroll in a specific PEI. There are some well-crafted studies that use larger samples to examine the selection of a PEI. However, they examine aggregate choice decisions such as the selection of a private PEI over a public PEI or the selection of a high-status PEI over a lower status PEI. Research on the choice stage employs a variety of univariate and multivariate statistical designs, as well as qualitative techniques. Missing, however, are studies that employ experimental designs that permit the utilization of causal modeling techniques.

This section on the choice stage will first examine the student correlates of choice. Some of the same variables, such as socioeconomic status or ability, will be used to organize the discussion of student correlates; however, there is little information available about the impact of variables such as gender, peer encouragement, high school quality, or labor market considerations on the choice stage. In this discussion of the choice stage, the institutional correlates of choice (of the institutional characteristics that are associated with selecting one type of public institution over another or in the decision to attend a specific PEI) will be discussed. These institutional characteristics include nonfinancial attributes (e.g., perceived quality and location) and financial attributes (e.g., tuition costs and financial aid). Finally, some of the process characteristics of the choice stage will be described.

Socioeconomic Status

Although different studies have reported conflicting results as they have attempted to determine the impact of SES on the choice stage, the weight of the evidence suggests that SES is related to both the cost and the quality of PEIs which students apply to and attend. Leslie et al. (1977) did not find a strong correlation between SES and the cost of the institution that students attended. Tierney (1980a, b) used multiple-regression analysis to analyze NLS data and a sample of high school seniors in Pennsylvania. In both studies he found that SES did not affect the cost of the institutions that students applied to, but it was related to institutional status. Lower SES students were less likely to apply to high-status institutions. Maguire and Lay (1981) used discriminant analysis to study the choice stage of applicants to Boston College; they found that low-SES students were just as likely to attend private institutions as high-SES students. Interestingly, Dahl's (1982) analysis of the choice stage for Kentucky high school seniors showed that low-income students were even more likely to choose private PEIs.

Hearn (1984), however, used multivariate techniques to analyze the college choice preferences in a longitudinal sample of students and reported that low-SES students were less likely to apply to high-status PEIs. Spies (1978) used multiple regression to analyze data from a sample of high-ability students. He discovered that middle- and low-income students were less likely to apply to high-status institutions. Maguire and Lay (1981) also found similar results. R. Chapman (1979) concluded that high-SES students are more interested in quality than the cost of attendance. Zemsky and Oedel (1983), in a study sponsored by The College Board, examined the PEI application patterns of students in the New England states. They found that high-income students were more likely to apply to PEIs that were out-of-state with more selective admissions standards. The cumulative evidence suggests that student SES does affect the choice stage of student college choice. High-SES students are more likely to apply to and attend selective PEIs. Surprisingly, however, SES does not seem to be associated with the cost of the PEIs students select.

Ability

Existing research on student ability suggests that it affects the choice stage of student college choice. Dahl (1982) found that high school graduates with the strongest academic credentials were the most likely to select an out-of-state PEI. They were also more likely to attend more selective PEIs. Hearn (1984) also reported that high-ability students were more likely to enroll in more selective institutions. The NLS data analyzed by Jackson (1978) revealed similar student choice patterns. Zemsky and Oedel (1983) found that student ability was directly related to the selectivity of the PEI students applied to as well as where the institutions were located. As student ability rose, the likelihood that students would apply to more selective, out-of-state PEIs also increased. In a single institution study, Maguire and Lay (1981) found that students with higher GPAs were more likely to apply to more selective institutions. Further, their results demonstrated that the preferences of students with high GPAs were more stable; these students were less likely to change their minds. In total, these studies indicate that student ability is positively associated with institutional selectivity. As student ability rises, the selectivity of the PEIs in a student's choice set also increases.

Ethnicity

Fewer studies have been conducted on the impact of ethnicity on the choice stage. In Hearn's (1984) study of this stage, which used longitudinal data from PSAT files, SAT/ACT files, and CIRP data, he found that black students were less likely to apply to more selective institutions. Stewart et al. (1987), in a descriptive study of freshmen at Michigan State University, reported that black students were more concerned about financial aid. He did not control, however, for student SES or ability. Based on these limited findings, we conclude that black students may be less inclined to apply to or enroll in selective PEIs and that they may be more concerned about financial aid and the cost of attendance. Although research has examined the choice stage for black students, little is known about this stage for other minority groups. This is an area that merits future study.

Parental Levels of Education

The research on this factor is limited. Litten et al. (1983) conducted an investigation into the postsecondary plans of high-ability students in six market regions (Baltimore/Washington, DC, Chicago, Dallas/Ft. Worth, Denver/Boulder, Minneapolis/St. Paul, and San Francisco/Oakland) from which Carleton College attracted students. Using multidimensional scaling they analyzed the characteristics of different market segments in each market region. They found that levels of parental education were positively associated with a preference for private colleges. Gilmour et al. (1978) and Lewis and Morrison (1975), both of whom utilized interview techniques, found that students with college-educated parents applied earlier and to more PEIs. Gilmour et al. (1978) noted that they also made their decision to attend a specific institution earlier. Hearn (1984) concluded that parental education had a positive impact on attending more selective institutions. In total, these studies suggest that as levels of parental education increase, students enter and complete the choice stage earlier and are more likely to choose and attend selective institutions.

Family Residence Characteristics

Where students live may exert a small influence on the choice stage of student college choice. The most thorough discussion of the role of residence is found in Anderson et al.'s (1972) analysis of student enrollment patterns in separate data sets. Anderson and his colleagues analyzed the postsecondary participation patterns of Wisconsin students between 1957 and 1964; and they also examined SCOPE data (from the states of California, Illinois, Massachusetts, and North Carolina) which contained information about the enrollment patterns of twelfth-graders in 1966. The authors employed multiple-regression techniques to analyze the data. They found a weak association between the presence of a local college option and college attendance. However, SES, parental level of education, student ability, and historical college enrollment patterns in various communities and regions had a larger effect upon enrollment rates than the presence of a nearby two- or four-year institution. Litten et al. (1983) and Lewis and Morrison (1975), as well as two single institution studies (Lay and Maguire, 1980; Muffo, 1987), reported that distance from home was negatively related to the likelihood of student application or enrollment. R. Chapman (1979) concluded that for students applying to Carnegie-Mellon University, distance was irrelevant.

Maguire and Lay (1981) used multivariate techniques in their study of the application pool at Boston College and found that students who planned to attend a PEI near their homes were more likely to implement their plans. It appears that residence characteristics have a limited effect on choice. While multi-institution studies suggest that residence characteristics have a small impact, single-institution studies suggest that distance has a stronger effect. Factors such as institutional prestige, selectivity, and drawing power may explain the differences across institutions.

Parental Encouragement

The level of parental encouragement for students appears to be correlated with attendance at more selective institutions. Conklin and Dailey (1981) provide the most persuasive evidence of the importance of parental encouragement. Their findings showed that as the level of parental encouragement increased, the likelihood increased that students would (1) attend a PEI, (2) attend a four year PEI, and (3) attend a selective PEI. Keller and McKewon (1984), in a descriptive study of Maryland National Merit finalists, found that students who planned to enroll in private institutions reported more parental support for their educational plans. Welki and Novratil (1987), in a single-institution study that employed conditional logic analysis, also found that parental preference played an important role in the decision to attend the institution. Litten et al. (1983), in his x-market study of the Carleton College applicant pool, noted similarities between the postsecondary preferences of parents and students. The results, however, concluded that parents did not have an effect upon the final matriculation decision. This does not rule out the possibility that parents influenced students' decisions to consider attending selective institutions such as Carleton. These studies suggest that parental encouragement plays a role in the choice stage: however, it would appear to be a subtle one which is not currently fully understood. Perhaps the most important parental role comes during the predisposition stage, when parental attitudes greatly influence student aspirations, and during the search stage, when parents may set some of the parameters on net cost and distance from home. During the actual choice stage, parents may not play a central role.

Peer Encouragement and Support

By the time students reach the choice stage, peers do not appear to have an impact. Jackson (1978), in his analysis of NLS data, did not find any relationship between peers and the actual matriculation decision. Gilmour et al. (1978), in his longitudinal study of high school seniors, also reported that peers did not play a role in the decision to attend a specific PEI.

High School Quality

Only one of the studies reviewed examined the relationship between school quality and the choice stage. Falsey and Heyns (1984) concluded that students enrolled in private schools are more likely to enroll in high-status PEIs. They did not control for background characteristics, however, and their findings may be the result of a higher proportion of high-ability and high-SES students attending private schools.

Institutional Attributes

Up to this point in this chapter, the unit of analysis has been the student. Student variables related to predisposition, search, and choice have been examined. This would suggest that PEIs have no impact on the student college choice process. In fact, PEIs have little impact on the predisposition phase. During the predisposition phase students have not sufficiently formulated their postsecondary plans, so that factors such as net cost, size of institution, distance from home, or reputation are not relevant factors. PEIs may, however, have an impact on the search stage; since this stage has not been studied, the effect of institutions on search is unknown. It is likely that students do begin to establish parameters for cost, distance from home, institutional size, specialized programs, and institutional selectivity during the search stage. These probably become important attributes during the search stage, but more research is needed to verify this. Nevertheless, by the time students reach the choice stage, it is clear that their plans are more fully developed and that institutional attributes are important determinants of where students enroll. There is sufficient research on the choice stage to examine some of these institutional attributes.

D. Chapman (1981) described factors such as two- and four-year institutions, academic reputation, size, public or private, and location as "fixed institutional characteristics." Since factors such as public and private, selectivity, and two- and four-year institutions are highly correlated with tuition levels, a discussion of cost is also included. This discussion of cost will focus both on the "list cost" (tuition and fees before financial aid had been awarded) and "net cost" (the cost of attending after financial aid has been awarded). In addition, there are what Hossler (1984) has described as "fluid institutional characteristics," which refer to marketing strategies, offering off-campus programs, and academic program changes designed to attract students. Many studies assert the efficacy of such strategies to attract more applicants and matriculants. For the purposes of this chapter, however, these studies have not been included. Most of these studies rely on anecdotal evidence or lack control groups that permit researchers to assess the effectiveness of such activities. In addition, the literature on this topic would move into a discussion of marketing which is beyond the scope of this chapter. This section will focus on two types of institutional attributes: nonfinancial attributes and financial attributes. Nonfinancial attributes include factors such as academic reputation and social life. Financial attributes include discussions of list and net cost.

Nonfinancial Attributes. A number of studies have been conducted that investigate the characteristics that students rate as most important when they decide to apply to or attend a PEI. Although the precise order of these characteristics varies from study to study, the most frequently mentioned characteristics are listed below in rank order:

1. Special academic programs (major area of study)

2. Tuition costs

3. Financial aid availability

4. General academic reputation/general quality

5. Location (distance from home)

6. Size

7. Social atmosphere

(Sources: Douglas et al., 1983: Bowers and Pugh, 1973; Dahl, 1982; Keller and McKewon, 1984; Konnert and Giese, 1987; Lay and Maguire, 1981; Litten, 1979; Litten et al., 1983; Stewart et al., 1987; R. Chapman and Jackson, 1987).

There are variations in the weighting of these factors by different student populations and for different PEIs. R. Chapman and Jackson (1987) investigated the choice stage of 2,000 academically talented students. Using conditional logic analysis to analyze the data, they concluded that institutional quality was the single most important determinant of the choice stage. Furthermore, they concluded that for high-ability students distance was irrelevant. In their six-market study of academically talented students, Litten et al. (1983) concluded that academic quality had the largest impact on the choice stage. They found. however, that nearness to home, lower costs, and smaller size were also preferred by students in the sample. Keller and McKewon's study of Maryland National Merit Finalists (1984) showed that students planning to attend out-of-state PEIs rated quality as the most important factor in selecting an institution. For students planning to attend an in-state PEI, costs were the most important factor. Leslie et al. (1977) studied the choice stage of 1,000 Pennsylvania high school seniors. They concluded that cost was the most important reason for selecting a PEI among low-income students.

In a study of the applicant pool at Boston College, Lay and Maguire (1980), using factor analysis, determined that the most important factors in deciding who came to Boston College were financial aid (negative), parental preferences, specific academic programs, size, location, and athletic and social activities. In a factor-analytic study of 231 athletes, Mathes and Gurney (1985) found that scholarship athletes placed more emphasis on the academic programs of the institution, while athletes in non-revenue-producing sports placed more emphasis on the coaching staff. In a study of athletes enrolled at colleges in a small college conference that did not award athletic scholarships, Konnert and Giese (1987) indicated that the opportunity to play intercollegiate sports was an important college selection factor for student athletes. Institutional quality and some measure of costs consistently appeared as the two most important reasons that students attend a specific PEI. However, these studies also reveal that there is great variation among students and types of institutions.

Moving beyond the effects of individual institutional attributes, Astin and others (1980) and Zemsky and Oedel (1983) revealed that state policies and the aggregate characteristics of PEIs in a region can influence the choice stage. In states with more generous state scholarship programs, Astin and others (1980) found high school students were more likely to enroll in private PEIs. In addition, students who resided in states with larger private PEI sectors were proportionately more likely to enroll in private PEIs. Zemsky and Oedel (1983) also found that in states with a large and diverse range of PEIs, such as Massachusetts, high school students were less likely to attend an out-of-state PEI. It appears that the perceived availability of aid and presence of specific types of PEIs may raise the awareness levels of high school students about postsecondary educational options. Increased awareness may lead to higher attendance rates at all types of PEIs.

Financial Attributes. As already noted in the section on non-financial attributes, students do consider costs when selecting a college in which to enroll. In this section the effects that costs have upon the attendance patterns of different types of students and institutions will be examined. Student self-reports suggest that cost and financial aid are important considerations when applying to a PEI, or when selecting a PEI in which to enroll. Fenske et al. (1979) reviewed several previous studies they had conducted on recipients of Illinois State Scholarships. In 1976-1977, 40% of all of the respondents indicated that they would not have been able to attend the PEI they selected without a state scholarship. An additional 59% indicated that they would not have been able to attend at all without their state aid (pp. 149–151). Fenske et al. estimated that between 15% and 25% would have attended a public instead of a private PEI if they had not had state scholarships (p. 153). Leslie et al. (1977) indicated that only 25% of their sample of Pennsylvania seniors would not have attended any institution without aid. However, 43.5% of those who indicated that they were only able to roll in a PEI because of aid were low-income students (p. 280). Lam and Hoffman (1979), in a single-institution study, found that students who did not enroll were more likely to report financial reasons as the cause for their nonattendance.

Although student self-reports suggest that financial aid influences the choice stage of student college choice, multivariate studies demonstrate that the relationship between cost and the choice stage is more complex. Dahl (1982) used discriminant analysis to examine the college enrollment patterns of high school graduates in Kentucky. He reported that those seniors who had planned to enroll but did not were more likely to indicate that low cost and financial aid were important factors in their decisions not to enroll. Hearn (1984), in his longitudinal study of high school students, found that the amount of variance in a student's choice of a PEI that was explained by institutional costs was not very high. Jackson (1978) analyzed NLS data using multiple regression and reported that the amount of aid only increased the likelihood of attending a specific institution by 8.5% (p. 566). Using High School and Beyond data in 1986, Jackson again reported similar results. R. Chapman and Jackson (1987) used conditional logic analysis to study the role of financial aid in the choice stage of academically talented students. They concluded that perceived quality has a greater impact on the choice stage than does the net cost. Their findings showed that on the average, the PEIs that students entered were more expensive than the institutions they did not attend. Furthermore, they found that it would have taken $4,000 in financial aid to move a second-choice institution to be the student's first choice, and $6,000 in financial aid to move a third-choice institution to first choice (p. 38). Freeman (1984), using a sample of students from private colleges in the Great Lakes region who had been awarded no-need merit-based aid, reported similar results.[4] Tierney (1980a) used multiple regression to examine the college choice patterns of 6,444 high school students included in the NLS data set. He found that as private institutions offered more aid, the likelihood of students' enrolling in a private PEI increased. Furthermore, he noted that as the tuition gap between public and private PEIs increased, students were more likely to enroll in a public institution.

An analysis of the impact of cost from the perspective of individual institutions, however, presents a somewhat different set of results. Supporting the findings already cited, R. Chapman (1979), who studied the applicant pool at Carnegie Mellon University, reported that cost had no effect on matriculation patterns. Lay and Maguire (1981), as well as Maguire and Lay (1981), in two investigations of the applicant pool at Boston College, found that the amount of aid did influence the matriculation decision of students. They found that better aid offers from competitor institutions resulted in 32% of their applicants' attending those institutions, even though they had rated Boston College as their first choice (p. 83). In a study of the applicant pool at Virginia Technical University, Muffo (1987) used multivariate techniques and concluded that high-ability nonmatriculants were more likely to report better financial aid offers from other institutions. This was especially true of high-ability black students. Litten et al. (1983) and Kehoe (1981) also found that students who (1) initially expressed interest in attending out-of-state PEIs and/or private PEIs, but who (2) also stated concerns about the cost of attendance, were more likely to decide to attend a less expensive private or in-state PEI. R. Chapman and Jackson (1987) indicated that when a high-ability student is undecided among two institutions, $1,000 in aid can shift a student's decision in favor of the awarding institution (p. 38).

By this point it should be evident that the relationship between cost and the choice stage is complex. In the aggregate, it appears that aid is not as important as student perceptions of quality. In fact, in the aggregate, net cost exerts only a modest influence on the choice stage. However, individual institutions do not function in the aggregate, and it appears that aid can make a difference to students who are undecided about two or more PEIs. The challenge for most PEIs is that they lack sufficient information about students to know in advance what the effect of financial aid will be. With the rising use of merit aid (Hossler, 1984), it appears that many institutions have decided to make Type I errors, erring on the side of awarding financial aid in order to attract students even though the additional funds may either not be needed or not be sufficient to move the institution to a first-choice institution. In addition, most of the evidence on the impact of financial aid at the institutional level focuses on high-ability students; little is known about the impact of financial aid upon less talented students.

In total, the choice stage of student college choice is a complex phenomenon which exhibits variation among students and institutions. Table four summarizes the correlates of the choice stage.

Process Characteristics of the Choice Stage

Although the correlates of the choice stage provide insights into this stage, the correlates do not adequately describe how students enter and complete it. The choice stage has two phases. In the first phase students identify their application list of PEIs. In the second phase students select a PEI to attend. Two qualitative studies of high school seniors provide the most detailed information about this stage (Gilmour et al., 1978; Lewis and Morrison, 1975). The search stage of student college choice ends sometime between the end of the junior year in high school and January of the senior year for most high school students (Lewis and Morrison, 1975).

Stewart et al. (1987), in a retrospective study of freshmen attending Michigan State University, reported that 10% of the students made the decision regarding where they would enroll in their junior year, 70% made the decision sometime during their senior year, and 20% made the decision after their senior year (p. ?). The choice stage begins with a list of the PEIs students are considering. Students consult a variety of sources while they are evaluating institutions to which to apply. At this point the role of parents and peers diminishes (Gilmour et al., 1978). Cibik (1982), in a

Table 4
The Correlates of Choice

Student variables	Strength of association
Ability	Strong; high ability is associated with attending more selective PEIs
Parental encouragement	Strong; positively associated with attending more selective and 4-year PEIs
SES	Strong; positively associated with selectivity
Ethnicity	Moderate; blacks less likely to attend
Parental education	Moderate; students with college educated parents more likely to prefer private PEIs and high-status PEIs
Family residence	Uncertain
High school quality	Weak

Nonfinancial institutional variables	
Academic quality	Strong
Location	Moderate/strong
Financial aid availability	Moderate
Scope of postsecondary system in region	Moderate
Size	Weak
Social atmosphere	Weak

Financial institution variables	
Net cost	Strong
Receipt of aid	Weak/moderate; depends on student preferences

descriptive study of high school seniors, found that students were more than twice as likely to report that they alone had the greatest impact on the choice stage (self, 59%; relatives, 21%) (p. 101). Ebberly (1987), however, in a retrospective investigation of freshmen attending Michigan State University, indicated that students used the following sources of information in evaluating their application set: other college students (77%), friends (72%), high school counselors (70%), and family (61%) (p. 7). Lewis and Morrison (1975) reported that students use global constructs such as size and general quality, as well as specific criteria, such as the quality of the chemistry program, in evaluating PEIs. The reasons for some of the discrepancies reported among other indices are difficult to determine. Sample size and sample representativeness, as well as the types of questions asked, may account for the differences. More systematic research is needed in order to understand how students form and evaluate their application set.

Dahl's (1982) longitudinal study of Kentucky high school seniors, as well as Litten et al.'s (1983) six-market study, shed light on shifts in institutional preferences that take place during this evaluation process. Dahl's (1982) data enabled him to compare stated student preferences with where they actually enrolled. He observed that 75% of all students were involved in a shift among various sectors of postsecondary education (public, private, two-year, and four-year PEIs) in Kentucky (p. 15). Most changers stayed within their stated preference of two- or four-year institutions; however, they shifted either from public to private, from private to public, or from out-of-state to in-state PEIs. Approximately 66% of all changers shifted from the private sector to the public sector (p. 19). Thirty-three percent of the students who planned to enroll in a PEI out-of-state ended up enrolling in-state (p. 21). Only 13% of those students who planned to enroll in two-year PEIs shifted to another sector (p. 21). The public sector had the best holding power: 88.8% of all students who indicated that they planned to enroll in a public four-year institution followed through on those plans (p. 20). Litten et al. (1983) also found change in students' stated plans and actual enrollment patterns. They found that almost 50% of all students who had indicated a

Table 5
The Process Characteristics of Choice

Duration	Fall of senior year to spring of senior year
Key influences	Students perceive choice as their own decision, and also recognize importance of parents and peers
Stability of choice	Moderate to high, though some shifting takes place
Application period	50% send in all applications in a 7-week period; there is great variability for the remaining 50%

preference for private PEIs in February of their senior year expressed a preference for public PEIs by the summer (p. 102). They also reported an even larger group of changers who had shifted from a preference for highly selective institutions to less selective institutions. Although the time frames on the evaluation process are different as a result of the variance in when these data were gathered, Lewis and Morrison (1975) concluded that evaluation was continuous from early October to early April. After April the application set is established for most students.

The application period varies widely for students. Half of all students apply over a seven-week period, one-fourth of all students send in all of their applications at the same time, and 10% take 21 weeks to send in their applications (p. 22). Black students apply to more PEIs, are accepted by more PEIs, and are rejected by more PEIs. Women start the application process and end the process earlier than men. Jackson (1986) reports that over 90% of all college applicants are accepted by their top-choice institution; 97% are accepted to one of their top three choices (p. 7). By the end of May, most students have received their acceptance notifications and know where they are going to enroll (Lewis and Morrison, 1975).

As Table 5 demonstrates, the process characteristics of the choice stage appear to be the most logical and straightforward of the three stages. This may indeed be the case, or this may be because more attention has been paid to the process characteristics of this phase. Further research on the process characteristics of this stage, as well as the other two stages, is needed.

Student college choice is a complex phenomenon that has not yet been sufficiently researched using theoretical models and a systematic set of questions. There are a number of questions still to be examined regarding the process characteristics of choice. In addition, the role of financial aid and other institutional characteristics in student college choice is poorly understood. At the end of this chapter these questions will be examined. In the context of the research already reviewed, the next section of this chapter will examine methodological issues and questions of theory development.

Conclusions

Student college choice is a complex phenomenon. It is not a single event, but the result of a process that begins at an early age for most students with a predisposition toward postsecondary education and ends in the selection of a PEI. For public policy-makers and institutional policy-makers questions of access, equity, and institutional vitality make student college choice a topic worthy of investigation. At each stage of the college choice process, a better understanding of college choice can facilitate more effective policy decisions. At the predisposition stage, the importance of parental encouragement indicates that any efforts to improve postsecondary participation rates should be targeted at parents as well as students. Furthermore, process research on predisposition reveals that most students have made their postsecondary plans by the end of the ninth or tenth grade. Thus, intervention programs need to begin early.

Research on the search stage indicates that developmental events such as taking the PSAT or academic tracking decisions influence the search stage. If public policy-makers wish to intervene during the search stage, the role of these events must be examined. More importantly, the dearth of research on the search stage makes it more difficult for policy-makers to develop intervention strategies. For instance, since little is known about how students identify potential PEIs and evaluate them, the effects of the marketing activities of individual PEIs are uncertain.

During the choice stage, institutional policy-makers can use an enhanced understanding of college choice to improve both marketing activities and student-institution fit. Research on the choice stage provides institutional policy-makers with a reverse lens that enables institutions to see themselves as students see them. This ability to see oneself through students' eyes could be used to recruit prospective students who are more likely to find that the institution meets their expectations.

With respect to marketing, institutional policy-makers can exert some influence by emphasizing quality and cost. Research on the process characteristics of the choice stage also reveals when students begin to apply to and evaluate PEIs. This can be useful information for institutional policy-makers. Nevertheless, many questions regarding the impact of institutional marketing efforts and financial-aid-awarding practices need further examination.

In addition to these applied questions a number of questions remain for the research community to address. This chapter points out the need for "middle-range" theories (Merton, 1957) that can be used to develop theoretical models for each stage of student college choice as well as models for different ethnic and other minority groups. In the search and choice stages, future studies should include large student sample sizes that examine the search and choice stages for multiple PEIs. Longitudinal studies which follow high school students from their early years in high school to their first year after high school would also be beneficial. Given the importance of parental encouragement, such studies should include the parents of the students. At the search and choice stages, causal modeling techniques should be employed that will enable researchers to untangle the interrelationships among a diverse set of variables.

Systematic, theory-driven research on college choice can enhance the accumulated knowledge on student college choice. It can lead to more effective policy decisions at the federal, state, and institutional levels. Students may also benefit from an improved understanding of college choice, which can lead to aid policies, high school guidance activities, and marketing activities that make college more accessible to students and that increase the likelihood of student fit. This would benefit the research community and policy-makers and extend our understanding of postsecondary institutions and students.

Notes

1. As many as thirteen separate activities were identified by Lewis and Morrison (1975).

2. The income differential between high school graduates, usually computed over a lifetime. For example, an estimated rate of return of 10% indicates that when background characteristics are controlled, the typical college graduate earns 10% more over a lifetime when compared to the typical high school graduate.

3. SEARCH is a service marketed by The College Board in which the names and addresses of potential students are sold to PEIs. PEIs then send these students unsolicited information about themselves. Although ACT and other educational marketing firms also sell prospective student names the term *search* has become synonymous with this approach to marketing.

4. R. G. Chapman and Jackson (1987) and Freeman (1984) used student samples that were academically talented. There are no high-quality studies using students of average or below-average ability. As a result, the effects of no-need aid on less talented students are unknown.

References

Adkins, D. L. (1975). *The Great American Degree Machine.* New York: McGraw-Hill.

Alexander, K., et al. (1978). *Status Composition and Educational Goals: An Attempt at Clarification.* Washington, DC: National Institute of Education. (ED 160 537)

Alwin, D. F., and Otto, L. B. (1977). Higher school context effects on aspirations. *Sociology of Education* 50: 259–273.

Anderson, C., Bowman, M. J., and Tinto, V. (1972). *Where Colleges Are and Who Attends.* New York: McGraw-Hill.

Astin, A., and others. (1980). *The Impact of Student Financial Aid Programs on Student College Choice.* Washington, DC: Office of Planning. (ED 187 368)

Attanasi, L. (1986). Getting in Mexican-American student's perceptions of their college-going behavior with implications for their freshman year persistence in the university. Paper presented at Annual Meeting of the Association for the Study of Higher Education, San Antonio, March.

Baird, L. L. (1973). *The Graduates: A Report on the Characteristics and Plans of College Seniors.* Princeton, NJ: Educational Testing Service.

Bird, C. (1975). *The Case Against College.* New York: David McKay.

Bishop, J. (1977). The effect of public policies on the demand for higher education. *Journal of Human Resources* 5(4): 285–307.

Blau, P. M. and Duncan, O. D. (1967). *The American Occupational Structure.* New York: Wiley.

Bowen, H. R. (1977). *Investment in Learning: Individual and Social Value of American Education.* San Francisco: Jossey-Bass.

Bowers, T. and Pugh, R. (1973). Factors underlying college choice by students and parents. *Journal of College Student Personnel* 220–224.

Boyer, E. L. (1987). *College: The Undergraduate Experience in America.* New York: Harper & Row.

Boyle, R. P. (1966). The effect of the high school on student aspirations, *American Journal of Sociology* 71: 628–39.

Brown, K. G. (1982). Postsecondary plans of high-school seniors in 1972 and 1980: Implications for student quality. Presented at the AIR Forum, Denver, May. (ED 220 060)

Campbell, R., and Siegel, B. N. (1967). The demand for higher education in the United States. 1919–1964. *American Economic Review* 57: 453–499.

Carpenter, P. G., and Fleishman. J. A. (1987). Linking intentions and behavior: Australian students college plans and college attendance. *American Educational Research Journal* 24(1): 79–105.

Chapman, D. W. (1981). A model of student college. *Journal of Higher Education* 52(5): 490–505.

Chapman, R. C. (1979). Pricing policy and the college choice process. *Research in Higher Education* 10: 37–57.

Chapman, R. C. (1984). Toward a theory of college selection: a model of college search and choice behavior. Unpublished manuscript, Alberta, Canada: University of Alberta.

Chapman. R. C., and Jackson, R. (1987). *College Choices of Academically Able Students: The Influence of No-Need Financial Aid and Other Factors,* Research Monograph No. 10. New York: The College Board.

Chressanthis, G. A. (1986). The impacts of tuition rate changes on college graduate head counts and credit hours over time and a case study. *Economics of Education* 5(2): 205–217.

Chronicle of Higher Education (1978). 16(5, November 13): 8.

Cibik. M. A. (1982). College information needs. *College and University* 57: 97–102.

Clark, B. R., Heist. P., McConnell, T. R., Trow, M. A., and Yonge, C. (1972). *Students and Colleges: Interaction and Change.* Berkeley. CA: Center for Research and Development in Higher Education.

Coelho, G. V., Hamburg, D. A., and Murphey, E. B. (1963). Coping strategies in a new learning environment: A study of the American college freshman. *Archives of General Psychiatry* 9: 433–443.

Coleman, J. S. (1966). Peer culture and education in modern society. In T. M. Newcomb and E. K. Wilson, (eds.), *College peer groups: Problems and Prospects for Research.* Chicago: Aldine.

Conklin, M. E., and Dailey, A. R. (1981). Does consistency of parental encouragement matter for secondary students? *Sociology of Education* 54: 254–262.

Coombs, C. H. (1982). *A Theory of Data.* New York: Wiley.

Corazzini, A. J., et al. (1972). Determinants and Distributional aspects of enrollment in U.S. higher education. *Journal of Human Resources* 7: 26–38.

Dahl, R. W. (1982). College attendance and institutional choice. Results from the Kentucky longitudinal study. Paper presented at the Annual Forum of the Association of Institutional Research, Denver, June. (ED 220 227)

Denison, E. F. (1971). In R. W. Wykstra, (ed.) *Human Capital Formation and Manpower Development.* New York: Free Press.

Douglas, P., et al. (1983). Factor in the choice of higher educational institutions by academically gifted seniors. *Journal of College Student Personnel* 24: 540–545.

Dresch, S. P., and Waldenberg, A. L. (1978). *Labor Market Incentives, Intellectual Competence, and College Attendance.* New Haven, CT: Institute for Demographic and Economic Studies.

Ebberly, C. G. (1987). Information sources used by high school seniors. Paper presented at the Annual Meeting of the American Association of Counseling and Development, New Orleans, March.

Ekstrom, R. B. (1985). *A Descriptive Study of Public High School Guidance: Report to the Commission for the Study of Precollegiate Guidance and Counseling.* Princeton, NJ: Educational Testing Service.

Elsworth, G., et al. (1982). *From High School to Tertiary Study: Transition to College and University in Victoria.* Hawthorn, Victoria: Australian Council on Education.

Erlich, I. (1975). On the relation between education and crime. In F. J. Juster (ed.), *Education, Income and Human Behavior.* New York, McGraw-Hill.

Falsey, B., and Heyns, B. (1984). The college channel: Private and public schools reconsidered. *Sociology of Education* 57: 111–122.

Fenske, R. H., Boyd, J., and Maxey, E. J. (1979). State financial aid to students: a trend analysis of access and choice of public or private college. *College and University* 54: 139–155.

Fields, C., and LeMay, M. (1973). Student financial aid: Effects on educational decisions and academic achievement. *Journal of College Student Personnel* 14: 425–429.

Freeman, R. (1976). *The Over-educated American.* New York: Academic Press.

Freeman, H. B. (1984). Impact of no-need scholarships on the matriculating decision of academically talented students. Paper presented at the Annual Meeting of the American Association of Higher Education, Chicago, March.

Fuller, W., Manski. C., and Wise, D. (1982). New evidence on the economic determinants of postsecondary schooling choices. *Journal of Human Resources* 17(4): 472–498.

Garfinkel, I., and Haveman, R. (1977). *Earnings Capacity, Poverty and Inequality.* Institute for Research on Poverty Monograph. New York: Basic Books.

Gilmour, J., et al. (1978). *How High School Students Select a College.* Pennsylvania State University. (ED 208 705)

Glaser, B. G., and Strauss, A. L. (1967). *The Discovery of Grounded Theory.* Chicago: Aldine.

Hanson, K. H., and Litten. L. H. (1982). Mapping the road to academia: A review of research on women, men, and the college-selection process. In P. Perun (ed.), *The Undergraduate Woman: Issues in Education.* Lexington, MA: Lexington Books.

Harnqvist, K. (1978). *Individual Demand for Education.* Analytical report. Paris, France: OECD. (ED 159 119)

Hause, J. C. (1969). Ability and schooling as determinants of lifetime earnings, or if you're so smart, why aren't you rich. *American Economic Review* 59: 289–298.

Hearn, J. (1984). The relative roles of academic ascribed and socioeconomic characteristics in college destinations. *Sociology of Education* 57: 22–30.

Hilton, T. L. (1982). *Persistence in Higher Education.* New York: The College Board.

Hossler, D. (1984). *Enrollment Management: An Integrated Approach.* New York: The College Board.

Hossler, D., and Gallagher, K. S. (1987). Studying student college choice: A three-phase model and the implications for policy-makers. *College and University* 2(3): 207–221.

Hossler, D., and Stage, F. (1987). *An Analysis of Student and Parent Data from the Pilot Year of the Indiana College Placement and Assessment Center.* Bloomington: Indiana College Placement and Assessment Center.

Hossler, D., and Stage. F. (1988). Family and high school experience factors' influence on the postsecondary plans of ninth grade students. Paper presented at the Annual Meeting of American Education Research Association. New Orleans, April.

Jackson, G. A. (1978). Financial aid and student enrollment. *Journal of Higher Education* 49: 548–574.

Jackson, G. A. (1982). Public efficiency and private choice in higher education. *Educational Evaluation and Policy Analysis* 4(2): 237–247.

Jackson, G. A. (1986). MISSA, the fall of Saigon, and college choice, 1972 to 1980. Paper presented at the Annual Meeting of the Association for the Study of Higher Education, San Diego, February.

Jencks, C., et al. (1972). *Inequality: A Reassessment of the Effects of Family and Schooling in America.* New York: Basic Books.

Johnson, R. H.. and Chapman, D. W. (1979). An assessment of college recruitment literature: Does the high school senior understand it? Presented at Annual Forum of the Association of Institutional Research, San Diego, June. (ED 174 079)

Kehoe, J. J. (1981). Migrational choice patterns in financial aid policy making. *Research in Higher Education* 14(1): 57–69.

Keller, M. J., and McKewon, M. P. (1984). Factors contributing to postsecondary enrollments decisions of Maryland National Merit Scholarship Semifinalists. Paper presented at Annual Meeting of the Association for the Study of Higher Education, Chicago.

Kohn, M. G., Manski, C. F., and Mundel, D. (1976). An empirical investigation of factors influencing college going behaviors. *Annuals of Economic and Social Measurement* 5(4, Fall): 391–419.

Kolstad, A. J. (1979). The influence of high school type and curriculum on enrollment in higher education and postsecondary training. Paper presented at the Annual Meeting of the American Educational Research Association, San Francisco, April. (ED 173 627)

Konnert, W. and Giese, R. (1987). College choice factors of male athletes at private NCAA Division III institutions. *College and University* 63(1): 23–48.

Kotler, P. (1976). Applying marketing theory to college admissions. In *A Role for Marketing in College Admissions*. New York: The College Entrance Examination Board.

Kotler, P. and Fox, K. (1985). *Strategic Marketing for Educational Institutions*. Englewood Cliffs, NJ: Prentice-Hall.

Kuntz, S. S. (1987). A study of student's cognitive structure for colleges. Paper at the Annual Meeting of the American Educational Research Association, Washington, DC, April.

Lam, J., and Hoffman, D. (1979). The study of sequential student participation in University in a changing environment. Manitoba, Canada: Brandon University. (ED 198 785)

Lay, R., and MaGuire, J. (1980). Identifying the competition in higher education. *College and University* 56(1): 53–65.

Lay, R. and Maguire, J. (1981). Coordinating market and evaluation research on the admissions rating process. *Research in Higher Education* 14(1) 71–85.

Leslie, L. L., et al. (1977). The impact of need-based student aid upon the college attendance decision. *Journal of Education Finance* 2: 269–286.

Leslie, L. L., and Brinkman, P. T. (1986). Rates of return to higher education: An intensive examination. In J. Smart (ed.) *Higher Education: Handbook of Theory and Research* Vol III. New York: Agathon Press.

Lewis, G. H., and Morrison, J. (1975). *A Longitudinal Study of College Selection* Tech. Report No. 2. Pittsburgh: School of Urban Public Affairs, Carnegie-Mellon University.

Litten, L. H. (1982). Different strokes in the applicant pool: some refinements in a model of student college choice. *Journal of Higher Education* 53(4): 383–402.

Litten, L. H. (1986). Perspectives on pricing. In D. Hossler (ed.), *Managing College Enrollments*, New Directions of Higher Education, No. 53. San Francisco: Jossey-Bass.

Litten, L. H ., et al. (1983). *Applying Market Research in College Admissions*. New York: The College Board.

Maguire, J., and Lay, R. (1981). Modeling the college choice process. *College and University* 56(2): 123–139.

Manski, C. F., and Wise, D. A. (1983). *College Choice in America*. Cambridge, MA: Harvard University Press.

Mare, R. D. (1980). Social background composition and educational growth. *Demography* 16: 55–71.

Marini, M. M., and Greenberger, E. (1978). Sex differences in educational aspirations and expectations. *American Education Research Journal* 15(1): 67–79.

Mathes, S., and Gurney, G. (1985). Factors in student athletes' choices of colleges. *Journal of College Student Personnel* 26: 327–333.

Mattila, J. P. (1982). Determinants of male school enrollments: A time series analysis. *Review of Economics and Statistics* 64: 242–251.

Mayer, R. R., and Greenwood. E. (1980). *The Design of Social Policy Research*. Englewood Cliffs. NJ: Prentice-Hall.

Merton, R. K. (1957). Priorities in scientific discovery. *American Sociological Review* 2: 635–659.

Miller, I. (1983). Higher education: The demography of opportunity. *Journal of College Admissions* 101: 10–13.

Miller, P. W., and Volker, P. A. (1985). On the determination of occupational attainment and mobility. *The Journal of Human Resources* 20(2): 197–213.

Muffo, J. A. (1987). Market segmentation in higher education: A case study. *Journal of Student Financial Aid* 17(3): 31–40.

Murphy, P. E. (1981). Consumer buying roles in college choice. *College and University* 57: 141–150.

Nolfi, G. J. (1978). *Experiences of Recent High School Graduates.* Lexington, MA: Lexington Books.

Parents, Programs and Pennsylvania Student Plans (1984). Harrisburg: Pennsylvania Association of Colleges and Universities.

Parrish, R. E. (1979). *Survey of Educational Goals: Ocean County High School Juniors and Seniors, Spring 1979,* Report 78–79–05. Toms River, NJ: Ocean County College. (ED 179 255)

Perlman, R. (1973). *The Economics of Education: Conceptual Problems and Policy Issues.* New York: McGraw-Hill.

Peters, W. B. (1977). *Fulfillment of Short-Term Educational Plans and Continuance in Education.* Washington, DC: National Center of Educational Statistics.

Powers, S., and Douglas, P. (1985). Gender differences in selecting of an institution of higher education: a discriminant analysis. *Psychological Reports* 56: 295–278.

Radner, R., and Miller, L. S. (1970). Demand and supply in U.S. higher education: a progress report. *American Economic Review* 30: 327–334.

Rumberger, R. W. (1982). Recent high school and college experiences of youth: Variations by sex, race and social class. *Youth and Society* 13: 449–470.

Russell, C. N. (1980). *Survey of Grade 12 Students' Postsecondary Plans and Aspirations.* Manitoba, Canada: Department of Education, September. (ED 201 225).

Schultz, T. W. (1961). Educational and economic growth. In N. B. Henry (ed.), *Social Forces Influencing American Education.* Chicago: National Society for the Study of Education.

Sewell, W. H., Haller, A. O., and Ohlendorf, G. (1971). The educational and early occupational status attainment process: replication and revision. *American Sociological Review* 35: 1014–1027.

Sewell, W. H., Haller. A. O., and Portes, A. (1969). The educational and early occupational attainment process. *American Sociological Review* 34: 82–92.

Sewell, W. H., and Hauser, R. M. (1975). *Education, Occupation and Earnings: Achievement in Early Career.* New York: Academic Press.

Sewell, W. H., and Shah, V. P. (1978). Social class, parental encouragement, and educational aspirations. *American Journal of Sociology* 3: 559–572.

Sewell, W. H., et al. (1972). The educational and early occupational status attainment process: replication and revision. *American Sociological Review* 40(1): 1014–1027.

Silber, E., et al. (1961). Competent adolescents coping with college decisions. *Archives of General Psychiatry* 5: 517–527.

Solmon, L. C., and Taubman, P. J. (1973). *Does College Matter?* New York: Academic Press.

Soper, E. L. (1971). *A Study of Factors Influencing the Postsecondary Educational Plans of Utah High School Students.* Washington, DC: National Center for Educational Statistics.

Spaeth, J. L. (1967). Occupational prestige expectations among male college graduates. *American Journal of Sociology* 73(5): 548–558.

Spiegleman, R. G. (1968). A benefit/cost model to evaluate educational programs. *Socio-economic Planning Sciences* 1: 443–460.

Spies, R. (1978). *The Effects of Rising Costs on College Choice, A Study of the Application Decision of High Ability Students.* New York: The College Board.

Stage, F., and Hossler, D. Differences in family influences on college attendance plans for male and female ninth graders. *Research in Higher Education* 30: 3.

Stewart, N. R., et al. (1987). Counselor impact on college choice. Paper presented at the Annual Meeting of the American Educational Research Association, Washington, DC.

Tierney, M. (1980a). Student college choice sets: Toward an empirical characterization. Paper presented at the Annual Meeting of the Association for the Study of Higher Education, Washington, DC, March.

Tierney, M. (1980b). The impact of financial aid on student demand for public/private higher education. *Journal of Higher Education* 51: 527–545.

Tillery, D. (1973). *Distribution and Differentiation of Youth: A Study of Transition from School to College.* Cambridge, MA: Ballinger.

Tillery, D., and Kildegaard, T. (1973). *Educational Goals, Attitudes and Behaviors: A Comparative Study of High School Seniors.* Cambridge, MA: Ballinger.

Trent, J., and Medsker, L. (1967). *Beyond High School: A Psychological Study of 10,000 High School Graduates.* San Francisco: Jossey-Bass.

Tuttle, R. (1981). *A Path Analytical Model of the College Going Decision.* Boone, NC: Appalachian State University. (ED 224 434)

Update. (1986, January). A report from the Washington Office of the College Board. Washington, DC: The College Board.

Welki, A. M., and Novratil, F. J. (1987). The role of applicant's perceptions in the choice of college. *College and University* 62(2): 147–160.

Williams, T. W. (1984). Recruiting graduates: Understanding student institutional fit. In D. Hossler (ed.), *Enrollment Management: An Integrated Approach.* New York: The College Board.

Willingham, W. W. (1970). *Free Access to Higher Education.* New York: The College Board.

Yang, S. W. (1981). Rural youth's decisions to attend college: aspirations and realizations. Paper presented at the Annual Meeting of the Rural Sociological Association, Guelph, Ontario, July. (ED 207 765)

Young, M. E., and Reyes, P. (1987). Conceptualizing enrollment behavior. *Journal of Student Financial Aid* 17(3): 41–49.

Zemsky, R., and Oedel, P. (1983). *The Structure of College Choice.* New York: The College Board.

The Transition to College:
Diverse Students, Diverse Stories

Patrick T. Terenzini, Laura I. Rendón,
M. Lee Upcraft, Susan B. Millar, Kevin W. Allison,
Patricia L. Gregg, and Romero Jalomo

While much is known about the role of student involvement in various dimensions of student change and development, considerably less is known about how students become involved as they make the transition from work or high school to college. This paper describes the results of a series of focus-group interviews with 132 diverse, new students entering a community college; a liberal arts college; an urban, commuter, comprehensive university; and a large research university. The study identifies the people, experiences, and themes in the processes through which students become (or fail to become) members of the academic and social communities on their campus.

According to Astin (1985), "Students learn by becoming involved" (p. 133). This notion of student learning has its roots in both the learning theory concept of time-on-task and the Freudian notion of cathexis—the investment of psychological energy. Astin suggests five basic postulates of involvement: (1) Involvement requires the investment of psychological and physical energy in "objects" (e.g., tasks, people, activities) of one sort or another, whether specific or highly general; (2) involvement is a continuous concept—different students will invest varying amounts of energy in different objects; (3) involvement has both quantitative and qualitative features; (4) the amount of learning or development that occurs is directly proportional to the quality and quantity of involvement; and (5) the educational effectiveness of any policy or practice is related to its capacity to encourage student involvement (pp. 135–136).

Pace (1984) speaks of "quality of effort" rather than "involvement," but the two concepts are highly similar. Pace argues that, "All learning and development require an investment of time and effort by the student. Time is a frequency dimension. Effort is a quality dimension. . . . Quality of experience and quality of effort are similar concepts, connected with one another in that the likelihood of having high-quality experience depends on investing high-quality effort" (p. 7).

Student effort and involvement have been shown to be positively related to gains or changes in a wide array of educational outcomes, including various dimensions of verbal, quantitative, and subject matter competence; higher-order cognitive skill development; and psychosocial, attitudinal, and moral development (e.g., Astin, 1993; Pace, 1990; Pascarella and Terenzini, 1991). Surprisingly, however, little research has been done on the personal and organizational mechanisms and processes by means of which students *become* "involved."

Tinto (1988) suggests parallels between Van Gennep's (1960) notion of rites of passage as a three-stage process (separation, transition, and incorporation) and the processes by which students become integrated into the academic and social systems of a college or university. As yet, however, there has been no empirical test of the validity or closeness of these parallels. Rodriguez

(1974–75, 1982) and Rendon (1992) offer compelling personal accounts of the emotionally wrenching experiences of being a first-generation, Mexican-American college student. With a few exceptions (e.g., Christie and Dinham, 1991; Hays and Oxley, 1986; London, 1989; Perl and Trickett, 1988), however, the organizational and interpersonal dynamics, mechanisms, and processes through which students make the transition from work or high school to college have gone largely unexplored.

This paper describes the National Center on Postsecondary Teaching, Learning, and Assessment's "Transition to College Project," which sought at least preliminary answers to the following questions:

1. Through what social, academic, and administrative mechanisms do students new to a campus become involved in the academic and social systems of their institutions?

2. What processes are involved in the transition from high school or work to college?

3. Who are the important people who facilitate or impede that process?

4. What experiences play a major positive or negative role in the success or failure of that transition?

5. Is the nature of the transition process different for different kinds of students? For similar students entering different kinds of institutions?

Methodology

Study Design

Because of the lack of information about which variables may be involved, their relative importance, or the dynamics operating among them in the transition-to-college process, a cross-sectional, focus-group interview research design was adopted. Data were gathered in interviews with groups varying in size from one to eight students.

Institutional Sample Selection

Four institutions were selected that promised to afford considerable variation on both student characteristics (e.g., race/ethnicity, gender, age, socioeconomic class) and institutional traits (e.g., mission, size, curricular emphasis, type, and the presence/absence of residential facilities). (All institutional names are fictitious.)

Southwest Community College (SCC): A relatively new community college in a major southwestern metropolitan area. One-third of the students are Hispanic and about 18 percent are African-Americans; about 3 percent are Native Americans. Enrollment: 3,200.

Bayfield College (BC): A predominantly white, residential, liberal arts college in a Middle Atlantic state. Enrollment: 4,300.

Urban State University (USU): A predominantly black, urban, commuter, comprehensive state university in a major midwestern city. Enrollment: 7,100.

Reallybig University (RBU): A large, eastern, predominantly white, residential, research university. Enrollment: 36,000.

Student Sample Selection

Institutional contact persons were sent information on the characteristics of students sought for participation (see below). Potential participants were advised that the interview would be a group session, that it would last about an hour, and (on three of the four campuses) that they would be compensated for their participation (no compensation was offered at the fourth site because none was requested by the institution).

Because little is known about the nature of the process or about the people and experiences that play important roles in it, the guiding concern in student selection was to ensure that students from diverse personal and academic backgrounds be invited. Participants were not selected randomly or to be proportionally representative of the new student population (or subgroup thereof) on a given campus or of the national population of students entering higher education in the Fall of 1991. Rather, contact persons were asked to form a specified number of groups consisting of students with characteristics generally typical of the overall entering student population on each campus. Sometimes groups were to be homogeneous with respect to a particular characteristic (e.g., race/ethnicity, gender, or place of residence), while other groups were purposefully heterogeneous (e.g., a group of commuting students, mixed by gender).

| | Profile of Students Interviewed | | | | |
Site	Groups	Men	Women	Minority	Total
Southwest Community College	5	8	14	15	22
Bayfield College	6	8	10	2	18
Urban State University	12	20	11	30	31
Reallybig University	13	21	40	9	61
Totals	36	57	75	56	132

Interview Protocol and Data Collection Procedures

The interview protocol was purposefully open-ended and broadly structured to prompt students for information about their backgrounds and decisions to go to college; their expectations for, and the reality of, college; the significant people and events in their transition; selected characteristics of the transition itself; and the general effects students felt college was having on them. Questions were constructed to minimize as much as possible leading students to any particular response. For example, rather than ask if faculty played an important role in their transition, students were asked, "Who are the most important people in your life right now?" Whether students mentioned institutional faculty and staff members or not, their responses would be equally revealing.

Data Analysis

All interview sessions were tape-recorded, and the member of the seven-person research group who had conducted the interview transcribed and/or summarized the tapes. Both individual and group analyses of the interview transcripts (over 200 pages) were conducted, identifying themes that ran through each interview session and through the set of interviews for each campus. Research group discussions of these interviews focused on each campus, seriatim. When the transcripts for each institution had been reviewed and discussed by the entire research group, analysis focused on the identification of themes that were common across campuses and subgroups of students, as well as on thematic differences distinctive to a campus setting or student subgroup.

Limitations

This study is limited in several respects. First, as noted, subjects were not selected randomly or to be proportionally representative of any given population (although they were chosen to be more or less typical of students enrolling on each campus). Thus, generalizations to larger populations are not possible. That fact, however, does not affect the power of this study to identify important or valid themes. It simply means that nothing can be said about the frequency with which such themes might occur in a larger population. Second, the institutions at which the interviews were done were selected to obtain variability on a number of student and institutional characteristics; no claim is made that these institutions are typical of other institutions in their general category.

Third, the study is cross-sectional and, thus, no claims can be made about any relations between a successful transition to college and subsequent academic success or persistence (although where students claimed or implied such linkages, they are noted). Fourth, because our respondents were invited by institutional staff members to participate in this study, the students interviewed are more likely than those not interviewed to have been "successful" in their transitions. Finally, it is quite possible that relevant themes other than those discussed here have gone undetected.

Summary of Findings

Our interviews indicated that the transition from high school or work to college is an exceedingly complex phenomenon. The nature and dynamics of the process vary according to the student's social, family, and educational background; personality; educational and occupational orientations and aspirations; the nature and mission of the institution being attended; the kinds of peers, faculty, and staff members encountered; the purpose and nature of those encounters; and the interactions of all these variables. The process is a highly interrelated, web-like series of family, interpersonal, academic, and organizational pulls and pushes that shape student learning (broadly conceived) and persistence. Despite this sometimes bewildering complexity, however, and despite the limitations on this research summarized above, several potentially important themes, common across settings and kinds of students, emerged. Some themes, of course, vary within setting or across kinds of students.

The Place of College in the Life Passage

College as Continuation: Traditional Students

The educational portion of the American Dream is a story of uninterrupted study and progressively greater academic accomplishment, beginning in kindergarten and culminating in college or graduate or professional school. For many Americans (primarily, but not exclusively, white), this passage is completed as expected. At Reallybig University and Bayfield College, for example, when asked what had gone into their decision to attend college, virtually all students were surprised by the question, indicating that they had never considered *not* going to college. For example, two traditional-age, white students at Reallybig University explained their "decision" to go to college:

> Going to college . . . was never even, like, a question! Um, both my parents went to college and I guess they figured that all their kids would go to college. I mean . . . it was never even too much a question. Um, both my sister and I did pretty well in school and so college was just like the definite thing to follow high school.

Another student chimed in:

> Yeah, I agree. Uh, going to college was never a question. You know, that's never something I thought about, whether I'm gonna go to college or not, that was kind of a given.

These students (and many others like them) and their parents have assumed all along that going to college is what one does after completion of high school. College was simply the next, logical, expected, and desired stage in the passage toward personal and occupational achievement. The passage actually originated in the educational attainment of parents, older siblings, or close relatives who have at least attended, and frequently completed, college (Pascarella and Terenzini, 1991). The new student from such a background, entering a college like Bayfield or a university like Reallybig, had accepted and was simply extending an established set of family and sociocultural values and tradition. For most of these students, the very fact that they had been admitted to a moderately selective college or university was evidence that academically they "belong" at their institution.

While these students occasionally expressed some concern about their ability to meet the academic competition, making new friends dominated their conversation. For them, the most threatening disjunction was interpersonal, not academic. A new student at Reallybig University described his experience:

> I hated it. [Another student: "So did I. I cried."] Like, for the first couple of . . . I, I hated it, 'cause I was like, here I am in a situation where I know absolutely nobody. I mean, it's like, it's like you're just dropped in, it's like here you go! And you know no one. You know, you had all these close friends and good friends, and you're always having a good time. And I had a great time in high school, and I, you know, a really great time. And I got here and I knew nobody. And it was just like, it was terrifying. . . . When I first got here, I wanted to transfer. I was like, "That's it! Send me to a branch campus! I'll commute from home." . . . Then I started thinking of it, like, "Okay. It has to get better." And like, it's great. I love it now.

College as Disjunction: First-Generation Students

On the surface, the educational transition for first-generation students may seem much like that of traditional students entering "traditional schools" like Bayfield or Reallybig. For all students, the transition involves adaptation to a new set of academic and social systems. Among nontraditional, primarily first-generation, college students, however, the adaptation to college was far more difficult. Indeed, for many, going to college constituted a major *disjunction* in their life course. For these students, college-going was not part of their family's tradition or expectations. On the contrary. Those who were the first in their immediate family to attend college were *breaking*, not continuing, family tradition. For these students, college attendance often involved multiple transitions—academic, social, and cultural. A young Native American student explained her motivation for attending Southwest Community College:

> Right before [my mother] died, she took me out to the reservation, and when we were outside the reservation, and she pointed it out to me and said, "Do you want to be like this? Sitting around and doing nothing? Or do you want to go on?" So it was probably the reason why I went to college. Because they really have no life out there. She goes, she goes, "The majority," she told me that the majority of the Indians that, that don't, don't, that don't go to college or don't finish school just move back to the reservation and just sit there.

A young African-American student at Urban State described being beaten up in high school by classmates who disapproved of his interest in ideas and his attention to his schoolwork. Later in the interview, when asked what was special about USU, he replied without hesitation: "Well, like I said before. It's very open-minded here. . . . You can read in the hall or on the steps, and nobody will throw a brick at you." A classmate (in another interview) described his reasons for going to college:

> I have a lot of reasons, but I guess, basically, because of where I live, a lot of kids are killed often, and, you know, I decided to further my education just to get away from it. I, I don't like the fact that people are, you know, constantly shooting at you. It, it's, uh, it's bothersome. You don't want to be bothered with these gang bangers gettin' you, rising up, so I said, "Either I make a difference or I get out of here." And I said, "I'll do both."

Because of their family and educational backgrounds, going to college often constituted a significant and intimidating cultural transition for the first-generation students in our study. Attending and completing college carried the potential for radical changes in these students and the lives they led. Indeed, for many (such as the two young people quoted above) the decision to go to college was a conscious decision to escape the occupational dead-ends and hopelessness their life courses otherwise promised.

Several cautions are warranted here. Further research is needed about the subtle and complex ways first-generation students negotiate separation. Cultural disjunction does not necessarily imply that all students need or want to separate totally from their culture to attain success (Rendon, 1992), and further research should probe how nontraditional students maintain or reject their personal cultural integrity and succeed or fail in college as a result of this process. Not all students are like Richard Rodriguez (1982), who attributes his academic success to shedding his Mexican-American identity. In fact, many college students maintain strong ethnic affiliation values and achieve a moderate to excellent level of academic success (Gurin and Epps, 1975; Rendon, 1992).

For many of these nontraditional students, the academic transition to college was the most challenging. When asked what they expected to find in college and what they actually found, most spoke of the anticipated academic rigors of college in comparison with high school. Most came expecting to have to study hard. Most found what they had expected, but others (a relatively small minority) commented that college was not all that much more difficult than high school had been. The majority, however, appeared to be deferring involvement in the nonacademic activities and life of the campus until they felt they had their academic lives under control.

In contrast, traditional students spoke more frequently of worrying about making new friends, or (at Reallybig) of becoming lost in the crowd. But if the academic transition was of greater concern, making friends was commonly cited as being the key to "feeling connected" or "a part" of their institution. Several students spoke of looking forward to the time when, once they were on their feet academically, they could devote more time to out-of-class activities and people. For a number of Southwest Community College students, the academic and interpersonal activities often overlapped, easing the transition in both spheres. These students spoke positively of meeting other students in their classes or on the student union's patio, and engaging in both social conversation and group discussion of what was going on in their classes. Several identified these sorts of sessions as among the most effective learning experiences they had (along with in-class discussions of course material).

High School Friends: Assets and Liabilities

The interviews also made clear that high school friends were instrumental in how successfully these new students made the transition to college. When a student knew high school friends who were also new students (or friends or siblings already enrolled) at the same institution, these precollege friends functioned during the early weeks or months of college as a bridge from one academic and interpersonal environment to the next. Such earlier acquaintances provided (and may themselves have received) important support during the transition. Friends performed this "bridge function," however, for a limited period of time. As a student's friendship network began to extend beyond the set of high school acquaintances, the student developed closer relationships with students not known before college, and high school friends slowly faded in importance.

While high school friends who went to the same college appeared to serve a similar "bridging" function for new students at schools like Southwest Community College and Urban State University, high school friends who did not go on to college may have served to complicate and hinder the transition. Such high school friends may have functioned as interpersonal anchors, tending to hold the student in the network of friends and pattern of activities and interests of the precollege years. A commuting student at Bayfield (quoted earlier) alluded to the interpersonal pull of high school friends who did not go on to college. A recent high school graduate attending Urban State described an encounter with a high school friend:

> Well, after we graduated, I seen him last week, matter of fact, and, um, he was just hanging on the mailbox, just, just, telling me, "What's up man? What you doin'?" And, you know, he seen the bookbag on my shoulder. "Aw, man! You goin' to school? Aw, man, that ain't nothin', man." You know, I just looked at him and hugged my shoulder bag, and left. You know, 'cause, um, see, he, he's not going to succeed in life. He's gonna be the one that's on the corner with the wine bottle, or he gonna end up dead. See, me, I'm gonna end up in school, you know, probably with a high-paying job, doin' what I like. [Another student comments: "Or at least a job."]

A young woman at Southwest Community College experienced similar pressures:

> My friend . . . plays basketball. But she, like, goes out partying and things like that. But she's after me. She [says]: "You're getting boring. You just stay home and study." I [say]: "No,

> I'm going [to college]. . . . It's something I'm paying for. And . . . I wanna learn something . . . I'm gonna be needing [it] . . . in the future."

Thus, it would appear that one's high school friends were not unalloyed assets to students trying to make connections with a new college or university. Depending on the individuals involved and the circumstances, they could be assets or liabilities.

The Family: Asset and Liability

There can be little doubt about the important role new students' families played in providing encouragement to attend college and to persist and succeed while there. With very few exceptions, when asked, "Who are the most important people in your life right now?" students unhesitatingly named one or more members of their immediate family. The sense of debt to parents for their support was greater among students at SCC and USU, but it was also apparent at BC and RBU. Among students at the latter two institutions, the more muted response seemed to reflect more their taking parental support for granted rather than an indication that they enjoyed any less parental support than their commuting peers. Residential students appeared to be developing greater personal independence and autonomy from family and, thereby, to be redefining the nature of the relationship they had with parents to be more one based on the equality of adults rather than on any superordinate-subordinate, parent-child relationship.

For some students, however, particularly those from black, Hispanic, or Native American families, some parents may have tried to maintain a relationship they recognized may be changing. This dimension of the transition process for these students, of course, was intimately related to the cultural disjunctions described above. Some parents may well have recognized that their college-going children—as proud of them as they were—might, metaphorically, never return home. For example, a Southwest Community College student described this loving tension. Asked who the most important people in his life were, he replied:

> My grandmother. Even though she is a big inspiration to me, uh, she has this way of clinging. She hates to let go of things. And I can understand. I think that's why she takes in a lot of us, as we're going along. She hates to let go. And my cousin and I have told her that we're going off, goin' to college. She goes, "I can't believe you're gonna leave." You know, "I need you here with me to do this or do that." "Listen, Grandma, life goes on. This may sound cold, but when you're gone, we're still here. And, uh, we need to do some things to prepare for our future." And she's startin' to understand that.

Sensing such fears, some of the students of these parents appeared to find their anxiety levels rising in ways and to degrees probably unimagined by most middle-class white students, faculty members, and administrators.

The Importance of "Validating" Experiences

A number of the nontraditional students who had entered Southwest Community College and Urban State were experiencing serious self-doubts and indicated an array of needs that we came to describe generically as the need for "validation." By that term we refer to a process similar to that described by Belenky, Clinchy, Goldberger, and Tarule (1986). Validation is empowering, confirming, and supportive. It is a series of in- and out-of-class experiences with family, peers, faculty members, and staff through which students come to feel accepted in their new community, receive confirming signals that they can be successful in college and are worthy of a place there, have their previous work and life experiences recognized as legitimate forms of knowledge and learning, have their contributions in class recognized as valuable, and so on. Validation can be something that is done for and in conjunction with the student, but for some students it may also be a self-affirming process as the student discovers new competencies or reaches levels of achievement previously thought unattainable.

In many cases, these students' high school experiences had signaled to them in various ways that they were not seen as serious or competent learners and, thus, were expected to fail. For example, one returning woman reported: "I expected to fail. Two weeks and I was out. I didn't think I could study. I didn't think I could learn." Another student felt she would be "just a number." Yet another student reported she had chosen to attend a community college "because I saw my brother go to a four-year college and he barely made it. He said it's hard. His advice was to go to a community college." Such experiences failed to confirm or validate the student as one capable of learning and deserving of a place in a college classroom.

Some students described invalidating experiences with their college instructors. An African-American woman who held a General Education Degree (GED) and attended Southwest Community College described such an experience:

> I went to secretarial school and I started working on Wall Street for an investment firm. I went in as a file clerk . . . And within about two or three years, I was making my $35,000-$40,000 a year. . . . But when I came to [the campus where she was enrolled] I was made to realize that I was a young black woman with hardly any education. . . . To come [here] and have someone speak to me as if I had the education of a five-year-old . . . that was a real bummer.

Other students talked about invalidating classroom experiences. Said one community college student:

> My math teacher . . . he has a number [for me] . . . I was a number, you know, instead of calling us by name, he would call us by our social security number. There aren't many people in class for him to go through all that and it's quicker for him to say my name than my number.

An RBU student described an encounter in an elevator with one of her large-class instructors. When she commented that she was in the instructor's class, he replied: "So what?"

Some students, however, had enjoyed highly validating, even transforming, college experiences. They spoke of teachers who communicated to them that they were capable of learning, who brought schoolwork to the home of a student who was ill, and who structured learning activities that allowed students to experience themselves as successful learners. Some students spoke of instructors who, through the time, energy, and interest they invested in their students, had instilled a sense of obligation to succeed. These students felt they could not let these instructors down. Out-of-class validation was equally important and came from the support of family and peers, who (as noted earlier) were often the most important people in the students' lives.

In contrast, students attending the two predominantly white, residential institutions had already experienced academic encouragement and success in elementary and secondary school and were further validated academically simply by being accepted by their institutions. For these students, the importance of the validation process was more social (being accepted by their peers) than academic.

The Transition and the "Real Learning"

When asked, "Where does the *real* learning occur around here?" a number of students, as might be expected, spoke of the classroom and various formal instructional activities, or of the preparations made for class. When encouraged to define "learning" broadly, however, it was clear that for a substantial number "real learning" meant learning about oneself, discovering abilities or personal sources of strength, developing pride in one's ability to survive, and becoming more independent and self-reliant. Such learning included developing "survival" skills (e.g., money and time management skills, personal goal setting); developing the self-discipline to "just do it" when a task or obligation was recognized; taking responsibility for one's physical, financial, and academic well-being; and developing a clearer understanding of oneself and one's goals through interactions with faculty and peers who held goals, attitudes, or values different from the student's. For some residential students, the transition represented an opportunity to explore a "new self," to try on a different "persona," to redesign one's self in ways that were impossible for students living at home. For some nontraditional students, as described above, the transition *required* a redefinition of self and values.

The most consistent element of this theme, however, was the pride students took in their achievement. Students who had made the transition were very proud of what they had accomplished. New vistas had opened up, new abilities were discovered, and new goals were considered, giving these students deep personal satisfaction.

The Transition as a Cooperative Activity

For residential students, the transition was an ordeal to be shared and experienced together. There was strength in numbers and some solace in the thought that, "We're all in this together." It appeared to be seen as the process (if not rite) of passage that one must make on the road to "a good job." What they were going through was to be expected and part of the process of beginning "the college experience." For most (but by no means all), even if a bit intimidating, it was a time of exploration, wonder, discovery, and fun. The cooperative character of the process meant helping one another meet and make new friends, establish one's social network, and become established in those of others.

In the voices of many nontraditional students, while many of these same elements were apparent, their volume was more muted. There was also the sense, emanating from the dual nature of the transition as both an educational and cultural passage, that these were serious, potentially dangerous waters. These students supported one another by consciously avoiding criticism of one another's work or performance. The cooperative nature of the passage was evident in students' discussing classwork together outside class, learning from the comments others made in class, making sure too much fun did not interfere with getting schoolwork done, reminding each other in subtle ways that academics was the first priority. In some instances, the cooperative nature of the transition was brought directly into the classroom, as instructors required students to learn about, and then introduce, a classmate; constructed group assignments that required students to get to know each other and to work together on a common project; or invested so much of their own energy and time in helping students that the students came to feel a positive obligation to work hard to succeed.

Implications

A considerable amount of evidence (Pascarella and Terenzini, 1991) indicates that if students become involved in one or another aspect of their new college communities—that is, if the transition from high school or work to college can be negotiated successfully—the likelihood of student change, educational growth, and persistence are significantly increased. So what can we do to ease the transition? The themes identified in this study have a number of implications for faculty members, administrators, and institutional researchers:

1. *Promote awareness of the varying character of the transition process for different kinds of students.* Faculty and staff must carefully consider the varying characteristics of an institution's students and the corresponding variations in students' transition experiences. Such reflection may be particularly important for faculty and administrators whose backgrounds and college experiences resemble those of "traditional" students at Bayfield College and Reallybig University who probably entered a four-year college at age 18, directly from high school; were from middle-class, white parents who also went to college; and who lived on campus. Compared to their traditional peers, students from disadvantaged socioeconomic and educational backgrounds confront and undergo a dramatically different transition, one that is at once academic, social, and cultural. Most campuses' current instructional practices, academic regulations and policies, and workload expectations recognize few differences among students. Meaningful alterations in teaching styles and techniques, as well as the development of new learning experiences for increasingly diverse students, however, cannot be effectively designed in the dark.

Institutional researchers have a particular role to play here. Much information on the varying characteristics of entering students (and how those characteristics may be changing over time) is already available but only infrequently shared with faculty members, department heads, deans, and other academic administrators. Perhaps the best antidote to stereotypic thinking about students is information on how inaccurate those stereotypes are. It seems likely that faculty members would benefit from small group interviews (similar to those done in this study) focusing on the transition process for diverse groups of new students. While such research might be organized and coordinated by the institutional research office, the findings are likely to have greater impact if developed (and thereby endorsed) by respected members of the faculty.

2. *Early validation appears to be a central element in students' successful transition to college.* Whether academically or socially (and there are decided variations across institutional types), new students need to be reassured that they can succeed: that they can do college-level work, that their ideas and opinions have value, that they are worthy of the attention and respect of faculty, staff, and peers alike. Academic validation appeared to be particularly important for first-generation students. Faculty members must be made aware of the importance of such early reaffirmation, particularly for students for whom college attendance is such an emotionally risky venture. The "wounds" some students bring to college must be understood and accorded the attention, support, and gentleness they require. The validation of students need not be formal (e.g., graded work). It might take the form of words of encouragement, of constructive and reassuring critiques of student answers or work. The message may take many forms, but its content must be consistent and clear: Students can learn, they are valuable as people, their experiences and ideas have legitimacy in and out of the classroom, and the instructor and institution are there to help the student learn.

An important policy issue resides beneath the importance of validating students' worth and performance. There is reason to believe that such validation is critical to student persistence and degree attainment. If access to occupational success and "the good life" is not to be restricted according to socioeconomic status, race, ethnicity, or gender, then all students must have an equal opportunity to benefit from their educational experience (Astin, 1985; Pascarella and Terenzini, 1991). Moreover, in many of our interviews with students from disadvantaged backgrounds, there were clear indications of altruistic motives for wanting to go to college—not simply to rescue oneself from a grim future, but also to give something back to family and community. Denying such students the opportunities not only to attend but to succeed closes the door on potential social and economic multiplier effects that college completion may produce.

3. *Involve faculty members in new student orientation programs.* There is evidence in this study and elsewhere (e.g., Pascarella and Terenzini, 1986) that student orientation programs serve an important early socialization function. Through orientation, new students receive their first introduction to the attitudinal and behavioral norms of a new academic and social setting and to what will be expected of them in that community. Faculty members, as noted earlier, have been shown to play important roles (both inside and outside the classroom) in what and how much students learn on a broad front. It is important that new students make contact with faculty members as early as possible in their college careers. Indeed, such contact may in itself be a form of validation in that it reflects faculty members' interests in students and a willingness to help students find a home in their new academic community. If orientation, however, is little more than an early course registration and a general introduction to Old Siwash and the services it offers when there are various kinds of problems, then an important opportunity to help new students make connections with the academic and intellectual life of the institution will have been lost.

4. *Orient parents as well as students.* The evidence strongly indicates that parents/spouses play a key role in the support of new students adjusting to a new environment. Such support is needed most by first-generation students, whose parents/spouses may be least able to provide it, not having been through the transition experience themselves. Parents/spouses of all students, but particularly those of first-generation students, must be helped to understand the nature of the academic and time demands that will be placed on the students, what will be happening to students (and to the parents/spouses as well!), and how to deal with the stresses parents/spouses and students will be experiencing. Many institutions currently involve parents/spouses in their orientation programs, but the need may be particularly great for parents/spouses of first-generation students.

5. *The transition to college involves both in- and out-of-class experiences.* What happens to students outside the classroom shapes in important ways how students respond inside the classroom, and vice versa. While the implications of this are hardly new, academic and student affairs divisions on a campus must come to see and respond to the interlocking character of students' in- and out-of-class experiences in the transition process. Academic affairs administrators and faculty must recognize that substantial and important learning goes on outside of class, and student affairs administrators must begin to consider how the activities and programs of their division relate to the academic/intellectual mission of the institution.

6. *Institutional accommodations are required.* In the past, we have tended to develop new student support programs implicitly assuming that the challenge is to help students adapt to the institution. In some cases, and to a certain extent, this may have been appropriate. For nontraditional and diverse students, however, the logic needs to be reversed: Institutions must seek ways in which *they* can change so as to accommodate the transitional and learning needs of first-generation and other nontraditional students. Some students will flourish in their new environment without institutional intervention. Others, however, will require assistance that is initiated by institutional representatives—faculty and staff. Faculty cannot assume that their sole responsibility is to teach and advise, and that if students do not take advantage of what they have to offer it is the student's problem. The burden of responsibility for taking advantage of transition support mechanisms cannot rest with the student alone.

7. *Somebody has to care.* In some ways, perhaps no theme was more persistent throughout the interviews—regardless of race or ethnicity, gender, age, or institution attended—than new students' need for self-esteem in its many variant forms: self-confidence, a sense of being in control, pride in oneself and what one does, respecting oneself and being respected by others, valuing oneself and being valued by others. The important role of self-perceptions is apparent in such themes as the academic, social, and cultural character of the transition process for nontraditional students; in the need for early validation from faculty and peers (whether the validation is of an academic or interpersonal nature); in the need for connectedness and a sense of belonging at the institution; in the move to personal independence and autonomy; and in proving oneself capable of success, however the individual defines that concept.

For these new students, the sense that they were competent and mattered came from many sources: parents and other relatives, peers, faculty members, institutional staff. Most of the students we interviewed, and who appeared to have successfully made the transition from work or high school to college, identified someone who had clearly indicated to them that they cared. In many ways, a successful transition for any given student is a cooperative activity, involving the individual and the will to succeed and a variety of other people willing to make success for that student possible.

Conclusion

If involvement is a central mechanism by which students maximize the range and extent of their learning opportunities, the route to involvement remains a circuitous and as-yet poorly mapped one. This research project has identified a number of the dimensions of the transition individuals make from high school or work to college and suggested places where institutions and policymakers might intervene to facilitate the successful passage for most new students. Its purpose has been to shed some light on the nature of the process for different kinds of students attending different kinds of institutions and to identify some of the elements and dynamics of that process for additional examination.

References

Astin, A. W. (1985). *Achieving Educational Excellence: A Critical Assessment of Priorities and Practices in Higher Education.* San Francisco: Jossey-Bass.

Astin, A. W. (1993). *What Matters in College? Four Critical Years Revisited.* San Francisco: Jossey-Bass.

Belenky, J., B. Clinchy, N. Goldberger, and J. Tarule (1986). *Women's Ways of Knowing.* New York: Basic Books.

Christie, N. G., and S. M. Dinham (1991). Institutional and external influences on social integration in the freshman year. *Journal of Higher Education* 62: 412–436.

Gurin, P., and E. Epps (1975). *Black Consciousness,. Identity, and Achievement: A Study of Students in Historically Black Colleges.* New York: Wiley.

Hays, R. B., D. Oxley (1986). Social network development and functioning during a life transition. *Journal of Personality and Social Psychology* 50: 305–313.

London, H. (1989). Breaking away: A study of first-generation college students and their families. *American Journal of Education* 97: 144–170.

Pace, C. R. (1984). *Measuring the Quality of College Student Experiences.* Los Angeles: University of California, Graduate School of Education, Higher Education Research Institute.

Pace, C. R. (1990). *The Undergraduates: A Report of Their Activities and Progress in College in the 1980s.* Los Angeles: University of California. Graduate School of Education, Higher Education Research Institute.

Pascarella, E. T., and P. T. Terenzini (1986). Orientation to college and freshman year persistence/ withdrawal. *Journal of Higher Education* 57: 155–174.

Pascarella, E. T., and P. T. Terenzini (1991). *How College Affects Students: Findings and Insights from Twenty Years of Research.* San Francisco: Jossey-Bass.

Perl, H. I., and E. J. Trickett (1988). Social network formation of college freshmen: Personal and environmental determinants. *American Journal of Community Psychology* 16: 207-224.

Rendon, L. I. (1992). From the barrio to the academy: Revelations of a Mexican American scholarship girl. In L. S. Zwerling and H. B. London (eds.), *First-Generation Students: Confronting the Cultural Issues* (pp. 55–64). New Directions for Community Colleges, No. 80. San Francisco: Jossey-Bass.

Rodriguez, R. (1974–75). Going home again: The new American scholarship boy. *The American Scholar* 44: 15–28.

Rodriguez, R. (1982). *Hunger of Memory: The Education of Richard Rodriguez.* Boston: Godine.

Tinto, V. (1988). Stages of student departure: Reflections on the longitudinal character of students leaving college. *Journal of Higher Education* 59: 438–455.

Van Gennep, A. (1960). *The Rites of Passage,* M. Vizedon and G. Caffee, trans. Chicago: University of Chicago Press.

Studying College Impact

A. Astin

Few people will argue with the premise that attending college can have a profound effect on one's life. With the possible exception of getting married or having children, few choices have more far-reaching implications than the decision about college. For most prospective college students, this decision involves three issues: (1) whether or not to go, (2) where to go, and (3) how to go. The matter of "whether" is particularly critical for that substantial minority of young people whose academic interests and achievements are minimal or whose financial situation is tenuous. Will I be able to succeed? Is it likely to be a worthwhile investment of my time and money? Among those for whom college attendance is a foregone conclusion—the college-bound students—the issues of "where" and "how" are paramount. The "where" of college choice involves which kind of institution to attend: large or small, public or private, religious or nonsectarian, and two-year versus four-year. The "how" of college attendance—a critical set of issues often poorly understood by counselors and parents—concerns matters such as financing (whether to borrow money or get a job), where to live (at home, in a dormitory, or in a private room), what to study (choice of major and electives), whether to attend full- or part-time, and which extracurricular activities to pursue.

But what is the impact of college attendance on students' personal, social, and vocational development? Are some students affected differently from others? Do different types of colleges produce different outcomes? And how important is it to attend college away from home, to attend full-time, to work, or to participate in extracurricular activities? Until recently, few research-based answers could be offered.

At the same time, public policy makers have questions of their own about the value of higher education. During the 1950s and early 1960s a substantial national investment in higher education was regarded as an insurance policy in the Cold War and as a way to enhance our technological and scientific position in world trade. Now, however, many public officials are asking whether the soaring costs of higher education are draining off resources that could be better used for other public purposes. Economic pressures have forced legislators to look for programs in which public spending can be cut, and the high level of federal and state investments in higher education underscores the need for better information on how colleges affect students. How does higher education influence students' career opportunities and aspirations? Does it have significant impact on their values, personality, behavior, and life-styles? Do they become more competent and knowledgeable? Are particular types of colleges or programs more effective than others? How can we improve undergraduate education in different types of institutions?

Why Study College Impact?

The sheer volume of publications on college impact (Feldman and Newcomb, 1969; Pascarella and Terenzini, 1991) might tempt one to conclude that a great deal is already known about the answers

66

to these questions. However, since much research is either limited in scope, inadequate in design, or outdated, there is surprisingly little one can say with confidence about the impact of college on contemporary students. Much early research failed to collect the data that would meet the two minimal requirements for adequately designed studies of college impact: (1) multi-institutional data, that is, information collected simultaneously from students at contrasting types of institutions, and (2) longitudinal data, that is, information on the ways in which students change between admission and some subsequent point in time. Other features missing from that research include large and diverse samples of students and institutions; multiple measures of entering student characteristics; multiple follow-up measures of student development, including both cognitive and affective outcomes; multivariate designs for controlling differences among students entering different types of institutions; and methodological provisions for separating college effects from maturational effects or the simple process of growing up. (For a detailed description of requirements for data and methods of analysis, see Astin, 1991.)

The original *Four Critical Years* (Astin, 1977) attempted to correct for these methodological and data limitations by relying on multi-institutional, longitudinal data collected from undergraduates during the late 1960s and early 1970s. (Many of the newer results summarized in Pascarella and Terenzini's 1991 *How College Affects Students* were based on a nine-year follow-up of the 1971 entering freshmen.) While the findings reported in *Four Critical Years* were of considerable value in helping us to understand how students are affected by various types of institutions and by different kinds of educational experiences, the decision to write an entirely new book on the same subject was prompted by several factors. First, considering the numerous ways in which higher education and its students have changed since the early 1970s, I was concerned that many of the earlier findings might now be outdated. And, second, the Higher Education Research Institute (HERI) at the University of California, Los Angeles (UCLA), was recently able to collect some new types of data that make it possible to explore a number of important educational questions and issues that got very little, if any, attention either in the earlier study or in Pascarella and Terenzini's (1991) more recent review, *How College Affects Students*. These new features, not available in *Four Critical Years* or in any other subsequent studies using data from the Cooperative Institutional Research Program (CIRP) (for example, Astin forthcoming; Pascarella, 1985b; Pascarella and Wolfe, 1985; Smart, 1986, 1988), include (1) an assessment of the student's cognitive development as measured both by performance on some of the major national tests used for graduate admissions and professional certification as well as by self-reported improvements in knowledge and competence during the undergraduate years, (2) extensive data on the characteristics of each institution's general education program, (3) measures of the characteristics of the student's *peer group* at each institution, and (4) measures of the characteristics of the *teaching faculty* (values, favored teaching methods, relationship with students, and so on) at each institution. The last two features were considered especially important, given the growing body of evidence suggesting that the undergraduate's development is substantially affected by interactions with both peers and faculty.

The purpose of this book is to answer questions about the effects of college that have been raised by students, parents, public officials, and educators themselves—and to answer them on the basis of data from an ongoing research program that was designed to overcome the limitations of earlier studies and to produce data for definitive studies of college impact: the Cooperative Institutional Research Program. CIRP was initiated at the American Council on Education (ACE) in 1966; since 1973 it has been conducted by the Higher Education Research Institute at the University of California, Los Angeles, with continuing sponsorship by ACE. It is now the largest ongoing study of the American higher education system, with longitudinal data covering some 500,000 students and a national sample of more than 1,300 institutions of all types. These data cover a wide range of cognitive and affective student outcomes, affording the opportunity to examine how the college experience affects more than eighty different measures of attitudes, values, behavior, learning, achievement, career development, and satisfaction. The size and scope of CIRP make it possible to employ highly sophisticated multivariate controls over a large number of potentially biasing variables—in particular, the characteristics of the entering students that might predispose them to pick particular types of colleges or programs.

The task of assessing how students are affected by their colleges is composed of three major undertakings: (1) understanding the meaning of student change, (2) developing a model or conceptual framework for studying student outcomes, and (3) designing the analyses of college impact. As an introduction to the findings discussed in later chapters, the following pages of this chapter describe how CIRP deals with each of these three requirements.

Understanding the Meaning of Student Change

In response to the question, How does college affect students? One can legitimately ask, In relation to what? While this response may seem flippant, it captures a fundamental truth regarding research on college impact: if students are not attending college, they are doing something else. "Thus the generic concept of "college impact" has meaning only in relation to what would happen if students either did not attend college or attended a different type of college.

In other words, potential students are in a continuous state of growth and change. These developmental processes go on whether or not students attend college and regardless of where they attend. If researchers could somehow put young people who do not attend college in cold storage or in a state of suspended animation, they might be able to obtain a "pure" measure of the effects of college attendance by comparing them after four years with students who went to college. But such a measure would make little sense. In the real world, those who do not attend may get married, join the armed forces or find other work, go on welfare, join communes, raise families, travel abroad, or stay home with parents while they figure out what to do with their lives—but they continue to develop and learn. The real issue in research on college impact is to determine what *difference* college attendance makes in the development of the individual.

Unfortunately, much of the literature on college impact looks merely at *change or growth* in students rather than impact as such. Typically, students complete a personality inventory or attitudinal questionnaire when they first enter college (in the jargon of educational research, a pretest) and again after one year, four years, or—in a few cases—many years following graduation (posttest). Change or growth is assessed by comparing the two measures. Most investigators, by equating measured change with college impact, have assumed that any observed changes result from the students' college experience. The major weakness of this approach is that it fails to consider whether the same changes would have occurred if the students had attended different colleges or had not gone to college at all.

For adequate research on "the impact of college," it is essential that observed changes in students over time be seen as having two major components: the first is change resulting from the impact of the college; the second is change resulting from other influences, such as maturation and the environment outside of college. Note that the first component may (1) bring about changes that would not occur under other conditions, (2) exaggerate or accelerate changes originating in other sources, or (3) impede or counteract changes originating elsewhere. One goal of CIRP and this report is to isolate changes brought about by the college experience from changes attributable to other sources.

Some investigators have concluded that the ideal solution to these inferential problems is a control group of young people who do not attend college. Such a college-noncollege research design may have some advantages over the traditional single-institution designs that are discussed later, in the section of this chapter entitled "Assessing the Impact of College Experiences," but the difficulty with the college-noncollege design is that it grossly oversimplifies the issue of college impact. As the proportion of high school graduates who went to college increased during the 1950s and 1960s and as the number and variety of postsecondary opportunities and institutions proliferated, the distinction between college and noncollege experiences grew increasingly blurred. Indeed, for many thousands of students these days, the college experience consists of little more than driving to campus for a few hours of classes and then driving home again. It is not unreasonable to suppose, for example, that the total environmental experiences and life-styles of those commuter students who work at off-campus jobs are much more similar to those of their nonstudent co-workers than to those of students attending, say, residential liberal arts colleges. Thus the variety of experiences possible within the collegiate sphere is so great that it renders virtually meaningless any simple comparison of college attendance with nonattendance. The real issue is not the impact of college but the impact of college *characteristics* or, more precisely, the comparative impact of different collegiate experiences. More information is needed on the relative impact of various *types* of collegiate experiences. The current study seeks to meet this need by focusing not only on differences among different types of institutions but also on differences in students' experiences (faculty, peer group, curriculum) at these institutions.

A Conceptual Framework for Studying Student Outcomes: The I-E-O Model

For nearly three decades I have been using what I call the input-environment-outcome (I-E-O) model as a conceptual guide for studying college student development. While this model has undergone a number of refinements over the years (Astin, 1962, 1970a, 1970b, 1977, 1991), the basic elements of the model have remained the same. *Inputs* refer to the characteristics of the student at the time of initial entry to the institution; *environment* refers to the various programs, policies, faculty, peers, and educational experiences to which the student is exposed; and *outcomes* refers to the student's characteristics *after* exposure to the environment. Change or growth in the student during college is determined by comparing outcome characteristics with input characteristics. The basic purpose of the model is to assess the impact of various environmental experiences by determining whether students grow or change differently under varying environmental conditions. Studying student development with the I-E-O model provides educators, students, and policy makers with a better basis for knowing how to achieve desired educational outcomes. A key problem, of course, is to specify the relevant outcomes, inputs, and environmental experiences that are to be assessed. In the next section, we examine the specific outcomes, input, and environmental measures used in this study.

Developing Outcome Measures of the College Experience

Trends in the CIRP surveys during the past two decades show that increasing numbers of students believe that the most important outcome of college attendance is economic (Dey, Astin and Korn, 1991). This view is reinforced by many educators who argue that having a college degree is supposed to help students develop cognitive skills that enable them to get better jobs and to make more money. But colleges potentially have a much more pervasive influence than this. An eighteen-year-old who is leaving home for the first time to attend college* is subject to wide-ranging influences from faculty, staff, curriculum, and fellow students. The possible influence of parents is reduced proportionately, simply because they are no longer present. Many freshmen experience their first intensive encounter with peers who have markedly different beliefs, backgrounds, and attitudes. For some students, enrolling in college may also provide their first direct experience with drugs, sex, alcohol, or political activism. For others, college presents the first real challenge to their academic motivation and skills. The fact that many students spend four or more years attending college under these circumstances highlights the great potential of the college experience for producing changes not only in knowledge and vocational skills but also in values, attitudes, aspirations, beliefs, and behavior.

A thorough examination of the impact of college must take into account a wide range of possible outcomes. There is no easy way to capture the impact of college adequately in one or two simple measures, such as credits and degrees earned or job placement. The need for a variety of outcome measures thus was anticipated in the design of CIRP. But rather than simply generating a list of miscellaneous measures, we developed a conceptual scheme to guide the selection of various measures. This "taxonomy of student outcomes," which was proposed several decades ago (Astin, 1970a), was also utilized by Pascarella and Terenzini (1991) in their recent comprehensive review of the college impact literature. It involves three major dimensions: type of outcome, type of data, and time.

Type of Outcome. Behavioral scientists have traditionally classified human performance into two broad domains: cognitive (sometimes called intellective) and noncognitive (sometimes called affective). Since cognitive outcomes involve the use of higher-order mental processes such as reasoning and logic, they are clearly relevant to the educational objectives of most students, faculty, administrators, trustees, parents, and others concerned with higher education. Noncognitive, or affective, outcomes refer to the student's attitudes, values, self-concept, aspirations, and everyday behavior and are important to students as well as to many educators. Information on affective outcomes is relatively easy to obtain through self-administered questionnaires, whereas measurements of cognitive outcomes often require more controlled conditions of administration and larger amounts of the student's time. But both deserve attention in a study of the impact of college.

Type of Data. The second dimension of the taxonomy, type of data, refers to the types of information gathered to assess the cognitive and affective outcomes. Again, two broad classes can be identified: *psychological* data, relating to the internal states or traits of the individual; and *behavioral* data, relating to directly observable activities. The measurement of psychological phenomena is usually indirect, in the sense that the investigator, from the student's responses to questions, infers some underlying state within that student. Behavioral measures, which might also be called sociological, directly reflect transactions between the student and the environment and are usually of intrinsic interest.

Any student outcome measure can be classified simultaneously by the type of outcome involved and the type of data (see Table 1). Each cell provides examples of different types of outcome measures obtained using different types of data. The cell on the upper left, for example, includes psychological measures of noncognitive or affective states: the student's ambition, motivation, and self-concept, as well as subjective feelings of satisfaction and well-being. The cell on the upper right includes cognitive measures such as the student's grade point average or performance on multiple-choice tests of ability and achievement. The lower-left cell includes sociological or behavioral features of the individual's development that reflect primarily affective states. Under personal habits, for example, one might include such behaviors as reading, eating, typical interactions with others, and use of drugs, tobacco, and alcohol. Citizenship would include such outcomes as voting behavior, participating in community activities, and earning special awards for community service or, on the negative side, welfare and arrest records. The lower-right cell gives examples of behavioral or sociological measures of cognitive outcomes. Basically,

Table 1
Classification of Student Outcomes by Type of Outcome and Type of Data

Data	Outcome	
	Affective	Cognitive
Psychological	Self-concept	Knowledge
	Values	Critical thinking ability
	Attitudes	Basic skills
	Beliefs	Special aptitudes
	Drive for achievement	Academic achievement
	Satisfaction with college	
Behavioral	Personal habits	Career development
	Avocations	Level of educational attainment
	Mental health	Vocational achievements:
	Citizenship	Level of responsibility
	Interpersonal relations	Income
		Awards or special recognition

Source: Data abstracted from Astin, Panos, and Creager (1967), p. 16.

this category contains outcomes that reflect the behavior of the student (or former student) in society and that usually require cognitive skills. Presumably, real-life achievements represent the behavioral manifestations of the cognitive traits listed in the cell immediately above it.

The two dimensions that make up Table 1.1 are really more continua than true dichotomies. For example, a person's earned income probably depends in part on cognitive abilities, but it almost certainly depends as well on noncognitive or personality traits.

Time Dimension. Since attending college can have both short and long-term effects, the four cells in Table 1 could be extended into a third dimension representing temporal differences in student outcomes. Table 2 shows examples of related measures taken at two points in time.

Although timing is seldom considered in discussions of educational outcomes, it is of fundamental importance. Most colleges hope to produce long-term rather than short-term changes. The goals stated in college catalogues, for example, imply that the institution is primarily concerned with making an impact that will last throughout a lifetime. The college, it would seem, tries to provide experiences that will help the student make the fullest possible use of his or her talents and become an effective, responsible member of society. Presumably, such effects will in turn result in a more satisfying and rewarding life.

For many prospective college students, however, such long-term effects may be too remote and too difficult to comprehend. These students are primarily interested in more immediate goals—their actual experiences during the undergraduate college years—rather than in how these experiences will affect their later development. Educators frequently do not recognize that the two, four, or eight years of college represent a sizable portion of the student's total life span. For students, then, college experiences are important in themselves, not merely for what they will mean later. We might add here that most professors and staff, if they focus at all on student outcomes, limit their attention to outcomes that can be assessed while the student is still enrolled. For these reasons, the study reported in this book will focus on those outcomes that can be observed during the "four critical years" after the student initially enrolls.

This outcome taxonomy, which has guided the selection of CIRP outcomes for the past twenty-seven years, has also been used to organize the major findings from the current study, as reported in Chapters Three through Nine. Affective-psychological outcomes are reported in Chapters Three ("Assessing Environmental Effects"), Four ("Personality and Self-Concept"), Five ("Attitudes, Values, and Beliefs"), and Nine ("Satisfaction with the College Environment"). Affective-behavioral outcomes are included in Chapter Six ("Patterns of Behavior"). Cognitive-psychological outcomes are reported in Chapter Seven ("Academic and Cognitive Development") and cognitive-behavioral outcomes are covered in Chapter Eight ("Career Development").

Outcome data for the study come from three different sources: the CIRP follow-up questionnaire administered during 1989–90 to samples of students who had originally entered college as

Table 2
Examples of Measures Representing Different Times, Types of Data, and Outcomes

Type of Outcome	Type of Data	Time 1 (During College)	Time 2 (After College)
Affective	Psychological	Satisfaction with college	Job satisfaction
Affective	Behavioral	Participation in student government	Participation in local or national politics
Cognitive	Psychological	Law School Aptitude Test (LSAT) score	Score on law boards
Cognitive	Behavioral	Persistence in college (staying in versus dropping out)	Income

freshmen in the fall of 1985; retention information on these same students, provided by the registrars of their institutions; and various national testing organizations that supplied us with results from the Scholastic Aptitude Test (SAT) and American College Test (ACT) taken by students prior to entering college, and from the Graduate Record Examination (GRE), Law School Admission Test (LSAT), Medical College Admission Test (MCAT), and National Teacher Examination (NTE) taken by these same students four years later. A total of eighty-two outcome measures was used, including twelve measures of personality and self-concept (Chapter Four), twelve measures of attitudes, values, and beliefs (Chapters Three and Five), nine measures of behavior patterns (Chapter Six), twenty-six measures of competency and achievement (Chapter Seven), nine measures of career development (Chapter Eight), and fourteen measures of satisfaction with the college environment (Chapter Nine). Details of how each outcome measure has been constructed will be provided in the relevant chapter.

Student Input Characteristics

A student's performance on some outcome measure such as the Graduate Record Examination (GRE) is, by itself, of little value in telling us how that student has been affected by the undergraduate experience. However, a GRE score takes on much greater significance when we can compare it to the student's performance on a similar measure, such as the SAT taken four years earlier, prior to college entry. This relationship holds for almost any other outcome measure: when the student's outcome (posttest) performance can be compared with input performance four years earlier, we can develop a measure of *growth* or *change*.

A long history of research on college impact (Astin, 1977; Bowen, 1977; Feldman and Newcomb, 1969; Pascarella and Terenzini, 1991) shows that the student's outcome performance can be affected by a number of other input characteristics besides the pretest performance. Since many of these input characteristics are also related to the kinds of environments to which students are exposed, the possibility remains that any observed correlation between an environment and an outcome measure may reflect the effect of some input characteristic rather than the effect of the college environment. In other words, our assessments of how outcomes are affected by environments will be biased unless we measure and control for as many student input characteristics as possible. The Cooperative Institutional Research Program (CIRP) was initiated in 1966 specifically to collect input data that would make it possible to apply the I-E-O model to a national study of student outcomes in American higher education.

In the study reported here, we had pretests available from the CIRP freshman questionnaire and from various college admissions test scores for approximately half (44) of the eighty-two student outcome measures. The main reason pretests were not available for all eighty-two outcomes is that some outcome measures do not lend themselves to pretesting. A good example is the outcome of student retention (completing a degree versus dropping out): since anybody who drops out of high school (the pretest) will, by definition, be eliminated from the college sample, it is obviously not feasible to have an adequate pretest for an outcome such as college retention. The best alternative in this situation is to make sure that those input characteristics that are known to predict retention (high school grades and admissions tests scores, for example) are available as input measures.

Another way to deal with outcome measures that have no obvious pretest at the input stage is to obtain students' *predictions* or *expectations* with respect to the outcome measure in question. One class of outcomes for which no appropriate pretests are available is measures of student *satisfaction*. In lieu of pretests one can ask students whether they *expect* to be satisfied with college. One can also ask students to estimate their chances of completing a degree or dropping out. Since self-predictions of this type have some accuracy (Astin, 1977), our input variables included the forty-four pretest measures plus a list of twenty-six different self-predictions by which the student was asked to indicate whether there was a very good chance, some chance, very little chance, or no chance of a particular outcome event occurring during college. Sixty-one other input characteristics included the number of high school courses taken in eight different subject matter fields (8 measures), preliminary choice of a career (12 measures), the importance (very important, somewhat important, not important) given to each of eleven reasons for attending college (11 measures), religious preference (6 measures), parental occupation (11 measures), parental income, parental education (2 measures), and a variety of demographic measures, including the student's race or ethnicity (6 measures), age, gender, marital status, and citizenship. Altogether, we used a total of 131 input measures. If we also consider the freshman's preliminary choice of a major field of study as an input rather than an environmental variable (see later in this chapter, and Chapter Two), there is a total of 146 input measures.

Environmental Measures

Earlier in this chapter I indicated that one of the major differences between this sequel to *Four Critical Years* and the original work is the inclusion of a number of environmental measures not available in that or any other previous study. The inclusion of these additional measures was made possible in part because of grants from the Exxon Education Foundation and the National Science Foundation, which provided funding for an expansion of the 1989–90 student follow-up questionnaire as well as for a special survey of all teaching faculty in each of the CIRP institutions selected for this study. (A more complete description of the CIRP sample used in the study is given later in this chapter.)

The 192 environmental measures used in this study include 16 measures of institutional characteristics (such as type, control, size), 35 measures of the student's peer group characteristics (for example, socioeconomic status, academic preparation, values, attitudes), 34 measures of faculty characteristics (such as favored methods of teaching, morale, values), 15 measures of the curriculum (such as true core, type of requirements), 15 measures of financial aid (such as Pell grants, Stafford loans), 16 measures of freshman major field choice, 4 measures of place of residence (for example, college dormitory, private room), and 57 different measures of student involvement (hours spent studying, number of classes taken in different fields, participation in honors programs, and so on). Because of the number and complexity of the various environmental measures used, a detailed description of the construction of each measure will be provided in the next chapter (Chapter Two). Comprehensive summaries of the outcomes affected by each environmental measure are provided in Chapter Ten ("Summary of Environmental Effects") and Chapter Eleven ("Effects of Involvement"). The last Chapter (Chapter Twelve) summarizes the effects by key input variables and discusses the theoretical and policy implications of the major findings.

Assessing the Impact of College Experiences

Assessing the impact of college experiences on students involves two basic problems. The first, as discussed earlier, is to identify the relevant outcome variables. The second and more complex task is to determine how these outcomes are differentially affected by various college programs or experiences. The widespread confusion about how to handle this second task is reflected in the variety of methods and procedures that has been used in research on college impact. Investigators often forget, however, that each methodology implies a somewhat different conception of the purposes of higher education and the nature of the college experience. For this reason, it is important at the outset to describe the particular conception of higher education that underlies this study and to sketch in some detail the methodology employed to assess the impact of higher education on student development.

Two models from outside education are most commonly used in describing the functioning of colleges and universities: those of industry and medicine.

The Industrial Model of Higher Education

Budgetary constraints in recent years have forced many college administrators to come to grips with such issues as institutional accountability and the efficiency of institutional management. Many administrators have responded to these pressures by experimenting with computerized management information systems, by introducing "outcomes assessments," by hiring management consultants, by embarking on elaborate programs of "enrollment management," and by instituting such procedures as program budgeting, management by objectives, and Total Quality Management (TQM). One consequence of this business orientation is that it portrays students and their degrees as "produced" by the institution, in much the same way an automobile is produced at a factory.

Manufacturing is a physical process in which raw materials are fabricated into parts that are put together on an assembly line. The finished product is a result of the manufacturing process. But graduates of college are clearly not produced by the institution in this way. Their personal characteristics at the time of graduation may, to be sure, have been influenced by their college experience, but their physical and psychological makeup depends heavily on background and environmental factors largely independent of the institution. Students, in other words, are fully functioning organisms before they get to college; the purpose of our higher education system is presumably to enhance the student's functioning, or to "develop the talent of its students" (Astin, 1985, p. 60).

A major assumption of the current study is that industrial analogies of this kind are simply not applicable to higher education institutions. Although it is possible to assess the impact of a plant in terms of the number and quality of its products, the actual impact of college is not necessarily reflected in the number of its graduates or even in the quality of their achievements.

The Medical Model of Higher Education

A better institutional analogy for the college is the hospital, clinic, or doctor's office. The main function of both medicine and education is to improve the condition of their clients. Patients (students) are admitted to treatment facilities (colleges) because they need or want medical assistance (education). Medical facilities administer treatment programs based on a diagnosis of the patient's illness; colleges administer educational programs that presumably are relevant to the student's education needs. Just as some patients do not benefit from medical treatment, so some students do not benefit from college education. At the same time some patients improve and some students learn, even if their treatment (educational) programs are ineffectual.

Although the medical model is clearly inappropriate in one respect—in that students are not ill—students and patients are both seeking some sort of personal service to improve their circumstances. Most important, both colleges and medical treatment facilities attempt to bring about desirable changes in the condition of their clients. For this reason, a critical ingredient in the assessment of college impact is to measure *change* in the characteristics of students over time.

We have already suggested that student change should not be equated with institutional impact. Does the same hold true for patient change? Can the hospital always take credit when the patient gets better? Should the hospital always take the blame if the patient's condition shows no change or gets worse? Can one assume that the hospital has had no impact? In medicine there is a convenient means for dealing with such conceptual issues: the *prognosis*. When the newly admitted patient has a poor prognosis (input), the treatment program may be judged highly successful if the condition of the patient simply stabilizes (outcome). By the same token, a treatment program could be judged a failure if a patient with a highly favorable prognosis (input) fails to improve after admission (outcome). Thus, a patient whose condition remains unchanged could be judged either a success or a failure, depending on the initial prognosis. In other words, neither the patient's status at discharge nor changes in the patient's condition between admission and discharge provides an adequate indication of the success or failure of a treatment program. Such information has meaning only in the context of the initial prognosis.

The concept of change from admission to discharge is simpler than the relationship between outcome and prognosis (input). For example, a patient with a high fever caused by a bad cold will generally have a favorable prognosis, regardless of treatment. Fevers caused by bad colds usually disappear without any treatment. Thus, the positive change from high to low fever is not remarkable, given that the prognosis was favorable. Fevers caused by other factors (such as pneumonia) may not present such a favorable prognosis in the absence of treatment.

If we recast this last discussion in terms of the I-E-O model, we could say that our initial focus is on a single input measure—the patient's fever— and that we are interested in whether the fever can be reduced (from input measure to outcome measure) through treatment (environment). But it is not enough simply to have a single input measure (the "pretest" fever) in order to make an accurate diagnosis and to prognosticate about what the outcome ("posttest" fever) will be after a period of time. We also need other input data, such as the patient's history, other symptoms, information from a physical exam, and possibly X-rays and laboratory tests of various kinds. By putting together all of this information we are in a much better position to make a prediction (prognosticate) about the outcome (posttest fever). If this other input information leads us to conclude that the patient has a bad cold (diagnosis), we would predict that the fever will disappear after a few days, regardless of what treatment (environment) the patient receives. If we conclude instead that the patient has pneumonia or some kind of bacteriological infection, then we would make a more pessimistic prognosis, especially if no treatment (environment) is administered.

Clinical medicine thus utilizes two types of prognoses: those that assume no treatment and those that assume particular treatment. Diseases for which no effective treatment exists have the same prognosis, regardless of treatment. The essential aspect of an effective treatment is thus that it *changes the prognosis.*

In many ways, assessing the impact of an educational program is analogous. People will continue to grow and develop (from input to outcome) regardless of whether or where they attend college, and, because human behavior tends to be consistent over time, it is possible to predict (prognosticate) from current information (input) what a person will be like at some later time (outcome). High achievers in secondary school (input), for example, tend to be high achievers in college (outcome). But we can make a better prediction as to whether this high achiever in high school will also be a high achiever in college if we have more input information on the student's ability, motivation, and family background. The basic issue, then, is whether attending a given college or being exposed to a particular type of environment *changes the prediction* of how the student will develop.

Medical prognosticating relies on collective experience showing that the illness of patients who show particular patterns of entry information (medical history, symptoms, laboratory findings, and so forth) frequently follow predictable courses. This is basically a statistical matter: particular illnesses under specified conditions frequently produce similar outcomes. In many ways, studying the development of college students is analogous: particular outcomes (for example, high grades in college) tend to be associated with particular input characteristics at entry (high grades in high school, high test scores, and so forth). The precise weight assigned to each entering freshman characteristic depends on the outcome predicted.

Modern statistical procedures can be used to combine such input information into a "best prediction" (prognosis) about how the entering student will perform later on the outcome measure. Just as the physician arrives at a prognosis using data from a patient's present symptoms, history, physical examination, and laboratory tests, the educational researcher can combine input information on an entering freshman's past achievements and behavior to predict that student's subsequent performance. Separate predictions can be developed for each student outcome. In predicting whether the student will complete a baccalaureate degree, for example, considerable weight will be given to past academic record, degree aspirations, and social background (Astin, 1975). In predicting such affective outcomes as political beliefs at graduation, considerable weight should be given to the student's initial beliefs at college entry. Put more simply, an entering student who espouses conservative beliefs (input) is much more likely to hold similar beliefs at graduation (outcome) than is an entering student who espouses liberal beliefs (see Chapter Three).

Whether such predictions are changed by particular college experiences is analogous to the medical question of whether particular treatments change the prognosis. A conservative freshman's chances of remaining a conservative during college are reduced if she enrolls at a college where her peers are mostly liberals (see Chapter Three). The environmental "treatment" (liberal peer groups) can thus change the "prognosis" (predicted political affiliation four years after entering). One major difference between medicine and education, however, is that the *causal* connections between certain treatments and certain medical outcomes are much better understood than are the causal connections between educational programs (environments) and student outcomes. This difference underscores the need for better studies in education where many student characteristics, such as input pretests, sex, ability, and socioeconomic status, are measured at entry and then statistically controlled in an effort to identify causal connections between educational experiences and outcomes. The actual statistical procedures used to control for entering student characteristics and to assess the impact of environmental experiences are described in Chapters Two and Three.

College Impact

So far we have discussed the problem of how to assess the impact of various *environmental characteristics and experiences* on student outcomes. Here we consider the more general question of how to assess the overall impact of college attendance. *College impact* is a generic concept that lumps together all the varieties of college experiences and tries to compare their effects with the effects of *noncollege.*

Some scholars in higher education believe that a definitive study of college impact should include a control group of persons who never attended college. By comparing such a group with college attenders, the investigator would presumably be able to differentiate purely maturational changes caused by noncollege influences from changes specifically attributable to the effects of college.

The current study takes a somewhat different approach to the task of identifying college effects. Rather than comparing college attenders with nonattenders, we look at three possible sources of systematic influence on student development: college, maturation, and social change.

College

To estimate the extent to which "college" may influence a particular outcome, we sorted students into groups according to their *degree of exposure* to the college experience. The underlying rationale for this approach is quite simple: if certain outcomes are facilitated by the experience of attending college, the likelihood of such outcomes should be greatest for those students who have the greatest exposure to the college environment. However, if an outcome is not affected by going to college, its occurrence should not depend on how much exposure to college the student has had.

Because of the great diversity of institutional types and the substantial variations in college attendance patterns, students differ widely in their degree of exposure to the college experience. The current study approaches the issue of exposure from two perspectives: *time* of exposure and *intensity* of exposure.

Time of Exposure. Time or degree of exposure can be handled quite simply: How long does the student stay in college? Some students register for college and never show up for their first class. Others drop out before completing the first term. Still others persist as full-time students for the entire four undergraduate years or longer. In subsequent chapters, the presence of college effects is assessed by determining answers to two questions: (1) Are changes in people who stay in college for a short time comparable to changes in people who stay longer? (2) Are the effects of particular college characteristics stronger for people who stay longer?

The lowest point on the time continuum lacks the extreme case of a group that had *no* exposure to college (the control group of the non-college attendees). Nevertheless, this continuum-of-exposure approach has certain advantages over the college-noncollege design. In laboratory experiments, the control group is supposed to be comparable to the experimental group in all respects except the "treatment" variable—in this case, degree of exposure to the college environment. Clearly, high school graduates who enroll in college are different in many respects from their classmates who do not enroll. It may be that a group of students with little exposure to college (say, those who left during their first term) is a less biased control group than one whose members have never attended college. The latter group would differ from college attenders in certain critical respects: most would not have gone through the process of applying to college, and presumably many were never motivated to attend college in the first place. Although it is true that college dropouts differ from nondropouts in such characteristics as ability and achievement (Astin, 1971a, 1975), similar differences between those who do and do not attend college may be even greater (Sewell and Shah, 1968; Trent and Medsker, 1967; Cooley and Flanagan, 1966). Furthermore, since much is known about factors that predispose students to drop out of college (Astin, 1975), this knowledge can be utilized to control for pre-existing input differences between early dropouts and college completers.

One problem with using time of exposure to the college environment is that student dropout rates differ widely among different types of institutions. Students entering private universities, for example, are much more likely to complete four years of undergraduate work than are students initially entering other types of institutions. Ignoring such institutional differences would confound *time of exposure* with *type of institution* attended. To deal with this problem, analyses of the effect of time of exposure to the college environment are conducted only *after* all institutional and other environmental differences have been controlled (see Chapter Three).

Intensity of Exposure. The quality or *intensity* of the student's exposure to the college experience is assessed using two environmental measures: the frequency of interaction with other students and the frequency of interaction with faculty. The rationale for defining intensity of exposure in such terms is that many of the effects of college are mediated through the student's contact with fellow students and with faculty. For example, if being exposed to a particular peer group of fellow college students has certain effects on student development, we would expect the magnitude of these effects to be proportional to the degree of exposure to that peer group: the more frequently the student interacts with peers, the greater the change will be. In other words, if we find that certain overall changes observed in our sample of college undergraduates are greatest for those who have the most exposure to faculty or students and smallest for those who have the least exposure, then we would have some reason to conclude that the observed change can be attributed to the effect of college attendance.

Maturation

One simple way to estimate the possible presence of maturational effects is by the age of the entering student. If a particular change from input to outcome is in part the result of maturation, the older students should show less change than younger students. That is, if a particular change occurs in most young people during the interval from eighteen to twenty, regardless of whether the person attends college, then it is reasonable to expect that students who are already twenty when they first enter college would be less likely to exhibit these changes than students who are seventeen or eighteen. In short, a negative relationship between any given change and age at college entry would constitute evidence that the change is in part maturational.

Social Change

The problem of assessing "the impact of college" is not complicated just by maturational effects. Students can also show systematic changes over time because of social changes that have little to do with either maturation or college impact (Gurin 1971). What if we had included a question in the 1985 freshman survey that measured something like "fear of the Soviet Union"? If we were to posttest this measure six years later, in 1991, we probably would see a sharp decline in "fear of the Soviet Union." It would make little sense to attribute such a change to college impact and even less sense to attribute it to maturation. Clearly, the change would be primarily attributable to external social events.

Because CIRP assesses the attitude and behavioral patterns of each new entering freshman class, we can monitor such social trends during the same period of time that the 1985 freshmen were attending college. Thus, in attempting to interpret longitudinal changes in the attitudes and behaviors of the 1985 freshmen that occurred between 1985 and 1989, we will look at responses to the same attitudinal and behavioral questions to see how they may have changed in the five consecutive freshman surveys conducted between 1985 and 1989.

Limitations of the Study

One major limitation of this study is that separate analyses have not been done by gender, race, ability, socioeconomic status, or other key student characteristics. While these characteristics have been included among the input variables and their effects on student outcomes summarized in the final chapter (Chapter Twelve), space limitations have made it impossible to do separate subgroup analyses (for example, for men and for women). HERI staff are currently conducting such analyses to identify possible interaction effects, and the highlights are expected to be published in a forthcoming series of journal articles.

Another limitation is the four-year longitudinal span. While the results reported in subsequent chapters show clearly that the first four years of college are indeed critical in many respects, the four-year limit precludes systematic study of other interesting and important phenomena, such as graduate and professional education and the link between higher education and employment. Given the rich data resources that have already been assembled on each of these students, we hope that further funding can be secured to support longer-term studies.

Summary

This chapter has considered a number of conceptual and methodological problems associated with studying college impact, presenting in some detail the general design of the impact analysis used in Chapters Three through Nine.

First, just the fact that students change in certain demonstrable ways while attending college does not mean that college attendance per se has produced the change. One also needs some basis for judging whether the same change would have occurred if the student had attended a different college or no college at all.

Second, because the college experience has the potential to affect any aspect of the students' lives, the impact of college cannot be adequately assessed from one or two simple outcomes such as attaining a degree or earning a certain income. An adequate assessment requires a variety of cognitive and affective outcome measures.

Third, the factory or production model of higher education, in which credits, degrees, and graduates are "produced" by the institution, has been rejected as a conceptually inadequate representation of the process of higher education. To assess college impacts, a medical or treatment model is a more appropriate analogy, primarily because both medical and educational institutions provide services designed to enhance the development of the individual. The effectiveness of these services cannot be assessed solely in terms of the status of the individual at some end point; rather, the person's final status must be evaluated in relation to initial status at the point of entry into the institution. Initial status (the person's educational potential) is analogous to a medical prognosis.

Fourth, much of the previous research on college impact has produced inconclusive findings, primarily because of limitations in the data and methods of analysis. The I-E-O model (Astin, 1991), which provides the conceptual framework for this new study of college impact, requires three types of information: *input* data describing the student at the point of entry, *environmental* data assessing the student's educational experiences after entering college, and *outcome* data describing the student after exposure to the college environment. The Cooperative Institutional Research Program (CIRP), which provides the principal basis for the findings reported in Chapters Three through Nine has a number of advantages in studying college impact. Its input data are collected from students as they enter a wide variety of collegiate institutions representing all major types. Environmental data describing the characteristics of each student's institution and experiences within those institutions, together with a variety of outcome measures covering both cognitive and affective as well as psychological and behavioral outcomes, are collected from institutions, faculty, testing organizations, and students via follow-up questionnaires. And CIRP data are longitudinal, with both freshman input pretests and posttests available for most outcome measures. Freshman input data also cover a wide range of personal and background information, which makes possible control of numerous potentially biasing variables.

Fifth and finally, many investigators have assumed that the "ideal" study of college impact requires comparing college attenders with a control group of nonattenders, but that design oversimplifies the college impact problem. Given the great variety of institutions and programs, it is necessary to assess the impact of college *characteristics* and collegiate *experiences* rather than "college" as such.

Note

* Like the original *Four Critical Years,* the current study will focus primarily on the experience of recent high school graduates who are attending college on a full-time basis. This is not to say that adult and part-time college students, whose numbers have been growing rapidly in recent years, are not important populations that are worthy of study in their own right. There are, however, good theoretical and practical reasons for focusing on the first-time, full-time student. For example, the sampling of part-time students in CIRP surveys is probably not representative of the entire population of such students. Moreover, since the environmental factors affecting full-time traditional-age students may be very different from those that are important to adults and part-timers, lumping these three populations together in a single study may well confound these different effects.

PART II
THE COLLEGE ENVIRONMENT

Introduction

If you read the Astin chapter before beginning this section, you will have read about the potential influences of both student characteristics and the collegiate experience on student outcomes and on student development. The first three articles in this section focus directly on the college student. In "The fulfillment of promise: Minority Valedictorians and Salutatorians", Arnold traces both the personal and collegiate factors that impact the college experiences and achievement of African-American and Latina/o students. More importantly, her study provides clear evidence that non-college environmental factors have direct consequences for students of color. For example, Arnold illustrates the negative influence of the socio-economic conditions of the communities in which the families of these students live. The second article by G. Kuh combines both qualitative and quantitative methods to examine the influence of "out of class" experiences of 149 college seniors. "In their own words: What students learn outside the classroom" describes the out of class activities associated with both personal development and learning.

"Latino students' sense of belonging in the college community: Rethinking the concept of integration on campus" by Hurtado and Carter retests a "mainstream" concept developed from research on traditional White college student samples. The authors intentionally cast their study in that nexus between the conventional and the transformational research perspective. They do so by distinguishing "between perceptions of group cohesion (based on the individual's perception)" and "observed cohesion, which is based on the researcher's assumptions of what constitutes cohesion (Bollen & Hoyle, 1990)." Thus, "sense of belonging" is operationalized from the student's perspective. The authors conducted this study with the goal of developing "research models that place the minority student experience at the center, with the clear purpose of improving their educational progress".

The samples studied by the researcher in the first three articles all consist of traditional aged or high achieving (by one measure or another) college students. The next two articles turn our attention to other types of college students. In "A conceptual model of nontraditional undergraduate student attrition" Bean and Metzener review the research on older, part-time, and commuter college students. The authors also present a model for studying these students. Nora, Attinasi, and Matonak focus on the community college student. They examined the persistence of community college students using Tinto's theoretical model of college students persistence. However, they incorporate factors in their study that were first examined in a naturalistic study of Mexican-American student retention (Attinasi, 1986). As such, this study too can be seen as bridging the conventional and transformational research perspectives. Finally, Olivas offers a perspective on the dangers of relying exclusively on quantitative research for information on college students.

The Fulfillment of Promise: Minority Valedictorians and Salutatorians

Karen D. Arnold

Thirty-five years ago today, my mother graduated valedictorian of [City Vocational] High School. My father graduated from Jackson State University during a time when blacks encountered various racial difficulties in attending college in the South.

My father died on August 10, 1977, one month before I entered my freshman year at [Urban] High School. On June 16, 1978, the last day of school for my freshman year, my mother also died.

On that day I made a commitment that I would be the number one student in my class. I thank God and my family for the strength and guidance that enabled me to fulfill my promise.

A capacity crowd of several thousand parents and friends heard a young African American man speak these words, without notes, as he began his high school valedictory address in June 1981 in an urban auditorium. As the student spoke, the audience rose silently to their feet then, as he finished his introduction, broke into an ovation that went on and on. Many audience members were moved to tears, including Terry Denny, the white researcher who had, until that moment, felt conspicuous among the almost completely African American assembly. After some time, the audience returned to their seats and the valedictorian to his speech. He reminded the graduates and their families that eleven hundred students had begun the freshman year with him four years previously and that only six hundred graduating seniors were seated in the auditorium. He called on the graduates and their families to continue their success and to care for the community of which they were the achievers. Mike (a pseudonym) titled his valedictorian speech: "Academic Persistence."

Denny's exploration of the meaning of academic success in high school had brought him to the study of high school valedictorians. He attended nearly forty high school commencement exercises that spring, including several others where the valedictorian or salutatorian was a minority; but Mike's valedictory address was the most extraordinary. The first extended interview with Mike, in the spring of the following year, confirmed the extraordinary talents of this handsome young man. Interpersonally gifted, ambitious, and involved in music, visual arts, and athletics, Mike was studying mechanical engineering at a Chicago private college. After this interview, Denny wrote in his field notes: "Mike is going to be somebody."

Mike entered mechanical engineering because he, like his auto-mechanic father, enjoyed working with his hands and with machines. He chose the nearby college on the advice of his sister's boyfriend and because he received a scholarship. Mike knew no practicing engineers. Unlike the close relationships he had experienced with high school teachers, he made no personal contact with any of his college professors. Mike couldn't imagine himself "sitting behind a desk with a white shirt and tie on. I like to get into work and do things." What he enjoyed was his job at a Chicago television station, work that combined his creative, interpersonal, and mechanical skills. Mike transferred to another area college to study television production. As in his original college, Mike made no informal contact with his faculty. He felt he was "floating" at school. The man who had hired him at the television station left Chicago, and his replacement did not rehire Mike. Although Mike was upset about losing his job, he did not challenge the decision. His broadcasting career and college education suddenly lost their primacy when his girlfriend of several years became pregnant. He dropped out of school, temporarily he said, and sought steady work with good pay, first as a city bus driver and then as a delivery truck driver. He and his girlfriend married.

Twelve years after high school, Mike is a manager for a delivery company and the married father of a son and a daughter. Because of the influence of his wife, he has become far more religious than he was in high school, and he considers his family and their economic and emotional well-being the center of his life. He has no plans to complete his degree. He continues some physical exercise but is no longer active in music, calligraphy, photography, or martial arts.

Mike considers himself a success and doesn't see his lack of a college degree as a career obstacle. "Family happiness motivates me more right now than anything," he says. "I look at my job as a means to an end. Seeing accomplishments in the home first and then the accomplishments that come after that are secondary. I mean, they're great, but those things don't last and your family does last."

Mike's life after high school had a clear turning point, but his story is not simple. Economic realities, cultural and family values, lack of engagement with college faculty, and a bounded view of the world of work are just some of the factors that shaped the sequel to Mike's "Academic Persistence" address.

Minority Student Achievement

The phenomenon of success in American schools is less well understood than the dimensions of failure. The ratio of studies of educational failure to studies of success is particularly high in investigations of urban African American and Latino youth. Researchers, demographers, and education policymakers have documented underachievement and obstacles to higher education for African American and Latino college students (Allen, 1992; Hodgkinson, 1985; Nettles, 1988; Pascarella, Smart, & Stoecker, 1989; Tracey & Sedlacek, 1984). Poor high school preparation, financial difficulties, and lack of role models impede the college entrance of students of color (Oden, Kelly, Ma, & Weikhart, 1992; Smith, 1989; Stampen & Fenske, 1988). Once enrolled in predominantly white colleges and universities, students contend with the additional factors of low institutional expectations, lack of informal faculty contact and support, and an often inhospitable social environment (Astin, 1982; Beckham, 1987/1988; Fleming, 1984).

First-generation college students, especially from non-Anglo cultures, often lack sophisticated knowledge of the rules and opportunities of the college and career system. Instead of multicultural sponsors, mentors, and interpreters of the educational system, students of color encounter faculty and peer neglect or active racism and sexism (Commission on Minority Participation, 1988). Statistical accounts of poor academic preparation, insufficient college enrollment, and low levels of degree attainment anchor this extensive literature.

The literature on minority achievement in postsecondary education described above comes from the dominant educational research tradition in which attainment is seen as a function of individual ability, achievement, motivation, and experiences in social institutions. Mainstream models of college student achievement, for example, describe the determinants of educational and occupational attainment as student characteristics in interaction with campus settings (Astin, 1982, 1984; Pascarella & Terenzini, 1991). Vincent Tinto's (1975, 1987) influential theory of student attrition views voluntary departure from college as a function of poor integration into the academic and social systems of a particular campus environment. Undergraduates who are academically able remain at colleges whose values they perceive as congruent with their own. They connect with a campus through significant interactions with peers and, especially, with faculty. The importance of engagement with faculty and active involvement in campus life are consistent themes in research and theory on college student development (Astin, 1977, 1984; Kuh, Schuh, & Whitt, 1991; Pascarella & Terenzini, 1991).

Studying barriers to achievement within this framework of individual and group characteristics, according to many sociologists and anthropologists, ignores the embeddedness of individual experience in larger social and economic structures. Instead, many educational theorists view minority achievement in terms of larger social relations (Ogbu, 1989; Trueba, 1988; Weis, 1985). Structuralist accounts document how the organization and content of schooling maintain inequitable labor force hierarchies in the larger society (Anyon, 1984; Bowles & Gintis, 1976). Cultural reproduction theorists consider the role of oppressed groups themselves in recreating existing class structures through the meaning systems, or cultural forms, they create in response to school (Ogbu, 1974, 1987, 1988; Weis, 1985; Willis, 1977).

Cultural forms come from a group's historical experience and from the meanings that are collectively constituted among interacting groups (Lubeck, 1988). Students consciously or intuitively develop understandings (or cultural models) of American society and assess their likely prospects for success in the dominant culture (Ogbu, 1974, 1978). Based on their experience and models, minority and low-income youths anticipate an educational and occupational world which is effectively closed to them and in which they have little chance of succeeding. In a culture like that of low-income minority communities, students take part in various forms of resistance or opposition to the dominant culture of schools. The resulting cultural forms are adaptive within the student's particular minority subculture but do not conform to the mobility strategies of the dominant white middle-class society (Ogbu, 1987).

Both structuralist and culturalist formulations have been criticized as reducing collective behavior to static issues of economics and class respectively (McCarthy & Apple, 1988). Researchers from various theoretical perspectives are currently examining the interrelations of race, class, and gender as separate concepts that cannot be reduced to a primary category such as class (Grant & Sleeter, 1986; McCarthy & Apple, 1988). The role of meaning-making in behavior also preoccupies scholars from various theoretical orientations. Perceptions and interpretations of experience determine the behavior of individuals and groups. Humans shape systems of meaning according to their individual and shared understandings (Lincoln & Guba, 1985).

Academic achievement therefore, can be viewed from the perspective of mainstream educational theory or from emerging constructions of individual attainment as a function of racial, class, and gendered social structures and cultural forms.

The Study

The Illinois Valedictorian Project began in 1981 by identifying eighty-one top high school graduates throughout Illinois, then exploring their academic success longitudinally—how students became top achievers, how they experience their academic attainment, and what consequences early academic promise holds for college and career achievement. This study is the first to examine top academic performers longitudinally in order to record student perceptions and experiences as they occur. My investigation traces the consequences of economics, family, and college experiences on the early adult achievement of eight academically talented African American and Latina students.

Unlike most cross-sectional quantitative studies of minority students in higher education, this project is a longitudinal naturalistic investigation of a small group of students whose academic performance and motivation should predict sustained educational and occupational attainment. Also termed ethnographic, constructivist, or post-positivist naturalistic research begins with the premise that human interactions and understandings are value laden and that people in particular contexts collectively construct their own realities (Guba & Lincoln, 1989; Lincoln & Guba, 1985). As investigator and nonneutral actor in that research process, I sought to discover the perceived world of study participants and to retain the complexity and rich context of their lives. The framework for understanding what is told or observed involves a continuing interplay between data and interpretation in the search for the most adequate theoretical accounting of study findings (Strauss & Corbin, 1990). Recent related work from this methodological orientation includes Dorothy Holland and Margaret Eisenhart's (1990) ethnographic study of twenty-three African American and white women at two Southern colleges. Louis Attinasi (1989) investigated Latino college student retention by considering the meanings that Mexican-American undergraduates ascribed to their freshman year experiences. Like the Illinois Valedictorian Project, these studies began with a general area of inquiry, discovering the lived meanings of their study members through open-ended interviewing and a dialectic interplay between data collection and theory generation.

Sample and Data Sources

In 1980, Terry Denny surveyed all Illinois high schools to determine if they named a valedictorian. Of the 550 high schools that responded, 270 formally identified the top-grade earner as valedictorian and had him or her present a valedictory address at commencement. Salutatorians were included on the urging of valedictorians in a 1980 pilot study. High schools were chosen from among the 270 with a nonrepresentative maximum variation sample (Patton 1980) designed to include the greatest possible spectrum in types of schools, communities, and geographic locations. The resulting sample of thirty-three high schools included large and small schools; city, rural and suburban; parochial, independent, and public; and those with predominantly African American, Anglo, and Latino student bodies. Chicago and East St. Louis were the sites of the five high schools with minority valedictorians and salutatorians. Two schools with predominantly African American student populations were public high schools in some of the most depressed urban areas in the country. Two were urban Catholic high schools with primarily Latino populations. (One valedictory was delivered in Spanish.) The fifth was a private school with a mixed race population.

The forty-six females and thirty-five males in the larger study were valedictorians and salutatorians at the identified high schools. All eighty-one remained active in the study ten years after high school graduation. (I refer to the group as valedictorians for the sake of conciseness.) This report focuses on eight valedictorians, five African Americans and three Mexican Americans. The minority valedictorians all grew up in lower-income families and inner city minority communities. Seven of the eight are first-generation college students. The three Latina valedictorians, all women, immigrated from Mexico during childhood and speak English as their second language. The minority students scored lower than the Anglo valedictorians on the ACT, with scores ranging from the national mean for college attenders (20) to the mean for the project group (25). Each received financial aid to attend college.

Terry Denny and I, both white, have followed the valedictorians since their spring 1981 high school graduation. Denny attended all the commencement exercises to witness the public recognition of the valedictorian and to gain first-hand a sense of each community and school context.

We also held hour and a half semi-structured interviews annually for each of the first four years of the study. Interviews were conducted in person at the student's home, college room, or workplace by one of the two researchers; both of us eventually interviewed most valedictorians. We encouraged students to discuss their experiences and preoccupations in their own terms, using interview protocols as guidelines to open-ended conversations about academic lives, families and relationships, and aspirations. The first interview wave in 1981–82 used field notes from the graduation ceremonies as the basis for a discussion of pre-college schooling and how students perceived their top high school honors. We also drew early questions from a pilot study of a small group of valedictorians at the University of Illinois.

Salient themes from previous interviews formed the basis for subsequent interviews, which covered college and graduate school experiences, career planning and work, and relationships. We asked students to react to group findings and to statements they had made in previous years as a form of member check (Lincoln & Guba, 1985). A set of questions about activities, goals, and difficulties recurred each year. The last annual conversation took place during the 1984–85 academic year. We interviewed the valedictorians again in 1990–91. A final interview wave is in progress.

In addition to interviews and field notes from commencement and interviewer observations, students have provided us with letters, resumes, writings, and art work. Quantitative data sources include standardized and project-designed questionnaires measuring attitudes, gender roles, achievement motivation, work and family values, and aspirations. We administered survey instruments in 1981, 1984, 1985, 1988, and 1991.[1]

Data Analysis

Researchers read and reread the approximately two-hundred pages of typed interview transcripts as well as interview and commencement field notes, resumes, correspondence, and open-ended survey responses for each of the eight students. Data analysis proceeded inductively, beginning with open coding in which transcripts were examined line-by-line for meanings and issues and continuing with the development of larger conceptual categories from clusters of descriptive codes (Strauss, 1987). For each valedictorian, we composed a longitudinal case study, or life history. The most salient themes in individual cases and the most frequently recurring issues across cases formed the basis for the organization of the data report (Spradley, 1979).

Study Group Status in 1991

Briefly, all eighty-one valedictorians attended college in the fall following their May 1981 graduation, with two-thirds of the group choosing majors in business, engineering, or science. The study group as a whole achieved spectacular undergraduate academic success, with numerous academic honors and a group mean grade point average of 3.6 on a four point scale. Four of the seventy-two white students and two of the eight minority students dropped out of college. African American and Latino students college graduates generally took longer than Anglo students to complete degrees.

Thirty-five of the valedictorians (43 percent) earned graduate degrees or were active graduate students ten years after high school. Most of the graduate degrees among the larger valedictorian group are Ph.D., law, and medical degrees. Only one minority valedictorian, a black female engineer, has earned a master's degree. Table 1 presents the educational, occupational, and family status of the minority valedictorians in 1991.

Personal Voices

This statistical profile of the achievements of minority high school valedictorians masks the common themes and experiences that these academically talented students reported over a ten-year period. The simple outcome data minimize the struggles that literally all of them faced. The healthy educational and career statistics of the group, furthermore, fail to reveal how the fulfillment of promise among students of color differs systematically from the patterns of academically able Anglo men and women.

Money

Disentangling the effects of culture, race, and ethnicity from the confounding influence of economic status is an extraordinarily difficult task. Margarita graduated salutatorian at a predominantly Latino Catholic high school. Now working as a nuclear engineer, Margarita sees her story as more about money than ethnicity:

> It's not so much being a minority. It's whether or not you have the opportunities that money can bring, that money can buy . . . Also, I never had a parent who could give me advice on college choices or on professional matters. I never had role models that I could look at and talk with about such matters as college. So it's not so much being a minority as it is that most minorities don't have the financial backing to take them along their career paths as smoothly as those who do have that kind of financial base.

Table 1
Valedictorial 1991 Educational, Occupational, and Family Status

Valedictorian	Degree/Time Required	Undergraduate Major	Occupation: 1991	Marital Status: 1991
Barbara*	B.S./5 years	engineering	electrical engineer	single
Eric*	2 institutions; B.S./9 years	engineering	electrical engineer	married with three adopted children
Karla*	B.A./5 years, 1 year law school	communications, pre-law	group insurance plan enroller	single
Mike*	2 institutions; 2 years completed	engineering, communications	delivery company supervisor	married, two children
Patrice*	B.S./4 years, MBA/4 years night study	engineering	utilities engineer	single
Anita**	2 institutions; 3 years completed	communications	administrative assistant	married, one child
Luisa**	B.A./6 years	accountancy	bookkeeper	single, lives with parents
Margarita**	B.S./5 years	engineering, computer science	nuclear engineer	single, lives with parents

*African American
**Mexican American
All names are pseudonyms.

Margarita, like other black and Latino valedictorians, explicitly considered whether the secretarial or waitressing wages she would forego in college were worth the eventual financial returns from a professional position. Like the other Latina women in the study, she worked twenty to forty hours a week throughout college and, like almost all of the minority valedictorians, contributed income to her parents and siblings while she was in college.

Statistically, family socioeconomic status is a predictor of early career achievement for the men in the study but not for the women (Arnold, 1993). Beyond this quantitative group finding, however, is a consistent pattern of explicit concern for economic survival and financial self-sufficiency on the part of the academically talented African American and Latino students. These students have seen family and friends work for low wages or suffer long periods of unemployment. They know that their families have no financial resources to offer. Avoiding the trap of economic dependency was a primary educational motivator for Barbara, an African American engineer who seriously considered dropping out of college after her sophomore year but returned to school because "I had to have some sort of an education in order to support myself. Money calls a lot of shots, you know. If I didn't have some sort of degree or some sort of a job, I don't really know where I would be." Taking care of herself financially was a primary goal for Barbara, who saw education as her means to economic self-sufficiency and life options.

Mike, on the other hand, came to see education as an expensive luxury in the face of immediate family needs. His decision not to complete his college degree rests largely on his perception that his future earnings and advancement will not be adversely affected by the lack of a college degree, especially since he feels that he will be able to receive the continuing training he needs inside his company.

Anita, a Latina woman without a degree, expresses a deep desire to finish college, a goal she sees as unreachable because of financial obstacles. "I wish I could have finished school. I mean, I would have loved to have finished school. It's very difficult if you don't have money. School is so expensive, and with the baby and everything. I'd love to go. I wonder how people do it." Anita tried to finish school as both she and her husband worked two jobs and as she continued to help her parents and siblings. Not only is she eager to finance her last year of college, Anita is struggling to help pay for a vocational program for her husband. Worst of all, she spends little time with her infant son: "My sister is raising him."

Possibly, Anita has missed sources of funding for completing college. Eric, for instance, an African American student, now knows he limited his educational options because he lacked information about financial aid possibilities.

> I really blew it coming out of high school. I didn't apply to enough colleges because money—just my understanding and coming from my family—I probably blew a lot of scholarships and things that I probably could have received given my ranking and my overall activities at school. I possibly could have gotten a full scholarship somewhere if I had applied for it.

Money is a consistent theme in the self-narratives of the gifted students of color—as a motivator for education, as a competitor to education, and as an obstacle to education.

Family

As the valedictorian stories demonstrate, family structures, like economics, play a crucial, sometimes determining role in the lives of the African American and Latino valedictorians. Nowhere is this clearer than in Eric's extraordinary success story. Of the seven children in his family, only he and one brother completed high school. This brother subsequently attended a proprietary business school but was unemployed when Eric started college. "I always looked to him, but since he's been lagging, there's not really anything I can look towards, anyone else. I believe if I were to graduate from a university I'd be the only one in my entire family and extended family also that has done that."

Furthermore, Eric described his home atmosphere as an "uproar. There was always so much noise and distraction and I've always been the only one that really sat down and studied." During high school, Eric worked to earn bus fare and lunch money and to help the family with their bills—with "the struggle," as he put it. Perhaps his desire for an education stemmed from some crucial time he spent living with a grandmother, highly supportive elementary school teachers, and/or an early, enduring love of reading. In any case, he developed very young the ability to detach himself from noise and confusion and to concentrate deeply on what he was reading.

Having graduated as class salutatorian, Eric entered a local university to study engineering; but he could not start the engineering sequence for the first year and a half and did poorly academically. Family problems were at the core of his disappointing start in college:

> I never really got a sensing there at the university, never really got my feet on the ground as far as studies. Seems like ever since high school, my family was always getting up and moving. Seemed like every 2–3 months. Family problems such as no one to pay the bills, that's one of the reasons why I chose to stay in the area at first, to try to help out my family with bills. . . . I just thought there was the obligation. A personal thing. The family was so close, had a lot of younger brothers and sisters trying to help them as I went along . . . And after a while I just sat back and promised myself that "Eric, what you're doing is really hurting yourself more than helping the family to go along. You're still not doing well in school; the family's going to survive whether I'm there or not. And that's what happened. I decided to go.

Eric left the university and transferred to a historically African American college in another state. In its co-op engineering program, he worked full time as an engineering intern between semesters of academic study. Proximity to his family, especially through an illness of his mother, motivated Eric to choose co-op placements and a post-graduate position in his home city. Immediately following graduation, he and his new wife adopted her three elementary- and preschool-aged sisters and brother.

Eric's story demonstrates how a family without economic stability or values for formal education can impede the educational achievement of even an able, motivated student. Perhaps more important, however, his story demonstrates the importance of family to Eric and his continuing affirmation of his freely chosen obligation to care for his mother, siblings, and stepchildren. Eric never wanted to break his primary family ties; he demonstrated his ability to achieve while continuing to prize his family relationships.

Equally compelling is the centrality of family for the gifted Latina women in this study. High school valedictorian and voted most likely to succeed by her classmates, Luisa told me in her first year of college: "When I was in high school I wanted to have my whole life figured out. My whole life. Since then, I have come to realize that I cannot do that. Every decision I make must involve my parents. They have always relied on me for everything. I am the only child. They cannot speak English. It must be this way. They are in my thoughts all the time in every important decision I make. This will not change."

After two years of college, Luisa left her city university and her state scholarships to move south with her family. The move, prompted by the illness of a grandparent, meant a year away from school as Luisa waited to become eligible for financial aid in the new state. Entering the local college meant a change to a lower-ranked institution and a more limited accountancy curriculum. Although she was unhappy about the move, Luisa felt she "had no choice" about going with her family and never considered negotiating to stay in Illinois. Graduating at the top of her college class, Luisa was restricted in her job search to the town where the family lived. The small businesses in the area all wanted experienced accountants, according to Luisa, "so I gave up." Luisa took a job as a bookkeeper at a local department store, a job that did not use her accounting degree and paid $4.00 an hour. Recently, she switched to a similar job at a small business in town. Although she describes her duties as "limited work," Luisa enjoys her coworkers and the challenge of setting up a new computerized bookkeeping system for the business.

Anita also defines her life in terms of her mother and siblings, as well as her husband and child. When Anita was an unmarried college junior, Terry Denny wrote about her:

> Anita is an able person whose values are principally, if not exclusively, rooted in the commitments that surround family and friendships. Her culture bombards her with the appropriateness and importance of getting married and having children—but she resists the message. She does want to marry and have children but she also wants to finish school and to try her hand in the television world first. No small measure of her strength comes from her mother who apparently has supported her for some time against the conventional wisdom of getting married and having children at a young age. She continues to give yeoman service to her family through her mother, brother, sister-in-law while persisting in her quest for an undergraduate degree in communications.

Seven years later, this assessment of Anita remains accurate, although Anita's strong academic and career motivations were apparently unable to resist the even stronger financial and family pressures she continues to feel.

All three Latina valedictorians know that their gender dictates their position within the extended family sphere. Moving away for college and work was not an option for them. "I'm sure that if I had been born a male, I would be out living on my own," says Margarita. But clearly, none of the three *wishes* such a physical and emotional detachment. Margarita continues: "I wouldn't leave my parents and I wouldn't want to. I don't want to do it." Conflict arises not because the women are blocked from desired autonomy, but because their strong educational and career motivations are difficult to sustain in the face of family involvement, the cultural primacy of relational ties, and limited opportunities within a circumscribed geographic area. These Latina valedictorians are strongly achievement oriented, but their routes to achievement must take family into account (Jordan, 1991).

Educational and Work Climate

Economics and family create one set of struggles for the valedictorians, a set of sociocultural factors that students bring with them to education. Another set of obstacles meets academically talented African American and Latino students once they enter college and careers. Every one of these gifted students described lack of support, racism and/or sexism, and limited understanding of the system in their undergraduate education and early careers.

The most successful Latina valedictorian, Margarita, works as an engineer for a public utility. Margarita's determination to fulfill her academic potential was fueled by her high school teachers and counselors: "They told me that I had the talent and the promise to go on and that I could be successful." Once in college, however, Margarita told Terry Denny she was not finding "any support, or I can't find any interest. Like if I see that somebody is interested in me or somebody is concerned about how I'm doing. You know, that pushes you to go ahead. I'm really trying hard and I see no motivation coming from anywhere." In her sophomore year, Margarita said her professors weren't interested in students. "They just go and lecture, they don't care." One professor, she said, wouldn't even let her talk when she had a question.

Without support or guidance from faculty or practitioners in her field, Margarita was unable to find work in her field, even though she remained in college an extra year to add a computer science major on the casual recommendation of a summer job interviewer. Determined to work in engineering, she took a pay cut to enter a government position as an environmental engineer. Margarita soon found that her position was an unchallenging "bean counting" job without advancement potential. The promise of funding for a master's degree was rescinded. Finally, she found a job as a nuclear engineer, a responsible professional position in her field. The job isn't perfect; Margarita worries about radiation exposure in the field and reports, "It's lonely in the office. In the field, I'm not in a competitive situation; in the office I am, so I feel very much alone. It's the fact that you know that they are not willing to help you. I guess I don't like to be at the mercy of others." Yet in twelve years, Margarita has never even hinted at stepping away from the struggle, instead consistently listing her "ultimate" goal as "having the respect and the success in my job that I seek."

Other students of color also reported that they failed to find supportive faculty in their undergraduate institutions. Some were hard put to name any influences after high school, though all pointed to supportive teachers and counselors before college. When I asked who influenced him, Mike was silent for a time before he said: "My life has taken so many turns. I don't know, career wise, no one who has been a mainstay. People have been in and out, in and out."

For a few, lack of support and mentoring went further into harsh experiences of racism or sexism. An African American engineering student, Barbara, attended one of the most prestigious private universities in the country. Barbara earned average grades in the engineering program. Despite her ability and adequate college performance, Barbara describes a constant struggle with professors in which she was often ignored, once told she was stupid, and repeatedly urged to change her major to something "easier."

> I was very disappointed with the education that I received at [the university], very disappointed. For the most part, some of the key professors in the engineering department, they had problems both with women and with minorities They specifically had problems that way and it showed in the way they talked to you, the amount of effort they put in trying to help you—I mean, it was there. And I think some of the professors, specific ones, they just kind of worked to destroy that program for minorities; and when I look at everything objectively, it seems like it was more just because my skin was black than it was because I was female or anything else—well, maybe it was because I was black and poor. This is the way I feel.

Barbara describes going to tutorial sessions to learn from the questions the other students asked but knowing she would not speak or be called on. "I'd have all kinds of stuff to say. I really tried, okay?" At such sessions, Barbara said, she might be the only student present who had worked on every assigned problem until she was unable to continue "I was always very studious and I was always trying very hard. There were a lot of times when I did poorly on tests where I just made a 'C' or whatever because that was the only thing I could teach myself." Barbara would survive a class and believe the next would be easier. "Every time I got someplace and I thought, okay, this isn't going to happen again and I would forget—I'd be caught sleeping again, you know. People always assumed that it was going to be easier to attack me because I was black and then also I was a woman."

The worst experience of her college years came outside the classroom. Barbara became ill at the beginning of her sophomore year.

> I started having terrible, terrible stomachaches. The doctor at the university clinic kept telling me it was my nerves. She told me that I needed to see a psychologist and needed to change my major, that I just couldn't handle school and all this and all that. Well, by January, you know, because I was in that mindset, I felt like I was just doing this to myself and I was causing these stomachaches. I did kind of believe this woman because she was so definite, she was so sure.

Barbara avoided returning to the medical center because "I just didn't really want this woman to tell me how silly I was and how I needed to see a psychologist." When she finally became unable to attend classes. Barbara did return to the clinic, where she received an emergency appendectomy. "If I'd gone to class that day and done what I intended to do, I think I probably would have died . . . and in a lot of ways I feel that this was done to me because I was both black and female."

The following semester, Barbara began classes, but withdrew after several weeks. "I was emotionally burned out. It was a very difficult time. I had too many problems to be effective in school. I wasn't even sure I wanted to be an engineer any more." Barbara returned to school only because she felt that a college degree was an economic necessity.

Without experienced family members or supportive teachers to elucidate the unspoken rules and methods of the educational system, students of color miss opportunities and misunderstand strategies for success. Anita dropped out of college only twelve credit hours from completion of her degree. She approached a college counselor to explain that she was able to afford only one class at a time toward her remaining degree requirements.

> I couldn't understand her. I mean, I want to go back and graduate there. It's a very good school. And I asked her to explain it to me and the way she explained it to me, she said, "You're better off taking six credits. If not, you're going to lose credits." And I did not understand it. I came home and I was depressed. After I took the class, I was still paying for it. Because I took more than six credits because she said, "You have to." For just an English class or something like that. It didn't make any sense to me. Is that the way they do it? That's why I haven't gone back. It was so expensive.

Unable to pay for multiple classes, Anita gave up her plan to graduate from that college. Her broadcasting career had started with great promise with a cable television internship where she was given a great deal of responsibility. "I loved it." She took a pay cut to take a secretarial position at another television company, a position she was assured would lead to broadcasting opportunities. "And I told them I'd like to move up. I told them what I was studying. They said, 'No problem.' And when I started talking to the girls there in the office, they said, 'Once he has you here, he's not going to let you move.' And that's it." Lack of assertiveness, especially in the face of dominating authority, has been a problem for the Latina valedictorians. Even more daunting, however, has been the total lack of sponsors to help these able women negotiate novel achievement settings.

The study's African American women have also suffered professionally from uncertainty about how to negotiate careers. Choosing colleges, majors, and early professional positions by starting salary, haphazard advice, and proximity to home is not a sophisticated way to build top-level careers. Patrice, for instance, an African American valedictorian, has known since high school that she is interested in business, not engineering. She entered engineering because "in high school they were pushing engineering. If you were strong in math and science, that's all they really pushed." Her goals are still "owning my own business, doing something that I really love, or making a critical difference in someone's life," but she has little idea of the steps required to reach them.

Achievement Factors

If academically able students of color consistently encounter personal and institutional barriers to adult achievement, what enables them to persist in college and careers? The study's African American and Latina valedictorians share a number of personal qualities that are the bedrock of their determination and achievement. First, the valedictorians were deeply affected by their early academic success. They believe in their potential. Margarita, for instance, said that being valedictorian "prompted me to pursue a career because I realized that I had potential. You have to live up to your talents. You have to use your talents, and without schooling and education it's not likely that you will." During her first year of college, Margarita revealed the motivating power of her high school achievement: "I will always try to strive for something higher because I know I did it once. I have to keep doing it. I'm not going to drop dead. Just because I was successful once, I want to be successful again."

Patrice, a successful engineer, is deeply motivated by the need to fulfill her academic promise and to produce socially useful work:

> Sometimes people would ask me, because I was valedictorian, they would say things like, "Hey, weren't you the smartest girl at [City High]?" It seems like I was destined for more than being an engineer for [a public utility company]. I mean, its okay and it pays the bills but it really doesn't make a difference. It really doesn't matter. At this point I thought I would be further along. Some people look at me and say, "Well, you're really doing great. You're an inspiration, but I really don't feel like I am. . . . When I was in high school and college, there was a lot of attention, but somehow this just seems kind of a let down. But its more—I guess I owe to these people who thought so highly of me to get further than where I am now. Not necessarily like in a corporation, but something that is going to make a difference, like having my own business, eventually being able to hire black people.

The valedictorians never rested on their high school records. They are without exception hard-working students and employees. Barbara saw her hard work as her only guarantee that she wouldn't be stopped in educational goals:

> For some reason I've always tried to do the best that I could, when I had a goal to reach, and my goal in high school was to get to college and be prepared, so I felt like, work your tail off in high school and if you are prepared for college then it won't be as easy for them to flunk you out as it might be for somebody else. And I think that was the number one goal and the number one reason why I tried so hard in high school.

Determination and persistence are additional entries on this somewhat old-fashioned list of character traits that the valedictorians share. Barbara reacted to her distressing college experiences by facing them. "It was just best that I go ahead and I deal with the system because I knew if I didn't, nothing would ever be right. It was painful. It was very painful, but I don't regret it. . . . If I set my mind to it and if I believe in myself, I don't think there's too much I can't do."

During her own struggle to complete her degree, Margarita told interviewers: "I don't quit. I don't give up. I insist and insist." Eric also exemplified the ability to persevere in the face of obstacles: "I've always considered myself blessed with the ability to keep trying, if something else failed, just to keep trying, never give up. I always say that I might lose a couple of rounds but I'm here for the long run." Eric remembers his elementary school teachers telling him: "To keep working. To keep working."

Self-sufficiency also characterizes this group of high school achievers. Luisa, for example, told interviewers, "I'm used to settling things by myself and so that's the way I do it." Eric echoed this idea: "Don't be constantly coming to someone for help. You should be trying to help yourself."

Presented with so few role models, the valedictorians reached beyond acquaintances for inspiration and validation. Margarita was encouraged by the reputation of the African American woman who had preceded her in her job: "She was well respected and had earned her reputation. I haven't earned mine as yet and the respect is not there, but I don't think it's because I'm a minority or just because I'm a woman. If she did it, I can certainly do it." Eric was impressed by the success story of a high school dropout who returned to college on the GI bill and eventually became a physician: "And I thought to myself, Eric, here you were coming out of high school being considered one of the top students in the city, or one of the 'cream of the crop' students and you can do better than what you're doing for yourself. So, that story always stayed in me."

Alone among the African American and Latina valedictorians, Eric had direct support from college faculty at his predominantly African American college. Although continuing family problems affected his academic success as a new transfer, Eric reported receiving "a lot of respect from my instructors because they knew how good a student I was or how good a student I could be." Professors told Eric he would be able to complete the normal five-year program in four years if he worked hard to master the fundamentals. Not only did Eric follow this advice, but he also became more and more challenged and involved in his academics as his courses got more difficult.

In contrast to his experience at his original, predominantly white university, where he reported being "on the edge" of the institution, Eric got involved in campus life and activities at his new college. "I got a start in what I considered college life, getting comfortable in school. Doing something I always wanted to do." His confidence was bolstered further when one of the top engineering students at the college asked Eric for academic help.

Eric's involvement in college life and the support he received from faculty were unique among the students of color in the valedictorian study. More commonly, students in predominantly white universities found support in African American and Latino student organizations. Barbara feels she graduated because of the African American engineering organization. "The only reason I made it through [the university] is because the network among the black students there was tight. It is unbreakable." Margarita provided volunteer clerical work for the Latino student organization "because they did so much for me." She made friends through her classes: "And a good thing they were there. I don't know why. I look for Hispanics, and I met Hispanics. I feel more at ease with them. I don't know why. Most of the time I'm talking half in English, half in Spanish. Friends don't have to be Hispanics, because I had a black friend and a Chinese friend. But I've never had a white friend."

Finally, the students of color relied on interpersonal skills and service commitments to support their achievement. Virtually all of the group mentioned their genuine liking for people and their ability to work with others. Margarita sees her sensitivity to people as an important and unusual quality in her profession: "I take pride in my work and when I work with people I see them as humans not as a means of getting something out of them or using them to go further up the ladder. I see people as humans." Patrice considers her ability to relate to people as one of her greatest strengths: "I really do care about people and where people are coming from and that may relate to being black and being a woman. I take the time for whatever reason to find out where people are coming from. I really do care what's going on with people and how they feel about things." Mike also speaks of his interpersonal skills as his greatest career asset and his primary pleasure in work.

In contrast with the Anglo valedictorian group, nearly all the African American and Latina valedictorians contribute to their communities through service activities. Helping others, being seen as a role model, using their interpersonal skills, and deepening their awareness of the advantages of education are all important reasons for volunteering.

In summary, the valedictorians have consistently demonstrated strong personal qualities of persistence, determination, and hard work. They rely on peers, indirect role models, and the rewards of interpersonal engagements and community service to nourish their already strong motivation. Above all, the valedictorians rely on their deep belief in their talent, their potential, and their goal of an economically sustaining and personally fulfilling life.

Discussion

The process of higher education and early careers has produced a leveling effect on the aspirations and attainment of African American and Latino high school valedictorians. Educational attainment is lower, and underemployment and work dissatisfaction higher among the minority group as compared to the Anglo study members. Seven of the eight valedictorians developed an identity in high school as academically talented, and all eight believed as teenagers that school achievement was worthwhile.

John Ogbu (1988) and others have noted the identity and peer/community pressures to conform that face high-achieving African American students who seek to adopt the white cultural frame of reference. "Students who do relatively well in school while still [being] accepted by their peers are those who are either simultaneously successful in sports and other activities regarded as black or students who have found ways to camouflage their academic efforts and outcomes" (1988, 176). This statement did not hold true for the five African-American valedictorians in this study, all of whom perceived themselves as accepted and active members of their high school social communities. Eric, as we have seen, was dissuaded from education by his family, not his school community. The African American and Latino valedictorians saw their status as an honor and never expressed feelings of conflict between academic performance and social belonging. Some of the group perceived themselves as representatives of their communities to the larger world.

What might account for the comfort with which the valedictorians maintained their anomalous standing as serious students in inner city high schools? Possibly, they were uncritically accepting of white middle-class goals and schooling practices, seeking consciously or unconsciously to assimilate (Helms, 1990). Perhaps the dilemma of crossing into white honors student groups never arose in an all-minority high school context. In any case, novel problems arose for the valedictorians once they entered the predominantly white universities.

The valedictorians revealed an imperfect match with middle-class white values and a critical lack of tacit knowledge about higher education and careers. Their own cultural reference system framed college as a site for job preparation in vaguely understood high paying fields, leading them to approach college and choice of majors with a "getting over" orientation (Holland & Eisenhart, 1990). Only Patrice discussed college in terms of her intrinsic interest in subject matter, and even she chose a major because high school officials "pushed it." The goal of college was instrumental: economic security and respect in the community. Mike considers himself a success because he has achieved these ends, even without college. Anita, the other college drop-out, still has poorly paying, low-level work. She longs to finish college.

Tacit knowledge encompasses understanding that is not directly taught and which may not be consciously accessible by the knower (Polanyi, 1966; Sternberg & Wagner, 1986). The specialized tacit knowledge of those in marginalized groups is often unacknowledged and unproductive in the wider society. In contrast, the web of white middle-class family and school structures provides Anglo students with tacit knowledge in such areas as academic strategies, college and major choice, and management of careers (Wagner, 1987). The acquisition of tacit knowledge is an interpersonal process. The interactive nature of talent development, apparent in the valedictorians' early careers, ceased during college for all but the single student who attended a predominantly African American institution. Without models, supporters, and guides to the wider post-high school world, talented students faltered. Class factors limited economic resources and opportunities and, along with racism and sexism, constrained interactions with college academic and social systems (Tinto, 1987). In contrast with Tinto's thesis, however, the valedictorians stayed in school despite severe social disconnection. Allen (1992) found similar patterns in his study of African-American college students. Latina women were further constrained by culture-specific gender expectations and the minority women engineers by gender stereotyping. Ignored by faculty and outside the central college academic and social structures, the valedictorians at predominantly white institutions never had the opportunity to develop the subtle skills of translating intrinsic academic interests into clearly formulated career goals and effectively managed educational and professional activities.

The former valedictorians can be viewed as highly successful. All have completed some college. All are productive workers. However, the encounter of academically talented African American and Latino students with postsecondary education resembles the patterns documented in the literature on minority student underachievement. In contrast to Anglo study participants, minority valedictorians have been more likely to drop out of college, to end their education with vocationally oriented bachelor's degrees, and to perceive themselves as dissatisfied workers.

They have been channeled and have channeled themselves into skilled worker and lower professional levels.

Given their encounters with postsecondary education and workplaces, the valedictorians have been forced to reexamine their identity as achievers. Patrice and Eric currently perceive themselves as continuing to find meaning in work and both explicitly incorporate connections to African American culture in their activities and goals. After experiencing race and gender discrimination in her technical field, Patrice plans to leave engineering and use her MBA to set up a business that employs and serves African Americans. Eric finds meaning through balancing intrinsically interesting work with care for his extended family and community. These two students are successful in terms of their attainment, satisfaction, and continued achievement motivation, although Patrice spent ten years in a field she disliked and Eric took nine years to earn his degree.

Luisa and Mike appear to have reconciled themselves to their attenuated achievement outcomes. Torn in high school between development of her talent and family responsibilities, Luisa abandoned her achievement strivings for the affiliative role of a traditional Mexican daughter. After a time of conflict in which he considered divorce, Mike has centered his life on family and religion and works only for money.

Karla, Anita, and Barbara perceive themselves as unhappy. Karla, who graduated with a B.A. in communications and prelaw, feels trapped in her unchallenging but highly paying job as a group insurance plan enroller. Anita is stuck in a cycle of poorly paying work that prevents her from either returning to college or remaining at home with her child. Of the eight valedictorians, Barbara is the most consciously aware of race and gender discrimination. She persists in her job, as in college, by distancing herself from her work and basing her identity on being labeled a professional. Margarita also struggles toward the goal of respected occupational status. Margarita is the most clearly assimilationist of the valedictorians. She believes wholeheartedly in the American dream of upward mobility through education and hard work, counting on her individual efforts to overcome her unsatisfactory job situation.

The valedictorians perceive their struggles as an individual problem, not a collective one. The gifted students pit individual persistence and resolution against structural barriers. Like Mike, most of the lower achievers view their outcomes as a function of personal choices. Institutionalized oppression and the effects of race, gender, and class are seldom central to the meanings valedictorians ascribe to their lives.

Conclusion

The valedictorians demonstrate that even the top students of color experience the difficulties that face almost all African American and Latino high school graduates. Both psychologically based and critical theories of schooling can be used to examine the valedictorians' stories. Economic disadvantage and marginalized undergraduate experiences have emerged as central constraints in the fulfillment of promise in academically talented minority students.

Moving beyond the level of the individual reveals structuralist and culturalist interpretations of the valedictorian study. The predominantly white universities that the students attended mirrored and replicated larger oppressive structures in society. Along with institutionalized racism and unequal opportunities, high schools and colleges failed to provide the tacit knowledge that leads to effective career strategies among white privileged students. As cultural reproduction theory might suggest, the valedictorians themselves participated in their attenuated outcomes by redefining their identities as achievers and by continuing to use strategies, such as persistence, without the accompanying interpersonal framework of talent development (Bloom, 1985).

Most of the students recognized instances of race and gender discrimination. Without larger understandings of oppressive social structures, however, they did not engage in collective resistance. Instead, individuals coped with intuited societal barriers by trying harder, distancing themselves from traditional achievement arenas, or adopting alternative visions of identity.

Success in college and careers should not have to require such extraordinary personal strength that we marvel at the valedictorians' success. The valedictorian stories, along with research literatures on women and minorities, point to the need for improved financial assistance and accommodation of family and cultural ties. College environments must provide role models and mentors who not only support and encourage students but who also offer active assistance in negotiating the institution and making the transition into postgraduate career achievement. Clearly, talented students of color would benefit from the recognition, opportunities, and above all, interactions with faculty that were so important to them in high school. The valedictorian study substantiates the need for college environments with active student involvement and interactions that free students from the debilitating effects of racism and sexism.

High school valedictorians are the students who should succeed. The African American and Latina members of the Illinois Valedictorian Project have succeeded: each is an educated, competent, contributing member of multicultural communities. However, the stories of these academically talented men and women of color do not reassure us about the inevitability of success for top African American and Latino high school students. These capable, motivated, hardworking valedictorians have struggled for their success in higher education. They continue to struggle in careers. The top high school students of color make it through persistence, hard work, and almost unbelievable personal will. Instead of documenting how minority students fail, the Valedictorian Project illuminates how higher education fails even the "best" African American and Mexican American students.

Note

1. Complete descriptions of Illinois Valedictorian Project instruments are provided in study reports which utilize quantitative data sources (Arnold, 1993). The small sample size and qualitative focus of the current investigation restrict the analysis to longitudinal interview data.

Bibliography

Allen, Walter R. "The Color of Success: African-American College Student Outcomes at Predominantly White and Historically Black Colleges and Universities." *Harvard Educational Review* 62, no. 1 (1992): 26–44.

Anyon, Jean. "Social Class and the Hidden Curriculum of Work." *Journal of Education* 162 (1984): 67–92.

Arnold, Karen D. "The Illinois Valedictorian Project: Academically Talented Women in the 1980s." In *Women's Lives Through Time: Educated American Women of the Twentieth Century,* edited by Kathleen D. Hulbert and Diane T. Schuster, 393–414. San Francisco: Jossey-Bass, 1993.

Astin, Alexander W. *Four Critical Years: Effects of College on Beliefs, Attitudes, and Knowledge.* San Francisco: Jossey-Bass, 1977.

———. *Minorities in Higher Education: Recent Trends, Current Prospects, and Recommendations.* San Francisco: Jossey-Bass, 1982.

———. "Student Involvement: A Developmental Theory for Higher Education." *Journal of College Student Personnel* 25, no. 4 (1984): 297–308.

———. *Achieving Educational Excellence: A Critical Assessment of Priorities and Practices in Higher Education.* San Francisco: Jossey-Bass, 1985.

Attinasi, Louis C. "Getting In: Mexican Americans' Perceptions of University Attendance and the Implications for Freshman Year Persistence." *Journal of Higher Education* 60, no. 3 (1989): 247–77.

Beckham, Barry. "Strangers in a Strange Land: Blacks on White Campuses." *Educational Record* 68/69, no. 4/1 (1987/1988): 74–8.

Bloom, Benjamin S. *Developing Talent in Young People*. New York: Ballantine, 1985.

Bowles, Samuel, and Herbert Gintis. *Schooling in a Capitalist America*. New York: Basic Books, 1976.

Commission on Minority Participation in Education and American Life. *One-Third of a Nation: A Report of the Commission on Minority Participation in Education and American Life*. Washington, D.C.: American Council on Education, 1988.

Fleming, Jacqueline. *Blacks in College: A Comparative Study of Students' Success in Black and in White Institutions*. San Francisco: Jossey-Bass, 1984.

Grant, Carl A., and Christine E. Sleeter. "Race, Class, and Gender in Education Research: An Argument for Integrative Analysis." *Review of Educational Research* 56 (1986): 195–211.

Guba, Egon G., and Yvonna S. Lincoln. *Fourth Generation Evaluation*. Newbury Park, Calif.: Sage, 1989.

Helms, Janet E., ed. *Black and White Racial Identity: Theory, Research, and Practice*. New York: Greenwood Press, 1990.

Hodgkinson, Harold. *All One System: Demographics of Education, Kindergarten Through Graduate School*. Washington, D.C.: Institute of Educational Leadership, 1985.

Holland, Dorothy C., and Margaret A. Eisenhart. *Educated in Romance: Women, Achievement, and College Culture*. Chicago: University of Chicago Press, 1990.

Jordan, Judith. *Women's Growth in Connection: Writings from the Stone Center*. New York: Guilford Press, 1991.

Kuh, George D., John H. Schuh, Elizabeth J. Whitt, and Associates. *Involving Colleges*. San Francisco: Jossey-Bass, 1991.

Lincoln, Yvonna S., and Egon G. Guba. *Naturalistic Inquiry*. Beverly Hills, Calif.: Sage, 1985.

Lubeck, Sally. "Nested Contexts." In *Class, Race, and Gender in American Education*, edited by Lois Weis. Albany: State University of New York Press, 1988.

McCarthy, Cameron W., and Michael W. Apple. "Race, Class, and Gender in American Educational Research: Toward a Nonsynchronous Parallelist Position," in *Class, Race, and Gender in American Education*, edited by Lois Weis, 9–39. Albany: State University of New York Press, 1988.

Nettles, Michael T., ed. *Toward Black Undergraduate Student Equality in American Higher Education*. Westport, Conn.: Greenwood Press, 1988.

Oden, Sherri, Mario A. Kelly, Zhenkui Ma, and David P. Weikhart. *Challenging the Potential: Programs for Talented Disadvantaged Youth*. Ypsilanti, Mich.: High Scope Press, 1992.

Ogbu, John U. *The Next Generation: An Ethnography of Education in an Urban Neighborhood*. New York: Academic Press, 1974.

_____. *Minority Education and Caste: The American System in Cross-Cultural Perspective*. New York: Academic Press, 1978.

_____. "Variability in Minority School Performance: A Problem in Search of an Explanation." *Anthropology and Education Quarterly* 18, no. 4 (1987): 312–34

_____. "Class Stratification, Racial Stratification, and Schooling," in *Class, Race, and Gender in American Education*, edited by Lois Weis, 163–79. Albany: State University of New York Press, 1988.

_____. "The Individual in Collective Adaptation: A Framework for Focusing on Academic Underperformance and Dropping Out Among Involuntary Minorities." In *Dropouts from School*, edited by Lois Weis, Eleanor Farrar, and Hugh G. Petrie, 181–204. Albany: State University of New York Press, 1989.

Pascarella, Ernest T., John C. Smart, and Judith Stoecker. "College Race and the Early Status Attainment of Black Students." *Journal of Higher Education* 60, no. 1 (1989): 82–107.

Pascarella, Ernest T., and Patrick T. Terenzini. *How College Affects Students*. San Francisco: Jossey-Bass, 1991.

Patton, Michael Q. *Qualitative Evaluation Methods*. Beverly Hills, Calif.: Sage, 1980.

Polanyi, Michael. *The Tacit Dimension*. Garden City, N.Y.: Doubleday, 1966.

Smith, Daryl G. *The Challenge of Diversity: Involvement or Alienation in the Academy?* ASHE-ERIC Higher Education Report, No. 5. Washington, D.C.: School of Education and Human Development, George Washington University, 1989.

Spradley, James. *The Ethnographic Interview*. New York: Holt, Rinehart and Winston, 1979.

Stampen, Jacob O., and Robert H. Fenske. "The Impact of Financial Aid on Ethnic Minorities." *Review of Higher Education* 11, no. 4 (1988): 337–53.

Sternberg, Robert J., and Richard K. Wagner. *Practical Intelligence: Nature and Origins of Competence in the Everyday World*. New York: Cambridge University Press, 1986.

Strauss, Anselm. *Qualitative Analysis for Social Scientists*. New York: Cambridge University Press, 1987.

Strauss, Anselm, and Juliet Corbin. *Basics of Grounded Theory Methods*. Beverly Hills, Calif.: Sage, 1990.

Tinto, Vincent. "Dropout from Higher Education: A Theoretical Synthesis of Recent Research." *Review of Educational Research* 45 (1975): 89–125.

_____. *Student Leaving: Rethinking the Causes and Cures of Student Attrition*. Chicago: University of Chicago Press, 1987.

Tracey, Terence, and William Sedlacek. "The Relationship of Noncognitive Variables to Academic Success: A Longitudinal Comparison by Race." *Journal of College Student Personnel* 26, no. 5 (1984): 405–10.

Trueba, Henry T. "Culturally-based Explanations of Minority Students' Academic Achievement." *Anthropology and Education Quarterly* 19, no. 3 (1988): 270–87.

Wagner, Richard K. "Tacit Knowledge in Everyday Intelligent Behavior." *Journal of Personality and Social Psychology* 52, no. 6 (1987): 1236–47.

Weis, Lois. *Between Two Worlds: Black Students In an Urban Community College*. Boston: Routledge and Kegan Paul, 1985.

Willis, Paul. *Learning to Labour: How Working Class Kids Get Working Class Jobs*. New York: Columbia University Press, 1977.

Karen D Arnold is assistant professor of higher education at the Boston College School of Education, Chestnut Hill, Massachusetts, and director of the Illinois Valedictorian Project, a study conducted since 1981 with Dr. Terry Denny, Professor Emeritus at the University of Illinois at Urbana-Champaign. The research for this article was supported in part by the North Central Regional Educational Laboratory, Boston College, and the University of Illinois Bureau of Educatio·*nl Research.*

In Their Own Words: What Students Learn Outside the Classroom

George D. Kuh

In most college impact models, student and institutional characteristics have substantial effects on student learning (Pascarella & Terenzini, 1991). The purpose of this study was to discover the impact of out-of-class experiences on outcomes of college attendance considered important by students. From interviews with 149 seniors at 12 colleges and universities, 14 categories of learning and personal development were distilled. These categories subsequently were reduced to five outcome domains: Personal Competence, Cognitive Complexity, Knowledge and Academic Skills, Practical Competence, and Altruism and Estheticism. Contrary to the literature on college impact, student background characteristics were not related to differences in outcomes; however, students attending small, private colleges with liberal arts missions more frequently reported changes in Cognitive Complexity, Knowledge and Academic Skills, and Altruism and Estheticism.

I've learned a lot about a lot of things . . . I care more about how I interact with other people. That is, I care about helping people learn and sharing my ideas with others. I definitely feel more confident in conveying what I have to say. I can express myself better . . . An important part of what I've done [is] the classes and seeing how things connect and seeing how things work in an in-depth way. (Earlham College senior)

Assessments of student learning in college usually focus on academic aspects of the undergraduate experience—the classroom, laboratory, studio, and library. Transcripts and test scores, however, reflect only a fraction of how students change (Light, 1992). Wilson (1966), for example, estimated that more than 70% of what students learn during college results from out-of-class experiences. According to Moffatt (1989):

For about 40% of the students, the do-it-yourself side of college [what took place outside the classroom] was the most significant educational experience. And for all but 10%, extracurricular learning had been at least half of what had contributed to their maturation so far in college (p. 58).

Other scholars also have linked many of the benefits of attending college to out-of-class activities and experiences (Astin, 1977; Bowen, 1977; Boyer, 1987; Chickering, 1969; Feldman & Newcomb, 1969; Pace, 1979, 1990; Pascarella & Terenzini, 1991; Thomas & Chickering, 1984). These benefits include, among other things, gains in confidence, self-esteem, and altruistic values (Astin & Kent, 1983; Pascarella, Ethington, & Smart, 1988). Out-of-class experiences that contribute to these and other aspects of student learning and personal development include conversations with faculty after class and collaboration in research and teaching projects, living in a residence hall, working on or off campus, participating in institutional governance, involvement in clubs and organizations, and voluntarism.

For the most part, the research methods used to assess the impact of college have been quantitative and positivistic (Pascarella & Terenzini, 1991). Such methods require that researchers determine both the questions to be asked and the response categories. Attinasi (1992) argued that "progress in understanding college student outcomes . . . has been retarded by our failure to adequately take into consideration the meanings that the phenomenon of going to college holds for students" (p. 68). This view holds that it is impossible to understand the human experience *without* taking into account the complicated, mutually shaping events, actions, and motivations of the individual or group under study. According to Bogdan and Biklen (1982), "people act, not on the basis of predetermined responses to predefined objects, but rather as interpreting, defining, symbolic animals whose behavior can only be understood by having the researcher enter into the defining process" (p. 38). Attinasi (1992) recommended use of "phenomenological interviews" whereby the inquirer gains access to the meanings individuals attach to their own experience using a semistructured interview guide.

There is a tradition of using qualitative research methods (e.g., phenomenological interviews) to discover what happens to students during college (Freedman, 1967; Madison, 1969; White, 1966). Several such inquiries culminated in popular, widely-used theories of college student development (i.e., Chickering, 1969; Kohlberg, 1984; Perry, 1970). However, the bulk of qualitative research about college students was conducted 25 years ago with traditional-age (18–22) students enrolled full time who lived on campus. Today, only about one sixth of undergraduate students fit that description (Levine, 1989). As Pascarella and Terenzini (1991) concluded, "specifying the effects of college for the vast numbers of non-traditional students . . . may be the single most important area of research on college impacts in the next decade" (p. 632). Through the use of interviews, we may be able to discover those aspects of college considered important by students whose frames of reference were not taken into account when many of the current research instruments and models of college impact were developed.

Purpose

The purpose of this study was to discover, by asking undergraduates to reflect on their college years, the impact of out-of-class experiences on their learning and personal development. Three research questions guided the study: (a) What did students learn from their experiences outside the classroom? (b) In what ways have they changed since starting college? and (c) Do the outcomes considered by students to be important differ by type of institution attended and student background characteristics?

Although seniors from multiple institutions participated, this study did not seek to obtain generalizable results. Rather, the purpose was to generate an accurate and trustworthy picture of the perceptions and experiences of learning and personal development of undergraduates as told by the students themselves. As we shall see, most students found it difficult to bifurcate their college experience into two separate categories of learning; that is, one linked to experiences outside the classroom and the other a function of the formal curriculum.

Conceptual Framework

According to Pascarella and Terenzini (1991), studies of what happens to students during college follow one of two general approaches: developmental and college impact.

Developmental Approaches

The vast majority of theory-driven research on change during the college years is developmental (Kuh & Stage, 1992). Inquiries grounded in this perspective emphasize discrete periods or stages of development that are presumed to emerge in an orderly and hierarchical manner. Developmental models are heavily influenced by psychological theory; therefore, intrapersonal dynamics are considered to be more important to development than the environment. Some developmental theories focus on the *content* of the changes in cognitive, affective, and behavioral domains (e.g., psychosocial, typological) that occur during college while others describe the *processes* (cognitive-structural, personal-environment interaction) by which these changes take place (Kuh & Stage, 1992; Pascarella & Terenzini, 1991; Rodgers, 1989).

An example of the latter is Baxter Magolda's (1992) study of cocurricular influences on intellectual development. Using the Epistemological Reflection model, Baxter Magolda found that students' ways of knowing or epistemologies, influenced their interpretations of the importance of out-of-class experiences. For example, when asked to talk about important aspects of the collegiate experience, absolute knowers (i.e., students who assume knowledge is certain) tended to talk about how they had to "adjust" to college life (e.g., take more responsibility for their own affairs); transitional knowers described the importance of peers to learning how to function effectively in the college environment; and independent knowers talked of how they "discovered their own voices" (Baxter Magolda, 1992, p. 211) through dealing with people different from themselves.

College Impact Approaches

The study reported in this paper uses the college impact approach to discover outcomes that college students associated with out-of-class experiences. To account for learning and personal development, college impact models emphasize interactions between students and the institution's environments (broadly conceived). For example, in Pascarella's (1985) model, outcomes (learning and cognitive development) are a function of reciprocal influences among the structural and organizational characteristics of the institution (e.g., enrollment, control, selectivity, affluence), student background characteristics (e.g., sex, aspirations, aptitude, ethnicity), the perceptual and behavioral environments created by interactions with peers and institutional agents (e.g., faculty seem friendly and helpful, peers are competitive), and the "quality" of effort (i.e., time and energy) students invest in educationally purposeful activities.

Various outcome taxonomies have been developed to account for changes that occur during college (Astin, 1973; Bowen, 1977; Lenning, 1976; Micek, Service, & Lee, 1975). These taxonomies typically encompass two types of outcomes, affective and cognitive, which can be assessed using either psychological instruments or observations and reports of behavior, or both. (Astin, 1977; Kuh, Krehbiel, & MacKay, 1988; Pascarella & Terenzini, 1991). An example of an affective outcome is enhanced aesthetic awareness, which could be assessed psychometrically, such as with the estheticism scale of the *Omnibus Personality Inventory* (Heist & Yonge, 1968). A behavioral measure of aesthetic awareness could be observations or self-report information about frequency of participation in cultural events.

The most comprehensive synthesis of college outcomes is Pascarella and Terenzini's (1991) review of 2,600 studies. They divided affective and cognitive outcomes into nine domains: knowledge and subject matter competence, cognitive skills and intellectual growth, psychosocial changes, attitudes and values, moral development, educational attainment, career choice and development, economic benefits, and quality of life after college. Pascarella and Terenzini found that, in general, college attendance typically was associated with "net" and "long-term effects" for each of the domains. Net effects are changes due to attending college, as contrasted with changes resulting from maturation or experiences other than college. Long-term effects refer to whether the changes that occur during college persist after college.

Research conducted using the college impact approach reflects aggregated group effects. Although not every student changes on every domain, on average, college attendance is associated with modest gains in verbal and quantitative skills, substantial gains in knowledge (particularly in the major), and increased cognitive complexity; greater social maturation, personal competence, and freedom from irrational prejudice; increases in appreciation for the aesthetic qualities of life; clarification of religious views; substantial gains in personal autonomy and nonauthoritarianism; and modest decreases in political naiveté and dogmatism. Also, college students become more introspective and more aware of their own interests, values, and aspirations. The crystallization of these diverse aspects of personality functioning into a sense of identity is one of the most important outcomes of college (Bowen, 1977; Chickering, 1969; Feldman & Newcomb, 1969; Pascarella & Terenzini, 1991). Equally important, the college experience leaves a "residue" (Bowen, 1977) manifested as an openness to new information and ideas, a facility for meeting and dealing with a wide variety of persons, and a practical sense of competence and confidence that enables a college-educated person to successfully cope with novel situations and problems.

Methods

To determine the impact of out-of-class experiences on student learning and personal development, seniors were interviewed from 12 institutions in different regions of the continental United States.

Participants

Participants were students classified as seniors at the following institutions: Berea College, Earlham College, Grinnell College, Iowa State University, Miami University of Ohio, Mount Holyoke College, Stanford University, The Evergreen State College, University of California, Davis, University of Louisville, Wichita State University, and Xavier University of Louisiana. These institutions were selected because they were known to provide rich out-of-class learning and personal development opportunities for their students (Kuh et al., 1991). Each institution was visited twice by a team of two to four investigators; the interviews with students on which this study is based were conducted during the second visits to these colleges.[1]

The institutional contact (typically someone designated by the chief student affairs officer) was asked to identify 10 to 12 seniors who, as a group, reflected a range of involvement in various aspects of the undergraduate experience. For example, we asked that no more than half the students selected for interviews be a highly visible student leader (e.g., editor of the student newspaper, varsity athlete, president of a social organization); the remainder, then, would likely be more typical of undergraduates at that institution in their level of campus involvement. We also requested that several students from historically underrepresented racial and ethnic groups be invited to participate. For the two metropolitan colleges, Louisville and Wichita State, a proportionate number of older, part-time, and commuting students were represented.

Problems related to scheduling and other vagaries (e.g., some students did not show up at the appointed hour) resulted in fewer than 10 students being interviewed at some institutions (i.e., Iowa State = 7; Xavier = 7; UC Davis = 9). Because members of the research team were employed at two of the institutions, they were able to conduct some interviews beyond the target number of 10. As a result, 28 students from Stanford University and 18 students from Wichita State University are included among the respondents.

In all, 149 seniors were interviewed: 69 men, 80 women; 101 whites, 30 African Americans, 6 Hispanics, 6 Asian Americans, and 6 international students; 129 students of traditional age (18–23) and 20 older than 23 years of age. Even though the numbers of students from most of the institutions are relatively small, as a group the participants reflect the diversity that characterizes undergraduate students enrolled in institutions of higher education in the United States.

Data Collection

A semistructured interview protocol was developed for this study and was field-tested during the first campus visit during the fall of 1988. The protocol subsequently was reduced to four general probes designed to elicit the most important things that the respondent learned during college—about oneself, others, interpersonal relations, cultural differences, academics, and so on—rather than the interviewer suggesting specific categories of outcomes. The four probes were: (a) Why did you choose to attend this college and in what ways has it been what you expected? (b) What are the most significant experiences you had here? (c) What are the major highlights of your time here? Low points? High points? Surprises? Disappointments? and (d) How are you different now than when you started college?

Interviews were conducted between January and June of 1989. Prior to the interviews, students received a letter from the investigators outlining the purpose of the study. By informing them in advance about the topics to be covered, some students were able to give the topics considerable thought before the interview.

Interviews were conducted by eight people. Seven of the interviewers were members of the College Experiences Study (CES) research team; by the time these interviews were conducted (during the second visit to the institutions), all the CES project staff had acquired extensive interviewing experience. The eighth interviewer, a graduate student in higher education, conducted 16 of the 28 interviews with Stanford students as part of an internship.[2]

No systematic effort was made to match interviewers and respondents on gender, race, and ethnicity. The interviews occurred in private rooms in campus buildings (e.g., administration buildings, libraries, student unions) that were reserved for this purpose. Interviews ranged in time from 35 minutes to 1 and one-half hours; the modal length was about 1 hour. All interviews were tape-recorded and transcribed verbatim.

Data Analysis

Transcribing interviews required 16 months (April, 1990 through July, 1991). Four people participated in the analysis of interview transcripts. Three were doctoral students in higher education with some training in qualitative research methods. They did not conduct any of the interviews. The fourth person (the author) conducted 21 of the interviews.[3]

To accomplish the purpose of the study, a two-stage, multimethod data analysis procedure was used. The first stage was inductive and the second deductive. As Reichardt and Cook (1979) argued:

> There is no need to choose a research method on the basis of a traditional paradigmatic stance. Nor is there any reason to pick between the two polar opposite paradigms . . . There is every reason (at least in logic) to use them together to satisfy the demands of . . . research in the most efficacious manner possible. (p. 27)

The inductive stage began by examining what respondents said were—for them—important benefits of attending college that they associated with out-of-class experiences. The interview transcripts were analyzed using a five-phase iterative procedure. First, each transcript was reviewed by one of the doctoral students who assigned an identification number to the transcript including the institution, a student identification number, and the student's age, sex, and ethnicity. This initial reading of the transcripts yielded a set of eight categories reflecting outcomes mentioned by the participants (Miles & Huberman, 1984). Second, another reader analyzed several dozen transcripts and, based on her suggestions, the initial set of outcome themes was revised and expanded to 10 categories. Third, a transcript was selected which was read by all four readers to determine how well these themes accommodated the student-reported outcomes contained in this transcript. This revised set of themes was then discussed at some length by the four readers. The product of these discussions was a taxonomy comprised of 13 outcome categories. Fourth, four additional transcripts were selected; each reader read a copy of all four. The experience of coding these transcripts was discussed, and several minor revisions were made to the taxonomy including the addition of the miscellaneous "other" category. Finally, all 149 transcripts were read and coded by the author, which included assigning outcome category numbers in the margin of the transcript next to relevant passages. Thus, a single "human instrument" was responsible for analyzing and interpreting all the data, thereby avoiding potential interrater reliability problems.

The second stage of data analysis was deductive. As Miles and Huberman (1984) suggested, one can more quickly analyze massive amounts of data in the form of words by transforming categories of information into numbers; in addition, numbers can protect against investigator bias, thus ensuring intellectual honesty. Following Miles and Huberman, after the transcripts were coded, quantitative data analysis procedures were used to identify patterns in the data that had empirical and conceptual integrity, not to test hypotheses about out-of-class experiences and student learning.

Measures of central tendency were computed for each outcome category. A factor analysis was performed to determine whether the outcome categories (excluding the miscellaneous "other" category) could be reduced to a more wieldy number of outcome domains. Using the factor solution, t-tests and analysis of variance (ANOVA) were used to determine if the outcomes mentioned by students differed by certain student background characteristics (age, sex, ethnicity) and institutional size (large = 5,000 or more undergraduates, which included Iowa State, Louisville, Miami, Stanford, UC Davis, and Wichita State; small = fewer than 5,000 undergraduates, which included Berea, Earlham, Evergreen State, Grinnell, Mount Holyoke, and Xavier); control (public = Evergreen State, Iowa State, Louisville, Miami, UC Davis, Wichita State; private = Berea, Earlham, Grinnell, Mount Holyoke, Stanford, Xavier), and mission (liberal arts = Berea, Earlham, Evergreen State, Grinnell, Mount Holyoke, Xavier; metropolitan = Louisville, Wichita State; comprehensive = Iowa State, Miami, Stanford, UC Davis).

Results

The presentation of the results is divided into three sections. The first section presents the taxonomy of outcomes and the five outcome domains produced by the factor analysis. In the second section, the words of selected participants describe many of the changes that occurred during college and the areas of learning considered to be important to the students themselves. Finally, differences in outcomes by student and institutional characteristics are presented.

Outcomes Taxonomy

The inductive analysis of the transcribed "voices" of respondents yielded 14 categories of learning and personal development (Table 1). Eight outcomes were mentioned at least once by 60% of the respondents. They were, in order of frequency mentioned: social competence (84%), reflective thought (72%), altruism (70%), autonomy (66%), knowledge acquisition (65%), confidence (63%), practical competence (62%), and self-awareness (60%) (Table 2). Outcomes mentioned least often included aesthetic appreciation (10%), vocational competence (16%), and knowledge application (25%).

The factor analysis (Table 3) reduced the 13 outcome categories (excluding the miscellaneous "other" category) to five factors or outcome domains: Personal Competence (self-awareness + autonomy + confidence + social competence + sense of purpose); Cognitive Complexity (reflective judgment + application of knowledge); Knowledge and Academic Skills (knowledge + academic skills); Practical Competence (practical competence + vocational competence); and Altruism and Estheticism (altruism + estheticism).

In Their Own Words

In this section, the voices of students illustrate what they learned and how they changed during college for each of the five outcome domains produced by the factor analysis.

Personal Competence. Five outcome categories comprise this domain: self-awareness, autonomy, confidence, social competence, and sense of purpose (See Table 3.)

A Hispanic student at UC Davis said:

> I've changed a lot. People notice it, too. They say, 'You act a lot more older, a lot more mature than when you left.' I say, 'Yeah, I've noticed that, too' . . . When I saw my high school friends last summer, they were still doing the same things we used to do in high school. I didn't want to seem snotty, but what they were doing was really boring to me . . . They hadn't changed . . . That's what really shocked me . . . I've learned a lot about myself and grown a lot.

Table 1
Taxonomy of Outcomes Reported by Seniors

1. Self-awareness (includes self-examination, spirituality)

2. Autonomy and self-directedness (includes decision making, taking initiative and responsibility for one's own affairs and learning, movement from dependent to independent thinking)

3. Confidence and self-worth (includes esteem, self-respect)

4. Altruism (includes interest in the welfare of others, awareness of and empathy and respect for needs of others, tolerance and acceptance of people from racial, ethnic, cultural, and religious backgrounds different from one's own)

5. Reflective thought (includes critical thinking, ability to synthesize information and experiences, seeing connections between thinking and experiences, seeing different points of view, examining one's own thinking)

6. Social competence (includes capacity for intimacy, working with others, teamwork, leadership, dealing with others, assertiveness, flexibility, public speaking, communication, patience)

7. Practical competence (includes organizational skills such as time management, budgeting, dealing with systems and bureaucracies)

8. Knowledge acquisition (includes academic and course-related learning, content mastery)

9. Academic skills (includes learning how to study, to write, to conduct independent research)

10. Application of knowledge (includes relating theory to practice and using skills learned in the classroom, laboratory, library, and so on in other areas of life, such as using political science theory and research methods when working in a law office)

11. Esthetic appreciation (includes appreciation for cultural matters as in the arts, literature, theatre, esthetic qualities of nature)

12. Vocational competence (includes acquiring attitudes, behaviors, and skills related to post-college employment)

13. Sense of purpose (includes clarifying life goals and the work one will do after college, sometimes by discovering what one is *not* well suited to do)

14. "Other" (includes such concepts as movement from conservative to liberal attitudes or vice versa, change in physical features, growing apart from a spouse, and so on)

Note. $N = 149$.

The definition of self that undergirds the development of personal competence was captured by a Mount Holyoke student:

> I became more aware of who I am. By going to a women's college you are forced directly or indirectly to take account of who you are . . . First I'm Susan and then second I'm Susan a woman, and then also a Black woman. Those have different meanings for me and I'm trying to figure them out. So I think Mount Holyoke was responsible for making me realize there are so many different parts of myself.

A Mexican American woman at Evergreen said:

> I had a teacher once point at me and say, 'The dark one,' meaning she wanted me to come [to her], and me just kind of shrugging my shoulders and just, well, 'Yeah, that's me.' Now, I look back and see that I should have called her on that. I should have said, 'Hey, you could have said the person with curly hair. You could have said the person with the blue shirt. You could have identified me any other way, but to first identify me with color, that makes me uncomfortable.' To hold people accountable, I've become more confident in doing this.

She continued:

Table 2
Standard Deviations of the Number of Times an Outcome Category Was Mentioned

Category	M	SD	Numbers of Times Mentioned[2]					
			0	1	2	3	4	5 or more
Self-awareness	1.07	1.19	40	33	11	11	4	1
Autonomy	1.33	1.37	34	29	18	12	3	3
Confidence	1.20	1.29	37	32	15	8	5	3
Altruism	1.53	1.51	30	27	19	15	5	4
Reflective thought	1.64	1.53	28	24	23	14	5	6
Social competence	1.83	1.37	16	28	31	13	5	6
Practical competence	1.13	1.28	38	31	21	4	3	3
Knowledge acquisition	1.11	1.19	35	38	17	6	2	3
Knowledge application	0.38	0.75	75	15	6	4	0	0
Academic skills	0.57	0.78	59	27	12	2	0	0
Esthetic appreciation	0.15	0.54	90	7	2	1	1	0
Vocational competence	0.27	0.78	84	11	1	1	1	1
Sense of purpose	0.60	1.03	59	28	11	1	1	1
Other	0.56	0.76	58	31	9	3	0	0

Note: n = 149.

[2]Expressed in percentages of respondents who mentioned the outcome.

Table 3
Factor Analysis of Outcomes Reported by Seniors to Be Associated With College Attendance

Outcomes	Factor matrix (Varimax rotation)					Communality estimates
	Practical competence	Personal competence	Cognitive complexity	Knowledge and academic skills	Altruism & estheticism	
Self-awareness	-.13	.32*	.10	.06	.11	.39
Autonomy	.10	.43*	.20	-.15	-.27	.48
Confidence	-.16	.38*	-.04	.29	-.18	.56
Altruism	-.10	.05	.03	-.11	.59*	.67
Reflective thought	-.15	.06	.51*	-.05	.17	.69
Social competence	.08	.38*	-.15	-.06	.08	.51
Practical competence	.46*	-.01	.02	.01	.03	.54
Knowledge acquisition	.19	-.04*	.07	.40*	.16	.49
Knowledge application	.14	-.01	.53*	-.08	-.08	.57
Academic skills	-.10	-.09	-.11	.63*	.12	.73
Aesthetic appreciation	.24	-.27	-.05	.16	.47*	.57
Vocational competence	.50*	-.04	-.03	-.09	.00	.57
Sense of purpose	.04	.28*	-.31	-.21	.20	.48
Eigenvalue	2.30	1.44	1.27	1.22	1.01	
Proportion of variance	17.7	11.0	9.8	9.4	7.8	
Total variance accounted for:	55.7					

I'm learning all along, all this time. I'm learning about me. I'm learning about my cultural heritage as well as I'm interacting with other groups, other ethnic groups, Native Americans, and African Americans. So, I'm learning a whole lot about people, these cultural roots, where I fit in the bigger picture . . . I've experienced racism for the first time and was validated in that. To say, 'Yeah, yes, of course, you have.' All these years it just wasn't your imagination; it was really happening . . . Somehow, you don't know when and you don't really quite know how, but somehow you're different.

Experiencing the "imposter syndrome" (i.e., occasional feelings of incompetence when surrounded by bright, inquisitive people; Saufley, Cowan, & Blake, 1983) was not uncommon. But students generally did not find such feelings to be debilitating or to inhibit their personal development. An Xavier student said:

When I came here, even though I had done very well in high school and went to one of the best high schools in the city, I still wasn't sure whether what I was doing was good enough. I thought maybe I had slipped through the cracks and they didn't know that I wasn't as bright as they thought. Now, I still sometimes feel that way, but I have more confidence in myself. I know that I can do anything.

In the words of a Stanford woman:

I was very insecure when I came here. I was scared because I didn't know anybody here, but I was also insecure because you're learning about yourself. I was pretty good about hiding it. Could I make friends in a new place? . . . I've gotten really confident in learning how to meet people.

A Grinnell student described this as a shift from

cockiness to confidence . . . I was "great" when I came out of high school. I was very cocky, arrogant as well. I have changed a lot.

A senior at Xavier described her growing sense of independence and autonomy:

I've been on my own. This has taught me a lot of responsibility . . . I paid for my apartment . . . and education through loans, because I decided to be on my own . . . I decided that my parents couldn't do it although I had them if I needed [them] to fall back on. And [doing it on my own] has allowed a greater sense of worth. And you appreciate everything more because you know how hard you had to work for it.

A Berea student talked about personal competence in terms of spiritual development:

I've done a massive amount of growing in many ways. Spiritually just being exposed to many different people from different religious backgrounds . . . I don't think [now] that people have to be religious to be spiritual and that's been good for me, to be exposed to people who are not religious and are very spiritual beings, people who are not Christians [but] who are more "Christian" than many others.

A Stanford student achieved a better understanding of her purpose in life by discovering what *not* to do:

The loans I had to pay back have been a pressure from my freshman year . . . I felt that I had to do something, major in something that was going to make money so I could pay for my education. I now laugh when I think back to that, but I'm very glad I didn't go the premed route . . . I also started seeing that I really didn't enjoy chemistry classes, didn't want to take physics, didn't enjoy calculus, so then it probably wasn't the right road for me.

The development of personal competence can be particularly challenging for athletes:

When I came to Iowa State I was somebody that people always looked up to. When I got here it was kind of like I was thrown back down to the floor and it was like, 'Now is your chance. You've got to prove to yourself and prove to others that you can do it.' In the first couple of months I was like an outcast.

This, too, was a success story as the interview continued:

> I grew so much as a person. I built on that, and I think academically I've become more knowledgeable as far as what I've learned, but I think also I've learned what I want to do with my life.

The words of another Iowa State senior echoed what many participants said they gained from attending college:

> My parents always stressed that college isn't all about just schoolwork. It's about being with people too, because when you get out into the real world it's about being with people. You've got to know what you are doing, but it's about being with people.

Cognitive Complexity. This outcome domain includes reflective thought (e.g., critical thinking, ability to examine different points of view) and knowledge application (e.g., ability to relate theory to practice and to use information presented in one class to other classes or to other areas of life). (See Tables 1 and 3.)

A woman from Mount Holyoke College described how her thinking changed:

> I try to wait, you know, see both sides more so than I used to, and not place myself on either until I know all of the facts, all of what's going on. That's one thing I didn't do before I came here.

An African-American male at Grinnell told us, "When I got back after my freshman year, I started to change . . . I was more open minded." A Berea student described his increased capacity for critical thinking:

> The people I met, the teachers I had, changed my whole way of thinking. Not that I don't want to be successful financially. Sure, I go to school for four years and get a degree, but to think, and by think I mean not just go with what everybody says, but to be able to question things critically on my own. So in that way, my whole idea of success and what I wanted kind of changed.

A 29-year-old male student at Wichita State told us:

> Ten years ago I would have said that I'm the type of person that the world owes me a living. "I'm here. Give it to me." I didn't do very well in high school. I had a C average. I lived in Florida during my junior and senior year, and fifth and sixth period the surf was up, so I didn't spend a lot of time at school . . . but I did graduate . . . Over the semesters that I've been here my need for intellectual stimulation has just skyrocketed. I have to have it; it's almost like an addiction . . . I have to keep my mind active.

Another Wichita State student, this one a 37-year-old woman, said:

> I'm a much more questioning person . . . I don't accept just anything without saying, "Well, that could be true or it may not," and I'd have to research that for myself or talk to other people. I'm less likely to just take one person's opinion or even the department's opinion than I would 5 years ago.

An Earlham senior demonstrated a capacity to explore alternative points of view:

> Earlham taught me how to look at things in many different ways and to see how things work and how things work out, and who has a part in that and what all the factors are. I see things now critically, not destructively. You realize that in every decision there is some sense of goodness. I mean every decision is made so that something good will come of it, maybe not for everyone but for the most part, every decision that's made is made on a basis of getting the best or getting the most of what's possible. The problem is that those things don't always satisfy every party involved. So you have to look at it and realize which parties are being satisfied and why . . . So you have to get a more definite idea of when certain ideas apply and where those ideas apply. It's not a matter of learning what your professor thinks and then writing that down because that's not learning at all. So these things we learn in class we can apply to all aspects of our lives, to all sorts of circumstances.

In a similar vein, a Stanford senior reflected:

> I am constantly challenged to think here about what I believe and what I want . . . My thinking is more rigorous. When I look at issues and things I think I've been a more critical thinker. All those things that were told to me the day I arrived I think are true. Stanford does make you a better thinker.

Knowledge and Academic Skills. In this section, students reflect on the importance of the knowledge and skills they obtained during college, both in and outside of class. (See Tables 1 and 3).

A Berea student talked about how his academic skills improved:

> One of my jobs [every student at Berea is required to "labor" or work at the College] really opened my skills. I feel like I have good library research skills, laboratory research skills, writing skills. [Being at Berea] really improved my writing and reading skills.

An African-American student at Mount Holyoke told us:

> We used to write papers for this [Religion and Social Change] professor, and he was so hard on our papers. I said to him, "I can't believe you're marking up my papers like that." He said, "You're a really good writer." He was very encouraging . . . He felt that the work I was doing was publishable.

A 31-year-old male student at Evergreen State said:

> My time here has been pretty much devoted to academics . . . environmental studies, environmental sciences. I'm pursuing independent film and video work this quarter . . . because I think it's a very important communication tool. In one [core program] . . . I did a 60-page research paper with 35 literature sources . . . They were subjects that I was very interested in and . . . so I went into more depth.

A Grinnell student reflected:

> As a result of taking the Introduction to Women's Studies class, I became very, very much aware of the feminist movement. I went to Washington, DC, on a march. I was the only male [who went from Grinnell]. A lot of my interest is linked to the course because I had no idea about a lot of these issues. I mean, I've always looked for equality. I've always thought that equality was natural, you know, the way it should be. But I never understood why it was any other way and why it was a male-dominated society.

Another Grinnell student talked about the development of academic skills:

> I have written maybe 100 papers here . . . Learning how to structure my thoughts was very important. I almost failed one class; I got a D in it because the prof knew I was trying so hard. That class taught me a lot about how to structure and organize my thinking.

Practical Competence. This domain reflects an enhanced capacity to manage one's personal affairs (e.g., time management, balancing a checkbook), to be economically self-sufficient, and to contribute to society through, among other ways, involvement in community affairs. (See Tables 1 and 3).

A Xavier student spoke of the importance of learning how to cope beyond the campus:

> I have always had a sense of independence, but not to the extent where I could leave home. And after going to New York [for an internship], I learned that I could do it—that I could go out and make my own friends, and find places that suited me, get involved in the community, learn different things about another place outside New Orleans. That is very important because I knew if I wanted to be successful in my career, then traveling would have to be a big part of my life and I would have to move to a different city.

An important practical competency a Stanford senior described was negotiating "the system" by learning how the institution worked or, as they say at Stanford, learning how to play "the game":

One way in which I'm different now is that I've learned how to play "the game" very well . . . I just began to realize how the wheels of Stanford worked. I didn't know how, I just watched for a while—other people getting money for activities [like the dorm sponsoring a Little League Team]. Now I really know how to play "the game": how to play the money game, how to play the power game, how to play the position game, how to just thank the right people, to ask favors of the right people, when it's right, and ask them what is right, and ask them properly. I just learned that very well here at Stanford.

Even older students talked about the importance of developing practical competencies. A 33-year-old Wichita State student told us:

Time constraints were becoming severe. I had too many meetings to attend. Now I'm able to schedule those so that I don't lose any time with my daughter because she's number one [in priorities]. School is number two. Work is number three and I run a poor number four! But the extracurricular is still an important part of the educational process. You're learning how to lead. You're learning how to be in charge. You're learning how to work with people and to compromise and sometimes to back off.

And an older student at Evergreen said:

There is so much you have to learn, and not all of it is in books . . . how to talk with people and how to negotiate contracts, how to do budget proposals, how to ask for funding. I learned to manage a $40 thousand budget—not in my academic program, outside of my academics. I learned how to produce an event. I learned about lighting . . . about the media . . . about the whole process of getting a speaker to come to campus from outside of the state.

Altruism and Estheticism. This domain represents an increase sensitivity to the needs of others, learning about and how to work with people different from oneself, and developing an appreciation for the esthetic qualities of life and the natural world. (See Tables 1 and 3).

A Mount Holyoke student said:

Mount Holyoke, unlike a lot of colleges, stresses community service. I had never been involved [in that] before coming here . . . As a result, I'm more sensitive to the differences of people from different cultures, from different political perspectives, people who have different lifestyles than my own. You learn to accept them and you learn from their experiences.

An international student at Berea spoke of the importance of meeting different types of people:

[They were] people who I would not have met at home. Africans, South Americans, Europeans, Asians from all parts of Asia, and it just makes you more tolerant of differences . . . makes you more broad-minded . . . What I learned from that whole experience is that people are all different, but basically we are—at the same time—all very much the same.

The "Xavier Way," to give back to the community, is expressed in the words of one senior:

Buy a Mercedes? I couldn't. That is not me. I would have to donate money to some foundation, or to Xavier, or somewhere. I couldn't keep it all to myself like some people [who] make lots of money and don't participate in the community. I am a big believer of giving back because I have grown up and seen other Blacks succeed and just abandon the whole Black community, and I think that is wrong.

An Earlham student mentioned in passing how dorm life influenced his views and respect of others:

Small things like playing the music too loud and disturbing other members of the hall can be great lessons in respect and mutual understanding.

A Berea student said:

Since being here I worked with a group of kids in a youth ministry program here on campus ... I was the director ... It got me into working with kids, you know? Since then, I've started a Big Brother program. The guys [in the dorm] enjoy it because it gets them working together. It's great working with the kids, camping out, seeing them learn from different things.

Finally, a male Stanford senior told us:

I think I've become less enamored with reason and rationality and more interested in feelings and relationships, and that seems really strange to me, but it's true. ... Some of the things that really bother me, the reason they bother me is because they affect the way I feel, not the way I think. When I think about poverty, I think less about whether it's just and unjust and more about how it must be for people who are in it and how painful it must be; I don't think so much in terms of right and wrong and what doesn't make sense, but more so in terms of the actual consequences for people's lives.

"Other" Changes. Some learning experiences during college did not fit cleanly into these categories. In addition to changes encompassed by the five outcome domains, respondents also talked about some other areas of their lives that were influenced by attending college, such as developing more sophisticated political and social values and changes in physical appearance:

When I first came [to Mount Holyoke] I was very conservative politically. But most of it was based just on not being very aware ... just kind of going along with whatever. Then I came here and my beliefs and what I took for granted were really challenged.

My first year [at Evergreen] I was more relaxed in my dress. I guess there is a definite influence to dress like a "Greener." When I would go back into Portland, I would go back wearing city clothes ... For me, having my hair cut short is an example ... I didn't do it to look different. I did it more, I guess, to affirm who I was.

Differences by Student and Institutional Characteristics

The final guiding question was whether institutional characteristics and students background characteristics were associated with self-reported outcomes as suggested by Pascarella's (1985) college impact model. Sex was the only background variable that was related to a statistically significant difference in outcomes; compared with women, men reported more changes on Cognitive Complexity ($t = 2.10$, $df = 147$, $p < .05$). An analysis of the two scales that make up this factor, reflective thought and knowledge application, revealed that this difference could be attributed to the latter category; that is, one third of the men, compared with 17% of the women mentioned at least once using information from classes in other areas of their life (knowledge application) such as a job or student organization.

All three institutional characteristics (control, size, mission) were related to differences in outcomes. Compared with their counterparts at public universities, students at private institutions were more likely to report changes in Cognitive Complexity ($t = 2.00$, $df = 147$, $p = <.05$) and Altruism and Estheticism ($t = 3.35$, $df = 147$, $p < .001$). Students at small colleges were more likely than students at large institutions to mention changes in Cognitive Complexity ($t = 2.94$, $df = 147$, $p < .01$), Knowledge and Academic Skills ($t = 2.35$, $df = 147$, $p < .05$), and Altruism and Estheticism ($t = 2.52$, $df = 147$, $p < .01$). Seniors at liberal arts colleges reported more changes in the domains of Cognitive Complexity, Knowledge and Academic Skills, and Altruism and Estheticism than did students at comprehensive universities and metropolitan universities (Table 4); similarly, students at comprehensive institutions reported more changes in these areas than did their counterparts at metropolitan institutions (Table 4).

Discussion

This section is divided into four parts: (a) the contribution of the study to the literature, (b) reflections on using interview data to assess college outcomes, (c) limitations of the study, and (d) thoughts on using quantitative data analysis procedures with qualitative data.

Contribution of the Study

The outcome categories that emerged from the inductive analysis of senior interview transcripts were, for the most part, similar to those developed by others to define and categorize college outcomes (e.g., Bowen, 1977; Ewell, 1984; Feldman & Newcomb, 1969; Lenning, 1976; Micek, Service, & Lee, 1975). For example, compared with the categories used by Pascarella and Terenzini (1991), the only outcomes *not* mentioned by seniors were those that cannot be determined until after graduation—educational attainment, economic benefits, and quality of life after college.

Given the focus of the study—learning and personal development associated with out-of-class experiences—it was not surprising that some outcomes, such as academic skills, were mentioned less frequently than other outcomes, such as autonomy and confidence. At the same time, it is disappointing that knowledge application was not mentioned by more than a quarter of the respondents. Collegiate environments offer innumerable opportunities to use information obtained from many courses of study (e.g., political science, psychology, sociology) in dealing with the problems and challenges of daily life. To encourage more knowledge application, faculty could structure assignments that require students to illustrate how they are using class material in other areas of their lives. Institutional agents whose primary work is with students outside the classroom (e.g., student affairs staff, academic advisors) could promote more knowledge application by asking students on a regular basis to apply what they are learning in class to life outside the classroom. Simple illustrations of how this might work are the residence hall director who routinely invites students during casual conversation to share the three or four most important things they learned that week, or the student government advisor who challenges student leaders

Table 4
Analysis of Variance of Outcome
Factor Scores by Institutional Missions

Factor	Liberal arts		Comprehensive		Metropolitan		F-ratio
	M	SD	M	SD	M	SD	
Practical competence	1.42	1.97	1.42	1.51	1.35	1.45	0.02
Personal competence	6.63	3.70	5.95	3.73	4.83	2.55	2.65
Cognitive complexity	2.52	2.22	1.87	1.50	1.14	1.48	5.90**
Knowledge and academic skills	2.03	1.78	1.74	1.52	0.79	0.86	6.49**
Altruism and estheticism	2.08	2.03	1.56	1.34	1.03	1.27	4.14
Number of respondents	65		55		29		

*$p < .05$, **$p < .01$.
Liberal arts = Berea, Earlham, Evergreen State, Grinnell, Mount Holyoke, and Xavier. Comprehensive = Iowa State, Miami, Stanford, and UC Davis. Metropolitan = Louisville and Wichita State.

to apply material from their political science, psychology, and communications classes to their student government role.

One outcome frequently mentioned by participants as important was learning about and gaining experience with people from different racial, ethnic, and cultural backgrounds (Altruism and Estheticism). Earlier studies of additional changes during college usually found increased tolerance for racial and ethnic differences (e.g., Clark, Heist, McConnell, Trow, & Yonge, 1972; Hyman & Wright, 1979; Winter, McClelland, & Stewart, 1981), an effective psychological outcome (Astin, 1973). This study suggests that experiences outside the classroom are an important venue where students not only develop an appreciation for people from backgrounds different from their own (the affective psychological outcome), but also cultivate skills that enable them to relate personally to such students (an affective behavioral outcome).

College impact models emphasize the influence of institutional and student characteristics on learning and personal development (Pascarella, 1985; Pascarella & Terenzini, 1991; Tinto, 1987; Weidman, 1989). Institutional control, size, and mission were associated with differences in Cognitive Complexity, Knowledge and Academic Skills, and Altruism and Estheticism. However, in this study sex was the only student characteristic associated with a difference in reported outcomes (Cognitive Complexity). That other student background characteristics were not systematically associated with differences in outcomes may be explained by the nature of the institutions. These institutions shared a number of properties, including cultural assumptions that every student can succeed and that every student is expected to participate fully in the life of the institution (Kuh et al., 1991). These colleges and universities have created something akin to a level playing field, an institutional context wherein student characteristics become neutral factors in terms of their learning and personal development (Kuh & Vesper, 1992).

Pascarella and Terenzini (1991) found that within-college differences (i.e., what a student does in college) were greater than between-college differences (i.e., type of institution attended). Few studies compared the effects of attending *specific* institutions on college impact, such as assessments of gains of students attending Indiana University, Ball State University, and Hanover College. Therefore, whether *individual* institutions have distinctive impacts on their students is not known because any differences in student outcomes that may be associated with salience and character of institutional mission become obfuscated by aggregating data from a number of institutions. For example, do students at colleges such as Berea, Earlham, and Grinnell, where the institutional mission emphasizes service to others, report patterns of outcomes that differ from those of their counterparts at other colleges and universities that do not emphasize service in their missions? Of course, institutions with salient service-oriented missions attract many students with humanitarian interests. Therefore, efforts to examine the relationship between institutional mission and student outcomes must attempt to estimate the relative contributions of the institutional environment and students' pre-college predilections to changes compatible with those valued by the institution's mission and philosophy. The contextual properties of these 12 colleges and universities differed in myriad, subtle ways that may influence student learning (Kuh et al., 1991), a point to which we shall return in the "Limitations" section.

Using Interviews to Assess Outcomes

The words of seniors describing the role of out-of-class experiences to their learning and development during college are compelling evidence of the value of using interviews to assess the impact of college on students. At the same time, using unstructured interviews to better understand what happens to students is not without potential pitfalls.

The quality of the information obtained from interviews is a function of the respondent's capacity to reflect on and discuss the topics under investigation and the interviewer's skill in creating the conditions which encourage the respondent to talk freely. Many seniors interviewed for this study spoke with clarity and precision about how they benefitted from out-of-class experiences. Others, when asked to reflect on changes associated with experiences outside the classroom, invariably used illustrations from both in-class and out-of-class experiences. In other instances, students described a seamlessness between learning in and out of the classroom, suggesting that the boundaries between academics and student life beyond the classroom—often perceived by faculty and administrators to be real—were blurred so as to be indistinguishable to students. Still others were not very articulate in talking about how or whether they had changed during college. The best example is a Rhodes Scholar who, during the course of a 75-minute interview, was asked three times to describe how he had changed. Each time, however, he took the conversation in other directions. In all likelihood, this student—who had achieved national honors and a spate of institutional recognitions—benefitted more from the undergraduate experience than his interview transcript revealed.

Finally, another plausible explanation for variation in the richness of interviews is the nature of a student's experiences in college. Some respondents may not have learned or changed very much as a result of experiences outside the classroom. Recall that seniors at small colleges with liberal arts missions were more likely to report changes in Cognitive Complexity, Knowledge and Academic Skills, and Altruism and Estheticism. Small classes and dorms place a greater obligation on students to actively participate; therefore, students at small colleges may have more opportunities to engage in activities—both in and out of the classroom—that require reflection and application of knowledge and skills (Barker, 1968; Chickering, 1969); thus, they have more practice in expressing themselves orally. At the same time, it may be that students who choose to attend small colleges are predisposed to such behavior and that these apparent differences in outcomes are a function of college recruitment, and not college impact (Pascarella & Terenzini, 1991).

Limitations

This study has several limitations. The first, and perhaps most important, is the nature of the institutions from which participants were selected. These colleges and universities were known to provide high quality out-of-class learning opportunities. Thus, it is possible that the range and degree of changes reported by students in this study may be richer than those of students at other institutions. Indeed, comparative analyses of *College Student Experience Questionnaire* (Pace, 1987) data indicated that students from these 12 institutions were more involved in their education (i.e., expended greater effort in their studies and educationally purposeful out-of-class activities) and benefitted more than their counterparts at other institutions (Kuh et al., 1991; Kuh & Vesper, 1992). Thus, the special qualities of these colleges and universities should be considered when determining the transferability of these findings.

Although these institutions are similar in that they provide rich out-of-class learning environments, they differed—as mentioned earlier—in other ways that influence student learning. More information about the contextual conditions of these colleges would provide a framework within which to interpret students' experiences and explain, perhaps, why what appear to be similar experiences and outcomes differ qualitatively. One example must suffice.

All of the quotations from students at The Evergreen State University mention their program of study. This may seem out of place in a paper focused on out-of-class experiences, unless one is familiar with the Evergreen ethos. At this college, many students have difficulty distinguishing between in-class and out-of-class learning. During our first visit to this campus, before we began interviewing for this study, we discovered that students viewed the terms, "in class" and "out of class" as irrelevant. At Evergreen, learning and personal development is a 24-hour-a-day activity, an expectation reinforced by an academic program that is markedly different from the traditional curriculum in which students select majors and take four or five courses a semester. Evergreen students ("junior learners" in the vernacular of that campus) match up with faculty ("senior learners") and form groups of 20 to 40 or so to study some topic in depth from an interdisciplinary perspective for a few months to, on occasion, a year. For many students, these groups, called "Programs," constitute one's primary academic *and* affinity groups. That is, the Program *is* the college experience, and to ask students to compartmentalize their learning experiences contradicts the mission of the institution and makes no sense to students. Hence, an understanding of the contextual conditions of these institutions would allow additional interpretations of these data.

Another limitation is the nature of the data—student reports of what happened to them since coming to college. Self-report data have been found to be moderately correlated ($r = .25$ to $r = .65$) with objective measures of knowledge acquisition (Pascarella & Terenzini, 1991). Nonetheless, memories are selective, and it is possible that students failed to mention certain changes. Recall could have been prompted by the use of a structured protocol based on an existing taxonomy of outcomes, such as Lenning (1976) or Micek, Service, and Lee (1975): This approach was rejected because it was incompatible with the phenomenological interview method. However, if respondents could have reviewed a verbatim transcript, or summary of their comments, they might have added other changes (Kvale, 1983). Therefore, the data reported in this paper almost certainly underestimate the benefits students derive from attending college in general and from out-of-class experiences in particular.

Finally, multiple investigators were needed to interview students at a dozen institutions in different regions of the country. Although all research team members were skilled in interviewing techniques, some were more successful than others in getting students to talk about the impact of out-of-class experiences on their learning and personal development.

A Note on Using Quantitative Data Analysis Procedures with Qualitative Data

The appropriateness of mixing quantitative and qualitative methods is the subject of continuing debate (Howe, 1988; Jick, 1979; Smith & Heshusius, 1986). The issues are complicated and cannot be resolved here; rather, the purpose here is to illustrate an important tradeoff associated with being "shamelessly eclectic" (Rossman & Wilson, 1991) in mixing methods: efficiency versus investigator influence. As mentioned earlier, employing quantitative procedures allows the researcher to more quickly identify patterns in large amounts of information (Miles & Huberman, 1984). However, using quantitative data analysis procedures limits the investigator's capacity to understand the nature, meaning, and impact of the information, the natural by-product of joining personal interpretations as one analyzes the data inductively (Peshkin, 1988).

This study took a middle road in that many weeks were devoted to the inductive analysis of more than 12 dozen interviews prior to employing quantitative techniques to distill patterns in the data. These procedures (e.g., factor analysis, ANOVA) allowed the researcher to classify the information in ways (e.g., by institutional type) that would have required substantially more time using the inductive approach exclusively.

Conclusions

This study provides a contemporary view of the changes students attributed to out-of-class experiences. Based on their "voices," four conclusions about student learning and personal development associated with out-of-class experiences are warranted.

First, consistent with earlier studies (e.g., Wilson, 1966), experiences beyond the classroom made substantial contributions to student learning and personal development. All students reported personally meaningful changes in one or more areas considered to be important outcomes of college (e.g., interpersonal and practical competence, critical thinking). The relationships among these outcomes were complex, suggesting cumulative and mutually shaping effects of knowledge, and enhanced capacity for critical thinking, personal reflection, competence, and self-direction. With all the attention given to outcomes assessment (Ewell, 1991), it is disappointing that the contributions of out-of-class experiences to learning and personal development have received so little attention, particularly given that students attach so much importance to such experiences.

Second, knowledge acquisition and academic skills were more frequently associated with classroom, laboratory, and studio activities than with out-of-class experiences. When talking about how they had changed during college many students mentioned skill areas such as writing and knowledge about specific subjects. The quotations illustrating this outcome domain suggest that students view the classroom as the primary source of these changes. At the same time, although students attributed gains in knowledge to classroom assignments and experiences, life outside the classroom provided ample opportunities to test the value and worth of these ideas and skills.

Third, student background characteristics were, for the most part, unrelated to the learning and personal development outcomes they considered important. The kinds and degree of changes reported by seniors in this study were similar, regardless of age and ethnicity. It is reassuring to know that the benefits associated with attending college reported by "new majority students" (i.e., students of color and those who are over the age of 23, attend college part time, live off campus, have families, or work more than 20 hours a week; Ehrlich, 1991, did not differ from those of traditional age and white students. The lone difference associated with sex regarding application of knowledge is a reminder that collegiate climates for learning often are less empowering for women than for men. If women are taken seriously in and out of the classroom by faculty and administrators, perhaps they will be encouraged to the same extent as their male counterparts to apply what they are learning.

Finally, the type of institution attended was related to differences in the frequency with which certain outcomes were mentioned. For example, students at the smaller colleges with a liberal arts mission more frequently reported changes in intellectual and aesthetic areas. To what degree precollege characteristics of students contribute to these differences cannot be determined from this study. However, others have argued that a salient, consistently articulated mission focuses student effort (Chickering, 1969; Keeton, 1971). To the extent that this is the case of these colleges, the results of this study affirm Bowen's (1977) conclusion that large size does not necessarily offer educational advantages.

There is more to discover about the contributions of out-of-class experiences to student learning and personal development. For example, studies that attempt to link various out-of-class experiences (e.g., voluntarism, student government, on-campus job) with specific outcomes would be useful to institutional decisionmakers responsible for weighing the merits of allocating resources to such activities. Because many of the benefits of college attendance seem to persist well beyond graduation, it would be instructive to examine the relationships between involvement in out-of-class activities and the long-term effects of college. The words of a senior from The Evergreen State College convey a thought consistent with this last point:

> My educational experience here, it's been more like preparing for my journey. [College] has been a journey within itself, but it's more a preparation for my real journey.

Notes

An earlier version of this paper was presented at the Annual Meeting of the American Educational Research Association, San Francisco, April 1992.

1. The research reported in this paper was funded in part by grants from The Lilly Endowment, Inc., the National Association of Student Personnel Administrators, and the Education Division of the Marriott Corporation. However, any endorsement by these agencies of the findings presented here should not be inferred.

2. I gratefully acknowledge the splendid work of collaborators on the College Experiences Study. Without them, the information on which this paper is based could not have been gathered: Rosalind Andreas, Herman Blake, James Lyons, Lee Krehbiel, Kathleen MacKay, John Schuh, Carney Strange, and Elizabeth Whitt. Also Jeff McCollough, while he was a graduate student at Indiana University, did an internship at Stanford (his alma mater), part of which included interviewing Stanford seniors.

3. The contributions of Caitlin Anderson, James Arnold, and John Downey, all doctoral students in higher education at Indiana University, were essential to completing this project. They played key roles in developing the outcomes taxonomy distilled from the interview transcripts and made many helpful comments on an earlier draft of this paper. Special thanks also are due to Nick Vesper of Indiana University who cheerfully, skillfully, and in a most timely fashion, performed the computer analysis of

outcomes data. Finally, I wish to acknowledge the helpful comments of John Centra and Elizabeth Whitt on an earlier version of this paper and the suggestions of the anonymous reviewers and John Rury.

References

Astin, A. W. (1973). Measurement and determinants of the outputs of higher education. In L. Solmon and P. Taubman (Eds.), *Does college matter? Some evidence on the impacts of higher education.* New York: Academic Press.

Astin, A. W. (1977). *Four critical years: Effects of college on beliefs, attitudes, and knowledge.* San Francisco: Jossey-Bass.

Astin, H. S., & Kent, L. (1983). Gender roles in transition: Research and policy implications for higher education. *Journal of Higher Education, 54,* 309–324.

Attinasi, L. C., Jr. (1992). Rethinking the study of college outcomes. *Journal of College Student Development, 33,* 61–70.

Barker, R. (1968). *Ecological psychology: Concepts for studying the environment of human behavior.* Stanford, CA: Stanford University Press.

Baxter, Magolda, M. B. (1992). Cocurricular influences on college students' intellectual development. *Journal of College Student Development, 33,* 203–213.

Bogdan, R. C., & Biklen, S. K. (1982). *Qualitative research for education: An introduction to theory and methods.* Boston: Allyn and Bacon.

Bowen, H. R. (1977). *Investment in learning.* San Francisco: Jossey-Bass.

Boyer, E. (1987). *College: The undergraduate experience in America.* New York: Harper & Row.

Chickering, A. W. (1969). *Education and identity.* San Francisco: Jossey-Bass.

Clark, B. R., Heist, P., McConnell, T. R., Trow, M. A., & Yonge, G. (1972). *Students and colleges: Interaction and change.* Berkeley: University of California, Center for Research and Development in Higher Education.

Ehrlich, T. (1991). *Our university in the state: Educating the new majority.* Bloomington: Indiana University.

Ewell, P. T. (1984). *The self-regarding institution: Information for excellence.* Boulder, CO: National Center for Higher Education Management Systems.

Ewell, P. T. (1991). Assessment and public accountability: Back to the future. *Change, 23*(6), 12–17.

Feldman, K. A., & Newcomb, T. M. (1969). *The impact of college on students.* San Francisco: Jossey-Bass.

Freedman, M. B. (1967). *The college experience.* San Francisco: Jossey-Bass.

Heist, P., & Yonge, G. (1968). *Omnibus Personality Inventory manual (Form F).* New York: Psychological Corporation.

Hyman, H., & Wright, C. (1979). *Education's lasting influence on values.* Chicago: University of Chicago Press.

Howe, K. R. (1988). Against the quantitative-qualitative incompatibility thesis or dogmas die hard. *Educational Researcher, 17*(8), 10–16.

Jick, T. D. (1979). Mixing qualitative and quantitative methods: Triangulation in action. *Administrative Science Quarterly, 24,* 602–611.

Keeton, M. (1971). *Models and mavericks.* New York: McGraw-Hill.

Kohlberg, L. (1984). *Essays on moral development: Vol. 2. The psychology of moral development: The nature and validity of moral stages.* New York: Harper & Row.

Kuh, G. D., Krehbiel, L., & MacKay, K. A. (1988). *Personal development and the college student experience: A review of the literature.* Trenton, NJ: New Jersey Department of Higher Education, College Outcomes Evaluation Program.

Kuh, G. D., Schuh, J. S., Whitt, E. J., Andreas, R. E., Lyons, J. W., Strange, C. C., Krehbiel, L. E., & McKay, K. A. (1991). *Involving colleges: Successful approaches to fostering student learning and personal development outside the classroom.* San Francisco: Jossey-Bass.

Kuh, G. D., & Stage, F. K. (1992). Student development theory and research. In B. R. Clark & G. Neave (Eds.), *Encyclopedia of higher education* (pp. 1719–1730). Oxford and New York: Praeger.

Kuh, G. D., & Vesper, N. (1992, April). *A comparison of student learning at "involving" and "other" metropolitan universities.* Paper presented at the Annual Meeting of the American Educational Research Association, San Francisco.

Kvale, S. (1983). The qualitative research interview: A phenomenological and hermeneutical mode of understanding. *Journal of Phenomenological Psychology, 14,* 171–196.

Lenning, O. T. (Ed.). (1976). *Improving educational outcomes.* San Francisco: Jossey-Bass.

Levine, A. & Associates. (1989). *Shaping higher education's future: Demographic realities and opportunities, 1990–2000.* San Francisco: Jossey-Bass.

Light, R. J. (1992). *The Harvard assessment seminars: Explorations with students and faculty about teaching, learning, and student life* (Second report). Cambridge, MA Harvard University Graduate School of Education and Kennedy School of Government.

Madison, P. (1969). *Personality development in college.* Reading, MA: Addison-Wesley.

Micek, S. S., Sevice, A. L., & Lee, Y. S. (1975). *Outcome measures and procedures manual.* Boulder, CO: National Center for Higher Education Management Systems, Western Interstate Commission on Higher Education.

Miles, M. B., & Huberman, A. M. (1984). *Qualitative data analysis: A sourcebook of new methods.* Beverly Hills, CA: Sage.

Moffatt, M. (1988). *Coming of age in New Jersey: College and American culture.* New Brunswick, NJ: Rutgers University Press.

Pace, C. R. (1979). *Measuring outcomes of college: Fifty years of findings and recommendations for the future.* San Francisco: Jossey-Bass.

Pace, C. R. (1987). *CSEQ: Test manual and noms: College Student Experiences Questionnaire.* Los Angeles: The Center for the Study of Evaluation, Graduate School of Education, University of California, Los Angeles.

Pace, C. R. (1990). *The undergraduates: A report of their activities and progress in college in the 1980s.* Los Angeles: University of California at Los Angeles, Center for the Study of Evaluation.

Pascarella, E. T. (1985). College environmental influences on learning and cognitive development: A critical review and synthesis. In J. Smart (Ed.), *Higher education: Handbook of theory and research* (Vol. 1). New York: Agathon.

Pascarella, E. T., Ethington, C. A., & Smart, J. C. (1988). The influence of college on humanitarian/ civic involvement values. *Journal of Higher Education, 59,* 412–437.

Pascarella, E. T., & Terenzini, P. T. (1991). *How college affects students: Findings and insights from twenty years of research.* San Francisco: Jossey-Bass.

Perry, W. G., Jr. (1970). *Forms of intellectual and ethical development in the college years: A scheme.* New York: Holt, Rinehart, & Winston.

Peshkin, A. (1988). In search of subjectivity—one's own. *Educational Record, 17*(7), 17–22.

Reichardt, C. S., & Cook, T. D. (1979). Beyond qualitative versus quantitative methods. In C. Reichardt & T. Cook (Eds.), *Qualitative and quantitative methods in evaluation* (pp. 7–32). Beverly Hills: Sage.

Rodgers, R. F. (1989). Student development. In U. Delworth & G. Hanson (Eds.), *Student services: A handbook for the profession* (pp. 117–164). San Francisco: Jossey-Bass.

Rossman, G. B., & Wilson, B. L. (April, 1991). *Numbers and words revisited: Being "shamelessly eclectic."* Paper presented at the Annual Meeting of the American Educational Research Association, Chicago.

Saufley, R. W., Cowan, K. O., & Blake, J. H. (1983). The struggles of minority students at predominantly white institutions. In J. Cones III, J. Noonan, & D. Janha (Eds.), *Teaching minority students: New directions for teaching and learning,* No. 16 (pp. 3–15). San Francisco: Jossey-Bass.

Shrader, W. (1969). *College ruined our daughter: Letters to parents concerning the baffling world of the college student.* New York: Harper & Row.

Smith, J. K., & Heshusius, L. (1986). Closing down the conversation: The end of the quantitative-qualitative debates among educational inquirers. *Educational Researcher, 15*(1), 4–12.

Thomas, R., & Chickering, A. W. (1984). *Education and Identity* revisited. *Journal of College Student Personnel, 25,* 392–399.

Tinto, V. (1987). *Leaving college: Rethinking the causes and cures of student attrition.* Chicago: University of Chicago Press.

Weldman, J. (1989). Undergraduate socialization: A conceptual approach. In J. Smart (Ed.), *Higher education: Handbook of theory and research (Vol 5).* New York: Agathon.

White, R. W. (1966) *Lives in progress* (2nd ed.), New York: Holt, Rinehart, & Winston.

Wilson, E. K. (1966). The entering student: Attributes and agents of change. In T. Newcomb & E. Wilson (Eds.), *College peer groups* (pp. 71–106). Chicago: Aldine.

Winter, D., McClelland, D., & Stewart, A. (1981). *A new case for the liberal arts: Assessing institutional goals and student development.* San Francisco: Jossey-Bass.

George D. Kuh is a Professor of Higher Education at the Center for Postsecondary Research and Planning in the Department of Educational Leadership and Policy Studies in the School of Education at Indiana University, 7th and Rose Ave., Room 4258, Bloomington, IN 47405. His specializations are college students, campus cultures, and student learning outside the classroom.

Latino Students' Sense of Belonging In the College Community:
Rethinking the Concept of Integration on Campus

SYLVIA HURTADO AND DEBORAH FAYE CARTER

Researchers have concluded that improving Latino student progress through the educational pipeline will require both institutional commitment and attention to issues that specifically affect these students (Rendon & Nora, 1988). However, part of the problem in addressing these issues is that we currently do not know enough about the unique experiences of Latino students, including those who have overcome significant barriers to attend four-year institutions. For example, only approximately one in five administrators reported in a national survey that their campus is able to provide a good climate for Hispanic students (El-Khawas, 1989). In addition, in a national sample of talented Latino students attending baccalaureate-granting institutions, 28 percent reported that Hispanics on their campus felt like they did not "fit in" (Hurtado, 1994). These facts are disturbing in light of both the growing numbers of Latino college-age students (Estrada, 1988) and consistent research which supports the view that it is the "integrating experiences" of involvement, engagement and affiliation that are central to student development and progress during college (Astin, 1984; 1993; Pace, 1984; Pascarella & Terenzini, 1991). We believe that Latino students' own views of their membership in a particular campus community is an important part of the process of inclusion in these college experiences. Understanding key factors that affect Latino sense of belonging with the college community may be important if we are to improve students' chances for success in higher education.

The objective of this study is to provide further clarification regarding what may constitute feelings of integration from the perspective of Latino students. We examine the extent to which a sense of belonging differs from most measures of integration used by higher education researchers. A second objective is to introduce elements of the college experience that may be distinct for the Latino college student. A final objective is to understand how students' sense of belonging in the third year of college is related to experiences that occur in the first and second year of college. Establishing the temporal sequence of such experiences may help us understand critical stages of the undergraduate experience that enhance Latinos students' sense of belonging with the college community.

Theoretical Perspectives

The concepts of social and academic integration in college has received much research attention in replication studies of the Tinto Model for retention and other college outcomes (Pascarella and Terenzini, 1991). It should be noted, however, that studies vary considerably in their conceptualization and measurement of these constructs. This problem stems from a major theoretical dilemma faced by both sociologists and researchers in higher education. Sociologists contend that there is a lack of theoretical clarity with which Durkeim articulates social integration, or cohesion (Bollen & Hoyle, 1990). Following from Durkeim's initial work, sociologists developed a line of research which attempted to address group cohesion that resulted in a confusing mesh of measures and findings (Bollen & Hoyle, 1990). Similarly, higher educational researchers' interpretations of Tinto's theoretical constructs of social and academic integration have lacked clarity and uniformity. This may be due, in part, to the fact that Tinto (1987) derives some of the central elements of his theory of student departure to social integration concepts articulated by Durkeim. However, it is primarily that researchers have often operationalized these constructs to reflect their own views of integration. The constructs also reflect differences in researchers' preferences for any number of measures that constitute formal and informal social activity, including effort or time spent in these activities, student perceptions, reported behaviors, satisfaction, interpersonal relations, objective performance criteria, or a combination of these measures in their models (see for example: Pascarella, Terenzini, & Wolfle, 1986; Stage, 1989; Cabrera, Castañeda, Nora, & Hengstler, 1992). It should be noted that despite this lack of uniformity, with a few exceptions that are noted below, there is amazing consistency in the effects of integration measures on retention and student outcomes.

Recent criticisms of the use of integration models suggest that there is an underlying assumption of acculturation stemming from this inquiry that ignores the cultural differences of ethnic groups that is potentially harmful in practice (Tierney, 1992). For example, Tierney (1992) demonstrated how administrators have interpreted the concept of integration to mean that "Native Americans need to become more acculturated to the university in order to persist" (p.613). Certainly, the word "integration" is a loaded term for racial and ethnic minorities, given the historical and contemporary problems in desegregating schools and colleges (Williams, 1988). Yet, previous research has not addressed the racial/ethnic dimension of "integrating experiences" for minority students. Researchers have used constructs that often reflect participation in mainstream collegiate activities without considering whether the social distance between racial and ethnic groups may inhibit participation in college activities (Hurtado, 1994b). Particular forms of affiliation that may reflect specific Latino student interests such as participation in ethnic student organizations and participation in cultural forms of expression on campus that may include religion, community service or activism, ethnic dance, music, and art have been excluded from social integration measures that include college activities. This may explain why some studies have found that social integration constructs are related to outcomes for majority students but are not significantly related to outcomes for Chicano (Nora, 1987) and other non-traditional students (Fox, 1986) in specific institutional settings. We have no clear understanding of how the variety of collegiate activities (mainstream and culturally-related) may contribute to a minority student's sense of membership in the college community. This suggests the need to assess specific forms of integration in college, and perhaps researchers' conceptualizations of integration, by using a conceptually distinct measure that captures the individual's view as to whether they feel included in college life.

Sociological research distinguishes between perceptions of group cohesion (based on the individual's perception) from observed cohesion, which is based on the researcher's assumptions of what constitutes cohesion (Bollen & Hoyle, 1990). Bollen & Hoyle's (1990) definition of "perceived cohesion" captures the extent to which individuals feel "stuck to" particular social groups, and it is composed of two dimensions: a sense of belonging and feelings of morale associated with group membership (p.482). Our study focuses on Bollen & Hoyle's first dimension of perceived cohesion, the Sense of Belonging Scale. Their view is that a "sense of belonging is fundamental to a member's identification with a group and has numerous consequences for behavior" (p.484). It contains both cognitive and affective elements in that, through cognitive processing, the individual evaluates their role in relation to the group and this evaluation often results in an affective response. Thus, a sense of belonging may be essential to understanding why some students chose to take part in college activities and whether such social interaction further enhances the individual's affiliation with the college. Bollen & Hoyle's (1990) overall Perceived Cohesion Scale has been tested on various populations including a mid-sized liberal arts college, a city, and several nations. Their perceived cohesion measure applies to large groups where face-to-face interaction or knowledge of everyone is not possible. This suggests that there are a variety of collective affiliations in large environments that are formed that can contribute to an individual's sense of belonging to the larger community.

Attinasi's (1989; 1992) qualitative work on Mexican American students sets the stage for understanding how students make sense of large environments and subsequently develop multiple communities on campus. Specifically, Attinasi found that students become integrated not because they share values and orientations with the majority of students at the institution, but because the specific collective affiliations they form help them acquire the skills to negotiate the social, physical, and cognitive geographies of large campus environments (Attinasi, 1992). This notion of cognitive mapping and the formation of multiple communities, or social niches, is useful in understanding minority students' collective affiliations on campus. These notions are important because they suggest that minority students can feel a part of the campus community without assimilating or adopting the values of the majority. In addition, it is the early experiences of college transition ("getting in" and "getting to know") that are key in determining how and whether students find their place in campus community. Newcomb (1962) supported this view of the importance of early post-matriculation experiences in his theory of peer group formation in college. These early experiences can also be facilitated by institutional intervention. For example, research has shown that an intensive two-day orientation can have a substantial effect on social integration during college (Pascarella, Terenzini, & Wolfle, 1986). Thus, student's transitional experiences in our study were hypothesized to play a key role in determining Latino students' sense of belonging.

At the same time that these early experiences are important in enhancing a sense of belonging, there are other elements of the minority experience that may inhibit this process. Research on student perceptions of the college environment has begun to reveal that the institutional climate for diversity can have considerable impact on campus social life for minorities. In a sample that included Chicano and other Latino students, Smedley, Myers, & Harrell (1993) reported that students face specific stresses associated with their minority status on predominantly white campuses. They found that minority freshmen exhibit considerable psychological sensitivity to the campus social climate, including interpersonal tensions with White students and faculty, and actual or perceived experiences of racism and discrimination. Oliver, Rodriguez, & Mickelson (1985) found reports of discrimination were associated with feelings of alienation among Chicano students in a university setting. Hurtado (1994a) also found that, among Latino sophomores and juniors, student perceptions of racial/ethnic tension and experiences of discrimination were related to student behaviors and informal social preferences on campus. These studies suggest that students are educated in distinct and variable racial climates that influence psychological processes, intergroup relations, and group cohesion. We hypothesize that students' perceptions of a hostile climate directly affects students' sense of belonging in their institution.

Figure 1. shows our hypothesized model of Sense of Belonging in relation to student background characteristics, college selectivity, ease in transition into college, and perceptions of a hostile climate. These relationships are ordered temporally in order to test the causal relationship between experiences that occur in the first two years of college and Sense of Belonging in the junior year. Longitudinal studies of students have begun to show how experiences at unique stages of a student's career can impact outcomes (Terenzini & Wright, 1987a; 1987b). For this reason, we selected measures to represent four specific time points: pre-college, first year, second year, and third year of college.

Gender and academic self-concept are depicted as exogenous variables (measured prior to college) that directly affect transition in the first year of college. College selectivity is also an exogenous variable which was hypothesized to directly affect student transition and perceptions of a hostile climate based on previous findings regarding these measures (Hurtado 1992; 1994). Ease in student transition in the first year of college was hypothesized to have a direct effect and indirect effect on Sense of Belonging, mediated by a hostile climate in the sophomore year. That is, we expect that excellent transitional experiences in the first year can be undermined by perceptions of a hostile climate in the second year. In addition, perceptions of a hostile climate in the second year will have a negative impact on Sense of Belonging in the third year of college.

Figure 1
Proposed Model of Sense of Belonging

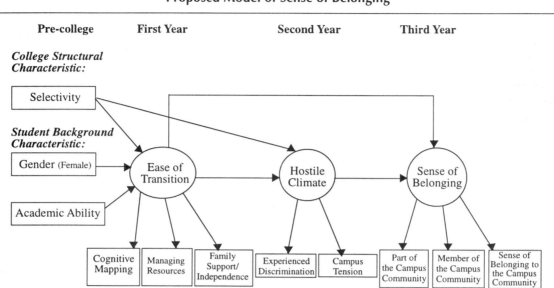

Methodology

Data Sources

This study utilized four primary sources of student data and is part of a national study of Latino college students who were among the top PSAT achievers identified as semifinalists for a national scholarship award (see Hurtado, 1994a for further details on the design). This national data constitute one of the few panel studies available on a select but important population of Latino students who demonstrate potential for academic success. Although the larger study focused on five cohorts of students, the current study focuses only on the cohort of Latino students who entered four-year colleges in 1990. Pre-college information was obtained from the Student Descriptive Questionnaire, a survey administered to students when they took the SAT examination. The survey is designed to obtain information about a student's background, high school preparation, and college preferences. Analyses were limited to cases that had both SDQ data and responses to longitudinal follow-up surveys at two subsequent time points in their college career.

The National Survey of Hispanic Students (NSHS) was developed as a comprehensive longitudinal survey of college student experiences. The survey was sent to 4,979 student home addresses, reported on semifinalist rosters, in the late summer of 1991. A reminder postcard was sent two weeks after the first wave of surveys, and two weeks subsequent, a second survey was sent to nonrespondents' homes. Surveys arrived throughout early Fall of the 1991-1992 academic year, with an overall student response rate of 49%. In addition to the survey data, information about each college the student attended was linked with data from the U.S. Department of Education's Integrated Postsecondary Educational Data Systems (IPEDS), *The College Handbook* (1992), and institutional data files maintained by the Higher Education Research Institute at UCLA. For this study, we relied primarily on the college selectivity data obtained from the two latter sources.

A 1993 follow-up survey of the NSHS was developed specifically to compare students' experiences and attitudes one year after completing the first survey. The survey used new measures and replicated measures from other research studies, including Bollen & Hoyle's (1990) Sense of Belonging scale, repeated questions from the first survey, and newly developed measures. We conducted two in-depth interviews with minority students, in their first and second year of college, in order to develop additional items regarding their transition experience. We developed a set of items that corresponded with their experience and reflected Attinasi's (1989) concepts of "getting in" and "getting to know" or cognitive mapping. Additional transition measures include survey items that reflected areas where students' appeared to have the most difficulty during the freshman year (e.g. managing time, money, schedules and issues regarding leaving the family). See Appendix A-1 for all variables, scales and measures in the model.

The second NSHS was sent to 1091 students who were members of two cohorts in early 1993. Follow-up postcards were sent two weeks after the first wave, and a second survey was sent to nonrespondents four weeks later. In the spring, phone calls were made to nonrespondents with valid phone numbers obtained from the first survey. Finally, a third mailing of the survey was sent in the late summer. Surveys were sent to parent's homes, college addresses when available, and updated addresses received the summer following administration of the first NSHS survey. These efforts produced an overall response rate of 57% for the most recent survey.

Sample

Analyses were limited to students who began college in the Fall of 1990 for several reasons. First, these students were college sophomores during the administration of the first NSHS survey. This enabled them to be relatively familiar with their early transition experiences, but unlike the 1991 cohort, they possessed time to adequately form opinions about the climate and begin participation in college activities that could be reflected in the first survey. Second, the cohort was able to provide sufficient information about their experiences in the third year of college that we attempted to capture in the second NSHS survey. This allowed for temporal ordering of variables and assessing change in attitudes, activities, and experiences. Only those students who had been matched with each of the sources of data (SDQ, first NSHS survey, second NSHS survey, and institutional data) were selected for analysis. A total of 272 students attending 127 colleges compose the sample. Females constitute 58.1 percent, Chicanos 43.4 percent, Puerto Ricans 22.4 percent, and Other Latinos (including Cubans, Central and South Americans) 34.2 percent of the sample.

Analyses

An exploratory factor analysis was conducted, utilizing principal axis factoring and a varimax rotation method, to reduce the number of measured variables for our small sample and to obtain adequate start values for our causal model. These results are available in Appendix A-2, along with alpha reliabilities. Factor analytic structural equation model (FASEM) analyses were conducted using version 3.0 of the EQS computer program. This software allows the researcher to confirm the factor structures of each of the constructs in the model and simultaneously test the hypothesized relationships among the constructs. It is a counterpart to LISREL that is used primarily in psychology although, increasingly, applications of the software and method are occurring in all fields (Bentler, 1989). The advantage of FASEM analyses over a traditional path analysis is that, in addition to assessing the overall fit of a hypothesized model, the researcher can take into account measurement error in order to obtain more precise coefficient estimates. However, it is difficult to hypothesize *a priori* the existence of correlated error terms in survey data analysis. In this case, the residual matrix revealed that the hypothesized model could be improved with additional paths placed between specific errors terms. These modifications were conducted in accordance with techniques used in previous FASEM analyses without disturbing the critical features of the structural model (Newcomb and Bentler, 1988).

Because membership in student organizations was measured as a series of dichotomous variables, these were not well-suited for inclusion in a structural equation model using normal distribution theory and the EQS software. However, understanding the Sense of Belonging construct in relation to mainstream and culturally-related organizations was important in understanding how each contributes to student's views of their membership in the entire college community. For this reason, we conducted t-tests to show how Sense of Belonging may significantly differ with membership in various organizations that constitute student communities on campus. We also show how these differ for students at two time points, the second and third year of college, in order to demonstrate how participation differs as a student reaches the upper-division stage of their student career.

Results

Sense of Belonging and Participation in Student Organizations

Table 1 shows the mean Sense of Belonging scores of students who are members of typical student organizations on a college campus. Conservative estimates for significance were used (two-tailed tests) in order to assess the differing levels of Sense of Belonging among members and non-members of each organization. It should be kept in mind that most of these students were extremely active in student organizations in high school and were likely to continue their participation in student activities during college. The overall participation of Latino students increases from the sophomore to the junior year in each activity. However, not all members of organizations have significantly higher Sense of Belonging than non-members. For example, only two organizational memberships show significant differences in the sophomore year. Students who belonged to religious organizations and members of sororities and fraternities are more likely to feel a strong Sense of Belonging with the campus community than non-members. Using a less conservative estimate (one-tail), one finds that participants in art, music, dance and social/community organizations also have significantly higher Sense of Belonging in the sophomore year.

In the junior year, student members of religious clubs, social/community organizations, student government activities, and athletics tend to have significantly higher Sense of Belonging than non-members. The strongest significant relationship is associated with membership in social or community organizations ($p = \leq .001$). Fraternity and sorority membership is no longer significant in the junior year, presumably because non-members have increased their participation rates in other types of activities. Using a less conservative estimate, it should be noted that membership in pre-professional or departmental clubs are also associated with significantly higher Sense of Belonging. These findings suggest there are some mainstream but primarily culturally-related activities (religious organizations, cultural expression, and social/community organizations) associated with Sense of Belonging. Members of ethnic student organizations, however, do not have a significantly higher Sense of Belonging than non-members in either year.

Sense of Belonging Model

Initial statistics revealed that the model fit the data moderately well but could be improved by adding parameters. The chi-square for the initial model was 80.841 and 39 degrees of freedom. The Comparative Fit Index (CFI) was .96, and Bentler-Bonnett Normed Fit Index (BBNFI) was .93, with a significant p-value of .001. Modification of the model was conducted by evaluating the residual matrix and the Lagrange Multiplier (LM) Test for additional parameters that would improve the fit of the model. Four parameters were added. Correlations were added between gender and academic self-concept, and between college selectivity and academic self-concept based on the LM Test and studies that support these relationships (Hurtado, 1994b; Astin, 1993; Pascarella, Smart, Ethington, & Nettles, 1987). In addition, a direct effect from the cognitive mapping scale to Sense of Belonging and a correlated error term from feeling a part of the campus community item to the disturbance term of the Transition factor was added to the model. The first change made theoretical sense because it indicates that only specific elements of the transition process may contribute to Sense of Belonging. Although it is difficult to anticipate correlated error terms, this second change also made logical sense because we had asked students to retrospectively assess their transition experience. These changes were added and improved the fit of our final model which is depicted in Figure 2. We have included error terms (variances and correlations) in Table 2 and omitted them from the figure in order to concentrate on the major relationships and to simplify the figure.

After these modifications, the CFI for the second model was .99 and the Bentler-Bonnett Normed Fit Index was .96, with a chi-square of 50.27, 36 degrees of freedom and a nonsignificant p-value of .06. This suggests that the final model fit the data well. Table 4 shows the parameter

Table 1
Means and Standard Deviations of Sense of Belonging Scale by Organization Membership in Second and Third Years

Organization/Activity	Non-Members		Members		T-value
	Mean	S.D.	Mean	S.D.	
Second Year					
Academic Honor Society	7.20 (235)	2.46	7.73 (37)	2.12	-.14
Athletics	7.09 (161)	2.49	7.55 (111)	2.28	-1.57
Ethnic organizations	7.21 (161)	2.39	7.44 (88)	2.50	-.70
Journalism, debating, drama	7.27 (243)	2.46	7.31 (29)	2.06	-.10
Art, music, dance	7.18 (231)	2.46	7.80 (41)	2.12	-1.68
Pre-professional or departmental	7.31 (216)	2.35	7.29 (54)	2.58	.06
Religious	7.10 (205)	2.44	7.80 (67)	2.30	-2.12*
Social or community	7.10 (176)	2.32	7.60 (96)	2.32	-1.66
Student government	7.21 (244)	2.38	7.79 (28)	2.71	-1.07
Sororities/fraternities	7.16 (235)	2.46	8.02 (37)	2.00	-2.35*
Third Year					
Academic Honor Society	7.18 (195)	2.40	7.52 (77)	2.46	- 1.03
Athletics	6.97 (125)	2.44	7.54 (147)	2.38	-1.95*
Ethnic organizations 1	7.41 (122)	2.42	7.16 (150)	2.41	.86
Journalism, debating, drama	7.23 (225)	2.48	7.49 (47)	2.07	-.75
Art, music, dance	7.21 (203)	2.43	7.47 (69)	2.38	-.78
Pre-professional or departmental	7.12 (195)	2.47	7.66 (77)	2.24	-1.74
Religious	7.01 (182)	2.51	7.82 (90)	2.12	-2.79**
Social or community	6.76 (132)	2.52	7.76 (140)	2.21	-3.47 ***
Student government	7.16 (236)	2.45	8.02 (36)	2.02	-2.31*
Sororities/fraternities	7.15 (212)	2.44	7.71 (60)	2.31	-1.61

Numbers in parentheses are the number of cases for each group. *p≤.05; **p≤.01; ***p≤.001

estimates for the final model. The Sense of Belonging equation accounted for 25 percent of the variance, the Hostile Climate equation accounted for 28 percent of the variance, and the Ease in Transition equation accounted for only 6 percent of the variance in the dependent variable. In terms of the latter equation, it was relatively surprising that neither gender nor academic self-concept is significantly related to Ease in Transition in this sample of students. The selectivity of the college, however, has a direct negative effect. This indicates that the higher the selectivity of the institution, the more likely that Latino students were to experience difficulty in their transition to college.

The Ease in Transition factor has a direct negative effect on student perceptions of a Hostile Climate in the second year of college. This indicates that the easier the transition into college, the less likely students are to perceive a hostile climate in the second year. No other significant direct or indirect effects are evident in this equation.

Perception of a Hostile Climate can have a negative direct effect on Sense of Belonging in the third year of college, indicating that Latino students are less likely to feel a part of the campus community if they perceive racial tension or experienced discrimination in their second year. The Ease of Transition has a indirect positive effect but does not have a direct effect on Sense of Belonging. However, one key element of the transition experience has a strong positive effect: the

Figure 2
Final Model of Sense of Belonging

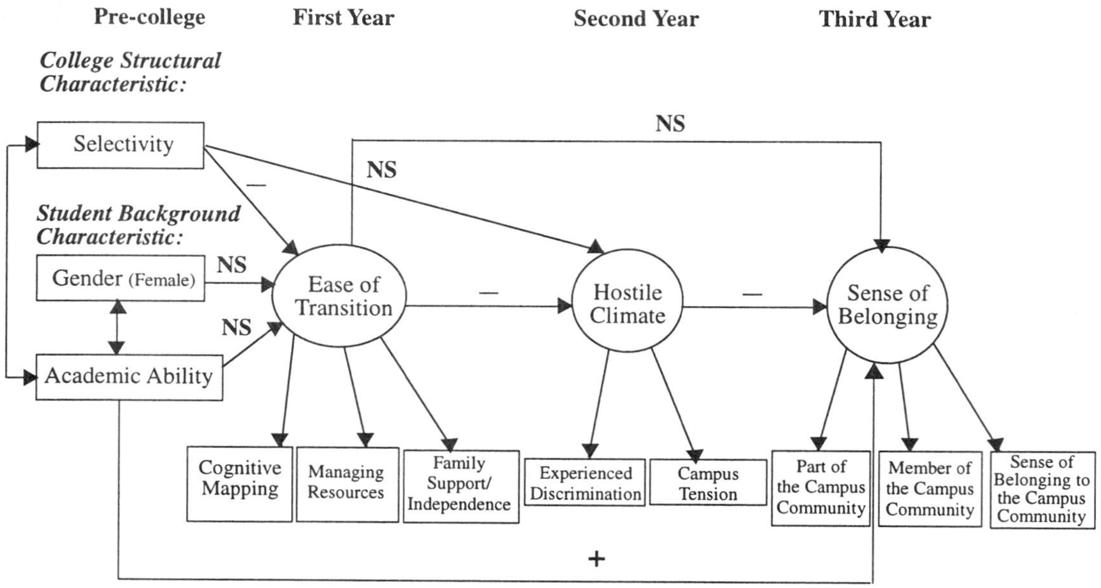

Table 2
Standardized Parameter Estimates for Causal Model

Effects of Observed and Latent Constructs		Regression Weights	Critical Ratio
Direct Effects on:			
Ease of Transition	V3 Gender (Female)	-.10	-1.32
	V5 Academic Self-Concept	.08	1.04
	V9 Selectivity	-.20	-2.50*
Hostile Climate	Selectivity	-.04	-.56
	Ease of Transition	-.53	-4.06***
Sense of Belonging	Ease of Transition	-1.36	-1.00
	Hostile Climate	-.29	-2.66**
	Cognitive Mapping	.43	5.02***
Indirect Effects on:			
Hostile Climate	Gender	.05	.58
	Academic Self-Concept	-.04	-.55
	Selectivity	.11	.57
Sense of Belonging	Gender	-.03	-1.22
	Academic Self-Concept	.02	.99
	Selectivity	-.04	-1.26
	Ease of Transition	.41	3.69***
Correlations	E18,D1	-.26	-1.98*
	Gender, Academic Self-Concept	-.21	-3.39***
	Academic Self-Concept, Selectivity	.13	2.25*
Percent Variance Explained			
	Ease of Transition	.06	3.52***
	Hostile Climate	.28	3.42***
	Sense of Belonging	.25	9.67***

Note: *p≤.05; **p≤.01; ***p≤.001

cognitive mapping or "getting to know" construct. We will return to discuss the implications of this finding in the final section of the paper.

Additional significant relationships in our model include correlations that were added during modification of the model. Specifically, at the pre-college level, academic self-concept is negatively related with gender and positively related with college selectivity. In addition, the error term of one item that composes the Sense of Belonging factor was correlated with the disturbance term of the Ease of Transition factor. We believe this may be due to the fact that students were asked on the second survey to reflect on their transition experiences during the first year of college.

Discussion

We examined a sense of belonging as an alternative approach to the idea of "integration" on college campuses in order to understand how Latino students view their membership in the college community. This allowed us to examine variation in student's sense of belonging in relation to membership in various student communities on campus, a formal type of social integration measure. Results show that specific forms of campus involvements are more likely to significantly enhance students' sense of belonging with the overall community, but these are not always the forms of involvement typically used by other researchers (Pascarella, Smart, Ethington, & Nettles, 1987). For example, membership in religious organizations and social/community organizational activity were strongly associated with student sense of belonging. Findings were somewhat suggestive of organizational involvements that may be culturally-related, although members of ethnic student organizations do not exhibit significantly more sense of belonging than non-members. Members had a higher sense of belonging in some of the more mainstream activities that include athletics, student government and, only in the second year of college, membership in sororities and fraternities. These activities all appear to require a high level of commitment, which may enhance students' sense of belonging. Students are also more likely to be involved in formal student organizations in their junior year, indicating that when a researcher chooses to assess student involvement may be critical to determining its relationship with other student outcomes.

Perhaps the most important finding of our study is that early experiences are key determinants of Latino sense of belonging in later years. As Attinasi (1989) has shown with qualitative data, we found that Latino students' ease in "getting to know" the institution in the freshman year is essential to finding their place in the college community. The overall transition experience has an indirect effect while cognitive mapping, one aspect of the transition process, has a strong positive effect on Sense of Belonging with the college community in the junior year. It is not so much the overall transition experience that includes learning how to manage resources (e.g. time and money) and maintaining family support/independence, but rather this process of negotiating the social, physical, and cognitive geographies of campus that appears to have a lasting effect on students. These findings provide further evidence that supports the importance of early experiences or post-matriculation activities for students that result in helping them to understand how they "fit in" the campus community.

Perceptions of a hostile climate in the second year had a depressing effect on Latino students' sense of belonging in the third year of college. This finding illustrates how important it is for campuses to minimize racial tension and increase cultural awareness, otherwise Latinos may begin to feel like outsiders in the college community. Research evidence regarding the campus climate has begun to show that what was once thought of as an intangible element, based on student perceptions of the college environment, appears to have real social and psychological consequences. These experiences are important to include in future models of minority progress in order to begin to fully assess the impact of the campus climate.

Given that Latino access to four-year institutions is the lowest among the ethnic groups and their attrition is relatively high, this study provides important information for college campuses. First, successful integration of Latino students in colleges and universities is directly dependent upon students having clear information about the campus from peers and faculty. Campuses can enhance Latino students' sense of belonging and facilitate students' cognitive mapping skills through orientations and freshman programs. Institutional efforts to reduce students' experiences of racial discrimination in the college setting and enhance an appreciation for multiculturalism also are important strategies to help Latinos feel like they are a part of the campus community.

Implications for Research

The current paper attempts to bring clarity to the problem of understanding Latino student cohesion with the college environment. It attempts to pinpoint issues in our thinking of integration concepts and incorporate measures that reflect the experiences of Latino students. This study also provides quantitative support for constructs derived from qualitative work on Mexican Americans as others have begun to do in the field (Nora, Attinasi, & Matonak, 1990). We encourage the development of concepts using naturalistic inquiry to discover constructs derived from student experiences that can be subsequently used to understand the dynamics that occur in large samples across many institutional contexts. Perhaps more importantly, the study illustrates that Latino student experiences require a marriage between diverse research methods that are based on students' own perspectives (Attinasi & Nora, 1992). This may include a reconsideration of traditional models and measures, as well as a questioning of our own assumptions regarding elements of the college experience that are important for student success. Future research models may also be improved by including distinct aspects of the minority experience, which involve the transition process and the climate for diversity, in order to better understand aspects of the college experience that can enhance engagement and affiliation on campus.

The next step in research is to expand the model to include more experiences in each of the years of college to identify critical stages in student development. Expanding the range of student experiences within each of the time points may help to identify the types of social experiences that impact students' sense of belonging and subsequent student outcomes. Of particular interest is additional information about students' early experiences, assessing the impact of various conceptualizations of social integration, and incorporating the unique elements of the racialized contexts in which students are educated. The ultimate goal is to develop research models that place the minority experience at the center, with the clear purpose of improving their educational progress.

References

Astin, A. W. (1984). Student involvement: A developmental theory for higher education, *Journal of College Student Personnel*, 25 (4): 297–308.

Astin, A. W. (1993). *What Matters in College? Four-Critical Years Revisited.* San Francisco: Jossey-Bass.

Attinasi, L. C. & Nora, A. The diverse student and complex issues: A case for multiple methods in college student research, in Frances K. Stage and Associates (Eds.), *Diverse Methods for Research and Assessment of College Students.* Alexandria, VA: American College Personnel Association.

Attinasi, L. C., Jr. (1989). Getting in: Mexican Americans' perceptions of university attendance and the implications for freshman year persistence. *Journal of Higher Education* 60 (3): 247–277.

Attinasi, L. C., Jr. (1992). Rethinking the study of outcomes of college attendance, *Journal of College Student Development, Vol.* 33: 61–70.

Bentler, P. M. EQS: *Structural Equations Program Manual.* Los Angeles: BMDP Statistical Software, 1989.

Bollen, K. A. & Hoyle, R. H. (1990). Perceived cohesion: A conceptual and empirical examination, *Social Forces* 69(2): 479–504.

Cabrera, A. F., Castañeda, M.B., Nora, A. & Hengstler, D. (1992). The convergence between two theories of college persistence, *Journal of Higher Education, Vol.* 63 (2): 143–164.

El-Khawas, E. (1989). *Campus Trends, 1989.* Higher education report no. 78. Washington, D.C.: American Council on Education.

Estrada, L.F. (1988). Anticipating the demographic future. *Change,* 20 (3): 14–19.

Hurtado, S. (1994a). The institutional climate for talented Latino students, *Research in Higher Education,* Vol. 35, (3): 21–41.

Hurtado, S. (1994b). Graduate school racial climates and academic self-concept among minority graduate students in the 1970s, *American Journal of Education,* Vol. 102 (forthcoming).

Pace, C. R. (1984). *Measuring the quality of college student experiences.* Los Angeles: Higher Education Research Institute.

Pascarella, E., Smart, J., Ethington, C. & Nettles, M. (1987). The influence of college on self-concept: A consideration of race and gender differences, *American Educational Research Journal, Vol. 24 (1):* 49–77.

Pascarella, E. & Terenzini, P. T. (1991) *How college affects students.* San Francisco: Jossey-Bass.

Pascarella, E., Terenzini, P. T., & Wolfle, L. M. (1986). Orientation to college and freshman year persistence/withdrawal decisions, *Journal of Higher Education, 57 (2):* 155–175.

Nettles, M. T., Thoeny, R. A., Gosman, E. J. (1986). Comparative and predictive analyses of Black and White students' college achievement and experiences. *Journal of Higher Education* 57 (3): 289–317.

Newcomb, M. D. and P. M. Bentler. "Impact of Adolescent Drug Use and Social Support on Problems of Young Adults: A Longitudinal Study." *Journal of Abnormal Psychology, 97,* no. 1, (1988): 64–75.

Newcomb, T. M. (1962). Student peer-group influence. In Nevitt Sanford (ed.), *The American College: A Psychological and Social Interpretation of the Higher Learning.* New York: John Wiley.

Nora, A. (1987). Determinants of retention among Chicano college students: A structural model, *Research in Higher Education,* 26, 31–59.

Nora, A., Attinasi, L.C., Jr., & Matonak, A. (1990). Testing qualitative indicators of pre-college factors in Tinto's Attrition Model: A community college population, *Review of Higher Education,* Vol. 13 (3): 337–356.

Oliver, M. L., Rodriguez, C. J., & Mickelson, R. A. (1985). Brown and black in white: The social adjustment and academic performance of Chicano and black students in a predominantly white university. *Urban review: Issues and Ideas in Public Education,* 17 (1), 3–24.

Rendon, L. I. & Nora, A. (1988). Hispanic students: Stopping the leaks in the pipeline. *Educational Record* (Fall/winter): 79–85.

Smedley, B. D., Myers, H. F., Harrell, S. P. (1993). Minority-status stresses and the college adjustment of ethnic minority freshmen, *Journal of Higher Education,* Vol. 64 (4); 434–452.

Stage, F. K. 1989. Reciprocal effects between the academic and social integration of college students, *Research in Higher Education,* 30: 517–530.

Terenzini, P.T. & Wright, T. M. (1987a). Students' personal growth during the first two years of college, *Review of Higher Education,* Vol. 10 (3): 259–271.

Terenzini, P.T. & Wright, T. M. (1987b). Influences on students' academic growth during four years of college, *Research in Higher Education,* Vol. 26, (2): 161–179.

Tierney, W. G. (1992). An anthropological analysis of student participation in college. *Journal of Higher Education* 63(6): 603–617.

Williams, J. B. III, (1988). *Desegregating America's Colleges and Universities.* New York: Teachers College Press.

Appendices

Table A-I
Variables and Scales for Statistical Model

		Mean	S.D.
Dependent Measure			
Sense of belonging to campus community	Scale Items in Table A-2	7.28	2.42
Student Background Characteristics			
Gender (Female)	Dichotomous: 1=male; 2=female	1.58	—
Academic Self-Concept	Scale Items in Table A-2	3.32	.46
College Structural Characteristics			
Selectivity	Mean SAT of entering freshmen scaled from 1=400 to 12=1600	7.84	1.44
College Transition Measures			
Managing Resources	Scale Items in A-2	2.17	.61
Family independence and support	Scale Items in A-2	2.69	.63
Cognitive Mapping	Scale Items in A-2	2.81	.62
General College Climate Measures			
Perceptions of racial/ethnic tension	Scale Items in A-2	2.00	.62
Experienced discrimination/exclusion	Scale Items in A-2	1.15	.29

Table A-2
Scales and Survey Items used in Analysis

Factors and Survey Items	Factor Loading	Internal Consistency (Alpha)
Sense of Belonging to Campus		.94
I see myself as a part of the campus community[a]	.91	
I feel that I am a member of the campus community[a]	.83	
I feel a sense of belonging to the campus community[a]	.82	
Academic Self-concept		.62
Self-rating of Mathematical Ability[b]		
Self-rating of Scientific Ability[b]		
Self-rating of Writing Ability[b]		
Cognitive Mapping		.70
Seeking help when I needed it[c]	.71	
Getting to know my way around[c]	.67	
Communicating with instructors[c]	.50	
Making new friends[c]	.47	
Managing Resources		.71
Staying on a schedule[c]	.87	
Managing my time effectively[c]	.80	
Managing money effectively[c]	.35	
Separation from family		.62
Being separated from family[c]	.72	
Been lonely or homesick (reversed for analyses)[d]	-.47	
Maintaining family relationships[c]	.43	
Experienced Discrimination/Exclusion		.61
Were insulted or threatened by other students because of your Hispanic background[e]	.60	
Heard faculty make inappropriate remarks regarding minorities[e]	.55	
Felt excluded from school activities because of your Hispanic background[e]	.48	
Perceptions of Campus Racial/Ethnic Tension		.63
There is a lot of campus racial conflict here[f]	.85	
Students of different racial/ethnic origins communicate well with one another (reversed for analyses)[f]	-.38	
There is little trust between minority student groups and campus administrators[f]	.33	

Note: [a]Eleven-point scale: from "strongly disagree"=0 to "strongly agree"= 10
     [b]Factor developed through exploratory procedures in Hurtado (1993).
      Four-point scale: from "below average"=1 to "highest 10%"=4
     [c]Four-point scale: from "very difficult"=1 to "very easy"=4
     [d]Three-point scale: from "not at all"= 1 to "frequently"=3
     [e]Three-point scale: from "not at all "= 1 to "frequently"=3
     [f]Four-point scale: from "disagree strongly" 1 to "agree strongly"=4

Table A-3
Measurement Model Estimates

Factors	Factor Loadings	Error Terms
Ease of Transition		
Cognitive Mapping	.61	.79
Managing Resources	.51	.86
Family Independence and Support	.65	.76
Hostile Climate		
Perceptions of Racial/Ethnic Tension	.65	.76
Experienced Discrimination/Exclusion	.66	.75
Sense of Belonging		
Part of campus community	.99	.25
Feel member of campus community	.91	.42
Sense of belonging to campus community	.93	.37

A Conceptual Model of Nontraditional Undergraduate Student Attrition

JOHN P. BEAN AND BARBARA S. METZNER

Older, part-time, and commuter students have composed an increasingly larger portion of college student bodies. The reasons why these students drop out of school are not well understood. The purpose of this paper is to describe the rise in nontraditional enrollments, define the nontraditional undergraduate student, and develop a conceptual model of the attrition process for these students. The chief difference between the attrition process of traditional and nontraditional students is that nontraditional students are more affected by the external environment than by the social integration variables affecting traditional student attrition.

Older, part-time, and commuter students have composed an increasingly larger proportion of undergraduate collegiate student bodies and are predicted to continue this trend as the number of traditional age college students decreases (Carnegie Council, 1980; U.S. Department of Education, 1982). While increasing in number, these nontraditional students show a higher rate of attrition from college than their traditional counterparts (Astin, 1975; Fetters, 1977). The reasons why these students drop out of school are not well understood.

The need for additional research about the attrition of older, part-time, and commuter undergraduate students enrolled in courses for college credit has been well documented (Knoell, 1966; Lenning, Beal, & Sauer, 1980; Tinto, 1975, 1982; Zaccaria & Creaser, 1971). Although older and part-time students have sometimes been included with traditional students in studies of attrition, little research has been devoted exclusively to these nontraditional students beyond a simple tabulation of the dropout rate. The attrition studies conducted with commuter students, particularly at community colleges, have been overwhelmingly descriptive. No theoretical model has been available to guide attrition research on the nontraditional student enrolled in institutions of higher education (IHEs).

The purpose of this paper is to develop a conceptual model of the dropout process for the nontraditional undergraduate student. The form (linkages) of the model is derived from models of traditional student attrition and other behavioral theories, and the substance (elements linked) comes from an extensive review of the literature on nontraditional students. Before proceeding with the development of the model, we will first describe the forces that resulted in the increase of this population, and then we will define nontraditional students.

Increases in Nontraditional Student Enrollment

Institutional, curricular, political, economic, and social factors led to the dramatic rise in the enrollment levels of nontraditional students. Of the 12 million college students enrolled today, over half of the undergraduate students are women, 2 of 5 are over 25 years old, more than 40% attend college part-time, and 1 of 6 is a member of an ethnic minority group (National Institute of Education [NIE], 1984).

Community colleges rely almost exclusively on older, part-time, and commuter students (Riesman, 1981). The community college sector experienced the greatest amount of growth since World War II, with over 600 of these institutions being formed since 1960 (NIE, 1984). Growth in this sector substantially contributed to the increased number of nontraditional college students, but these students were found in ever larger numbers at other types of institutions as well. By 1980, of full-time students, 68% of the students enrolled in public universities were commuters as were 66% of 4-year college students and 58% of private university students (Andersen & Atelsek, 1982).

Besides the rise in the number of community colleges whose missions often explicitly focused on nontraditional students, 4-year institutions also have accommodated new student demands. Projections for smaller numbers of 18- to 23-year-olds caused many administrators to believe that institutional survival depended on finding nontraditional students to replace the loss of traditional ones. Institutions expanded their curricular of offerings and missions, often from a liberal arts emphasis to the inclusion of a smorgasbord of vocationally oriented certification and degree programs. IHEs offered their courses at times and places convenient to students with family or employment responsibilities. Weekend and evening programs and courses taught in shopping malls or other central locations contributed to the growth in nontraditional student enrollment.

Political forces also contributed to this enrollment growth. The Allied victory in World War II was accompanied by democratic jubilation, including burgeoning support for democratic institutions. The main theme *of Higher Education for American Democracy,* the 1947 report of President Truman's Commission on Higher Education, was "education for all" (Trivett, 1973). The political popularity of institutionalizing this goal is reflected in the fact that by 1977, 1,240 community colleges existed in 426 of the 435 U.S. congressional districts (Gilder, 1980).

The Truman Commission Report also contained results from Army studies suggesting that "at least 49 percent of our population has the mental ability to complete 14 years of schooling" and "32 percent . . . has the mental ability to complete an advanced liberal or specialized professional education" (quoted in Trivett, 1973, p. 13). The Gl Bill (Public Law 346, passed in June 1944) became the chief instrument for access to higher education for Americans who might not have considered further study, and they enrolled in unexpectedly large numbers (Henry, 1975).

Another jolt to the educational system occurred after the Soviet Union's successful launch of Sputnik. This event gave impetus to the passage of the National Defense Education Act of 1958, followed by the Higher Education Act of 1965. Both Acts endorsed the political view that encouraging college attendance promoted the general welfare of the nation and that the federal government, in addition to state governments, had a legitimate role in financially supporting higher education institutions. More recently, Basic Educational Opportunity Grants, which were part of the Higher Education Act amendments of 1972, the Pell Grants which followed, and a variety of state financial aid programs indicated the continued political legitimacy of providing resources to many nontraditional students. In addition, the Carnegie Commission on Higher Education endorsed lifelong learning and universal access to educational institutions.

Economic factors have influenced the enrollment levels of nontraditional students. The decline in the blue-collar sector of the economy has had a profound effect on college enrollments, as large numbers of workers entering or reentering the labor force must choose either low-paying jobs in the service sector or higher paying jobs in the technical, business, or professional service areas which require specialized training. Higher education institutions have become the gatekeepers to many of these positions, and nontraditional students have enrolled in various vocational, technical, and professional programs to obtain access to preferred work. Viewing community colleges as a means of "cooling out" nontraditional students from the higher education system (Clark, 1960) has become a less useful interpretation of their role, given the increased acceptance of associate degree programs as a means of entry into skilled and technical careers. Placed in a flexible educational system and an economy based on jobs requiring specialized skills, large numbers of nontraditional students entered educational institutions for vocational purposes.

Finally, several norms in American society have been changing. Until World War II, women's roles in society were limited largely to traditional work roles, such as food service employees, secretaries, nurses, teachers, and unpaid housework and child care. As society's views of women's capabilities have changed, women have been drawn into educational programs that were once the exclusive domain of men, so that women now constitute the majority of both full-time and part-time students in American higher education. A second and related social change involves the structure of the American household. Many couples feel that two incomes are necessary for personal and financial reasons, and consequently enroll in educational programs they believe will lead to higher paying jobs. Couples are having fewer children and possess more discretionary money, not only for a child's higher education but for their own continuing study. Last, there has been widespread social acceptance of life-long learning for vocational and avocational reasons, including college attendance for older, part-time, and commuting students (Cross, 1981).

In spite of the spectacular growth in nontraditional student enrollments, the likelihood of nontraditional students finishing a degree program is much less than for traditional students. Before identifying the reasons for nontraditional student attrition, we will more clearly define nontraditional students.

Defining Nontraditional Students

Nontraditional students can be from any part of the country; from rural or urban settings; rich or poor; black, white, or Hispanic; 18 years old or older; not employed, working full- or part-time, or retired; male or female; with or without dependents; married, single, or divorced; and enrolled for vocational or avocational reasons in a single course or in a degree or certificate program. Due to this heterogeneity it is very difficult to develop a profile of a typical nontraditional student. For this reason, the focus of our definition is on the differences between traditional and nontraditional students.

Stewart and Rue (1983), in their essay defining the commuter student, identified nontraditional students as being 25 or older. Age alone does not seem to reflect completely what we would consider nontraditional. If one defines traditional students as residing on campus, 18–24 years old, and attending college full-time, it is easiest, though not completely satisfactory, to consider as nontraditional students those who lack one or more of these characteristics. At any rate, these three factors must be considered in a definition of nontraditional students.

A nontraditional student usually does not live in a college residence and therefore must commute to classes. Chickering (1974) believes this to be the most important distinction between the "new" and traditional students, because living arrangements have a profound influence on the socialization of the traditional student. The second characteristic that differentiates traditional from nontraditional students is age. Older students, who have already developed self-control and values typically identified with maturity, are less susceptible to socialization than their traditional counterparts. Thus, the types of development described by Chickering (1969) and Parsons and Platt (1973) for undergraduates may not occur for the older student. The third characteristic associated with nontraditional students is part-time attendance. Again, enrolling in an institution part-time reduces the amount of student-to-student and student-to-faculty contact and therefore the socializing influence of attending college (Pascarella, 1980).

The difference between traditional and nontraditional students is a matter of extent; traditional and nontraditional students cannot be easily classified into simple dichotomous categories. These two groups of students can be differentiated on the basis of age, residence, and full- or part-time attendance, not to mention ethnicity gender, or socioeconomic status, which might have differentiated traditional and nontraditional students a century ago. But it seems unlikely that a widely acceptable formula can be derived that precisely distinguishes traditional from nontraditional students. For example, it is questionable to say that a student who is enrolled for 8 credit hours one semester is nontraditional but that the same student who enrolls for 12 credit hours the next semester is traditional; yet to suggest that a student enrolled for 3 hours is similar to the one enrolled for 15 hours is unwise. It is necessary, but not sufficient, for a nontraditional student to have at least one of three characteristics (part-time, commuter, older than 24).

Nontraditional students are distinguished by the lessened intensity and duration of their interaction with the primary agents of socialization (faculty, peers) at the institutions they attend. As a result, the IHE is not a "total adult socializing institution" for them as suggested by Rootman (1972). Nontraditional (commuting) students are less likely to progress through the vectors of self-development than traditional students because they lack adequate contact with students and faculty (Chickering, 1969, 1974). For the same reason, they are less likely to change from an undifferentiated to a differentiated, more mature state due to attending a college or university (Parsons & Platt, 1973).

They will not become socialized to the values of their student peers or faculty members because their "net climate" (Rossi, 1966) of socializing agents remains largely what it has been. While traditional students attend college for both social and academic reasons (Tinto, 1975), for nontraditional students, academic reasons are paramount. Here, we do not wish *academic* to mean scholarly, but rather those factors associated with taking *courses* for vocational, avocational, certification, or other utilitarian reasons. Tinto (1975) described an economic analysis used by traditional college students for decisions about continued college attendance. With the focus on utility among nontraditional college students, it is very likely that they use a similar process, but emphasize utilitarian more than social outcomes.

Whereas the traditional student is in a social environment and a degree program, which are expected to have a long-term impact, the nontraditional student does not greatly change his or her social environment and may or may not be seeking a degree. Thus, we come to our appropriately cumbersome definition of a nontraditional student: A nontraditional student is older than 24, or does not live in a campus residence (e.g., is a commuter), or is a part-time student, or some combination of these three factors; is not greatly influenced by the social environment of the institution; and is chiefly concerned with the institution's academic offerings (especially courses, certification, and degrees).

The definition of student attrition can be equally perplexing (Tinto, 1982). For example, should a person who wants to take only a single course and successfully completes that course be considered a dropout because the person did not complete a degree? For the purposes of developing the model, a dropout is considered to be any student who enrolls at an institution one semester but does not enroll the next semester and has not completed his or her formally declared program of study. The two most obvious limitations of this definition are that the institutional perspective of dropout is used rather than a national perspective and that the period considered (semester to semester) is brief, so that stopouts would not be differentiated from dropouts. Since many nontraditional students drop out, stop out, or transfer, a researcher needs to be careful to choose an operational definition of attrition that is appropriate for the research problem to be investigated.

Structure of the Model

The most influential theoretical contributions to understanding the student attrition process, those of Spady (1970), Tinto (1975), and Pascarella (1980), relied heavily on socialization or similar social processes (e.g., shared values and friendship support) to explain the attrition process. One defining characteristic of the nontraditional student was the lack of social integration into the institution; therefore, a different theory must be used to link the variables in this model.

Older, part-time, and commuter students experience an environmental press (Murray, 1938) while attending college that differs from that of traditional age, full-time, residential students. For these nontraditional students, the environmental press includes (a) less interaction in the college environment with peers or faculty members and less interaction through extracurricular activities and the use of campus services, (b) class-related activities very similar to traditional students, and (c) much greater interaction with the noncollegiate, external environment. Pascarella and Chapman (1983) substantiated these differences between several residential and commuter institutions regarding the relative effect of the collegiate environmental press on student attrition. Unfortunately, no research was located that assessed the relative contribution of external environmental factors to explain the attrition process for traditional and nontraditional students. Thus, due to the unimportance of socialization in the college environment and the presumed importance of the noncollegiate environment, the underlying process of attrition proposed here differs for nontraditional students.

The theories of traditional student attrition contain elements other than socialization, which should not be ignored. Each contains a set of background variables expected to affect how a student will interact with the institution, each indicates that dropout is a longitudinal process, and each identifies a set of academic variables that are expected to affect attrition decisions. These relationships will be maintained in the model.

The conceptual model is presented in Figure 1. Briefly, the model indicates that dropout decisions will be based primarily on four sets of variables. Students with poor academic performance are expected to drop out at higher rates than students who perform well, and GPA is expected to be based primarily on past (high school) academic performance. The second major factor is intent to leave, which is expected to be influenced primarily by the psychological outcomes but also by the academic variables. The third group of variables expected to affect attrition are the background and defining variables—primarily high school performance and educational goals. These effects, however, may be mediated by other endogenous variables in the model. Finally, the environmental variables are expected to have substantial direct effects on dropout decisions.

In a path model, the indirect effects of a variable on dropout can be calculated, and the statistical significance of these effects can be tested. For example, although high school grades may not have a significant direct effect on dropout, high school grades would be expected to have a significant direct effect on college grades, and college grades, in turn, would be expected to have a significant direct effect on dropout. Thus, high school grades could have a significant indirect effect on dropout.

When estimating a path model, a common convention is to calculate both direct and indirect effects for each of the independent variables in order to find those variables having the greatest total (direct + indirect) effects on the dependent variable. Due to their importance in understanding the interrelationships between the variables in this model, and as a guide to further research, indirect effects of particular salience will be identified.

A variety of behavioral theories and models of student attrition were used as the basis on which to link the variables. The superficial similarity of this model to the previous models of Bean (1982a, 1985) should not mask the underlying differences especially in the variables themselves. These variables were identified as important predictors of nontraditional student attrition in the literature reviewed for this study.

Two compensatory interaction effects are included in the model and are indicated by dotted lines. The predicted interactions are similar to the compensatory effects between social and academic integration identified by Tinto (1975) and found by Pascarella and Chapman (1983). Environmental variables are presumed to be more important for nontraditional students than academic variables, which leads to the following results. When academic and environmental variables are both good (e.g., favorable for persistence), students should remain in school, and when both are poor, students should leave school. When academic variables are good but environmental variables are poor, students should leave school, and the positive effects of the academic variables on retention will not be seen. When environmental support is good and academic support is poor, students would be expected to remain enrolled—the environmental support compensates for low scores on the academic variables. For example, if students cannot make adequate child care arrangements, or adjust their work schedules, or pay for college, they will not continue in school regardless of good academic support. Students who are encouraged to remain in school by family and employers will probably do so despite poor academic advising or

Figure 1
A Conceptual Model of Nontraditional Student Attrition

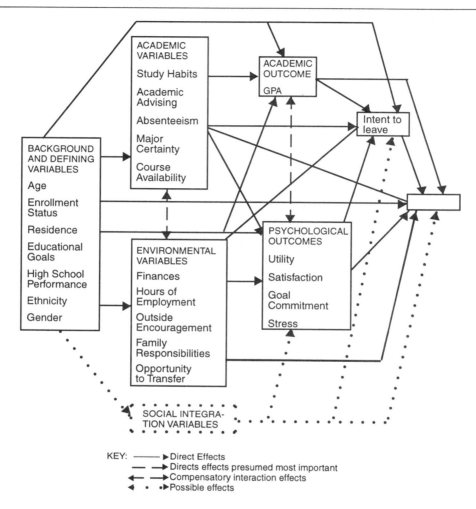

KEY: ———▶Direct Effects
        — —▶Directs effects presumed most important
        ◀———▶Compensatory interaction effects
        ◀ ∙ ∙ ●▶Possible effects

uncertainty of major. Thus, for nontraditional students, environmental support compensates for weak academic support, but academic support will not compensate for weak environmental support. These relationships can be examined empirically by an analysis of interaction effects.

The second compensatory effect is between the academic outcome, GPA, and the psychological outcomes. Students who score high in both should remain in school, while students who score low in both would be expected to drop out. However, students may drop out of school despite high GPAs if they perceive low levels of utility, satisfaction, or goal commitment, or have high levels of stress. Others may continue in school despite low GPAs if they receive positive psychological outcomes from attendance. Again, the nonacademic factors compensate for low levels of academic success, while high levels of academic achievement only result in continued attendance when accompanied by positive psychological outcomes from school.

The background variables are included not only because they appear in most conceptual models of student attrition (Bean, 1982a; Pascarella, 1980: Spady, 1970; Tinto, 1975), but also because past behavior is expected to predict future behavior (Bentler & Speckart, 1979). For example, high school percentile rank as an indicator of past academic achievement, should influence attrition decisions by affecting college GPA. Furthermore, the major defining variables of nontraditional students (age, enrollment status, and residence) are included as reminders that they must be controlled or they would be expected to interact with other variables. For instance, if a research project focused on part-time commuter students, these three defining variables were included to remind the researcher to assess the impact of age on attrition, since age was not a variable in sample selection.

Lewin (1935) described behavior as a function of the person and the environment. Whereas residential students are primarily concerned with the internal environment of the Institution, nontraditional students are much more closely connected with the external environment. The external environment, which may pull a student from the college environment, seems like a highly valuable source of variables related to nontraditional student attrition (Metzner, 1984; Staman, 1980). External contacts reduce the likelihood that students will be socialized by college contacts.

The academic variables represent the primary way in which nontraditional students interact with the institution. Such variables are expected to have a direct effect on academic performance (GPA). According to Tinto's model, the more a student interacts with the institution, the more likely the student will be committed to staying at the institution. Thus, these variables should also be negatively related to intent to leave.

According to Locke (1976), it is the evaluation of our past experiences that gives rise to our attitudes. Therefore, it is the student's experiences, both in and out of school, that influence the attitudes about his or her education and ultimately the decision to continue in school. The academic and environmental variables should directly influence the psychological outcomes and attitudes toward school. Besides psychological outcomes, Spady (1970) originally posited that college grades, which result from a student's past academic work and experiences in school, will directly affect attrition decisions. This relationship was specified because involuntary student attrition (dismissal) may be the direct result of low GPAs. GPA is therefore expected to directly affect dropout whether a student is traditional or not.

According to Fishbein and Ajzen (1975), attitudes lead to intentions, which in turn lead to behavior. In this instance, the attitudes toward the academic experience at school should affect the intent to continue in school, which in turn results in a student's actually staying in or leaving school. It is through the use of these theories that the sets of variables in the model are linked.

In contrast to the great importance assigned to the institution's social environment in the attrition process for traditional students, the social interaction variables in the current model are assumed to be of comparatively little importance. We do not wish to imply that informal contact with faculty or participation in extracurricular activities with peers are unimportant in individual cases—for some students they may be determining factors for remaining at a college. However, for most nontraditional students, especially as we have defined them here, such student participation is relatively rare and hence less important when compared to other factors.

Given the theoretical relationships between the various sets of factors in the model, the specification of particular variables to be included in the model must be done with great care. Decisions to include particular variables were made on the basis of their consistency with theory and the findings from an extensive search of the literature, including books, articles, ERIC documents, and dissertations. Literature from three major content areas was used: attrition research with traditional students attending residential institutions, descriptive literature about nontraditional students that did not measure attrition, and attrition research with nontraditional students. The remainder of the text reports the rationale for the inclusion of each variable in the study, as well as noting why others, which on an a priori basis should be included, were not.

The following literature review may assist in the design of future studies. The student attrition literature regarding traditional students is quite extensive; consequently, reviews of research have been periodically published to synthesize the findings from many empirical studies. Such publications will be designated as *codifications*.

Defining and Background Variables

Three defining variables—age, enrollment status, and residence—are included al this stage in the model. In addition, four background variables are expected to affect how nontraditional students interact with the institution and thus must be taken into account in modeling the attrition process.

These variables are educational goals, high school performance, ethnicity, and gender. Parents' education, important for traditional age student retention, is discussed but excluded from the model.

Age

The majority of codifications that addressed the relationship of students' age to attrition concluded that age per se was not a major factor, although some correlates of students' age, such as family responsibility and hours of employment, might be significantly associated with attrition (Lenning et al., 1980; Pantages & Creedon, 1978; Sexton, 1965; Skaling, 1971; Summerskill, 1962).

Several studies conducted at commuter institutions reported a positive association between students' age and attrition from college: *commuter-oriented 4-year institutions* (Gordon & Johnson, 1982; Pascarella, Duby, Miller, & Rasher, 1981; Smith, 1980; Tweddale, 1978); *2-year colleges* (Aiken, 1968; Brunner, Packwood, & Wilson, 1978; Gorter, 1978; Greer, 1980; Hunter & Sheldon, 1980; R. Johnson, 1980). Other research at these types of institutions, however, failed to note a significant association: *commuter-oriented 4-year institutions* (Louis, Colten, & Demeke, 1984; Pascarella & Chapman, 1983); *2-year colleges* (DeVecchio, 1972; Pascarella & Chapman, 1983; White, 1972).

In the model, it is assumed that older students will have more family responsibilities, hours of employment, and higher levels of absenteeism than younger students. The indirect effects of age on dropout should be through these variables.

Enrollment Status

This variable refers to the number of academic credits for which a student was enrolled during the term when the initial assessment of students occurred. Students are usually considered to be part-time if they enroll for fewer than 12 semester credit hours. Only one codification (Lenning et al., 1980) acknowledged a relationship between this variable and student attrition and concluded that part-time students showed a greater rate of attrition than full-time students.

Several studies at primarily commuter 4- and 2-year institutions furnished very strong evidence that students who were enrolled on a part-time compared to a full-time basis were more likely to drop out of college (Alfred, 1973; Behrendt, 1974; Brunner et al., 1978; Cohen, 1969; Everett, 1979; Fetters, 1977, Martin, 1974 Knoell, 1976; Smith, 1980; Tweddale, 1978).

Although most studies employed a dichotomous variable of part-time/full-time enrollment based on credit hours, some research used *credits attempted* as a continuous variable (Rice, 1983; Staman, 1980; Tata, 1981). In these latter studies, credits attempted during a term showed a negative association with attrition. One study (California State Coordinating Council, 1974) examined the relationship between credits attempted *within* the part-time student classification and still noted a negative relationship with attrition.

Most older students attend college on a part-time basis (Greer, 1980; Rauch, 1981; Solmon & Gordon, 1981). Staman (1980) reported a negative association between credits attempted and the attrition of older students who attended a commuter-oriented, 4-year college.

In the model, it is assumed that students often enroll on a part-time basis due to other responsibilities. Thus, older students are more likely to enroll part-time than younger students. Furthermore, there should be a substantial positive relationship between being a part-time student and hours of employment.

Residence

Commuter students are a diverse group about which generalizations must be made with caution. Nonetheless, these students appear to be dissimilar to residential students on several key factors that are relevant to retention decisions. Commuter compared to residential, students spend little time on campus outside of class (Chickering & Kuper, 1971; Flanagan, 1976; Lackey, 1977; Ward & Kurz 1969). Commuters generally have fewer friends at college, less contact with faculty members outside of class, and less participation in extracurricular activities (Chickering, 1974; Everett, 1979; Nelson, 1982; Ward & Kurz, 1969; Welty, 1976). Chickering and Kuper (1971), however, found little difference between residential and commuter students regarding academic activities, such as experiences in the classroom or time spent preparing assignments.

Commuters usually express a greater concern about financing their education than residents (Chickering, 1974; Fenske & Scott, 1972; Ward & Kurz, 1969). More commuters are employed and are more likely to have family responsibilities than residential students, a condition that often causes conflicts between time and priorities (Dressel & Nisula, 1966; Fenske & Scott, 1972; Kuh & Ardaiolo, 1979; Ward & Kurz, 1969). Gusfield, Kronus, and Mark (1970) summarily described commuter institutions as being composed of "student bodies without clearly developed student cultures" (p. 39). The absence of a student culture suggests a weak effect of on-campus social interactions on the attrition process.

In the model, it is assumed that few nontraditional students will reside on campus. Residence is, in fact, the most critical variable distinguishing nontraditional from traditional students. To estimate the model, residence would be controlled by using only commuting students in the data analysis.

Educational Goals

Students' educational goals at the time of matriculation include the highest level of college education sought, the amount of importance ascribed to obtaining a college education, and the likelihood of completing an educational goal at the present institution (a variable Tinto identified as institutional commitment). Seven codifications (Cope & Hannah, 1975; Lenning et al., 1980; Pantages & Creedon, 1978; Skaling, 1971; Spady, 1970; Summerskill, 1962; Tinto, 1975) acknowledged that students' initial educational goals may contain motivational influences that affect persistence at a college.

The following empirical studies demonstrated that one or more of students' pre-enrollment educational goals affected persistence at: *residence-oriented 4-year institutions* (Astin, 1972, 1975; Coker, 1968; Hackman & Dysinger, 1970; Marks, 1967; Mattox, 1984; Nelson, Scott, & Bryan, 1984; Panos & Astin, 1968; Peng & Fetters, 1978; Rossmann & Kirk, 1970); *commuter-oriented 4-year institutions* (Baumgart & Johnstone, 1977; Pascarella et al., 1981; Staman, 1980; Tata, 1981); *commuter 2-year colleges* (Astin, 1972; MacMillan, 1969; Peng & Fetters, 1978). Other researchers, however, did not confirm such findings at residence-oriented 4-year institutions (Munro, 1981; Pascarella & Terenzini, 1980, 1983; Slocum, 1956; Terenzini, Lorang, & Pascarella, 1981) or at a commuter university (Pascarella, Duby, & Iverson, 1983).

Two major models of student attrition (Pascarella, 1980; Tinto, 1975) incorporated students' initial educational goals, expectations, and commitments as background factors, which were expected to create indirect effects on persistence by influencing students' interaction with the college environment. In a test of Tinto's model at a residential university (Pascarella & Terenzini, 1983) and an urban commuter university (Pascarella et al., 1983), students' initial educational goals did not directly affect persistence; however, these goals produced significant indirect effects on persistence through students' academic and social integration at the residential university and through academic integration at the commuter university. No research was found that adequately examined the relationship between pre-enrollment educational goals and the persistence of part-time or older students.

Some writers (e.g., Alfred, 1973; Walleri, 1981) contended that many students at commuter institutions, especially community colleges, did not seek a college degree but enrolled in one or a few credit courses for job enhancement or personal enrichment. Furthermore, these students compared to degree-seeking students frequently showed inordinate rates of attrition, perhaps because their short-term educational goals had been completed (Behrendt, 1974; Brainard, 1973; Brunner et al., 1978). According to Alfred, such students are not comparable to students with a longer term goal of a college degree who prematurely discontinue progress toward a degree. Alfred suggested that students with short-term (non-degree) pre-enrollment educational goals be studied as a separate subgroup in attrition research. Measures of students' pre-enrollment educational goals might therefore contain response categories that permit this subgroup identification. No research was found that exclusively investigated attrition for such a subgroup.

Educational goals, then, have been included in the present model as background variables because of (a) empirical studies and previous models that indicate direct and indirect effects of these variables on persistence and (b) a possible need to identify a subgroup of students without degree aspirations. Educational goals should have significant indirect effects on dropout through major certainty, opportunity to transfer, goal commitment, and intent to leave.

High School Academic Performance

The following codifications reported a substantial positive relationship between students' persistence in college and their high school grade average, high school class rank, and precollege scores on standardized tests of academic ability: Summerskill, 1962; Sexton, 1965; Bucklin and Bucklin, 1970; Skaling, 1971; Tinto, 1975; Pantages and Creedon, 1978; Lenning et al., 1980. According to Tinto and Pantages and Creedon, high school grade average and high school rank are stronger predictors of persistence than scores on tests of academic ability.

Studies at primarily residence-oriented 4-year institutions revealed that students' persistence was positively related to their *high school* grade *average* (Astin, 1972, 1975; Coker, 1968; Dulniak, 1982; R. Johnson, 1980; Marks, 1967; Mattox, 1984), *high school class rank* (Astin, 1975; Blanchfield, 1971; Chase, 1970; Demitroff, 1974; Iffert, 1957; Peng & Fetters, 1978; Trent & Medsker, 1968), and *scores on tests of academic ability* (Astin, 1972, 1975; Coker, 1968; Dulniak, 1982; Marks, 1967; Mattox, 1984; Naylor & Sanford, 1982).

Several investigators (Chickering, 1974; Chickering & Kuper, 1971; Fenske & Scott, 1972) found that commuter students frequently possessed lower high school rank, grade averages, and scores on tests of academic ability than residential students. Furthermore, older students often demonstrated lower high school grade averages than traditional age students (Cross, 1981; Greer, 1980; Kuh & Ardaiolo, 1979; Solmon & Gordon, 1981).

Smith (1980), Staman (1980), Pascarella and Chapman (1983), and Pascarella et al. (1983) examined student attrition at commuter-oriented 4-year institutions. In these studies, persistence was positively related to high school grade average (Smith; Staman; Pascarella & Chapman), high school rank (Smith), and scores on tests of academic ability (Smith; Pascarella et al.). Staman reported that high school grade average discriminated between dropouts and persisters who were continuing students age 22–45 but produced no significant effect for beginning or continuing students age 17–21.

Some researchers (Jaffe & Adams, 1970; Pascarella & Chapman, 1983; Roueche, 1967; Weigel, 1969; White, 1972) failed to note a direct relationship between measures of high school academic performance and student persistence at community colleges. However, Astin (1972), DeVecchio (1972), Eagle (1979), and R. Johnson (1980) found that high school grade average was positively related to persistence. Peng and Fetters (1978) reported that high school rank was positively associated with the persistence of a national sample of students attending 2-year colleges.

In general, measures of high school academic performance currently seem to be among the strongest pre-enrollment predictors of persistence for students at both residence-oriented and commuter institutions, although extremely limited research has been conducted with older college students. In the model, the indirect effect of high school performance on attrition is expected to occur primarily through its influence on college GPA.

Ethnicity

Two codifications addressed the relationship between students' ethnicity and college student attrition. Lenning et al. (1980) stated that although black students showed a lower rate of retention (graduation) than white students, black students exhibited a higher rate of retention than white students when high school academic ability levels were controlled. Dunston, Richmond, and House (1983a, 1983b) provided a review of the literature regarding black student retention at predominately white colleges; while acknowledging that there were several differences in college experiences for blacks and whites, rates of black student attrition were generally higher.

Empirical studies at predominately white institutions typically measured students' eth according to the following categories: white, black; white, nonwhite; nonminority, minorit white, black, Hispanic. This research produced varied results about the association of ethnicity with attrition as presented below. MacMillan (1969), Astin (1975), and Bennett and Bean (1984) reported that black students had lower persistence rates than white students. In other studies, higher persistence rates were found for black versus white students (Alfred, 1973) and for black versus other ethnic groups (Nelson et al., 1984).

From research with two national samples of students who attended 4- and 2-year colleges, Astin (1972) and Peng and Fetters (1978) disclosed that black students at 4-year institutions showed greater persistence than white students when measures of past academic achievement, aspiration, and socioeconomic status were controlled. When such controls were applied to data from students attending 2-year colleges, however, Astin found that black students still exhibited greater attrition than white students, and Peng and Fetters reported no significant difference in attrition rates for blacks and whites.

The following studies revealed no relationship between students' ethnicity and attrition at *residence-oriented 4-year institutions* (Munro, 1981; Pascarella & Terenzini, l 980; Terenzini et al., 1981); *commuter-oriented 4-year institutions* (Gordon & Johnson, 1982; Louis et al., 1984; Pascarella et al., 1983; Smith, 1980); and *commuter 2-year colleges* (Brunner et al., 1978; California State Coordinating Council, 1974; Martin, 1974; Rice, 1983; Wetzel, 1977; White, 1972).

In the model, it is posited that the primary indirect effects of ethnicity for nontraditional students are through a strong negative influence on GPA due to the comparatively poorer education provided for minority students at the secondary level.

Gender

Few studies of nontraditional students were found that compared the reasons why men drop out as opposed to women (e.g., Costa, 1984). However, in research with traditional students, gender was found to interact substantially with other predictor variables. In these studies, attrition models for men and women were estimated separately (e.g., Bean, 1980, 1982c; Spady, 1971). For this reason, and because men and women still have distinctive (i.e., stereotypical) roles in the environment outside of college which may affect their enrollment decisions, it seems important to include gender in the model. Gender is likely to have indirect effects on attrition through family responsibilities (positive effects for women) and opportunity to transfer (negative effect for women).

Parents' Education

Skaling (1971) concluded from his literature review that parents' level of formal education was the most powerful predictor of traditional student persistence in college among the various indicators of parental socioeconomic status (SES) (e.g., income, occupation, education). Four codifications (Cope & Hannah, 1975; Skaling, 1971; Spady, 1970; Tinto, 1975) reported a positive relationship between parents' educational level and student persistence; however, Pantages and Creedon (1978) and Lenning et al. (1980) found equivocal results showing either a positive relationship or no significant association.

Several empirical studies at primarily residence-oriented 4-year institutions revealed a positive relationship between student persistence and *father's educational level* (Astin, 1975; Jaffe & Adams, 1970; Kowalski, 1977; Panos & Astin, 1968), *mother's educational level* (Astin, 1975; Chase, 1970; Panos & Astin, 1968), and *both parents' level of education* (Astin, 1975; Meyers, 1981; Panos & Astin, 1968). Rossmann and Kirk (1970) and Pascarella and Terenzini (1980) found no significant difference between dropouts and persisters according to the educational level of either parent.

Although commuter and older students exhibit considerable heterogeneity in family background characteristics, these students more than their traditional counterparts have been depicted in the literature as first generation college attenders from a blue collar family background containing a lower level of formal education (Chickering, 1974; Cross, 1981; Kimball & Sedlacek, 1971; Kuh & Ardaiolo, 1979; Solmon & Gordon, 1981; Welty, 1976). In the older student population, Solmon and Gordon found less parental education among part-time students than among full-time students.

Regarding commuter students at 4-year institutions, no significant difference was noted between student attrition and the educational attainment of either parent (Pascarella et al., 1981; Louis et al., 1984) or both parents (Pascarella et al., 1983). From research at 2-year colleges, Jaffe and Adams (1970) discovered no significant relationship between father's educational level and the persistence of students composing a multi-institutional sample. Studies by Cohen (1969), Astin (1972), and Alfred (1973) disclosed that mother's but not father's educational level was associated with persistence. Finally, Aiken (1968) and DeVecchio (1972) did not find a significant relationship between either parent's level of education and student persistence.

No study was located that investigated the effect of parents' educational level on the persistence of students who had been independent of their primary family for a substantial period. For this reason and due to only limited support from research with commuter students, the variable was not included in the model. If researchers had a special interest in including SES measures in their research, they would appear as background variables.

Academic Variables

Academic variables are prominent in models of traditional student attrition as indicators of academic integration (e.g., Tinto, 1975). These variables—study skills and habits, academic advising, absenteeism, major certainty, and course availability—are expected to have indirect effects on dropout through GPA, through the psychological outcome variables, especially satisfaction, and through intent to leave.

Study Skills and Study Habits

Four codifications (Bucklin & Bucklin, 1970; Lenning et al., 1980; Pantages & Creedon, 1978; Sexton, 1965) concluded that students who stated that they possessed poor study skills and study habits were more likely to drop out of college. Empirical studies by Chase (1970), Demitroff (1974), Astin (1975), Kowalski (1977), Smith (1980), and Taylor (1982) substantiated this conclusion. According to Timmons (1977), however, significantly more persisters than dropouts at a university said that they had difficulty developing good study skills. Regarding commuter students, Smith (1980) and Taylor (1982) found that students at two commuter 4-year institutions listed inadequate study skills and study habits among the major reasons for discontinuing enrollment.

Several writers (e.g., Apps, 1981; Burgess, 1973; Hughes, 1983; Mangano & Corrado, 1981; Solmon & Gordon, 1981) stated that many older students who entered college after a lengthy absence from a formal learning situation initially lacked confidence in their ability to succeed at college, rated their study skills as deficient, and requested assistance in learning better study skills and more efficient time management. No research was located, however, that examined an association between older students' ratings of their study skills and persistence in college.

According to Trent and Ruyle (1965) and Trent and Medsker (1968), persisters indicated that they spent more time studying than dropouts. Similar findings were reported by Baumgart and Johnstone (1977) for part-time as well as full-time students at a commuter university and by R. Johnson (1980) for full-time students attending several community colleges.

Kimball and Sedlacek (1971), Roelfs (1975), and Preston (1976) discovered that older students engaged in considerably more hours of study outside of class than traditional age students, even though older students were often enrolled in fewer courses. No research was located, however, that related amount of study time to the persistence of older students.

Academic Advising

This variable refers to students' evaluation of the quality of the academic advising they have received. One codification (Lenning et al., 1980) suggested that academic advising was related to student persistence. Most studies employing academic advising as a variable measured the frequency of student usage or students' evaluation of the service. Crockett (1978), however, advocated more extensive assessment: "length of contact, frequency of contact, topics discussed, accessibility, . . . student satisfaction, number of registration errors, . . . and [advisor's] knowledge of the institution" (p. 34).

Empirical studies that investigated an association between students' use of academic advising services and retention at primarily residence-oriented 4-year institutions produced inconsistent results. Trent and Medsker (1968), Pascarella and Terenzini (1977), Endo and Harpel (1979), and the University of California (1980) found that more persisters than dropouts had used academic advising services. Everett (1979) reported that significantly more dropouts than persisters had obtained academic counseling. Finally, no significant association between the use of academic advising services and persistence was noted by Johansson and Rossmann (1973), Kowalski (1977), and Disque (1983). Regarding commuter and older students, Staman (1980) found that the amount of time that students spent with an academic adviser was not significantly related to the persistence of continuing students age 17–21 or age 22–45 who attended a 4-year college.

Equivocal results were also apparent for students' evaluation of academic advising services (e.g., amount of satisfaction or ratings of quality) and persistence at 4- and 2-year institutions. Research found (a) no relationship between students' evaluation and persistence (Aiken, 1968; Bean, 1980; Enos, 1981; Kowalski, 1977; Staman 1980; Steele, 1978), (b) lower ratings of advising services by dropouts compared to persisters (Brigman, Kuh, & Stager, 1982; Louis et al., 1984; Meyers, 1981; Smith, 1980; Taylor, 1982), or (c) less favorable ratings by persisters than dropouts (Iffert, 1957; Timmons, 1977).

Smith (1980) and Louis et al. (1984) discovered from research at commuter-oriented 4-year institutions that dropouts were significantly less satisfied than persisters with academic advising. From research at a similar type of institution Baumgart and Johnstone (1977) reported that no significant difference in satisfaction with advising services was evident for persisters compared to dropouts who were male part-time students. These researchers also found that for male full-time students, voluntary dropouts were more satisfied with academic advising than dropouts who had been academically dismissed.

Staman (1980) found no significant difference in persistence according to the degree of satisfaction with academic counseling services expressed by continuing students under age 22 or by older continuing students at a commuter-oriented 4-year college. In many studies, commuter student dropouts registered their dissatisfaction with academic advising or indicated that improved advising services would have assisted them in remaining in college (e.g., Davis, 1971; Gorter, 1978; Smith, 1980; Taylor, 1982; Tweddale, 1978; White, 1972).

Absenteeism

This variable is defined as the extent to which students missed class and serves as an indicator of students' reduced interaction with their college. A perusal of the student attrition literature revealed that an association between absenteeism and student attrition has rarely been investigated. No codification was found that discussed this relationship.

Kowalski (1977) reported that dropouts showed significantly greater absenteeism than persisters. Bean (1981) indicated that absenteeism was positively related to dropout for full-time freshmen with low academic confidence; however, absenteeism had no significant effect on dropout for academically confident freshmen. Furthermore, Bean's study showed that among freshman women with low academic confidence, absenteeism had a strong negative effect on students' reported enjoyment of their role as a student. In another study (Bean, 1982b), absenteeism was positively related to attrition for students with lower college grade averages, but it was not significantly associated with absenteeism for students with better academic performance.

No study was located that examined the effect of absenteeism on the persistence of older, part-time, or commuter students. Greer (1980), however, assessed the precollege expectations of college experiences for older compared to traditional age freshmen who attended a public urban community college. She found that older students reported a significantly higher probability that they would miss classes and have to drop out of college because of job or family responsibilities.

Major Certainty

Three codifications (Bucklin & Bucklin, 1970; Sexton, 1965; Summerskill, 1962) concluded that students' degree of certainty about their academic major was positively related to persistence in college. A considerable number of empirical studies provided supporting evidence (Brigman et al., 1982; Curran, 1981, Demitroff, 1974; Demos, 1968; Dulniak, 1982; Everett, 1979; Kowalski, 1977; Krebs & Liberty, 1971; MacMillan, 1970; Newton & Gaither, 1980; Rice, 1983; Slocum, 1956, Smith, 1980; Staman, 1980; Timmons, 1977; White, 1972).

Major certainty was found to be positively related to the persistence of students attending primarily commuter 4-year institutions (Demos, 1968; Newton & Gaither, 1980; Smith, 1980; Staman, 1980) and 2-year colleges (MacMillan, 1970; Rice, 1983; White, 1972). Several researchers (Greer, 1980; Roelfs, 1975; Solmon & Gordon, 1981; Wallace, 1979) reported that older students were more certain of their academic major than traditional age students. Staman (1980) found that major certainty was strongly and positively associated with persistence among continuing students age 22–45 as well as continuing students under age 22 who attended a commuter-oriented 4-year college.

Course Availability

This variable indicates the extent to which students believe that they are able to take the courses they prefer at their present college. Factors involved in course availability include whether the desired courses are (a) offered by the college, (b) scheduled at times when students are able to enroll, and (c) have sufficient capacity for student demand. Two codifications (Lenning et al., 1980; Pantages & Creedon, 1978) briefly mentioned that course unavailability was related to student attrition.

The following empirical studies at 4- and 2-year institutions demonstrated that students' inability to take desired courses was a factor in dropout: Chickering and Hannah, 1969; MacMillan, 1970; Baumgart and Johnstone, 1977; Brunner et al., 1978; Gorter, 1978; Tweddale, 1978; Brigman et al., 1982; and Johnston, 1982. Moreover, Beal and Noel (1980, p. 44) disclosed from their survey of 947 2- and 4-year colleges that course unavailability was the second highest ranked item among 17 institutional characteristics that college administrators believed were positively associated with student attrition. Brigman et al. (1982) reported that course unavailability was the primary reason for the withdrawal of students who had transferred to another university.

Some studies with commuter students at 4-year institutions (Smith, 1980; Tweddale, 1978) and 2-year colleges (Brunner et al., 1978; Gorter, 1978; Johnston, 1982; MacMillan, 1970) showed that course unavailability was a factor in student attrition. From research at a commuter-oriented university, Smith (1980) found that a lack of desired courses or program of study was listed by students as a major reason for dropout; however, no significant difference between dropouts and persisters was evident regarding satisfaction with the scheduling of courses.

At a similar type of institution, Staman (1980) did not find a significant relationship between satisfaction with the scheduling of courses and the attrition of older students. In addition, students' dissatisfaction with the kind and variety of course offerings did not significantly discriminate between dropouts and persisters among traditional age or older continuing students. Finally, "courses not offered" (p. 25) was a major reason for withdrawal cited by part-time but not full-time students at a community college (Gorter, 1978).

Environmental Variables

These variables indicate those factors over which the institution has little control but which might pull the student from the institution. A perceived (or real) lack of finances, working for long hours, lacking encouragement, family responsibilities, and a perceived opportunity to transfer are presumed to have direct effects on attrition decisions as well as indirect effects on dropout through the psychological outcome variables.

Finances

In attrition research, students' ability to finance their college education has been measured by various indicators: parents' SES (e.g., occupation, education); students' or parents' income; and students' perceptions about their finances (e.g., financial problems, inadequate finances, degree of financial concern, extent of certainty about finances). From their review of studies conducted with students attending residence-oriented 4-year institutions, Summerskill (1962), Spady (1970), and Cope and Hannah (1975) questioned the validity of many students' responses that mentioned inadequate finances as a reason for dropout.

For example, Cope and Hannah reported that often family income was not highly correlated with students' listing of inadequate finances as a reason for withdrawal. These writers attributed this finding to many students' need to express more socially acceptable reasons for dropout than lack of commitment to a college education or other personal liabilities.

Nevertheless, five codifications (Lenning et al., 1980; Marsh, 1966; Pantages & Creedon, 1978; Skaling, 1971; Summerskill, 1962) concluded that students' reports of financial difficulty were positively related to attrition from college. A very large number of studies substantiated this conclusion for *residence-oriented 4-year institutions* (Astin, 1972; Curran, 1981; Demitroff, 1974; Iffert, 1957; Kowalski, 1977; Krebs & Liberty, 1971; Slocum, 1956), *commuter-oriented 4-year institutions* (Demos, 1968; Gordon & Johnson, 1982; Louis et al., 1984; Smith 1980; Staman, 1980; Tweddale, 1978), and *commuter 2-year colleges* (Aiken, 1968; Brainard, 1973; Bromley, 1973; Brunner et al., 1978; Davis, 1971; Fetters, 1977; Gorter, 1978; Hall, 1975; Hinrichsen & Schaumberg, 1976; Weigel, 1969; White, 1972). Research by Steele (1978) and Aitken (1982), however, failed to confirm this result at residential universities.

Several writers (Cross, 1981; Hughes, 1983; Kimmel & Murphy, 1976; Lenning & Hanson, 1977; Preston, 1976; Solmon & Gordon, 1981) stated that many older students expressed concern about their ability to finance a college education. For instance, Solmon and Gordon (1981, pp. 40, 103) reported from their longitudinal study of freshmen who attended a national sample of 4- and 2-year colleges that (a) 65% and 68% of the traditional age and older full-time students, respectively, indicated at least some financial concern, (b) 53% of the older part-time students mentioned some financial concern, and (c) since 1974, the percentage of older part-time students with financial concern has been increasing.

At a commuter-oriented 4-year institution, Gordon and Johnson (1982, p. 10) found no significant age difference between the percentage of students who listed inadequate finances as a reason for withdrawing during a semester: This reason was indicated by 42.5% of the students under age 21 compared to 47.8% of the older students. Finally, Gorter (1978) reported that financial difficulty was included among the two reasons most frequently mentioned by part-time as well as full-time students for their withdrawal from a community college.

Hours of Employment

Three codifications (Lenning et al., 1980; Pantages & Creedon, 1978; Sexton, 1965) stated that the number of hours per week that students were employed while attending college was related to their persistence in college. Numerous empirical studies supported this conclusion (Alfred, 1973; Anderson, 1981; Astin, 1972, 1975; Cohen, 1969; Everett, 1979; Hunter & Sheldon, 1980: Krebs & Liberty, 1971; Louis et al., 1984; Peng & Fetters, 1978; Smith, 1980; Staman, 1980; University of California, 1980).

Astin (1975) reported that students who were employed fewer than 20 hours per week exhibited greater persistence in college than unemployed students. Most researchers agreed that employment in excess of 20–25 hours per week was negatively related to persistence.

According to several investigators (Dressel & Nisula, 1966; Fenske & Scott, 1972; Hardwick & Kazlo, 1973), commuter students were likely to be employed and to work a greater number of hours per week than residential students. In studies at commuter-oriented 4-year institutions (Louis et al., 1984; Smith, 1980; Staman, 1980) and commuter 2-year colleges (Alfred, 1973; Astin, 1972; Cohen, 1969; Hunter & Sheldon, 1980), the extent of students' employment per week was negatively related to their persistence in college. Using a national sample of traditional age students, Peng and Fetters (1978) found that the amount of student employment per week (none, part-time, full-time) was negatively associated with persistence at 4-year institutions but created no significant effect on student persistence at 2-year colleges.

Older students appear to exhibit some heterogeneity regarding their amount of employment while attending college. Kuh and Ardaiolo (1979) found that older university students were more likely to be employed and to work a greater average number of hours per week than traditional age students. Lenning and Hanson (1977), Greer (1980), and Solmon and Gordon (1981) reported that more older students worked at full-time jobs than traditional age students who attended 4- and 2-year colleges.

Lenning and Hanson (1977) also noted that more older than younger community college students were not employed. Finally, Solmon and Gordon (1981) discovered that older and younger students were about equally likely to work at part-time jobs while attending 4- and 2-year colleges.

In a study by Staman (1980) at a commuter-oriented 4-year institution, the number of hours of employment per week was very strongly and negatively related to the persistence of continuing students under age 22 but showed no significant association for older continuing students. Berkove (1976), however, reported that a greater percentage of older female dropouts than persisters at three universities were employed while attending college.

Outside Encouragement

This variable measures the extent of encouragement to remain at a college that a student receives from influential persons in the student's life who are not employed by the college. Such persons include a student's parents or spouse, close friends, and an off-campus employer.

According to five codifications (Bucklin & Bucklin, 1970; Pantages & Creedon, 1978; Sexton, 1965; Spady, 1970; Tinto, 1975), the degree of parental encouragement toward a student's college attendance was positively related to student persistence in college. Several empirical studies primarily involving students at residence-oriented 4-year colleges supported this conclusion (Anderson, 1981; Hackman & Dysinger, 1970; Marks, 1967; Reed, 1968; Slocum, 1956; Trent & Medsker, 1968).

No research was located that exclusively examined the effect of parental encouragement on the attrition of students at commuter-oriented 4-year institutions. Although parental encouragement has rarely been studied in conjunction with attrition at 2-year colleges, MacMillan (1969) and Weigel (1969) found that persisters experienced significantly greater parental encouragement than dropouts.

No codification was reviewed that investigated the relationship between students' ratings of spouse encouragement toward continued college attendance and persistence in college. Some writers (e.g., Hughes, 1983; Malin, Bray, Dougherty, & Skinner, 1980; Mangano & Corrado, 1981; Roach, 1976) stated that older students considered family reaction to their college attendance to be an important aspect of satisfaction with the college experience. Berkove (1976) reported that older female dropouts compared to persisters at three universities rated their husbands as providing less functional help; however, husbands' degree of emotional support for their wife's college attendance did not exhibit clear differences among persisters and dropouts.

Several codifications (Bucklin & Bucklin, 1970; Lenning et al., 1980; Pantages & Creedon, 1978; Sexton, 1965; Spady, 1970) acknowledged that students' close friends affected decisions about persisting in college. However, few empirical studies employing friends' encouragement as a variable were located.

Although some close friends of commuter students may also attend the same college, commuter students often retain many friendships with persons in their community who do not attend their college (Chickering, 1974; Dressel & Nisula, 1966; Flanagan, 1976). For example, research by E. Johnson (1981, p. 57) revealed that only one-third or fewer of the commuter students in her study listed other students at the university as a source of close friends. A somewhat similar situation appears to exist for older students.

Anderson (1981) wrote, "While research has usually been limited to the influence of peers *within* the college, associations with peers who are not students can be just as important. . . . Peer attitudes can influence integration into college, achievement goals, and persistence" (p. 5). Anderson examined factors related to the persistence of a national sample of full-time traditional age freshmen who entered 4- and 2-year colleges. The results of this study indicated that peer discouragement of alternatives to college attendance, such as employment or vocational training, was positively related to student persistence. This effect was significantly greater for students who lived off campus than for residential students.

Baumgart and Johnstone (1977) found that among male full-time students the number of friends who considered withdrawing from a commuter-oriented university was positively related to attrition. Metzner (1984) reported that encouragement by friends to continue attending college was negatively related to intent to leave a public urban commuter university for traditional age full-time students, traditional age part-time students, and older part-time students. This relationship was stronger among traditional age than older students.

As discussed earlier, a substantial percentage of older, part-time, and commuter students are likely to be employed while they are attending college. The extent to which employers are supportive of students' college attendance not only provides students with psychological reinforcement for continued college study but may also affect student persistence by more pragmatic means such as adjustments in work hours around exigencies in academic schedules (Malin et al., 1980), college tuition and fee remission, and promotional opportunities. No codification or empirical research was found that investigated the relationship between an employer's encouragement of a student's college attendance and student persistence in college.

It is outside encouragement that replaces normative support in the models of Spady (1970) and Tinto (1975). In this model, the support for attending school comes from outside the institution and therefore is expected to be qualitatively different from the normative support of insiders. We do not wish to imply that no such internal support exists for nontraditional students, but rather that external encouragement is more important for nontraditional students because their reference group of peers, friends, family, and employers is thought to be largely external to the institution.

Family Responsibilities

No codification was located that examined an association between the degree of students' family responsibilities and dropout from college.

At a commuter university, Carter (1982, pp. 2–3) reported that family responsibilities were among the 5 most prevalent of 60 reasons for the attrition of older and part-time students during a semester; this reason was not frequently mentioned by traditional age or full-time students who withdrew. At a similar type of institution (Staman, 1980), the number of a student's children was negatively associated with persistence for continuing students age 22 or older but showed no significant effect for younger students. From research at three universities, Berkove (1976) discovered that for older female commuter students who were married and had at least one child living at home, dropouts reported significantly greater stress than persisters from family obligations. Baumgart and Johnstone (1977) found that anticipation of family problems was not significantly related to the withdrawal of part-time students attending a commuter-oriented university.

According to Brainard (1973), Martin (1974), and Hunter and Sheldon (1980), family pressures and obligations were listed as major reasons for withdrawal by students who attended 17 community colleges. Gorter (1978) corroborated this finding for part-time community college students. Reehling (1980) found that the older female students who failed to accomplish their original educational goal at several community colleges had a significantly greater number of children living at home than students who had attained their goal.

Opportunity to Transfer

Two codifications (Lenning et al., 1980; Spady, 1970) stated that student transfer was a major reason for students' withdrawal from their initial college. Some studies conducted primarily with students attending 4-year institutions revealed that a considerable proportion of students entered college with an intention of transferring and that indeed approximately 20% to 35% of student dropouts had transferred to a different college (Demitroff, 1974; Everett, 1979; Iffert, 1957; Kowalski, 1977; Trent & Medsker, 1968; Tweddale, 1978).

Additional research at a university (Bean, 1982c) showed that students' perception of how difficult it would be for them to transfer to another college was negatively related to attrition. Meyers (1981), Brigman et al. (1982), Gathers (1983), and Getzlaf, Sedlacek, Kearney, and Blackwell (1984) conducted a separate subgroup analysis for dropouts from residential universities who had transferred. Results of these analyses were different from the findings for dropouts who had not transferred. White (1972) reported a similar result for community college students. Research at numerous commuter institutions, nearly all of which are 2-year colleges, demonstrated that student transfer was a somewhat frequent reason for dropout (Behrendt, 1974; Brainard, 1973; Bucks County Community College, 1973; Eagle, 1979; Greive, 1970; Haas, 1974; Hall, 1975; Johnston, 1982; MacMillan, 1970; Selo, 1974; Snyder & Blocker, 1970; Stine, 1976; Taylor, 1982; Tweddale, 1978; Weigel, 1969).

A higher percentage of residential than commuter students (Nelson, 1982), full-time than part-time commuter students (Behrendt, 1974), and traditional age than older commuter students (Preston, 1976; White, 1972) show a likelihood of transfer. On the basis of this limited research, a probability of transfer may be greater for the more traditional students. Measures frequently correlated with persistence as reported in the literature about traditional students may be correlated with attrition in the case of dropouts who transfer, thus producing a *transfer effect,* defined as a reversal of the expected relationship between a variable and attrition due to students dropping out to transfer to another institution. A transfer effect may create some surprising results in studies at institutions with a substantial transfer rate.

For example, Staman (1980) and Pascarella et al. (1983) reported that the extent of students' social integration was negatively associated with persistence. The latter researchers speculated that students with high levels of social integration at a commuter institution may be more likely to transfer to a college with greater social opportunities. Tinto (1975) cited some studies in which students' academic aptitude was negatively associated with persistence and discussed the possible operation of a transfer effect at 4- and 2-year colleges of lower academic standing.

Finally, Metzner (1984) assessed students' intent to leave an urban commuter university and found that intent to transfer at the end of the semester or academic year was correlated with measures of college preparatory program, level of parents' education, recency of formal education, the number of known campus resources, and hours of employment.

Thus, in surveys at colleges with somewhat high transfer rates, researchers might include a control variable regarding students' likelihood of transfer to provide a possible explanation for findings atypical of those reported in the literature. Since beginning freshmen for a fall term might be more likely to transfer at the end of an academic year than at the conclusion of one enrollment term (Gell, 1974), studies of attrition at the end of a fall enrollment term may not be highly influenced by a transfer effect even at institutions with an eventually high transfer rate.

Social Integration Variables

Social integration refers to the extent and quality of students' interaction with the social system of the college environment. The models of Spady (1970) and Tinto (1975) assume that students who have extensive, high quality interaction with persons in this social system (i.e., greater social integration) are more likely to continue enrollment at their college. Measures of social integration typically include the following: the degree of students' participation in extracurricular activities, peer friendships on campus, and relationships with instructors outside of class; students' evaluation of the quality of these experiences, such as the amount of satisfaction with the relationship; and a global assessment of students' satisfaction with their social life or with the social opportunities at their college.

Several codifications of research with students attending *residence-oriented* 4-year institutions (Lenning et al., 1980; Sexton, 1965; Skaling, 1971; Spady, 1970; Tinto, 1975) concluded that students' degree of social integration, as assessed by one or more of these measures, was positively related to persistence in college. Numerous studies provided supporting evidence (e.g., Everett, 1979; Nelson et al., 1984; Panos & Astin, 1968; Pascarella & Chapman, 1983; Pascarella & Terenzini, 1980; Reed, 1968; Slocum, 1956; Spady, 1971; Steele, 1978).

The literature that compared commuter with residential students reported that commuter students exhibited less social integration at college (e.g., Chickering, 1974; Dressel & Nisula, 1966; Everett, 1979; Flanagan, 1976; Nelson, 1982; Ward & Kurz, 1969; Welty, 1976). Literature that contrasted older with traditional age students concluded that older students usually expressed relatively little interest in social integration and were less involved in social activities on campus (e.g., Greer, 1980; Kuh & Ardaiolo, 1979; Lenning & Hanson, 1977; Louis et al., 1984; Mangano & Corrado, 1981; Preston, 1976; Solmon & Gordon, 1981; Wallace, 1979; Wolfgang & Dowling, 1981).

Regarding attrition research with students who attended *commuter-oriented* 4-year *institutions*, 8 of the 16 studies used in this literature review (see Table I) contained measures of social integration. In three of these studies, no significant relationship between social integration and persistence was found: Baumgart and Johnstone, 1 977 (number of friends at the university, part-time students); Pascarella et al., 1981 (likelihood of joining a social organization); and Pascarella and Chapman, 1983 (weekends spent on campus, number of best friends on campus, extracurricular and social activities, informal contact with faculty members, and peer conversations). A fourth study (Carter, 1982) was an exit study, which indicated that measures of social integration (inability to meet friends, dissatisfaction with social life) were not among the more prevalent reasons that students listed for their withdrawal during a semester.

Two studies noted an equivocal association between social integration and attrition. Although Smith (1980) found that persisters were significantly more satisfied than dropouts with the extracurricular activities on campus, no significant difference between persisters and dropouts was apparent for students' satisfaction with social opportunities or the amount of contact with instructors.

Louis et al. (1984) reported that even though dropouts and persisters showed no difference in their amount of participation in social activities on campus, more dropouts than persisters felt that they had made fewer friends at the university. No significant difference was found between dropouts and persisters regarding the degree to which social life on campus met their initial expectations. Dissatisfaction with social life was among the reasons dropouts cited least frequently for their withdrawal. Finally, the extent of social problems, participation in campus social activities, and the formation of friendships at the university were not strongly correlated with persistence in a multivariate analysis.

In the final two studies, students' extent of social integration was negatively related to persistence. According to Staman (1980), participation in social and recreational activities and attendance at college sports events were significantly and negatively related to the persistence of continuing students under age 22 and older continuing students. Likewise, Pascarella et al. (1983) found a very strong negative association between persistence and measures of social integration (degree to which students formed peer friendships at the university, satisfaction with these relationships, extent of nonclassroom interaction with faculty, ratings of influence and satisfaction from these relationships).

•••

Regarding student attrition research at *2-year colleges*, 7 of the 40 studies used in this literature review (see Table I) included measures of social integration. The overwhelming majority of exit and autopsy studies did not contain response categories for social integration variables as probable reasons for attrition.

Four studies showed that social integration and attrition were unrelated: Roesler 1971 (not enough social life); White, 1972 (attitudes about student activities and fellow students); Martin, 1974 (dissatisfaction with social/cultural environment) and Pascarella and Chapman, 1983 (weekends spent on campus, extracurricular and social activities, number of best friends on campus, informal contact with faculty members, and peer conversations). In addition, Fetters (1977) found that students who were dissatisfied with social life on campus were likely to leave primarily residence-oriented 4-year institutions. This variable, however, was not related to attrition at 2-year colleges.

Two studies produced some limited evidence that social integration was positively related to persistence. Weigel (1969) reported that for approximately one-third of the dropouts, dislike of the social atmosphere was a reason given for withdrawal. This reason was the sixth most frequently mentioned among 14 items (p. 16). R. Johnson (1980) found that for full-time freshmen of primarily traditional age, close friendships on campus and some types of informal contact with instructors were positively but not significantly related to persistence.

In conclusion, there appears to be considerable empirical evidence indicating that students' degree of social integration at residence-oriented 4-year institutions is positively related to persistence. Social integration variables have not been included in the majority of attrition studies with commuter students. The literature comparing nontraditional with traditional students and most attrition research examining social integration at 4- and 2-year commuter institutions, however overwhelmingly, suggests that social integration is rarely a major factor in attrition decisions. Furthermore, it has not been found to be positively and significantly related to the persistence of nontraditional students. Thus, social integration has been omitted as a primary component of the model.

Nevertheless, researchers may be interested in determining the relationship between social integration and persistence in their samples of nontraditional students to contribute to further understanding of this relationship. For example, the finding of a negative association between social integration and persistence in two studies is particularly curious. Provision has therefore been made to incorporate social Integration variables as an adjunct to the model's main design.

Academic Outcomes

The direct effect of a low GPA on student attrition is often a matter of institutional policy: Failing to achieve a minimum level of performance becomes grounds for dismissal. Above this level, students may perceive grades as quasi economic rewards (Bean, 1980; Tinto, 1975), and the higher the level of this reward the more likely a student is to remain in school. The effect of GPA on attrition is therefore expected to be primarily direct. Students receiving poor grades, however may also be more likely to intend to leave school, and indirect effects through intent to leave would also be expected.

College Academic Performance (GPA)

Four codifications (Lenning et al., 1980; Pantages & Creedon, 1978; Summerskill, 1962, Tinto, 1975) concluded that students' grade average exhibited a strong negative relationship with attrition from college. In fact, Tinto (1975) wrote that "with respect to grade performance, many studies have shown it to be the single most important factor in predicting persistence in college" (p. 104).

Several empirical studies reported a negative association between students *first term grade average* and attrition at residence-oriented 4-year institutions (Beans 1982c, 1983; Blanchfield, 1971; Endo & Harpel, 1979; Marks, 1967); commuter-oriented 4-year institutions (Pascarella et al., 1981; Staman, 1980; Tata, 1981); and 2-year colleges (Costa, 1984; Knoell, 1976; Weigel, 1969; White, 1972). Other studies found a negative association between *cumulative grade average* and attention at residence-oriented 4-year institutions (Aitken, 1982; Bean, 1985; Johansson & Rossmann, 1973; Peng & Fetters, 1978; Spady, 1971); commuter-oriented 4-year institutions (Staman, 1980; Zaccaria & Creaser, 1971); and 2-year colleges (Aiken, 1968, Peng & Fetters, 1978; Rice, 1983).

Although older students tend to have inferior high school academic performance compared to traditional age students (Greer, 1980; Kuh & Ardaiolo, 1979; Solmon & Gordon, 1981), older students' academic performance at college has often been found to equal or surpass that of younger students (Greer, 1980; Kasworrn, 1980; Kimmel & Murphy, 1976; Lenning & Hanson, 1977; Preston, 1976; Von der Embse & Childs, 1979). Kimmel and Murphy and Greer, however, reported that older students were more likely to drop out of college than traditional age students in spite of having earned equivalent or better college grades.

Staman (1980) discovered that college grade average was positively related to the persistence of continuing students under age 22 but showed no significant relationship to the persistence of older continuing students who attended a commuter-oriented 4-year college. At a community college, however, Costa (1984) indicated that first semester grade average was a highly significant predictor of attrition for entering students age 25 or older.

For part-time and full-time students attending 32 community colleges, Knoell (1976) found that college grade average was negatively related to attrition; however, a greater proportion of part-time than full-time student dropouts earned higher grades. Gorter (1978) reported that the grade average for part-time student dropouts was above the average for all part-time students at a community college; full-time student dropouts earned a grade average that was considerably below the average for all full-time students.

To summarize, college academic performance has been a consistent and powerful predictor of persistence in numerous studies at various types of institutions. College grade average, however, may be relatively less predictive of persistence for part-time and older commuter students than for their more traditional counterparts.

Psychological Outcomes

The psychological outcomes—utility, satisfaction, goal commitment, and stress—are located in the model where attitudes are found in the Fishbein and Ajzen models (1975) and where emotions appear in the model of satisfaction described by Locke (1976). These outcomes are expected to be primarily the result of the academic and environmental variables; the primary effects of these outcomes are expected to be indirect, acting through intentions that are designated in this model as *intent to leave*. Utility, satisfaction, and goal commitment should reduce intent to leave, while stress should increase intent to leave.

Utility

This variable measures students' perceptions of the usefulness of their college education for employment opportunities (practical value) and personal development. Very little research has incorporated students' ratings of the value of their college education for future employment; however, one recent codification (Lenning et al., 1980) suggested that this variable was negatively related to attrition and might be especially important in light of some uncertainty in the job market for college graduates.

Empirical studies by Reed (1968), Davis (1971), White (1972), Terenzini and Pascarella (1977), and Taylor (1982) found that students' attitudes toward relevancy of a college education, certainty about the value of a college education, or the practical value of courses were negatively related to attrition. More specifically Bean (1983) reported a negative association between students' ratings of the utility of their college education for future employment opportunities and attrition from a university.

In several of Bean's studies (1980, 1982c, 1983), practical value was the third or fourth most powerful of 10 to 14 variables in total effect on dropout. Bean (1982c) concluded that the perceived value of a college education for future employment was an important student attitude affecting freshman attrition at residence-oriented universities. Similar findings for nontraditional students are expected on the basis of the following research.

According to some writers (e.g., Chickering, 1974; Flanagan, 1976; Garni, 1974 Klotsche, 1966), commuter compared to residential students were disproportionately interested in the practical benefits of college attendance for future employment. Furthermore, several researchers (e.g., Burgess, 1973; Lenning & Hanson 1977; Mangano & Corrado, 1981; Solmon & Gordon, 1981) reported that older students tended to emphasize career preparation as a primary motivation (or college attendance. Kuh and Ardaiolo (1979, p. 212), however, found some institutional differences: 75% of the older freshmen who attended a commuter university compared to only 40% of the older freshmen at a residence-oriented university listed career preparation as their primary reason for entering college.

Regarding attrition studies at commuter institutions, Davis (1971), Gell (1974) Taylor (1982), and Dennis-Rounds (1983) disclosed that students' perception of the relevancy of a college education was positively related to persistence. Weigel (1969) reported that significantly more persisters than dropouts had entered a community college to obtain a better paying job. Staman (1980) also discovered that this goal was related to persistence for continuing students age 22-45 who attended a commuter-oriented 4-year college.

Finally, Metzner (1984) reported that practical value produced a very strong negative association with students' intent to leave among part-time and full-time freshmen under age 22 and part-time freshmen age 22 or older at an urban commuter university. Practical value, however, created a smaller effect for older than for traditional age students.

Although college attendance may offer students the extrinsic reward of better employment opportunities, Spady (1970) wrote that a college education also affords an intrinsic reward of personal development. Two codifications (Spady, 1970; Tinto, 1975) concluded that students' perception of their amount of intellectual growth at their college was a personal developmental factor that was positively associated with their persistence in college. Several studies (Pascarella & Terenzini, 1980; Terenzini et al., 1981; Trent & Medsker, 1968; Spady, 1971) provided supporting evidence.

Two studies by Bean (1980, 1983) disclosed that personal development was not significantly related to dropout for traditional freshmen at two midwestern universities, however, personal development was positively and significantly associated with the extent to which students enjoyed the role of being a student. This latter variable was negatively related to an intent to leave and dropout.

In contrasting the impact of commuter and residence-oriented institutions on students' personal development, Harrington (1972) wrote, "The most important and unique role of the residential college is its provision of more decision-making opportunities, interaction with peers, development of interpersonal relationship skills, and the analysis of personal values" (p. 549). Many writers suggested that except for students' intellectual development through their course work, college attendance contributed minimally to the personal development of commuter students (Chickering, 1974; Chickering & Kuper, 1971; Dressel & Nisula, 1966; Garni, 1974; Harrington, 1972; Trivett, 1974; Ward & Kurz, 1969). Scott (1975) and Welty (1976) reported that commuter students at two universities exhibited less intellectual as well as other types of personal growth than did residential students.

Some writers (e.g., Burgess, 1973; Lenning & Hanson, 1977; Malin et al., 1980; Solmon & Gordon, 1981) asserted that older students enrolled in college primarily for vocational preparation. For example, Solmon and Gordon (1981) concluded from their research that "institutions wishing to attract . . . more adult students should emphasize students' career development rather than their personal, intellectual, and social development" (p. 113). Other writers (e.g., Berkove, 1976; Flaherty, 1978; Parelius, 1979; Wolfgang & Dowling, 1981), however, reported that personal development was the primary motivation for many older students' college attendance. In a descriptive study of adult students from six campuses of a university system, Sewall (1984) found that the single most important reason that these students had entered college was almost equally divided between career preparation and personal development. Similar results were obtained by Reehling (1980) for older female students attending several community colleges.

No study was located that adequately examined an association between attrition and ratings of personal development among older or commuter students.

Satisfaction

This variable is an indicator of the degree to which a student enjoys the role of being a student and reports a lack of boredom with college courses.

Few empirical studies were reviewed that investigated an association between students' role satisfaction and attrition from college. At residence-oriented 4-year institutions (Bean, 1983; Panos & Astin, 1968; Rootman, 1972), a commuter-oriented 4-year institution (Smith, 1980), and a 2-year college (Johnston, 1982) students' enjoyment and compatibility in the role of a student were negatively related to attrition. Metzner (1984) discovered that role satisfaction was negatively associated with intent to leave for traditional age full-time and part-time freshmen and for older part-time freshmen attending an urban commuter university. The effect of role satisfaction was greater for older than for traditional age students.

Role satisfaction might be a particularly effective variable in future research with nontraditional students given the possibility of (a) a preference for practical versus theoretical knowledge among a significant number of commuter and older students (Gell, 1974; Hughes, 1983); (b) the prevalence of outside commitments which may render academic activities a burden; (c) inferior academic preparation for college making course work initially more difficult; and (d) the prolonged period of enrollment prior to graduation experienced by part-time students, leading to possible "burnout. "

Four codifications (Cope & Hannah, 1975; Lenning et al., 1980; Pantages & Creedon, 1978; Summerskill, 1962) acknowledged that students' lack of interest in their courses was negatively related to persistence in college, although little research was cited. Several studies conducted primarily at residence-oriented 4-year institutions supported this conclusion (Astin, 1975; Brigman et al., 1982, Demitroff 1974; Iffert, 1957; Kowalski, 1977; Krebs & Liberty, 1971; Terenzini & Pascarella 1977; Timmons, 1977).

From research at commuter-oriented 4-year institutions, Haas (1974) reported that lack of interest was frequently cited by students as a reason for dropping out, and Baumgart and Johnstone (1977) disclosed that for part-time students, satisfaction with intellectual stimulation was positively related to persistence. Although Aiken (1968) did not find a difference between dropouts and persisters concerning boredom with courses at a community college, studies at other community colleges (MacMillan, 1970; Weigel, 1969; White, 1972) revealed that students' lack of interest in course work was a prevalent reason for attrition.

According to some writers (e.g., Kimball & Sedlacek, 1971; Lenning & Hanson, 1977; Roelfs, 1975), older compared to traditional age students expressed greater interest in and satisfaction with their courses. In a study of full-time freshman attrition at 15 community colleges (MacMillan, 1970), however, no major age difference was apparent regarding dropouts' lack of interest in their course work as a reason for discontinuing enrollment; course boredom was the second most frequently mentioned reason among 11 items (pp. 4–5).

Goal Commitment

This variable refers to the amount of personal importance that a student ascribes to obtaining a college education, typically defined as the importance of graduating from college, after a student has gained some experience in the college environment. Four codifications (Lenning et al., 1980; Pantages & Creedon, 1978, Spady, 1970 Tinto, 1975) reported a positive relationship between students' *prematriculation* goal commitment and persistence in college, as did several empirical studies conducted primarily at 4-year institutions (Baumgart & Johnstone, 1977; Hackman & Dysinger, 1970; Marks, 1967; Tata, 1981; Trent & Medsker, 1968). Other empirical studies noted a positive association between students' goal commitment *after matriculation* and persistence (Chickering & Hannah, 1969; Pascarella & Terenzini, 1980, 1983; Terenzini et al., 1981).

Pre- or postmatriculation goal commitment has rarely been included as a variable in attrition research at commuter institutions. Tata (1981), however, found that persisters compared to dropouts had a significantly higher level of prematriculation goal commitment at a commuter-oriented 4-year institution. A similar result was obtained by MacMillan (1969) in a study of full-time students at 23 community colleges.

Pascarella and Chapman (1983) incorporated postmatriculation goal commitment as a variable in a study involving full-time freshmen at three types of institutions. Goal commitment showed a small positive direct effect on persistence at residence-oriented 4-year institutions, no significant effect at commuter-oriented 4-year institutions, and a very large positive influence at 2-year colleges. No study was reviewed that exclusively explored the relationship between goal commitment and the attrition of older or part-time students.

It is expected that goal commitment is closely related to educational aspirations, and the findings for this variable are relevant here. Educational aspirations are defined as the highest level of college education that a student plans to obtain, traditionally measured by the highest degree sought. As was mentioned earlier, since some students attending commuter institutions may enroll in a few credit courses for job enhancement or personal enrichment without degree aspirations, this variable might contain such options for student response. Three codifications (Cope & Hannah, 1975; Lenning et al., 1980; Tinto, 1975) reported a positive relationship between students' prematriculation level of educational aspiration and persistence in college.

At primarily residence-oriented 4-year institutions, several empirical studies confirmed a positive relationship between student's *prematriculation* educational aspirations and persistence (Anderson, 1981; Astin, 1975; Coker, 1968; Marks, 1967, Mattox, 1984; Peng & Felters, 1978). Hackman and Dysinger (1970) and Rossmann and Kirk (1970), however, found no significant difference between dropouts and persisters. Anderson (1981) and Munro (1981) reported that students' *postmatriculation* educational aspirations were positively related to persistence.

Regarding commuter students, Fenske and Scott (1972) obtained data from a national sample of beginning freshmen and found that students attending college in their home community possessed lower prematriculation educational aspirations than students who attended college away from home. Research at a commuter-oriented 4-year institution (Staman, 1980) indicated that the prematriculation educational aspirations of beginning students age 17-21 were positively related to persistence. Pascarella et al. (1983), however, found no significant relationship between either pre- or postmatriculation educational aspirations for freshmen at a similar kind of institution.

Using national samples of students who entered community colleges, Astin (1972) and Peng and Fetters (1978) reported that prematriculation educational aspiration was positively related to persistence. Three studies involving community college students (DeVecchio, 1972; Reehling, 1980; White, 1972) disclosed similar results for postmatriculation educational aspiration.

In research conducted at 4- and 2-year colleges (Kuh & Ardaiolo, 1979; Lenning & Hanson, 1977; Solmon & Gordon, 1981), older compared to traditional age students showed a lower level of pre- and postmatriculation educational aspiration although Greer (1980) noted no significant age difference in prematriculation educational aspirations for students attending a community college. According to Staman (1980), however, postmatriculation educational aspiration was not significantly related to the persistence of continuing students age 22–45 at a commuter-oriented 4-year college. Reehling (1980) reported that postmatriculation educational aspiration was positively related to the persistence of older female students attending several community colleges.

Stress

This variable measures the extent to which students believe that they experience stress from factors that are not related to college attendance as well as from the amount of time and energy required for college study.

Regarding stress from sources unrelated to college attendance, several codifications concerning attrition at residence-oriented 4-year institutions acknowledged that such factors as students' poor health and family problems could affect withdrawal from college (Lenning et al., 1980; Marsh, 1966; Pantages & Creedon, 1978; Summerskill, 1962). The role of stress from sources outside the college environment, however, has generally received less attention in studies of residential student attrition than factors within the college setting.

Commuter compared to residential students spend considerably more time outside the college environment. The literature regarding commuter and older students suggests many types of personal stress from the noncollegiate environment: conflicts in the home between students, siblings, and parents about autonomy and values; personal and family illness; dating and marital discord; students' tribulations with their children; co-worker and other employment-related difficulties, problems with peers, relatives, and neighbors; and personal and family debt (Alfred, 1973; Chickering & Kuper, 1971; Garni, 1974; Harrington, 1972; Klotsche, 1966; Schuchman, 1974; Ward & Kurz, 1969).

Students' personal problems have often occupied some prominence in research regarding reasons for attrition at *commuter-oriented 4-year institutions* (Carter 1982; Demos, 1968; Gordon & Johnson, 1982; Louis et al., 1984, Smith, 1980; Tweddale, 1978) and *2-year colleges* (Behrendt, 1974; Bromley, 1973; Brunner et al., 1978; Davis, 1971; Dennis-Rounds, 1983; Gell, 1974; Hinrichsen & Schaumberg, 1976; Roesler, 1971; Stine, 1976; White, 1972).

Most of this research consisted of exit interviews or autopsy studies. Particular personal problems were frequently not identified or, if identified, students often exhibited little consensus about problems. Nevertheless, outside stress factors have appeared with sufficient frequency to warrant a conclusion that outside stress may significantly affect commuter student attrition. For example, Metzner (1984 p. 161) found that a global measure of outside stress was the seventh strongest of 14 significant variables predicting intent to leave for 1,382 freshmen attending an urban commuter university.

No codification was reviewed that examined a relationship between student attrition from college and the extent to which students experienced psychological stress from the time and energy requirements of college attendance. Research at a commuter-oriented 4-year institution (Louis et al., 1984) and a community college (Hall, 1975) indicated that lack of time for school was one of the most frequent reasons that students reported for withdrawing at the end of a semester.

Using the Omnibus Personality Inventory, Kuh (1980) measured personality changes during the freshman year for traditional age and older students who were enrolled in at least seven semester credits at one of two public universities. Compared to traditional age students, older students showed a higher level of stress for two semesters of their freshman year.

Furthermore, older male students reported a greater degree of stress as the number of college credits per term increased. Signs of such stress for these students were tenseness, more aggressive behavior, less tolerance for frustration, and strong feelings of social isolation. Kuh concluded that many older students should reduce their course load during their first year of college.

Poor high school preparation for college and a prolonged absence from a formal learning situation may initially result in less efficient study habits, thus increasing the time and energy required for college work among many older students (Apps, 1981; Burgess, 1973; Mangano & Corrado, 1981; Solmon & Gordon, 1981). In addition, more older compared to traditional age students may have extensive outside commitments, which limit the time and energy available for college attendance. Research by Burgess (1973), Preston (1976), Lance, Lourie, and Mayo (1979), Buckley (1980), and Malin et al. (1980) disclosed that lack of time for school work was a widespread problem among older students who attended public universities and community colleges.

In a study involving exit interviews at a public urban commuter university, Carter (1982) found that "courses are too demanding and time-consuming" (pp. 2-3) was the fourth and fifth most frequent of 60 reasons that older and part-time students, respectively, listed for their withdrawal from college during a semester. Carter did not find this reason to be a major factor in the attrition of traditional age, full-time students.

Intent to Leave

Several recent empirical studies (Bean, 1980, 1982c, 1983, 1985; R. Johnson, 1980; Nelson et al., 1984; Pascarella et al., 1983) found that students' intent to leave their college at the end of the current term or academic year was highly predictive of actual attrition. In each of these multivariate studies, intent to leave was the strongest single predictor of dropout. This finding was evident at residence-oriented 4-year institutions (Bean; Nelson et al.), at a commuter university (Pascarella et al.), and in a combined sample of 4- and 2-year institutions (Johnson).

Only one study was located that employed intent to leave solely with community college students. Alfred (1973, p. 46) reported that 65% of the students who had indicated an intent not to continue enrollment actually departed at the end of the semester; 69% of the students who planned to continue did, in fact, enroll the next semester. No research was found that exclusively investigated the association between intent to leave and the attrition of older or part-time students.

The location of this variable in the model follows from the theories of Fishbein and Ajzen (1975). Attitudes, here called psychological outcomes, are expected to be the best predictors of intent, and intent to leave is expected to be the best predictor of actual dropout.

Intent to leave is closely associated with postmatriculation measures of institutional commitment (Tinto, 1975). Institutional commitment refers to the importance students attribute to attending one particular institution, typically measured as the importance of graduating from the present college. Intent to leave indicates students' intention of leaving their present institution before graduating. Institutional commitment implies a longer commitment than intent to leave. Since the duration of attrition studies is typically 1 year, intent to leave should be a more accurate predictor of attrition than institutional commitment, because intent is predicting behavior over a shorter period.

Intent to leave rather than institutional commitment is used in this model because (a) prior research has consistently shown intent to leave to be an extremely strong predictor of dropout, even when institutional commitment is statistically controlled (see Pascarella et al., 1983); (b) intent to leave is more accurate than institutional commitment for short-term attrition studies; and (c) inclusion of both institutional commitment and intent to leave creates some redundancy and possible multicollinearity problems. It should be remembered that students who intend to transfer also intend to leave, and the potential transfer cannot be distinguished from students who intend to leave for other reasons. If information about students who intend to transfer is important to an institution, a postmatriculation measure of intent to transfer may be included as a control variable (see the discussion of opportunity to transfer).

Conclusions

Spady (1970), Tinto (1975), Pascarella (1980), and Bean (1985) described four models of the dropout process for traditional students which share many elements. The structure of the model developed here is similar to these others, but the content differs markedly. Each of the four models of traditional student attrition emphasizes the importance of students' social interactions with other members of the campus community. In this model, social integration variables should have only minimal effects on retention, partly due to the way nontraditional students were defined and partly because social variables from the outside environment are expected to be of greater importance than college social integration variables. In addition, other environmental variables, such as family responsibilities, can play a significant role in the attrition process for nontraditional students.

The model presented here is a tentative one and will undoubtedly need to be modified when more evidence from multivariate studies of nontraditional students becomes available. Nonetheless, the model should provide a framework for understanding past studies and should serve as a guide for conducting future ones. It can be used to identify variables for study at individual institutions and to specify the relationships among those variables. Not only can it lend coherence to a wide body of knowledge, but it can be extremely practical at the local level, especially as the number of nontraditional students increases.

The longitudinal process of attrition is expected to be similar for nontraditional students regardless of their institutional setting or student subgroup affiliation. The most important variables, however, are likely to differ for subgroups such as older students, part-time students, ethnic minorities, women, or academically underprepared students at different types of institutions, particularly 2-year, 4-year commuter, and 4-year residential colleges. The model is flexible enough to guide studies of different populations in various institutional settings. However, a model that tries to capture the general differences between traditional and nontraditional students will miss many of the details of the attrition process for nontraditional students and thus may fail to account for much of the variance found in specific nontraditional subpopulations.

If there is a particular factor, such as an extended orientation program, that was not included in the model due to insufficient empirical study, but that is assumed to be of importance at a particular institution, such a factor can be added to the model in its appropriate place (in this case, as an academic variable).

Finally, researchers may wish to concentrate their efforts on part of the model. It can be used as a guide to the study of GPA, satisfaction, stress, goal commitment or other intervening variables, each of which can be treated as a dependent variable.

References

Aiken, J. (1968). *A comparison of junior college withdrawees.* Palatka, FL: St. Johns River Junior College. (ERIC Document Reproduction Service No. ED 023 389)

Aitken, N. D. (1982). College student performance, satisfaction, and retention. *Journal of Higher Education. 53,* 32–50.

Alfred, R. L. (Ed.). (1973). *Student attrition: Strategies for action.* Kansas City, MO: Metropolitan Junior College District. (ERIC Document Reproduction Service No. ED 085 064)

Andersen, C. J., & Atelsek, F. J. (1982). *An assessment of college student housing and physical plant.* Higher Education Panel Report, No. 55. Washington, DC: American Council on Education.

Anderson, K. L. (1981). Post-high school experiences and college attrition. *Sociology of Education, 54,* 1–15.

Apps, J. W. (1981) *The adult learner on campus.* Chicago: Follett.

Astin, A. W. (1972). *College dropouts: A national profile.* Washington, DC: American Council on Education.

Astin, A . W. (1975). *Preventing students from dropping out.* San Francisco: Jossey-Bass.

Baumgart, N. L, & Johnstone, J. N. (1977). Attrition at an Australian university. *Journal of Higher Education, 48,* 553–570.

Beal, P. E., & Noel, L. (1980). What works in student retention. Iowa City, IA: American College Testing Program.

Bean, J. P. (1980). Dropouts and turnover: The synthesis and test of a causal model of student attrition. *Research in Higher Education, 12,* 155–187.

Bean, J. P. (1981). *Student attrition, intentions, and confidence: Interaction effects in a path model, Part I. The 23 variable model.* Paper presented at the annual meeting of the American Educational Research Association, Los Angeles.

Bean, J. P. (1982a). Conceptual models of student attrition: How theory can help the institutional researcher. In E. T. Pascarella (Ed.), *Studying student attrition* (pp. 17–33) San Francisco: Jossey-Bass.

Bean, J. P. (1982b). *The interaction effects of GPA on other determinants of student attrition in a homogeneous population.* Paper presented at the annual meeting of the American Educational Research Association, New York.

Bean, J. P. (1982c). Student attrition, intentions, and confidence: Interaction effects in a path model. *Research in Higher Education, 17,* 291–320.

Bean, J. P. (1983). The application of a model of turnover in work organizations to the student attrition process. *Review of Higher Education, 6,* 129–148.

Bean, J. P. (1985). Interaction effects based on class level in an explanatory model of college student dropout syndrome. *American Educational Research Journal, 22,* 35–64.

Behrendt R. L. (1974). *Attrition/retention patterns at HJC. Final report.* Hagerstown, MD: Hagerstown Junior College. (ERIC Document Reproduction Service No. ED 088 539)

Bennett, C., & Bean, J. P. (1984). A conceptual model of black student attrition at a predominantly white university. *Journal of Educational Equity and Leadership, 4,* 173–188.

Bentler, P. M., & Speckart, G. (1979). Models of attitude-behavior relations. *Psychological Review, 86,* 452–464.

Berkove, G. (1976). *Returning women students: A study of stress and success.* Paper presented at the annual convention of the Western Social Science Association, Tempe, AZ. (ERIC Document Reproduction Service No. ED 156 971)

Blanchfield, W. C. (1971). College dropout identification: A case study. *Journal of Experimental Education, 40,* 1–4.

Brainard, S. R. (1973). Student attrition: The student personnel climate. In R. L. Alfred (Ed.), *Student attrition: Strategies for action* (pp. 72–79). Kansas City, MO: Metropolitan Junior College District. (ERIC Document Reproduction Service No. ED 085 064)

Brigman, S. L., Kuh, G. D., & Stager, S. F. (1982). Those who choose to leave: Why students voluntarily withdraw from college. *Journal of the National Association for Women Deans, Administrators and Counselors, 45,* 3–8.

Bromley, A. (1973). *Two attrition studies at Santa Fe Community College.* Paper presented at the annual meeting of the American Educational Research Association, New Orleans. (ERIC Document Reproduction Service No. ED 075 022)

Brunner, W. D., Packwood, G., & Wilson, B. (1978). *Retention and attrition: Does it relate to students goals?* Paper presented at the annual meeting of the American Educational Research Association, Toronto. (ERIC Document Reproduction Service No. ED 153 682)

Buckley, P. G. (1980). The adults returning to higher education in an urban community college. *Dissertation Abstracts International, 40,* 2497A. (University Microfilms No. 79–24,585)

Bucklin, R. W., & Bucklin, M. L. (1970). *The psychological characteristics of the college persister and leaver: A review.* Washington, DC: U.S. Department of Health, Education, and Welfare. (ERIC Document Reproduction Service No. ED 049 709)

Bucks County Community College. (1973). *Follow-up study: Nonacademic attrition.* Newtown, PA: Author. (ERIC Document Reproduction Service No. ED 082 751)

Burgess, T. C. (1973). *The older student at Portland State University.* Portland, OR: Portland State University, Counseling Center.

California State Coordinating Council for Higher Education. (1974). *Through the open door: A study of persistence and performance in California's community colleges* (Report No. 3). Sacramento, CA: Author. (ERIC Document Reproduction Service No. ED 121 393)

Capoor, M., & Eagle, N. (1977). Dropouts in two-year colleges: Better prediction with the use of moderator subgroups. *Community/ Junior College Research Quarterly, 1.* 171–177.

Carnegie Council on Policy Studies in Higher Education. (1980). *Three thousand futures.* San Francisco: Jossey-Bass.

Caner, B. L. (1982). *Exit interview summary, fall, 1981.* Indianapolis, IN: Indiana University-Purdue University, Office of Student Services.

Chase, C. I. (1970). The college dropout: His high school prologue. *Bulletin of the National Association of Secondary School Principals, 54,* 67–71.

Chickering, A. W. (1969). *Education and identity.* San Francisco: Jossey-Bass.

Chickering, A. W (1974). *Commuting versus resident students.* San Francisco: Jossey-Bass.

Chickering, A. W., & Hannah, W. (1969). The process of withdrawal. *Liberal Education, 55,* 551–558.

Chickering, A. W., & Kuper, E. (1971). Educational outcomes for commuters and residents. *Educational Record, 52,* 255–261.

Clark, B. R. (1960). The "cooling-out" function in higher education. *American Journal of Sociology, 65,* 569–576.

Cohen, A. M. (1969). *The relationship among student characteristics, changed institutional practices and student attrition in junior college.* Washington, DC: U.S. Department of Health, Education, and Welfare. (ERIC Document Reproduction Service No. ED 032 074)

Coker, D. L. (1968). *Diversity of intellective and non-intellective characteristics between persisting and non-persisting students among campuses.* Stevens Point: Wisconsin State University. (ERIC Document Reproduction Service No. ED 033 645)

Cope, R. G., & Hannah, W. (1975). *Revolving college doors.* New York: John Wiley & Sons.

Costa, A. E., (1984), Selected correlates of achievement and persistence of adult community college students. *Dissertation Abstracts International, 44,* 2989A. (University Microfilms No. 84-01,974)

Crockett, D. S. (1978). Academic advising: A cornerstone of student retention. In L. Noel (Ed.), *Reducing the dropout rate* (pp. 29–35). San Francisco: Jossey-Bass.

Cross, K. P. (1981). *Adults as learners.* San Francisco: Jossey-Bass.

Curran, J. (1981). *Why do students leave the university?* Paper presented at the annual convention of the American Psychological Association, Los Angeles. (ERIC Document Reproduction Service No. ED 210 974)

Davis, B. H. (1971). The community junior college experience as perceived by students who have withdrawn. *Dissertation Abstracts International, 31,* 5659A. (University Microfilms No. 71-12,743)

Demitroff, J. F. (1974). Student persistence. *College and University 49,* 553–565.

Demos, G. D. (1968). An analysis of college dropouts—Some manifest and covert reasons. *Personnel and Guidance Journal, 46,* 681–684.

Dennis-Rounds, J. (1983). *Study of students leaving Cerritos College, spring 1983.* Norwalk, CA: Cerritos Community College. (ERIC Document Reproduction Service No. ED 233 762)

DeVecchio, R. C. (1972). Characteristics of nonreturning community college freshmen *Journal of College Student Personnel, 13,* 429–432.

Disque, C. S. (1983). The relationship of student characteristics and academic integration to college freshman attrition. *Dissertation Abstracts International. 43,* 3820A–3821A. (University Microfilms No. 83-02,569)

Dressel, P. L., & Nisula, E. S. (1966). *A comparison of the commuting and noncommuting student.* East Lansing: Michigan State University. (ERIC Document Reproduction Service No. ED 011 967)

Dulniak, D. I. (1982). Predicting freshmen dropouts at Montana State University using selected institutional data. *Dissertation Abstracts International, 42,* 3455A–3456A. (University Microfilms No. 82-01,177)

Dunston, F. M ., Richmond, P. A., & House, L. A., Jr. (1983a). *Annotated bibliography: Black student retention in higher education institutions.* Chapel Hill, NC: Research and Evaluation Associates. (ERIC Document Reproduction Service No. ED 228 911)

Dunston, F. M., Richmond, P. A., & House, L. A., Jr. (1983b). *Review of the literature: Black student retention in higher education institutions.* Chapel Hill, NC. Research and Evaluation Associates. (ERIC Document Reproduction Service No. ED 228 912)

Eagle, N. (1979). *Attrition and student progress at Bronx Community College for entering classes. Fall 1972 to fall 1976 (progress to fall 1978).* Bronx, NY: Bronx Community College. (ERIC Document Reproduction Service No. ED 192 856)

Endo, J. J., & Harpel, R. L. (1979). *A longitudinal study of attrition.* Boulder: University of Colorado. (ERIC Document Reproduction Service No. ED 174 095)

Enos, P. B. (1981). Student satisfaction with faculty academic advising and persistence beyond the freshman year in college. *Dissertation Abstracts International, 42,* 1985A. (University Microfilms No. 81-23,315)

Everett, C. L. (1979). *An analysis of student attrition at Penn State.* University Park: Pennsylvania State University, Office of Planning and Budget.

Fenske, R. H., & Scott, C. S. (1972). *A comparison of freshmen who attend college in their home community and freshmen who migrate to college.* Iowa City, IA: American College Testing Program. (ERIC Document Reproduction Service No. ED 067 567)

Fetters, W. B. (1977). *National Longitudinal Study: Withdrawal from institutions of higher education.* Washington, DC: U.S. Department of Health, Education, and Welfare, National Center for Education Statistics. (ERIC Document Reproduction Service No. ED 150 913)

Fishbein, M., & Ajzen, I. (1975). *Belief, attitude, intention and behavior: An introduction to theory and research.* Reading, MA: Addison-Wesley.

Flaherty, E. G. (1978). Higher education responds to the needs of the adult part-time student. *College Student Journal, 12,* 375–378.

Flanagan, D. (1976). The commuter student in higher education. *National Association of Student Personnel Administrators Journal, 13,* 35–41.

Garni, K. F. (1974). Urban commuter students: Counseling for survival. *Journal of College Student Personnel. 15,* 465–469.

Gathers, E. G. (1982). A retention study of horizontal transfer, vertical transfer, and native students at a selected university. *Dissertation Abstracts International, 43,* 3232A. (University Microfilms No. 83-04,858)

Gell, R. L. (1974). *A follow-up study of freshmen who left Montgomery College after just one semester of attendance.* Rockville, MD. Montgomery College. (ERIC Document Reproduction Service No. ED 097 054)

Getzlar, S. B., Sedlacek, G. M., Kearney, K. A., & Blackwell, J. M. (1984). Two types of voluntary undergraduate attrition: Application of Tinto's model. *Research in Higher Education, 20,* 257–268.

Gilder, J. (1980). Lifelong education: The critical policy questions. In B. Heermann, C. C Enders, & E. Wine (Eds.), *Serving lifelong learners* (pp. 69–86). New Direction for Community Colleges No. 29. San Francisco: Jossey-Bass.

Gordon, S. A., & Johnson, D. H. (1982). Characteristics of withdrawing students. In D. H. Johnson (Ed.), *Report of the Withdrawal Office: The who, when, why, and how of withdrawal at University of Maryland, Baltimore County, spring semester,* 1981 (pp. 4–21). Catonsville: University of Maryland. (ERIC Document Reproduction Service No. ED 231 282)

Gorter, S. (1978). *Non-returning students, spring 1978.* Trenton, NJ: Mercer County Community College. (ERIC Document Reproduction Service No. ED 161 473)

Greer, L. R. (1980). *Persistence and academic success among non-traditional age students at a Junior college.* Paper presented at the annual forum of the Association for Institutional Research, Atlanta, GA. (ERIC Document Reproduction Service No. ED 189 942)

Greive, D. E. (1970). *A study of student attrition at Cuyahoga Community College, part 1.* Cleveland, OH: Cuyahoga Community College. (ERIC Document Reproduction Service No. ED 038 976)

Gusfield, J., Kronus, S., & Mark, H. (1970). The urban context and higher education: A delineation of issues. *Journal of Higher Education. 41,* 29–43.

Haas, P. (1974). *Follow-up study of discontinuing students at Indiana University at South Bend.* South Bend: Indiana University. (ERIC Document Reproduction Service No. ED 104 261)

Hackman, J. R., & Dysinger, W. S. (1970). Research notes: Commitment to college as a factor in student attrition. *Sociology of Education, 43,* 311–324.

Hall, T. L. (1975). *El Paso Community College attrition studies, fall 1971–fall 1974.* El Paso, TX: El Paso Community College. (ERIC Document Reproduction Service No. ED 110 114)

Hardwick, M. W., & Kazio, M. P. (1973). *Designing and implementing a commuter services program. A model for change.* College Park: University of Maryland. (ERIC Document Reproduction Service No. ED 087 368)

Harrington, T. F. (1972). The literature on the commuter student. *Journal of College Student Personnel, 12,* 546–550.

Henry, D. D. (1975). *Challenges past, challenges present: An analysis of American higher education since 1930.* San Francisco: Jossey-Bass.

Hinrichsen, K. A., & Schaumberg. G. F. (1976). *The dropout: A look into the historical evaluation of long-standing implied policy at Cerritos College, California.* Norwalk, CA: Cerritos Community College. (ERIC Document Reproduction Service No. ED 129 361)

Hughes, R. (1983). The non-traditional student in higher education: A synthesis of the literature. *National Association of Student Personnel Administrators Journal, 20.* 51–64.

Hunter, R., & Sheldon, M. S. (1980). *Statewide longitudinal study, part 3.* Sacramento: California Community Colleges, Office of the Chancellor. (ERIC Document Reproduction Service No. ED 188 714)

Iffert, R. E. (1957). *Retention and withdrawal of college students.* Washington, DC: U.S. Department of Health, Education, and Welfare.

Jaffe, A. J., & Adams, W. (1970). *Academic and socioeconomic factors related to entrance and retention at two- and four-year colleges in the late 1960's.* New York: Columbia University, Bureau of Applied Social Research. (ERIC Document Reproduction Service No. ED 049 679)

Johansson, C. B., & Rossmann, J. E. (1973). Persistence at a liberal arts college: A replicated five-year longitudinal study. *Journal of Counseling Psychology, 20,* 1–9.

Johnson, E. F. (1981). Characteristics and needs of Indiana University freshman commuter students. *Dissertation Abstracts International, 42,* 102A. (University Microfilms No. 81–14, 958)

Johnson, R. H. (1980). The relationship of academic and social integration to student attrition—A study across institutions and institutional types. *Dissertation Abstracts International, 41,* 1868A. (University Microfilms No. 80-25,700)

Johnston, A. B. (1982). *Tallahassee Community College retention study, final report.* Tallahassee, FL: Tallahassee Community College. (ERIC Document Reproduction Service No. ED 224 524)

Kasworm, C. E. (1980). The older student as an undergraduate. *Adult Education, 31,* 30–47.

Kimball, R. L., & Sedlacek, W. E. (1971). *Characteristics of older undergraduates at The University of Maryland*. College Park: University of Maryland, Counseling Center. (ERIC Document Reproduction Service No. ED 165 523)

Kimmel, E. W., & Murphy, M. E. (1976). Back to school: The older than average student. *College and University*, 51, 679–692.

Klotsche, J. M. (1966). *The urban university and the future of our cities*. New York: Harper & Row.

Knoell, D. M. (1966). A critical review of research on the college dropout. In L. A. Pervin, L. E. Reik, & W. Dalrymple (Eds.), *The college dropout and the utilization of talent* (pp. 63–81). Princeton, NJ: Princeton University Press.

Knoell, D. M. (1976). *Through the open door: A study of patterns of enrollment and performance in California's community colleges*. Sacramento: California State Postsecondary Education Commission. (ERIC Document Reproduction Service No. ED 119 752)

Kowalski, C. (1977). *The impact of college on persisting and nonpersisting students*. New York: Philosophical Library.

Krebs, R. E., & Liberty, P. G., Jr. (1971). *A comparative study of three groups of withdrawal students on ten factor variables derived from a 36-problem self-report inventory*. Austin: University of Texas. (ERIC Document Reproduction Service No. ED 052 690)

Kuh, G. D. (1980). The *personality functioning of traditional-age students and adult learners during the first year of college*. Paper presented at the annual meeting of the American Educational Research Association, Boston.

Kuh, G. D., & Ardaiolo, F. P. (1979). Adult learners and traditional age freshmen: Comparing the "new" pool with the "old" pool of students. *Research in Higher Education, 10*, 207–219.

Lackey, P. M. (1977). Commuter students: Interaction in two types of college situations *College Student Journal, 11*, 153–155.

Lance, L., Lourie, J., & Mayo, C. (1979). Difficulties of re-entry students by sex and length of school interruption. *Journal of the National Association for Women Deans, Administrators, and Counselors, 42*, 39–42.

Lenning, O. T., Beal, P. E., & Sauer, K. (1980). *Retention and attrition: Evidence for action and research*. Boulder, CO: National Center for Higher Education Management Systems.

Lenning, O. T., & Hanson, G. R. (1977). Adult students at two-year colleges: A longitudinal study. *Community/Junior College Research Quarterly, 1*, 271–294.

Lewin, K. (1935). *A dynamic theory of personality: Selected papers*. New York: McGraw Hill.

Locke, E. A. (1976) The nature and causes of job satisfaction. In M. D. Dunnett (Ed.), *Handbook of industrial and organizational psychology*. Chicago: Rand McNally.

Louis, K. S., Colten, M. E., & Demeke, G. (1984). *Freshman experiences at the University of Massachusetts at Boston*. Boston: University of Massachusetts. (ERIC Document Reproduction Service No. ED 242 251)

MacMillan, T. F. (1969). *NORCAL project, phase 1, final report*. Los Angeles: University of California, Los Angeles. (ERIC Document Reproduction Service No ED 031 240)

MacMillan, T. F. (1970). *NORCAL project, phase 2, final report*. Los Angeles: University of California, Los Angeles. (ERIC Document Reproduction Service No. ED 039 879)

Malin, J. T., Bray, J. H., Dougheny, T. W, & Skinner, W. K. (1980). Factors affecting the performance and satisfaction of adult men and women attending college. *Research in Higher Education, 13*, 115–130.

Mangano, J. A., & Corrado, T. J. (1981). Easing academic re-entry. In F. R. DiSilvestro (Ed.), *Advising and counseling adult learners* (pp. 33–41). San Francisco: Jossey-Bass.

Marks, E. (1967). Student perceptions of college persistence and their intellective, personality, and performance correlates. *Journal of Educational Psychology, 58,* 210–221.

Marsh, L. M. (1966). College dropouts—A review. *Personnel and Guidance Journal. 44,* 475–481.

Martin, F. H. (1974). *Student follow-up 1: Attrition study.* Harriman, TN: Roane State Community College. (ERIC Document Reproduction Service No. ED 099 087)

Mattox, V. R. (1984). A study of a means for the early identification of potential college dropouts. *Dissertation Abstracts International, 44,* 2688A. (University Microfilms No. 84-00,254)

Metzner, B. S. (1984). An application and evaluation of a model of student attrition using freshmen at a public urban commuter university. *Dissertation Abstracts International, 44,* 2378A. (University Microfilms No. 83-28,8080)

Meyers, E. M., III. (1981). A comparative analysis of persisters, permanent dropouts, dropouts who transfer, and stopouts at St. Cloud State University. *Dissertation Abstracts International, 42,* 105A. (University Microfilms No. 81-13,988)

Munro, B. H. (1981). Dropouts from higher education: Path analysis of a national sample. *American Educational Research Journal, 18,* 133–141.

Murray, H. A. (1938). *Explorations in personality.* New York: Oxford University Press.

National Institute of Education. (1984). *Involvement in learning: Realizing the potential of American higher education.* Report of the Study Group on the Conditions of Excellence in American Higher Education. Washington, DC: U.S. Government Printing Office.

Naylor, P. D., & Sanford, T. R. (1982). Intrainstitutional analysis of student retention across student levels. *College and University, 57,* 143–159.

Nelson, J. E. (1982). Institutional assessment of a private university by commuter and resident students. *Dissertation Abstracts International, 43,* 90A–91A. (University Microfilms No. 82-13,169)

Nelson, R. B., Scott, T. B., & Bryan, W. A. (1984). Precollege characteristics and early college experiences as predictors of freshman year persistence. *Journal of College Student Personnel 25,* 50–54.

Newton, L L., & Gaither, G. H. (1980). Factors contributing to attrition: An analysis of program impact on persistence patterns. *College and University, 55,* 237–251.

Noel, L. (1976). College student retention: A campus-wide responsibility. *National Association of College Admissions Counselors Journal, 21,* 33–36.

O'Donnell, K. M. (1980). Older Learners: A viable clientele. In E. Greenberg, K. M. O'Donnell & W. Bergquist (Eds.), *Educating learners of all ages. New Directions for Higher Education, 8*(1). San Francisco: Jossey-Bass.

Panos, R. J., & Astin, A. W. (1968). Attrition among college students. *American Educational Research Journal, 5,* 57–72.

Pantages, T. I., & Creedon, C. F. (1978). Studies of college attrition: 1950–1975. *Review of Educational Research, 48,* 49–101.

Parelius, A. P. (1979). Age inequality in educational opportunity: The needs of adult students in higher education. *Adult Education, 29,* 180–193.

Parsons, T., & Platt, G. M. (1973). The American university. Cambridge, MA: Harvard University Press.

Pascarella, E. T (1980). Student-faculty informal contact and college outcomes. *Review of Educational Research, 50,* 545–595.

Pascarella, E. T., & Chapman, D. W. (1983). A multi-institutional, path analytic validation of Tinto's model of college withdrawal. American Educational Research Journal, 20, 87–102.

Pascarella, E. T., Duby, P. B., & Iverson, B. K. (1983). A test and reconceptualization of a theoretical model of college withdrawal in a commuter institution setting. *Sociology of Education 56,* 88–100.

Pascarella, E. T., Duby, P. B., Miller, V. A., & Rasher, S. P. (1981). Preenrollment variables and academic performance as predictors of freshman year persistence, early withdrawal, and dropout behavior in an urban, nonresidential university. *Research in Higher Education, 15,* 329–349.

Pascarella, E. T., & Terenzini, P. T. (1977). Patterns of student-faculty informal interaction beyond the classroom and voluntary freshman attrition. *Journal of Higher Education, 48,* 540–552.

Pascarella, E. T., & Terenzini, P. T. (1980). Predicting freshman persistence and voluntary dropout decisions from a theoretical model. *Journal of Higher Education, 51,* 60–75.

Pascarella, E. T., & Terenzini, P. T. (1983). Predicting voluntary freshman year persistence/ withdrawal behavior: A path analytic validation of Tinto's model. *Journal of Educational Psychology, 75,* 215–226.

Peng, S. S., & Fetters, W. B. (1978). Variables involved in withdrawal during the first two years of college: Preliminary findings from the National Longitudinal Study of the High School Class of 1972. *American Educational Research Journal, 15,* 361–372.

Preston, W. G. (1976). *Adults as regular community college students: A comparative analysis of some of their characteristics and perceptions and those of college-age students.* Pleasant Hill, CA: Diablo Valley College. (ERIC Document Reproduction Service No. ED 121 368)

Rauch, D. B. (1981). Education for the growing majority: Adults. *Life-long Learning, 5,* 10–13.

Reed, H. B. (1968). College students' motivations related to voluntary dropout and under-overachievement. *Journal of Educational Research, 9,* 412–416.

Reehling, J. E. (1980). They are returning: But are they staying? *Journal of College Student Personnel, 21,* 491–497.

Riesman, D. (1981). *On higher education: The academic enterprise in an era of rising student consumerism.* San Francisco: Jossey-Bass.

Rice, R. L. (1983). *USC-Lancaster: A retention study for a two-year commuter campus.* Lancaster: University of South Carolina. (ERIC Document Reproduction Service No. ED 231 440)

Roach, R. M. (1976). Honey, won't you please stay home. *Personnel and Guidance Journal, 55,* 86–89.

Roelfs, P. J. (1975). Teaching and counseling older college students. *Findings* (Vol. 2). Princeton, NJ: Educational Testing Service.

Roesler E. V, (1971). *Community college and technical institute follow-up study of students enrolled during one or more quarters: Fall, 1970 to fall, 1971.* Washington, DC: U.S. Department of Health, Education, and Welfare. (ERIC Document Reproduction Service No. ED 072 770)

Rootman, I. (1972). Voluntary withdrawal from a total adult socializing organization: A model. *Sociology of Education, 45,* 258–270.

Rossi, P. (1966). Research strategies in measuring peer group influence. In T. Newcomb & E. Wilson (Eds.), *College peer groups* (pp. 190–214). Chicago: Aldine.

Rossmann, J. E., & Kirk, B. A. (1970). Factors related to persistence and withdrawal among university students. *Journal of Counseling Psychology, 17,* 56–62.

Roueche, J. E. (1967). *Research studies of the junior college dropout.* Washington, DC: American Association of Junior Colleges. (ERIC Document Reproduction Service No. ED 013 659)

Schuchman, H. (1974). Special tasks of commuter students. *Personnel and Guidance Journal, 52,* 465–470.

Scott, S. H. (1975). Impact of residence hall living on college student development. *Journal of College Student Personnel, 16,* 214–219.

Selo, P. A. (1974). *The non-returning students: Who are they? Why have they not returned?* Oakland, CA: Laney College. (ERIC Document Reproduction Service No. ED 100 468)

Sewall, T. J. (1984). A study of adult undergraduates: What causes them to seek a degree? *Journal of College Student Personnel, 25,* 309-314.

Sexton, V. S. (1965). Factors contributing to attrition in college populations: Twenty-five years of research. *Journal of General Psychology, 72,* 301–326.

Skaling, M. M. (1971). Review of the research literature. In R. G. Cope (Ed.), *An investigation of entrance characteristics related to types of college dropouts, final report* (pp. 17–68). Seattle: University of Washington. (ERIC Document Reproduction Service No. ED 052 749)

Slocum, W. L. (1956). Social factors involved in academic mortality. *College and University, 32,* 53–64.

Smith, A. D. (1980). A study of selected variables among student persisters and nonpersisters enrolled in the general and the community and technical colleges. *Dissertation Abstracts International, 41,* 963A. (University Microfilms No. 80–19,117)

Snyder, F. A., & Blocker, C. E. (1970). *A profile of nonpersisting students: A description of educational goals and achievements, activities, and perceptions of non-graduates, spring 1969.* Harrisburg, PA: Harrisburg Area Community Colleges. (ERIC Document Reproduction Service No. ED 037 218)

Solmon, L. C., & Gordon, J. J. (1981). *The characteristics and needs of adults in postsecondary education.* Lexington, MA: D. C. Heath.

Spady, W. G. (1970). Dropouts from higher education: An interdisciplinary review and synthesis. *Interchange, 1,* 64–85.

Spady, W. G. (1971). Dropouts from higher education: Toward an empirical model. *Interchange, 2,* 38–62.

Staman, E. M. (1980). Predicting student attrition at an urban college. *Dissertation Abstracts International, 40,* 4440A. (University Microfilms No. 80–02,565)

Steele, M. W. (1978). Correlates of undergraduate retention at the University of Miami. *Journal of College Student Personnel, 19,* 349–352.

Stewart, S. S., & Rue, P. (1983). Commuter students: Definition and distribution. In S. S. Stewart (Ed.), *Commuter students: Enhancing their educational experiences* (pp. 3–8). San Francisco: Jossey-Bass.

Stine, V. (1976). *Some characteristics of students who withdrew from LACC spring 1975, spring 1974, and spring 1973.* Los Angeles: Los Angeles City College. (ERIC Document Reproduction Service No. ED 118 200)

Summerskill, J. (1962). Dropouts from college. In N. Sanford (Ed.), *The American college* (pp. 627–657). New York: John Wiley & Sons.

Tata, C., Jr. (1981). *The effect of an intrusive advisement program on first-term freshman attrition.* Paper presented at the annual forum of the Association for Institutional Research, Minneapolis. (ERIC Document Reproduction Service No. ED 205 096)

Taylor, W. D. (1982). A five-year attrition study of an undergraduate class at the University of Tennessee at Chattanooga. *Dissertation Abstracts International, 43,* 695A. (University Microfilms No. 82-17,304)

Terenzini, P. T., Lorang, W. G., & Pascarella, E. T. (1981). Predicting freshman persistence and voluntary dropout decisions: A replication. *Research in Higher Education, 15,* 109–127.

Terenzini, P. T., & Pascarella, E. T. (1977). Voluntary freshman attrition and patterns of social and academic integration in a university: A test of a conceptual model. *Research in Higher Education, 6,* 25–43.

Timmons, F. R. (1977). Freshman withdrawal from college: An empirical examination of the usefulness of "autopsy studies." *Psychological Reports, 41,* 672–674.

Tinto, V. (1975). Dropout from higher education: A theoretical synthesis of recent research. *Review of Educational Research, 45,* 89–125.

Tinto, V. (1982). Limits of theory and practice in student attrition. *Journal of Higher Education, 51,* 687–700.

Trent, J. W., & Medsker, L. L. (1968). *Beyond high school.* San Francisco: Jossey-Bass.

Trent, J. W., & Ruyle, J. (1965). Variations, flow, and patterns of college attendance. *College and University, 41,* 61–76.

Trivett , D. A. (1973) *Goals for higher education. Definitions and directions.* ERIC Higher Education Research Report No. 6. Washington, DC: American Association for Higher Education.

Trivett, D. A. (1974). The commuting student. *College and University Bulletin. 26,* 3–6.

Tweddale, R. B. (1978). *The non-returning student: Why do they leave and will they return?* Allendale, MI: Grand Valley State Colleges. (ERIC Document Reproduction Service No. ED 156 023)

University of California. (1980). *Retention and transfer: University of California undergraduate enroll-ment study.* Berkeley: University of California, Office of the Academic Vice President. (ERIC Document Reproduction Service No. ED 215 597)

U.S. Department of Education, National Center for Education Statistics. (1982). *The condition of education.* Washington, DC: Author.

Von der Embse, T. J., & Childs, J. M. (1979). Adults in transition: A profile of the older college student. *Journal of College Student Personnel, 20,* 475–479.

Wallace, D. (1979). A comparative analysis of the needs of undergraduate adults. *National Associa-tion of Student Personnel Administrators Journal, 16,* 15–23.

Walleri, R. D. (1981). *Student retention and attrition in the community college: A review and research design.* Gresham, OR: Mount Hood Community College. (ERIC Document Reproduction Service No. ED 210 064)

Ward, F. R., & Kurz, T. E. (1969). *The commuting student: A study of facilities at Wayne State University.* Final report of the Commuter Center Project. New York: Educational Facilities Laboratories.

Weigel, M. (1969). *A comparison of persisters and non-persisters in a junior college.* Coon Rapids, MN: Anoka-Ramsey State Junior College. (ERIC Document Reproduction Service No. ED 044 115)

Welty, J. D. (1976). Resident and commuter students: Is it only the living situation? *Journal of College Student Personnel, 17,* 465–468.

Wetzel, S. (1977). *Non-returning student survey, winter, 1976–fall, 1976.* Media, PA: Delaware County Community College. (ERIC Document Reproduction Service No. ED 145 906)

White, J. H. (1972). Individual and environmental factors associated with freshman attrition at a multi-campus community college. *Dissertation Abstracts International, 32,* 3709A. (University Microfilms No. 72–3745)

Wolfgang, M. E., & Dowling, W. D. (1981). Differences in motivation of adult and younger undergraduates. *Journal of Higher Education, 52,* 640–648.

Zaccaria, L., & Creaser, J. (1971). Factors related to persistence in an urban commuter university. *Journal of College Student Personnel, 12,* 286–291.

Testing Qualitative Indicators of Precollege Factors in Tinto's Attrition Model:
A Community College Student Population

Amaury Nora, L. C. Attinasi, Jr., and Andrew Matonak

During the 1970s, research on student retention saw the emergence of theoretically based studies, a departure from previous research which had been largely atheoretical. Although researchers have posited various theoretical explanations for retention in higher education institutions, to date few have explored them in the community college setting.

While many publications identify variables correlated with student attrition, relatively few theoretical conceptual models explain how and why these variables affect student attrition. These models include those of John Bean (1980, 1982), Ernest T. Pascarella (1980), William Spady (1970), and Vincent Tinto (1975). All of them emphasize that student retention is not the result of individual or institutional factors but rather the interaction between the two.

Alexander Astin (1975), Phillip Beal and Lee Noel (1980), and Vincent Tinto (1982) suggested that retention can best be explained by the interaction between the student and the institution. Their interaction theory contends that retention or attrition results from the holistic interactions between a student and the collegiate environment, and not solely from individual attributes, program components, and the environment.

Although each research theory incorporated the various characteristics of students and the institutions they attend, these interaction models focused on what happened to students once they arrived on campus and resulted in important insights about student integration into campus life. Dropouts were seen as less integrated into college life and less committed to obtaining a degree.

Over the past decade, Tinto's theoretical model of persistence has driven much of the retention research. Tinto's model examines the relationships among: (1) social and academic integration, (2) student commitments to their educational goals and to their respective institutions, (3) students' background characteristics, and (4) retention decisions. In sum, Tinto hypothesizes that higher levels of social and academic integration result in higher levels of commitment both to the institution and to educational goals. Most, if not all, student persistence studies have not found that precollege factors have a significant impact on retention, but this lack of extensive direct effects may result from misspecification errors because studies have not incorporated appropriate indicators in quantitative models.

Based on his naturalistic study of Mexican-American student retention, Louis C. Attinasi (1986) hypothesized two important precollege retention influences: experiences early in life which lead to students' beliefs or expectations that they will go to college and prematriculation on-campus experiences such as extended visits to college campuses. No one has previously analyzed

174

this construct in relation to Tinto's model. Incorporating this factor in quantitative models may reduce misspecification error and establish a stronger relationship between one measure of the precollege construct and retention.

Retention research has primarily focused on residential, senior institutions. Only a few studies in recent years have examined the relationship among variables affecting retention in community colleges (Rendon 1982; Seale 1984; Nora 1987). Our study helps develop an explanatory model of community college student retention. In addition, qualitative researchers have questioned findings from quantitative studies because they exclude important and necessary variables from causal models of student attrition. The misspecification of quantitative models could result in bias in parameter estimates or reduce the variance they explain. We address the issue of misspecification by quantifying and testing factors excluded in previous causal models but which, according to an ethnographic study, influence retention.

Our purpose was to investigate the predictive accuracy of Tinto's (1975) theoretical model of student attrition among academically underprepared students in a two-year community college. We examined the direct and indirect effects of four exogenous variables (family background, precollege schooling, getting ready, and encouragement by significant others) and three endogenous variables (initial commitments, academic integration, and social integration) on student retention. More important, this study quantifies and tests precollege characteristics identified in Attinasi's (1986) ethnographic study that previous quantitative models testing Tinto's model of student attrition have not used.

Figure 1 displays the hypothesized path model representing the four structural equations tested in the study. In each case, the direction of causation and the nature of the relationship are supported by previous research or hypothesized for the first time in the study (e.g., the effect of getting ready on each endogenous variable). The study hypothesizes that the four exogenous variables have direct effects on initial commitments. The study also hypothesizes direct and indirect effects (1) from three exogenous variables (family background, precollege schooling, and getting ready) on academic integration, (2) from two exogenous variables (getting ready and encouragement from significant others) on social integration, and (3) from two exogenous variables (getting ready and precollege schooling) on student retention. We hypothesized that initial commitments would have a direct effect on both academic and social integration, plus direct and indirect effects on student retention. We also hypothesized that academic integration and social integration would jointly have direct effects on student retention.

Research Design

The sample population included 1,036 first-time college freshmen enrolled in developmental education courses in a large, multi-campus community college in the Houston metropolitan area. We studied these students from the fall of 1984 through the, spring of 1987. The students returned a total of 253 usable surveys which resulted in a 24.4 percent response rate. We interviewed twenty-six nonrespondents, seeking differences in behavior patterns between those in the sample and those not responding to the survey; their characteristics were similar.

This study's survey instrument incorporated items developed by Ernest Pascarella and Patrick Terenzini (1980, 1983), Robert Seale (1984), and Amaury Nora (1987). Pascarella and Terenzini (1983) and others have thoroughly documented the content and predictive validity of the fifty-five items measuring three main variables in the causal model (initial commitments, academic integration, and social integration). Subsequent investigations (i.e., Pascarella ¶ Chapman, 1983) refined the scales through a series of factor analyses and reduced the fifty-five items to thirty. The Pascarella and Chapman study (1983) confirmed the construct and predictive validity of the measures by contrasting student retention among students at different types of institutions (including two-year colleges). Ernest Pascarella, Paul Duby, and Barbara Iverson (1983) and Richard Fox (1985) established the validity of the instrument while studying retention in a non-residential university setting. Laura Rendon (1982) and Nora (1987) established construct and predictive validity of the measures with a community college population. Additional data

Figure 1
Hypothesized Causal Model

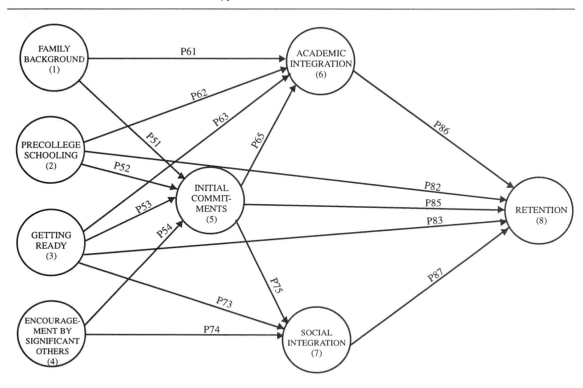

collection sources consisted of official forms and records of the college, including class rosters and college transcripts. In addition, we developed items to measure Attinasi's (1986) getting construct.

To estimate the construct validity of the present instrument with the study population, we performed a principal components factor analysis. Table 1 presents the factor loadings. The factor composition of the items representing academic integration, social integration, initial commitments, and encouragement by significant others were consistent with the dimensions specified by Tinto's model. Since path analysis requires one measure per variable, we computed a composite score for each scale and then added those scores, corresponding to the variables in the study, to obtain one measure of each variable. We computed Cronbach's alphas for each scale used to measure variables in the model. (See Table 1.)

Exogenous Variables

In measuring family background, we used the family socioeconomic status taken from the socioeconomic index based on 1983 labor force data compiled by the U.S. Department of Commerce and reported by Gillian Stevens and Joo Hyun Cho (1985). Operationally, we defined the family background variable as the greater of the father's socioeconomic status or the mother's socioeconomic status. If both parents' status equaled zero, we used the student's socioeconomic status.

The student's academic performance in high school represented the precollege schooling variable; operationally, we defined it as student self-reports of high school grades.

The getting ready variable consisted of two scales: (1) students' early expectations about going to college and (2) prematriculation on campus experiences. We combined three items to represent early college-going expectations (college expectations growing from family experiences in college, college expectations growing from friends' experiences in college, and the age when it first occurred to students that they would go to college). Three items provided a measure of prematriculation on-campus experiences (the number of times the student visited a college

Table 1
Factor Loadings and Alpha Reliabilities for Variables in the Model

Variables	Number of Items	Range of Loadings	Chronbach's Alpha
1. Family background	1		.44
2. Precollege schooling	1		.72
3. Getting ready	6	.14–.74	.83
College-going expectations			.64
On-campus experiences			.83
4. Encouragement by significant others	6	.54–.73	.77
5. Initial commitments	6	.49–.84	.72
Goal commitment			.76
Institutional commitment			.35
6. Academic integration	11	.44–.75	.73
Academic perceptions			.79
Academic involvement			.64
Study behavior			.48
7. Social integration	7	.51–.83	.71
Social perceptions			.75
Social involvement			.43

campus, the number of times the student visited with a college official while on a college campus, and the number of days a student spent on a campus before attending college).

The variable encouragement by significant others represented the interest and encouragement that high school teachers, high school counselors, parents, other close relatives, and friends expressed about having the student go to college. The variable was a composite of the items measuring interest and encouragement of all significant others.

Endogenous Variables

Operationally, we defined initial commitments as the sum of items measuring both initial goal commitments (highest expected academic degree, the importance of graduating from college, the importance of making good grades, and the importance of accomplishing educational goals) and institutional commitments (confidence in making the right decision in attending the community college and the importance of graduating from that institution).

Academic integration represented the students' perceptions of their academic experiences, the frequency of academic involvement, the frequency of study behavior, and their grade performance. Five items reflected the students' perceptions of their academic experiences, and three items represented the frequency of the students' academic involvement. To measure study behavior, we summed three questions indicating the frequency of library visits, hours spent studying, and academic counseling/advising sessions.

Social integration represented both the students' perceptions of their social interactions with faculty and students and also the frequency of their involvement in social activities. Operationally, we defined social integration as the sum of the measures of student perceptions and behavior pertaining to peer group and faculty interactions. Five items reflected the students' perceptions of their relationships with fellow students and instructors. We measured the frequency of students' social involvement by two items which reflected the students' nonacademic interactions with students and faculty.

This study operationally defined retention, the dependent variable, as the inverse of the ratio of semester hours attempted by semester hours earned over a three-year period multiplied by the number of semesters attended during that same period of time. This retention rate formula allowed us to analyze complete withdrawal from college. More important, this measure included partial dropouts (those dropping some, but not all, course) and stopouts (those who left for a semester or two but who later re-enrolled).

Data Analysis

To analyze the causal model in the study, we used path analysis, an application of multiple regression analysis in conjunction with causal theory. We posed a priori causal linkages and specified the causal theory in the path model. We tested the causal model to determine the overall fit of the model to the data through a chi-squared goodness of fit test. The goodness of fit analysis tested the hypothesized, or overidentified, model by comparing properties of the observed correlation matrix with the reproduced correlation matrix. We used determinants of these matrices to calculate a chi-square with degrees of freedom equal to the number of the restrictions for the overidentified model. A significant chi-square would result in rejecting the null hypothesis leading to the conclusion that the hypothesized model fit the data.

Once we found that the causal model supported the data, we examined the path coefficients to determine the total effects (effect coefficients) of the variables in the model. To assess the significance of the relationships stated in the hypotheses, we employed four regression equations. A comparison of the path coefficients examined the relative importance that exogenous and endogenous variables had on the dependent variable in the theoretical model.

Results

Of the 253 students, 113 (45.4 percent) were males and 137 (54.6 percent) were females. Approximately 83.7 percent of the respondents were white, while the second largest ethnic group was Hispanics with 12.2 percent. Blacks and Asians comprised the remaining 4.1 percent of the respondents. Seventy-four percent of the respondents were under twenty-three when they first enrolled. The sample population was primarily unmarried (74.3 percent). A breakdown of the students' high school rank revealed that 39.7 percent had graduated in the third quartile of their graduating classes, 40.5 percent had graduated m the first and second quartiles, and another 10.3 percent had received their GED. The respondents reported their high school grades as mostly A's and B's (30 percent), mostly B's and C's (47 percent), and mostly C's and D's (17 percent). The students' mean grade point average at the college was 2.36 on a 4.0 point scale.

Table 2 presents the means and standard deviations for the continuous variables employed in the causal model. The mean socioeconomic status for male parents was 31.695 compared to 27.428 for female parents and 28.281 for students. In the three-year period from summer semester 1984 to spring 1987, the students earned an average total number of semester hours of 27.652 which compared to an average number of semester hours attempted of 40.190. On the average, students attended 4.5 semesters during that same period. Table 3 summarizes the correlation coefficients for all exogenous and endogenous variables in the model while Table 4 presents the zero-order correlation coefficients among all factorially derived scales representing the variables in the model.

Table 2
Means and Standard Deviations for Continuous Variables

Variables	Mean	Standard Deviation
Father's socioeconomic status	31.695	27.288
Mother's socioeconomic status	27.428	18.449
Student's socioeconomic status	28.281	10.660
Total semester hours earned	27.652	19.316
Total semester hours attempted	40.190	21.654
Total number of semesters attended	4.542	2.767

Table 3
Correlation Matrix for all Factorially Derived Subscales
Measuring the Variables in the Model

Variable	Socio-economic Status (SES)	High School Grades	College Going Expectations	Getting In Behavior	Encouragement by Significant Others	Institutional Commitment	Goal Commitment
SES	1.000						
High school grades	−.040	1.000					
College going expectations	.157	.029	1.000				
Getting in behavior	.087	.097	.197	1.000			
Encouragement	.237	.092	.329	.089	1.000		
Institutional commitment	−.121	−.021	.074	−.115	.060	1.000	
Goal commitment	−.121	.129	.063	−.045	.106	.422	1.000
Academic perceptions	−.080	.014	.073	−.005	−.076	.294	.568
Study behavior	.059	.065	.067	.155	.106	.081	.261
Academic contact	−.022	.011	.091	.210	.060	.142	.309
Social perceptions	−.062	−.039	.202	.038	.132	.264	.489
Social contact	.094	−.006	−.033	.180	.056	.069	.253
College GPA	−.085	.206	−.200	.108	−.164	.030	.217
Semester attended	.076	−.171	−.091	.096	−.017	.013	.092
Hours earned	.100	.015	−.149	−.066	.059	−.068	.122
Hours attempted	.148	−.097	−.085	−.028	.158	−.047	.130

Coefficients ≥ .195 are significant at p < .05 for 100 df.

Measures of Goodness of Fit

We determined the overall fit of the causal model by a chi-squared goodness of fit test. This analysis tested the hypothesized statistical model by using properties of the observed and the reproduced matrices among the variables in the path model. Determinants of these matrices were used to calculate a chi-square with degrees of freedom equal to the number of overriding restrictions. A significant chi-square leads to the rejection of the null hypothesis and the conclusion that the model does not fit the data. A nonsignificant chi-squared test indicates a good fit of the model of the data (Pedhazur, 1982).

The hypothesized causal model fit the data ($X^2 = 11.0414$, df = 5), thus representing a plausible model for explaining retention among a population of academically disadvantaged students. Table 5 summarizes the decomposition of the effects of the variables in the model. Each causal relationship was decomposed into the direct, indirect, and total effects. The standardized path coefficients (beta weights) determined the direct effects. Standardized path coefficients indicated the amount and direction of change in the dependent variable for every unit standardized deviation increase in the predictor variable (Pedhazur, 1982). The standardized coefficient represents the direct effect of each of the paths in the structural model. Indirect effects represented the

Table 3
Correlation Matrix for all Factorially Derived Subscales
Measuring the Variables in the Model

Academic Perceptions	Study Behavior	Academic Contact	Social Perceptions	Social Contact	College GPA	Semesters Attended	Hours Earned	Hours Attempted
1.000								
.190	1.000							
.330	.368	1.000						
.611	.170	.291	1.000					
.253	.295	.458	.279	1.000				
.245	.105	.142	.042	.165	1.000			
.057	.122	.051	.040	.130	.325	1.000		
.087	.168	.064	.016	.189	.471	.659	1.000	
.045	.207	.068	.084	.175	.261	.704	.874	1.000

influence of each predictor variable on the dependent variable mediated through the intervening predictors in the model. By summing the direct and indirect effects for each predictor variable in the four structural equations, we determined the total effects. Table 6 reports the squared multiple correlations for both the just identified model and the hypothesized model. These correlations were used in analyzing the goodness of fit test. Figure 2 displays the full causal model with standardized path coefficients.

Initial Commitments

The first equation in the structural model examined the effects of four precollege variables on the students' initial commitments to the institution and to educational and career goals. The results of this structural equation yielded a squared multiple correlation (R^2) of .044. The proportion of variance explained by the exogenous variables was 4.4 percent. Of the four predictor variables, only family background (–.171) and encouragement by significant others (.146) were statistically significant. The inverse relationship between family background and initial commitments indicated that students whose parents had higher levels of socioeconomic status were less likely to have high initial commitments. Although we hypothesized that precollege schooling would have

Figure 2
Full Statistical Model

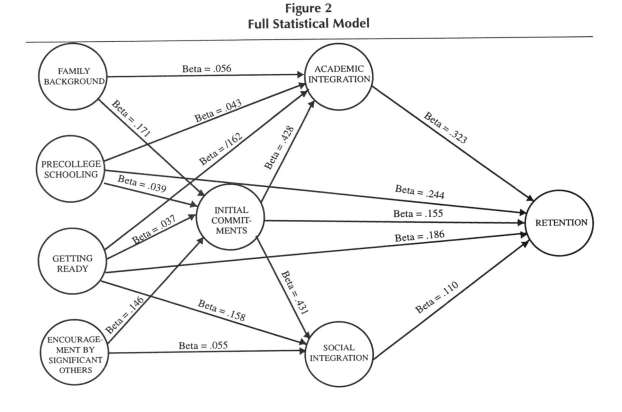

a direct effect on initial commitments, the standardized coefficient was merely .039. The study found that getting ready, hypothesized to have a positive effect on institutional/goal commitments based on findings from Attinasi's (1986) ethnographic study, had a nonsignificant, negative effect (−.037) on initial commitments.

Academic Integration

The second structural equation in the model examined the effects of three exogenous variables (family background, precollege schooling, and getting ready) and one endogenous variable (initial commitments) on academic integration. The R^2 or proportion of variance explained was .220 (22 percent). Initial commitments (.428) and getting ready (.162) had significant direct effects on academic integration. Although we hypothesized that both family background (−.056) and precollege schooling (.043) would have a positive effect on academic integration, neither produced a significant standardized coefficient. Operating through initial commitments as a mediating influence, the indirect effect of family background was −.073, generating a total effect of −.130.

Social Integration

The third structural equation assessed the effects of initial commitments, family background, precollege schooling, getting ready, and encouragement by significant others on social integration. The squared multiple correlation (R^2) for the structural equation was .218. A comparison of the standardized coefficients revealed that both initial commitments (.431) and getting ready (.158) had significant direct effects on social integration. While encouragement by significant others did not have a significant direct effect (.055), the addition of an indirect effect (.063), mediated through initial commitments, resulted in a total effect of .118 on social integration.

Table 4
Correlation Matrix
For All Exogenous and Endogenous Variables In the Model

Variable	Family Background (SES)	Precollege Schooling	Getting Ready	Encouragement by Significant Others
Family background (SES)	1.000			
Precollege schooling	−.046	1.000		
Getting ready	.168	.066	1.000	
Encouragement by significant others	.221	.095	.261	1.000
Initial commitments	−.167	.060	−.056	.079
Academic integration	−.051	.084	.121	−.057
Social integration	.009	−.027	.134	.133
Retention	−.115	.265	−.142	−.131

	Initial Commitments	Academic Integration	Social Integration	Retention
Initial commitments	1.000			
Academic integration	.468	1.000		
Social integration	.414	.566	1.000	
Retention	.013	.174	.004	1.000

Table 5
Decomposition of the Effects from the Hypothesized Causal Model

	Direct Effects	Indirect Effects	Total Effects
Effects on Retention			
of academic integration	.3237[a]	.0000	.3237
of social integration	−.1101	.0000	−.1101
of initial commitments	−.1553[d]	.0912	−.0640
of precollege schooling	.2448[b]	.0116	.2565
of getting ready	−.1867[d]	.0376	−.1491
Effects on Academic Integration			
of initial commitments	.4285[b]	.0000	.4285
of family background	−.0568	−.0733	−.1302
of precollege schooling	.0438	.0167	.0606
of getting ready	.1628[c]	−.0161	.1467
Effects on Social Integration			
of initial commitments	.4311[c]	.0000	.4311
of getting ready	.1587[d]	−.0162	.1425
of encouragement	.0557	.0631	.1189
Effects on Initial Commitments			
of family background	−.1711[d]	.0000	−.1711
of precollege schooling	.0390	.0000	.0390
of getting ready	−.0376	.0000	−.0376
of encouragement	.1465[d]	.0000	.1465

[a] $p < .0001$ [b] $p < .001$ [c] $p < .01$ [d] $p < .05$

Retention

The last structural equation examined the effects of two exogenous variables (precollege schooling and getting ready) and three endogenous variables (initial commitments, academic integration, and social integration) on the dependent variable, retention. The squared multiple correlation (R^2) for the structural equation was .153. The standardized coefficients for the two exogenous variables hypothesized to affect retention directly indicated significant direct effects on retention. However, while precollege schooling had a significant positive direct effect (.244), the getting ready variable had a significant negative direct effect (–.186). Of the three endogenous variables hypothesized to positively affect retention, only academic integration (.323) produced a significant positive standardized coefficient. Both social integration (–.110) and initial commitments (–.155) yielded negative direct effects on retention. The indirect effects of initial commitments mediated through academic integration and social integration produced a standardized coefficient of .091, thus reducing the total negative effect to –.064.

In sum, the results supported the constructs in Tinto's model. The direct, positive effect of academic integration on retention was consistent with the theoretical expectations based on the model and with results of previous studies on commuter students (Nora, 1987; Fox, 1985). The negative influence of social integration on retention was inconsistent with the hypothesized model yet was consistent with previous research on similar populations (Fox, 1985; Pascarella, 1982). Although initial commitments accounted for a significant portion of the variance in academic integration and social integration, there was a nonsignificant negative relationship between initial commitments and retention. Initial commitments had a significant positive direct effect on both academic integration and social integration, however, but were negatively related to retention. The indirect effects of initial commitments, operating through academic and social integration, lessened the total negative effect of this variable. One exogenous variable, precollege schooling, had a positive relationship with retention.

Significantly, the study not only verified the inclusion of the getting ready construct in quantitative models but demonstrated its significantly large negative direct effect on retention. Students with higher levels of getting ready behavior were less likely to persist in higher education.

In addition, neither precollege schooling nor getting ready had a significant effect on initial commitments. Attinasi's (1986) ethnographic study suggested that students' beliefs or expectations of going to college and students' prematriculation visits to college campuses contributed to student retention. Our study found that prematriculation on-campus experiences and early college-going expectations did not significantly impact students' initial institutional and goal commitments and negatively impacted retention. One plausible explanation might be that these expectations and experiences are often directed toward four-year residential colleges. Therefore, students exhibiting more frequent prematriculation on-campus experiences and college-going expectations might see the community college merely as a stepping stone toward a four-year residential institution.

Table 6
Squared Multiple Correlation Coefficient
For Each Structural Equation

Structural Equation	R2 for Just-identified Model	R2 for Hypothesized Model
Effects on retention	.1505	.1530
Effects on academic integration	.2511	.2206
Effects on social integration	.2240	.2183
Effects on initial commitments	.0441	.0441

Bibliography

Astin, Alexander. *Preventing Students from Dropping Out*. San Francisco: Jossey-Bass, 1975.

Attinasi, Louis C. *Getting In: Mexican American Students' Perceptions of Their College Behavior with Implications for Their Freshman Year Persistence in the University*. Ph.D. diss., Arizona State University, 1986.

Beal, Phillip E., and Lee Noel. *What Works in Student Retention*. Iowa City, Iowa: American College Testing Program and the National Center for Higher Education Management Systems, 1980.

Bean, John. "Dropout and Turnover: The Synthesis and Test of a Causal Model of Student Attrition." *Research in Higher Education* 12, (1980): 155–87.

———. "Concept Models of Student Attrition: How Theory Can Help the Institutional Researcher." In *Studying Student Attrition*, edited by Ernest T. Pascarella. New Directions for Institutional Research, Monograph No. 36. San Francisco: Jossey-Bass, Dec. 1982.

Fox, Richard. "Application of a Conceptual Model of College Withdrawal to Disadvantaged Students." Paper presented at the annual meeting of American Educational Research Association, Chicago, Ill., 1985. Photocopy in our possession.

Nora, Amaury. "Determinants of Retention among Chicano College Students: A Structural Model." *Research in Higher Education* 26, (1987): 31–59.

Pascarella, Ernest T. "Student-Faculty Informal Contact and College Outcomes." *Review of Educational Research* 50 (1982): 545–95.

Pascarella, Ernest T., and David Chapman. "A Multi-Institutional Path Analytical Validation of Tinto's Model of College Withdrawal." *American Education Research Journal* 20, (1983): 87–102.

Pascarella, Ernest T., and Patrick T. Terenzini. "Predicting Freshman Persistence and Voluntary Dropout Decisions from a Theoretical Model." *Journal of Higher Education* 51, no. 1 (1980): 60–75.

———. "Predicting Voluntary Freshmen Year Persistence/Withdrawal Behavior in a Residential University: A Path Analytic Validation of Tinto's Model." *Journal of Educational Psychology* 75 (1983): 215–26.

Pascarella, Ernest T., Paul Duby, and Barbara Iverson. "A Test and Reconceptualization of a Theoretical Model of College Withdrawal in a Commuter Institution Setting." *Sociology of Education* 56, no. 2 (1983): 88–100.

Pedhazur, Elazar J. *Multiple Regression in Behavioral Research*. Chicago: Holt, Rinehart, and Winston, 1982.

Rendon, Laura. "Chicanos in South Texas Community Colleges: A Study of Student and Institutional-Related Determinants of Educational Outcomes." Ph.D. diss., University of Michigan, 1982.

Seale, Robert. "A Structural Model for Explaining Retention and Attrition in a Community College." Ph.D. diss., University of Houston, 1984.

Spady, William G. "Dropouts from Higher Education: Toward an Empirical Model." *Interchange* 2 (1971): 38–62.

Stevens, Gillian, and Joo Hyun Cho. "Socioeconomic Indices and the New 1980 Census Occupational Classification Scheme." *Social Science Research* 14, no. 2 (1985): 142–68.

Tinto, Vincent. "Dropout from Higher Education: A Theoretical Synthesis of Recent Research." *Review of Educational Research* 45 (1975): 89–125.

———. "Defining Dropout: A Matter of Perspective." In *Studying Student Attrition*, edited by Ernest T. Pascarella, 17–34. New Directions for Institutional Research, Monograph No. 36. San Francisco: Jossey-Bass, 1982.

Amaury Nora is an assistant professor in the College of Education at the University of Illinois at Chicago; Louis C. Attinasi, Jr., is assistant professor in the Department of Educational Leadership and Cultural Studies at the University of Houston; Andrew Matonak is Dean of Students at the Horry-Georgetown Technical College, Conway, South Carolina.

Trout Fishing in Catfish Ponds

Michael A. Olivas

I have prepared this outline as a summary of my remarks on the papers by Rebecca Zwick (1991a) and Shirley Vining Brown (1987, 1988). In addition, I have reviewed several other recent GRE reports on closely allied topics by Michael Nettles (1987, 1990) and a team headed by Joan Baratz-Snowden (1987). Had I written these, I would have approached the topics in much the same manner and probably arrived at many of the same conclusions. Nonetheless, I view the world differently and, in several respects, take issue with important premises and definitions of this terrible problem. I write to register three dissents and to suggest three areas where I think research is needed. Like Justice Thurgood Marshall, I would like to concur in part, dissent in part, and remand for reconsideration.

First, in the search for paradigms, I would like to enact a ban, or at least a temporary restraining order, on the "pool" and the "pipeline." Each of the reports employs these metaphors, prominently and uncritically. I am not merely quibbling, like the deconstructionists over original intent, or the theologians over articles of faith and morals. Rather, I believe the paradigms are inapt, both because they misconstrue the nature of the problems (as I define them) and because they misdirect attention. A pool is static, likely to turn brackish, and bounded. It requires restocking and resupply, and if it over-flows its bounds, it *is* no longer a pool. Most crucially, it can become stagnant and unusable without fresh water; it cannot replace itself. A pipeline is even worse as a metaphor, though I recognize its widespread use and recognition value. But think of it in its quotidian, oil-industry meaning. It is a foreign mechanism introduced into an environment, an unnatural device used to leach valuable products from the earth. It requires artificial construction; in fact, it is a dictionary-perfect artifice. It cuts through an ecosystem and has unintended and largely uncontrollable, deleterious effects on that environment. It can, and inevitably does, leak, particularly at its joints and seams, as Alyeska discovered. It can also rust prematurely, and if any part of it is blocked or clogged, the entire line is rendered inoperative. It may also be insulated with asbestos.

I prefer the metaphor of the river. It is an organic entity; one that can be fed from many sources, including other bodies of water, rain, and melting snow. It can be diverted to form other tributaries without altering its direction or purpose, feeding streams, canals, and fields; it can convey goods, drive mills and turbines, create boundaries, and irrigate land—all without diminishing its power. Although it can be fouled by unnatural pollutants, it has a natural filtration system to slough off impurities. Despite its natural flow, it can adapt to new flows and can even be reversed or altered by engineering and hydraulic interventions. Its surface can be frozen, yet its power will be undiminished beneath the floes.

This is the image I want to convey, rather than those conjured by pipelines, ladders, or pools, none of which have the sense of a river's power, purpose, potential, fecundity, or majesty. If this is a simple autobiographical quirk derived from my childhood in New Mexico, with its magnificent Rio Grande, then understand my search for a more apt metaphor.

Without making too much more of this point, I'll say that the difference in paradigm is important for its characterization of the problem, for the evidence mounted to measure the problem, and for solutions proffered to resolve the problem. Let me illustrate briefly. Characterizing the problem of minority underenrollment at any level as a "pool problem" suggests a supply shortage or, at best, a failure to cast one's line in the right fishing hole. On the supply side, the data presented here and elsewhere make powerful claims that we produce too few qualified minority graduates to stock our faculties. The pipeline and ladder metaphors reinforce this view of the problem, suggesting that it is simply a delivery glitch, or that faculties would hire us if only they used better conveyances. After all, neither pipelines nor ladders produce anything of value; they only carry or convey products. While both the supply function and conveying function are important, they are not, individually, rich enough metaphors to portray the complex phenomenon of both functions intertwined to produce and propagate faculty. A river, in contrast, provides nutrients and conveys resources, unlike its more static counterparts that do one or the other, but not both. As a final trump, a river also creates demand through dynamic flow and natural, organic properties. It constantly changes form, seeking new flows and creating new boundaries. It can even wear down rock, as the Rio Grande Gorge and Grand Canyon will attest.

The Pernicious "Percent Change" Approach

Apart from the incompleteness or mischaracterization of the problem that these elliptic metaphors engender, the evidence offered to prove the extent of the dilemma is problematic. Each of the authors employs a technique I'd like to see banned from the discussion, the pernicious "percent change" approach. There are literally dozens of tables and figures in these reports showing how Asian and Hispanic percentages have increased—and increased substantially—while Black percentages have declined—and declined precipitously. While these characterizations, are in a narrow or crabbed sense, literally true, each is misleading. In my view, they are dangerously misleading because they misapprehend the truer measures available. I could cite many examples, such as Brown's overly generous suggestion in *Increasing Minority Faculty: An Elusive Goal* (1988, p. 17):

> . . . the increase in the appointment of Ph.D.s to full-time faculty positions among Hispanics (1.0 percent) and Asian Americans (1.2 percent) were slightly larger than for Black full-time faculty, whose proportions increased less than one percent (0.7 percent).

How's that again? Why the interethnic comparisons? These data do not justify any characterization as an "increase" and are not large enough or reliable enough to warrant anything but more carefully hedged analysis. The most obvious counter is the reminder that hiring a second when you have one is an "increase" of 100 percent. There is no statistical property in a variation of .7, 1.0, or 1.2. I think these comparisons and incremental measures, especially with such poor National Research Council (NRC) and Equal Employment Opportunity (EEO) data, are virtually meaningless.

I want to go into painful detail in one area, law enrollments, to show how such minute detail can obscure larger pictures. In *Minorities in the Graduate Education Pipeline* (1987, p. 12), the author notes:

> There were small Black enrollment gains and modest Hispanic gains in law. . . . White enrollment declined. . . .

Fine, except that I believe this picture is incomplete and misleading. Moreover, it doesn't square with law enrollment patterns that I have studied each year in my efforts to improve Latino law-faculty hiring practices. (In May 1990, only 51 of the 5,800 law teachers were Latino, an all-time high.) First, the 1980–84 data were calculated, presumably, as straight-line projections of 1976–80 trends; this method fails to capture the volatility of law applications and enrollments, which both increased sharply in the 1980s, particularly in the last five years. American Bar Association (ABA) enrollments reveal that Blacks were enrolled at all-time high levels in 1988–89 (6,321), up from 5,257 in 1979–80. Both White and overall enrollments were at an all-time high. Mexican American enrollments were at 1,657, down from 1,670 in 1979–80 (and their 1983 peak of

1,739). Puerto Rican enrollments in the 50 states and Washington, D.C., declined from 540 in 1979–80 to 478 last year; they peaked at 603 in 1980-81. Enrollments by Cubans and other Hispanics increased (tripled, in fact) from 714 in 1979 to 2,207 a decade later. Cubans, who comprise 10 percent of the Latino population (and a smaller percent of the 18- to 24-year-old cohort) enrolled in law schools more than did Chicanos and Puerto Ricans, who constitute three-quarters of the Hispanic population. Of course, this doesn't even take into account the growth of Latinos in the U.S. population as a whole, which renders "percentage increase" analysis even less useful. I suspect this important disaggregation and cohort context could account for much of the Hispanic "gains" characterized throughout these papers.

Two final points on law enrollments. Last year, for the first time, a historically White law school—Georgetown University—graduated more Blacks than did Howard University—the largest of the historically Black law schools. This phenomenon and the unsure futures of Southern University and North Carolina Central University do not bode well for continuing the exceedingly modest growth. (A footnote to this footnote: A March 8, 1990, *New York Times* article [Olivas, 1990] on recent ABA enrollments showed a 16 percent increase for Blacks in 1987-89. It all depends upon what is put in the numerator and denominator, and when you take the snapshot.) Second, because there are no historically Hispanic law schools, Latino students must rely on schools with no record of service to their community. For instance, three of the law schools with the largest Latino enrollments, University of Miami (220), University of Texas (200), and Georgetown University (105), have no Latino law faculty.

Data Disaggregation

I hope I have planted sufficient doubt about comparative "percentage increase" data analysis and intergroup measures, but I must make one other point about disaggregation. Imprecision about data can lead to serious distortions. No researcher, either Anglo or of color, would employ a cohort of West Indians or Haitians or Nigerians to make an important point about indigenous Black Americans, but carelessness or insensitivity have permitted researchers to make misleading points about Hispanic students. In spite of routine disclaimers in ETS/GRE publications, the data are not large enough or calibrated well enough to permit such generalizations as these in Nettle's *Black, Hispanic, and White Doctoral Students: Before, During, and After Enrolling in Graduate School (1990):*

> The Hispanic students were better off than their Black counterparts, in terms of their easier transitions into doctoral programs and better experience once enrolled in their doctoral programs.

> . . . [Blacks] had greater feelings that their graduate institutions were racially discriminatory as compared with the Hispanic and White students.

The institutional data that prompted these generalizations included not a representative sampling of Hispanics, but of Puerto Ricans. Additional discussions with the researcher revealed that the Puerto Ricans were nearly all from the Island, not the 50 states and the District of Columbia, and that no Mexican Americans were included in the sample, even though Mexican Americans constitute nearly 70 percent of the Latino population. I believe that these mischaracterizations skew the problem, misstate the extent of disadvantage, and fail to provide attention to the possible remedies.

What are these remedies? I would suggest that a start toward remedies would be to read Latino characterizations of the problem and its consequences. I was astounded to see this error of omission in the ETS/GRE papers: Not one book or article by a Latino scholar was read or cited in one of these five papers. Not one. Of course, this means my own children will never see the royalties or proceeds of my various books—available in fine bookstores everywhere!

More surprisingly, former or current ETS scholars such as Richard Duran, Maria Pennock-Roman, and Luis Laosa are completely ignored, while Alexander Astin's work is cited by nearly all the reports. No Asian scholars are cited either, even ETS scholar Jayjia Hsia. How could thorough research on minority students include Tinto but not Amaury Nora's (1987) important reconsideration of Tinto's theories for Chicanos? How could any study on GRE data and achievement of minority graduate students not take into account Pennock-Roman's and Duran's work on predictive validity of standardized tests for Latino students?

How could a study essentially on Puerto Rican doctoral students not refer to the *Prueba de Admision para Estudios Graduados* (PAEG) or the *Prueba de Aptitud Academica* (PAA), as suggested in *Latino College Students* (Olivas, 1986)? I have treated this anomaly of exclusion in detail in a *Chronicle of Higher Education* article (Olivas, 1989), so I'll not take time to do so here. Rather, I'll summarize by saying that this citation (or noncitation) pattern has consequences—in sociology of knowledge terms, characterization of expertise terms, and in academic colonialism terms. I regretfully expect this from Anglo scholars, but not from colleagues of color, and certainly not in discussions of minority students. If these discussions and papers are to have consequence, important basic reference literature and critical racial characterizations must be reckoned with, especially in a community such as this. Frankly, we need all the help we can get, especially within our own ranks. Enough said.

A Research Agenda

As a final matter, I would like to take the time remaining to sketch briefly the research agenda I envision as necessary. As befits my Catholic heritage, I have three suggestions for further research and advocacy. First, the quality of most quantitative databases is poor, and worsening. For example, several of the studies employed National Longitudinal Study (NLS) and High School and Beyond (HSB) data, which track students from their sophomore year in high school to graduate school. While these are often the best data available, they are inadequate for minority students, particularly Latinos, whose attrition occurs primarily in the transition from middle school (or junior high) to high school. I have attempted to analyze Latino financial aid patterns, building on my earlier work in this area, by using the new National Postsecondary Student Aid Study (NPSAS) database. This study, along with the ongoing NLS and HSB longitudinal data, will form the basis for basic research, as well as forthcoming Higher Education Act (HEA) reauthorization initiatives. Yet the minority subsamples, especially those for Latinos and Asians, are thoroughly inadequate.

I have already shown how attempts to fashion institutional databases can also run afoul and lead to mischaracterizations. Inasmuch as I am in Princeton, I feel compelled to add that the National Assessment of Educational Progress (NAEP) approach of using age cohorts will cause serious comparability problems for populations (such as Latinos) who are out of age-sync with most majority students. My analysis of data has shown that Hispanic elementary-secondary students fall behind in school, so that fully a quarter of the survivors (the 50 percent who do graduate—the statistical cream of the crop) are an average of two years older than are their Anglo counterparts, as a result of being held back in school. These and other important demographic features require specific expertise, technical capability, and access to information. You can't expect law professors, even those of us from New Mexico, to keep up with this stuff. More informed attention to all large-scale database construction is an essential first step. Good user practice, as I've stressed, is a crucial corollary.

Second, qualitative research skills are necessary, yet underappreciated by too many number crunchers. I may be prejudiced by my powers of observation being better than my computing capability, but important grounded-theory and anthropological research will likely contribute much to improving our understanding of racial achievement on campus. For example, I think Attinasi's (1989) recent piece on Chicano college-going has added more to my own understanding of this phenomenon than has almost anything else I've read, yet it was an intensive study of only a handful of students. Flora Ida Ortiz's (1977) ethnographic study of subtle resource allocation in classrooms is similarly revealing, in a way that national studies with chi-squares, Wilk's Lambda, and del statistics cannot approach.

Finally, knowing that legislators and policymakers are not any more convinced by social science (quantitative or qualitative) than anyone else, I believe that improving the quality of policy studies is essential for getting at the truth and devising workable solutions. Financial aid packaging studies, analyses of the effect of immigration "reform" on colleges, and critical evaluations of racial climate all will aid in increasing minority retention, as will measuring the impact of action projects, like Gary Keller's Project 1000—curiously omitted from all the papers on graduate education. Unfortunately, this type of scholarship is often fraught with the same unfamiliarity with minority literature, wrong headed assumptions, insensitive conclusions, and baleful data problems I have identified already in excruciating detail. Nonetheless, triangulating the truth is the only way I know to improve our lot and the lot of future students whose success will rely upon our efforts. It is this realization, forged in my eight years in the seminary, that leads me to preach. Nonetheless, I believe in preaching, and I believe in it evangelically.

References

American Council on Education. (1987). *Minorities in Higher Education.* Washington, DC: Author.

American Council on Education & Education Commission of the States. (1988). *One-third of a nation: A report of the commission on minority participation in education and American life.* Washington, DC: American Council on Education.

Astin, A. W. (1982). *Minorities in American higher education.* San Francisco: Jossey-Bass.

Attinasi, L. (1989). Getting in: Mexican-Americans' perceptions of university attendance and the implications for freshman year persistence. Journal *of Higher Education, 60,* 247–276.

Blackwell, J. E. (1987). *Mainstreaming outsiders The production of Black professionals.* (2nd ed.). Dix Hills, NY: General Hall.

Braddock, J. H. (1988, August). Minorities in sociology: Strategies for increasing partnership of students and faculty. Presented at the American Sociological Association Annual Conference.

Brademas, J. (1984). Graduate education: Signs of trouble. *Science, 223,* 881.

Brown, C., Choy, S., & Hoachlander, E. G. (1987). *High school and beyond student financial assistance: Student loans.* Washington, DC: U. S. Department of Education.

Brown, S. V. (1987). *Minorities in the graduate education pipeline.* Princeton, NJ: Educational Testing Service.

Brown, S. V. (1988). *Increasing minority faculty: An elusive goal.* Princeton, NJ: Educational Testing Service.

Chamberlain, M. K. (Ed.). (1988). *Women in academe: Progress and prospects.* New York, NY: Russell Sage Foundation.

The Committee for Economic Development, Research and Policy Committee. (1987). *Children in need: Investment strategies for the educationally disadvantaged.* New York, NY: The Committee for Economic Development.

Dawes, R. M. (1975). Graduate admissions variables and future success. *Science, 187,* 721–723.

Girves, J. E., & Wemmerus, V. (1988). Developing models of graduate student progress. *Journal of Higher Education, 59,* 163–189.

Harlem Youth. (1964). *Youth in the ghetto: A study of the consequences of powerlessness and a blueprint for change.* New York, NY: Opportunities Unlimited.

Hartnett, R. T. (1987). Has there been a graduate student "brain drain" In the arts and sciences? *Journal of Higher Education, 58,* 562–585.

Leggon, C. B. (1987). Minority underrepresentation in sciences and engineering graduate education and careers. In National Research Council, *Minorities: Their underrepresentation and career differentials in science and engineering: Proceedings of a workshop.* 151–158. Washington, DC: National Academy Press.

Mooney, C. J. (1989). Affirmative-action goals, coupled with tiny number of minority Ph.D.s, set off faculty recruiting frenzy. *The Chronicle of Higher Education, 35(1),* 10–11.

National Board of Graduate Education. (1976). *Minority group participation in graduate education.* Washington, DC: National Academy of Sciences.

National Research Council. (1986). *Summary report 1984: Doctorate recipients from United States universities.* Washington, DC: National Academy Press.

Nettles, M. (1987). *Financial aid and minority participation in graduate education.* Princeton, NJ: Educational Testing Service.

Nettles, M. T. (1990). *Black, Hispanic and White doctoral students: Before, during and after enrolling in graduate school.* Princeton, NJ: Educational Testing Service.

Nora, A. (1987). Determinants of retention among Chicano college students: A structural model. *Research in Higher Education, 26(1),* 31–59.

Olivas, M. A. (1986). *Latino college students* New York, NY: Teacher College Press.

Olivas, M. A. (1989, May 24). An elite priesthood of White males dominates the central areas of civil-rights scholarship. *The Chronicle of Higher Education, 35(37),* B1–B2.

Olivas, M. A. (1990, March 8). Minority enrollment efforts show gains at law schools. *The New York Times,* A20.

Ortiz, F. I. (1977). Bilingual education program practices and their effects on students. *Aztlan, 8,* 157–174.

Pearson, W. (1987). B*lack, science, and American education.* New Brunswick, NJ: Rutgers University.

Pruitt, A. S., & Isaac, P. D. (1985). Discrimination in recruitment, admission, and retention of minority graduate students. *Journal of Negro Education, 54,* 526–536.

Quality Education for Minorities Project. (1990). *Education that works An action plan for the education of minorities.* Cambridge, MA: Massachusetts Institute of Technology.

Rubin, D. B. (1980). Using empirical Bayes techniques in the law school validity studies. *Journal of the American Statistical Association, 75,* 801–816.

Snowden, J., Brown, S., Clewell, B., Nettles, M., and Wightman, L (1987). *Research Agenda for Graduate Record Examinations Board Minority Graduate Education Project.* Princeton, NJ: Educational Testing Service.

Thomas, G. E. (1987). Black students in U.S. graduate and professional schools in the 1980s: A national and institutional assessment. *Harvard Educational Review, 57,* 261–282.

Trent, W. T., & Copeland, E. J. (1987). *Effectiveness of state financial aid to the production of Black doctoral recipients.* Atlanta, GA: Southern Education Foundation.

Zwick, R. (1990). *The validity of the GMAT for the prediction of success in doctoral study in business and management.* Princeton, NJ: Educational Testing Service.

Zwick, R. (1991a). *Differences in graduate school attainment patterns across academic programs and demographic groups.* Princeton,NJ: Educational Testing Service.

Zwick, R. (1991b). *An analysis of graduate school careers in three universities: Differences in attainment patterns across academic programs and demographic group.* Princeton, NJ: Educational Testing Service.

Zwick, R. & Braun, H. I. (1988). *Methods for analyzing the attainment of school milestones: A case study.* Princeton, NJ: Educational Testing Service.

PART III
THE DEVELOPMENTAL EXPERIENCE

Introduction

This section includes articles on the affective and cognitive development of students (personal development and student learning). The research on college students up through the early 70s has been mainly descriptive. Since that time the work of Erikson and Chickering have helped us understand the psychosocial development of college students. The personality characteristics of our students have been neatly classified for us by Holland and by Briggs-Myers & Myers. Kohlberg and Gilligan have shed light on the moral perspectives of male and female students. And Cross and Helms have proposed models of racial identity development. Space limitations prevent us from including papers describing these and other theorists works. However, the chapter by Chickering and Reisser is an exemplar, providing a useful framework for understanding the development of "traditional" college students. We have included articles that focus on college student groups that, especially in developmental research, continue to receive minimal attention. It is our intention that they will reinforce the framework and help us understand our changing college student population.

Cheatham's chapter, "Identity development in a pluralistic society", urges us to incorporate the distinct sociocultural and psychological collegiate experiences of students of color. He urges us to recognize the role of shared historical, social and cultural antecedents (of "enforced isolation and disenfranchisement") on norms, attitudes, expectations and behaviors. McEwen, Roper, Bryant, & Langa's article proposes the addition of "dimensions" in order to extend the boundaries of student development theories. The nine dimensions they propose include the development of ethnic and racial identity, developing interdependence, and developing social responsibility.

In "The development of gay, lesbian, and bisexual identities", Levine and Evans review the progression of developmental theories. They begin by clarifying the terms used in studies of this population. The authors begin their review of various theories by distinguishing between social and psychological models. They include a discussion of pertinent gender differences not addressed by existing theories.

Key Influences on Student Development

ARTHUR CHICKERING AND LINDA REISSER

Our basic proposition is that human development should be the organizing purpose for higher education. That proposition rests on the knowledge, based on decades of research, that community colleges and four-year institutions can have significant impact on student development along the major vectors addressed in Part One. This is not to say that all institutions have positive impacts or make significant contributions. But it is clear that educational environments do exist and can be created that influence students in powerful ways. Part Two addresses seven key ingredients for encouraging human development, with a chapter devoted to each: (1) institutional objectives, (2) institutional size, (3) student-faculty relationships, (4) curriculum, (5) teaching, (6) friendships and student communities, and (7) student development programs and services. It concludes with a chapter suggesting ways to create and sustain educationally powerful environments.

In 1969, when the first edition of this book was published, we posed these ingredients of influence as "hypotheses" based on the evidence available then. The substantial evidence that has accumulated since then consistently validates those hypotheses. Since none of the hypotheses posed have been rejected, it is tempting to give up the language of hypothesis and move to simple assertion. But we resist that temptation. We stick with it not because the supporting evidence is weak or uncertain, but because there is much more to be learned. A hypothesis is primarily a theory or supposition tentatively adopted to account for certain facts and to shape the investigation of others. Although the general directions of change and sources of influence we identify are strongly anchored in research, we are a long way from understanding the intricate interactions among (1) students in their infinite variety, (2) psychological, sociological, and environmental ingredients in all their complexity, and (3) developmental outcomes across the full spectrum of human potentials. We were lucky that the first edition of Education and Identity provided a conceptual framework that helped others pursue some of these interactions. We hope that this revision, building on research since then, does the same.

For clarity and succinctness, we state our hypotheses baldly. We drop those ubiquitous terms "in general," "tend to," "probably," and "under normal circumstances" that educators and behavioral scientists use to protect their rears and obscure their meanings. Though we may seem to be dogmatic, we do have strong convictions and strong concerns about strengthening higher education's contributions to individuals and to society. It is just such concerns that drive our work. But we also encourage you to insert your own qualifiers, "yes buts," or elaborations that move our thinking toward greater accuracy and relevance.

Clear and Consistent Objectives

Hypothesis: Impact increases as institutional objectives are clear and taken seriously and as the diverse elements of the institution and its programs are internally consistent in the service of the objectives.

Of course it is not the simple statement of objectives that has an impact. Every college catalogue contains such statements. But where objectives are taken seriously, institutional impact is strengthened in three ways. First, policies, programs, and practices tend toward greater internal consistency. When faculty members sitting on ubiquitous committees make decisions in terms of commonly shared and explicit institutional objectives, then the various parts fit together with greater coherence and integration. The developmental impact of one element less frequently runs counter to another. Second, clear objectives help students make more explicit their own reasons for attending the college and their own purposes while there. The objectives help them use time and energy more directly in the service of those objectives they value. Third, it is important to be explicit about objectives because they contain within them strong value commitments. No institution is without commitments. Often they are absorbed unwittingly by students as matters not to be questioned. At some institutions, for example, the success ethic, rugged individualism, personal achievement, self-denial or conservative morality, and future-time orientation are among the dominant values assumed; at others, such values as sociability, a relativistic moral attitude, conformity, or a hedonistic present-time orientation is left unquestioned. Unconscious learning seals off these matters from conscious control and modification. Enter rigidity and dogmatism. When objectives are explicit and when the attendant values are overtly expressed, they can become the object of examination, disagreement, and challenge. Then the learning that occurs makes for more conscious and flexible integration of these values with other components of personality and behavior.

As institutional objectives remain salient and are clearly expressed, a distinctive atmosphere develops. It develops not only out of the conscious effort of those who stay with the institution for some time; more important, it develops because prospective students and prospective faculty who support the objectives and their modes of implementation are accepted and retained. Through this process, a community of shared values, which sustains its members and influences those who join, comes into being.

Institutional objectives are thus of primary importance. Not only do they influence the emphasis given to one vector relative to another—for one college competence is most important, for another integrity, for a third autonomy and purpose. But their clarity and the internal consistency with which they are implemented largely determine whether any substantial development will occur or whether the student, subject to opposing forces, remains fixed or changes only in response to other external pressures.

Institutional Size

Hypothesis: As redundancy increases, development of competence, mature interpersonal relationships, identity, and integrity decreases.

Barker and Gump (1964) use the term redundancy to describe the situation where the number of persons for a given setting exceeds the opportunities for active participation and satisfying experiences. When people are superfluous because Of excessive numbers, redundancy exists; if three runners end up on second base, two are redundant. Redundancy is one person driving from behind the wheel and another from the back seat, three persons to change the tire, or four to diagnose the engine failure. It is ten players per tennis court, a thousand golfers per golf course, ten thousand visitors per city park. And when redundancy occurs—when increasing numbers cause decreasing individual participation and satisfaction—forces operating for personal development diminish.

As redundancy sets in, the activities and responsibilities of those who do participate become more specialized and those with marginal qualifications are more quickly and more completely left out. A hierarchy of prestige and power develops, and evaluation shifts from an emphasis on the fit between abilities and the requirements of a job to an emphasis on how one person compares with another. Rules and standards for conduct become more formalized and rigid.

Under such conditions, the opportunities to cope with significant problems become more limited and challenges to existing skills and knowledge are encountered less frequently. Experience becomes less varied and self-testing more restricted. The range of different people to be dealt with in contexts important to one's own life decreases, and situations provoking examination of values and consideration of the consequences of one's actions have to be faced less often. Thus, development of competence is more limited except when provided by special ability or special interest; the development of identity, mature relationships, and integrity are fostered less than is the case when the ratio of people to settings is smaller.

Conceived in these terms, institutional size therefore sharply affects institutional impact. For as the number of persons outstrips the opportunities for significant participation and satisfaction, the developmental potential of available settings is attenuated for all.

Student-Faculty Relationships

Hypothesis: When student-faculty interaction is frequent and friendly and when it occurs in diverse situations calling for varied roles and relationships, development of intellectual competence, sense of competence, autonomy and interdependence, purpose, and integrity are encouraged.

The first step in moving through autonomy toward interdependence is redefining relationships with parents. After this step is taken, support of nonparental adults and peers is sought and idolization and idealization of warm, sensitive teachers and other adults occurs. Thus accessible adults, open enough to be known as real human beings, can have substantial impact, whether they be advisers, custodians, or professors. With them, the actions and reactions learned during childhood and habitual with parents or other authorities can be reexamined, and alternative behaviors can be tested. New modes of relationship with people in authority and with institutional expressions of authority can be developed. Movement from dependency or rebellious independence toward relationships of mutual respect can occur. Areas of interdependence can be recognized. Space for an autonomous existence can be carved out of the larger context. By demonstrating varied life-styles and value orientations, such adults can also help foster development of purpose and integrity. In them, students can see more clearly the rewards and frustrations of varied vocations and avocations, of varied marriage and family relationships. Of course, as Adelson (1962, p. 414) points out, a teacher may also serve as an "antimodel," as a lodestar from which the student sails away as fast as possible, saying, "Whatever he is, I will not be; whatever he is for, I will be against." But teachers who are such a force for repulsion also provoke development.

Curriculum

Hypothesis: An educationally powerful curriculum encourages the development of intellectual and interpersonal competence, sense of competence, identity, purpose, and integrity.

Curriculum, properly understood, includes the full range of activities and investments that a student's college experience comprises. We use the more restricted and conventional definition: "the courses of study offered by an educational institution." But we need to recognize that "course of study" involves both process and content. When faculty debate curricula, they generally focus on content; those debates seldom address four critical criteria for content selection. In our judgment, content should:

1. Be relevant to students' backgrounds and prior experiences

2. Recognize significant dimensions of individual differences among students

3. Create encounters with diverse perspectives that challenge preexisting information, assumptions, and values

4. Provide examples of, opportunities for, and activities that help students integrate diverse perspectives, assumptions, and value orientations

Selecting content based on these criteria will help foster the dimensions of development hypothesized above.

But the force of the "hidden" curriculum needs to be recognized as well. This curriculum resides in the assumptions and orientations that underlie curriculum and teaching and in the student behaviors and interactions that result. Palmer (1987, p. 22) clearly articulates the dominant assumptions underlying most curricula: "Objective, analytic, experimental. Very quickly this seemingly abstract way of knowing, this seemingly bloodless epistemology becomes an ethic. It is an ethic of competitive individualism, in the midst of a world fragmented and made exploitable by that very mode of knowing. The mode of knowing itself breeds intellectual habits, indeed spiritual instincts, that destroy community. We make objects of each other and the world to be manipulated for our own private ends." He does not advocate throwing out objectivity, analysis, and experimentation but calls for "a capacity for relatedness within individuals—relatedness not only to people but to events in history, to nature, to the world of ideas, and yes, to things of the spirit. We talk a lot in higher education about the formation of inward capacities—the capacity to tolerate ambiguity, the capacity for critical thought. I want us to talk more about those ways of knowing that form an inward capacity for relatedness" (p. 24).

Another kind of hidden curriculum exists. This curriculum involves how the student learns, not just what is learned. The professors' rhetoric may call for critical examination of diverse ideas, for creating one's own analyses and syntheses, for originality and developing one's own perspectives. But often, wittingly or unwittingly, evaluation and grading emphasize getting the right words in rote order or simple memorization for multiple-choice exams. Students quickly spot the disparity. They deliver what gets the best grade.

As Astin's (1991) research indicates, it is the behaviors provoked by the curriculum that have most impact, not the content. Among the most significant variables are (1) the amount of interaction and cooperation among students and between students and faculty, (2) the hours devoted to studying, (3) an institutional emphasis on diversity, and (4) a faculty that is positive about the general education program.

Curricula that recognize our four criteria for content and that strengthen interaction and cooperation among students and between students and faculty can make powerful contributions to key vectors of student development.

Teaching

Hypothesis: When teaching calls for active learning, encourages student-faculty contact and cooperation among students, gives prompt feedback, emphasizes time on task and high expectations, and respects diverse talents and ways of knowing, the following qualities are fostered: intellectual and interpersonal competence, sense of competence, mature interpersonal relationships, autonomy, identity, and purpose.

Intellectual competence does not just happen. An uneducated mind may be sufficient for trial-and-error behavior, but education is required to develop analytical, synthetic, and creative abilities. Evidence indicates that different teaching practices produce different kinds of cognitive operations and therefore may foster different kinds of intellectual competence. The differential effect of lectures versus discussion classes in most settings is well documented. Lectures are superior for the transmission of information (Barnard, 1942), either quite specific in nature or integrated in a way not otherwise held. Discussion classes provoke more active thinking than lecture classes (Bloom, 1953), and several experiments have demonstrated that active learning is more efficient than passive learning (McGeoch and Irion, 1952). Group discussion provides experiences in integrating facts, formulating hypotheses, amassing relevant evidence, and evaluating conclusions. When information encounters intellectual or emotional resistance, discussion can reveal the source so it can he examined and dealt with. And group membership can contribute to changes in motivation and attitudes because it is often easier to effect change with a group than with a single individual (Lewin, 1952). Research concerning student-centered teaching is also relevant. In ten of eleven studies reviewed by McKeachie (1962), greater changes in ability to apply concepts, in attitudes, in motivation, or in group membership skills were found for discussion techniques emphasizing freer student participation than for discussion with greater instructor dominance.

Evaluative procedures also influence cognitive behavior. When grades are based on memorization of details, students memorize. When grades are based on integrating diverse materials and applying principles, students will try to develop such abilities. Meyer (1936) and Terry (1933) found that an upcoming essay exam leads to study emphasizing the organization and interrelationships of facts and principles, while an upcoming multiple-choice exam leads to memorization. Dressel (1958) observed that the need to cover large masses of material leaves little time to reflect on the meaning, interrelationship, and applicability of the knowledge being gained. And even the able student often is reluctant to think independently, partly because such efforts are time consuming and difficult, but also because they apparently contribute little to better grades.

Sense of competence is also affected. Thistlethwaite (1962, p. 313) found that curricular flexibility, controversial instruction, informality, and warm student-faculty contacts characterized colleges "outstandingly successful in encouraging undergraduates to get the doctorate in humanistic fields." Davis (1964) found that intellectually elite colleges significantly underproduced graduate students in science and blames the competitive grading practices that restrict faculty encouragement to those few A students at the top of the curve—even though all the students may have an aptitude for science.

Teaching also has implications for developing the emotional and instrumental independence necessary to move through autonomy to interdependence. When teaching completely specifies what will be studied, when learning involves memorizing information and developing only the content and skills deemed important by the teacher, and when grades depend on absolute conformity to these requirements, emotional and instrumental independence do not flourish. These qualities are fostered when students can help define key areas of content and competence to be pursued and when objectives for learning are established collaboratively, taking account of individual interests and motives within general parameters set by the curriculum and course. Such development is strengthened when students must cope with diverse tasks that have consequences for themselves and when they must identify, find, and get to whatever resources are needed to achieve the objectives. It is also strengthened when they are asked to participate in defining the products or behaviors that will be evaluated, the methods to be used, and the criteria to be applied in making judgments about whether the desired learning has occurred.

But most teaching does not involve students in shaping course objectives in ways that recognize their priorities, in helping identify appropriate resources, and in specifying the products, processes, methods, and criteria required for effective evaluation. Instead, a limited set of skills and competencies is called on. A trip to the library and use of the card catalogue fill the demands for mobility, search, discovery, and learning resources. That is why successful course achievement adds so little to the coping abilities needed beyond the classroom. And that is why college grade-point averages show so little relationship to post-college success, satisfaction, and social contribution.

According to Erikson (1950) and Sanford (1966), development of identity is fostered by varied experiences and roles, meaningful achievement, and relative freedom from anxiety and pressure. Few colleges offer these conditions. Grading systems and detailed requirements work directly counter to the sampling and self-testing through which self-definition proceeds. High academic pressures make thinking for oneself risky. That all-important index of worth, the grade-point average, makes venturing into areas of weakness dangerous. Meaningful work can counterbalance a narrow role. But most college work is meaningless to most students. Observe student-taught courses and programs of study in "free universities." Teacher behavior, learning activities, student role, content, and evaluation depart markedly from the usual curriculum, lectures, and examinations.

Interpersonal relationships also are affected. Competitive grading pits one person against another. Grading on a curve means that your good grade makes mine more unlikely. And the problem is amplified if we are both training for the same kind of work, both in the same department shooting for graduate fellowships, assistantships, and other significant goodies. It is not so much that close friendships are precluded but that they have to carry such a burden. On the other hand, when the emphasis is on cooperative effort to complete complex tasks with excellence, then diversity of skill, perspective, and insight become valuable and the orientation is toward sharing and toward knowing different persons and being able to work With them. Then more wide-ranging friendships and easy relationships become possible and valued. Clinging together in couples and cliques becomes less necessary.

Friendships and Student Communities

Hypothesis: When students are encouraged to form friendships and to participate in communities that become meaningful subcultures, and when diversity of backgrounds and attitudes as well as significant interchanges and shared interests exist, development along all seven vectors is fostered.

The personal connections developed during college can have lifelong ramifications. Whether relating as casual acquaintances, classmates in a small-group discussion, teammates, roommates, club members, best friends, or committed partners, students often learn more from each other than from teachers. Dialogue clarifies values and purposes. Caring brings up dependency issues and an array of feelings to explore and manage. Mutual enjoyment stimulates shared adventures and the discovery of new interests and skills. Recognition from others bolsters self-esteem.

Communities on campus can include informal reference groups, residence halls, student organizations, and classes that emphasize student connections to each other and to content and process. Once a student identifies with a particular group, it becomes both an anchor and a reference point, influencing behavior and thinking powerfully if older ties to family and friends have loosened and if the group supports the individual's goals.

Residence halls can provide ready-made communities for students. Because the college can vary the mix of students, place trained student staff members on site, organize developmental activities, and alter the arrangement of rooms and furniture so as to balance privacy with interaction, residence halls have great potential for fostering development of competence, management of emotions, autonomy and interdependence, and mature interpersonal relationships. They can also inhibit development if they are operated *in loco parentis* or create an overly protective environment with few intellectual and social challenges. By applying developmental principles in programming, governance, architectural design, size of units, and matching of students, college administrators can amplify the positive aspects of residential living.

Student culture can affect the development of identity and purpose by encouraging wide-ranging exploration or curtailing it. The sense of self is strengthened by encountering different kinds of people and situations, observing their reactions, trying out different roles with varying degrees of investment and receiving useful feedback. But when the community validates a limited set of roles, development of identity suffers. Too little feedback or reflection time and too much passivity or premature commitment to a single alternative can countermand growth. When friendships and the intimate exchanges that accompany them are valued and promoted, identity and purpose become clearer. When the culture inhibits personal or cross-cultural connections, or assigns second-class citizenship to certain types of students or relationships, stereotypes are reinforced.

Learning communities involve innovative restructuring of curriculum by linking courses around a common theme and enrolling students in cooperative groups. Encouraging students to work together and explore engaging interdisciplinary topics enhances development by helping students to care, not only about their own work and each other, but also about what they are learning. By balancing "separate knowing" (objective analysis, debating positions, weighing evidence) with "connected knowing" (honoring feelings, personal experiences, and subjectivity), ideas can be shared as works in progress. This requires trust, support, and a nonjudgmental attitude in listeners, who, like midwives, help emerging insights struggle into being. For this collaborative approach to succeed, classmates need to know each other relatively well and must be able to tolerate their individual opinions and remarks.

For optimum development, the community, whether it takes the form of residence hall unit, sorority or fraternity house, student organization, or informal circle of friends, should have the following characteristics:

1. It encourages regular interactions between students and provides a foundation for ongoing relationships.

2. It offers opportunities for collaboration—for engaging in meaningful activities and facing common problems together. It is small enough so that no one feels superfluous.

3. It includes people from diverse backgrounds.

4. It serves as a reference group, where there are boundaries in terms of who is "in" and who is "out." It has norms that inform those with different roles, behaviors, and status that they are "good" members or that what they are doing is unacceptable.

Student Development Programs and Services

Hypothesis: When student development professionals define themselves as educators working collaboratively with faculty to apply student development theory, they increase the direct and indirect impact of programs and services on students' movement along all vectors.

Those responsible for helping students enter an institution, move through it, and exit successfully have been called "student personnel administrators," "student services staff," or "student affairs administrators." This vocabulary conveys an image of supervisors moving "personnel" through the system or of staff dispensing services to consumers. These terms may have been appropriate when staff members were seen as administrators shepherding individuals through the system, dispensing financial aid, issuing transcripts, or enforcing conduct codes. They evolved from faculty wardens living in colonial colleges with students aspiring to the ministry, molding students' character through prayer, indoctrination, and strict supervision. When colleges became more secular, these staff members became enrollment managers and deans charged with maintaining discipline. Later they transcended the trend toward specialized administrative functions and redefined a profession grounded in a concern for "the whole student" and in a growing body of theory and research on student development. They proactively defined themselves as equal partners with faculty in educating students. Yet often their actual status and mission did not match these aspirations, and they continued to be seen as service providers somewhat extraneous to the educational mission of the college.

During the past thirty years, research and theory on student development have continued to provide a foundation for the profession. We recommend that administrators of student programs and services redefine themselves as educators and refer to themselves as "student development professionals." Staff members well versed in theory and skilled in applying developmental principles can have profound influence on individual student growth and on an environment that intentionally provides a mix of challenge and support.

Knefelkamp (1974) identified one reason why the potential of student services had not been realized: administrators and faculty members continued to view student services as ancillary to the real work of the institution. After analyzing theorists and critics since 1950, she concluded that the profession itself stopped short of practicing what it preached. It "recognized the interrelationship between the intellectual and the affective but consistently failed to enter both areas of the student's life" (p. 31). Instead, it focused on learning outside the classroom—in workshops, small groups, and one-to-one interactions—as the solution. Yet those who are knowledgeable about student development, student characteristics, and individual differences have much to offer faculty. The opportunities for collaboration and communication are many. The 1984 Traverse City Statement *Toward the Future Vitality of Student Development Services* (American College Testing

Program, 1985), drafted by student development leaders at two-year colleges, affirmed "integrating student development into the educational experience" as one of seven major goals. It specifically emphasized "collaboration with faculty and other campus educators to incorporate student development concepts into the college mission, academic program competencies, co-curricular programs, and ultimately, course objectives" (p. 5). To be effective, student development professionals must also understand faculty priorities and feelings and find ways to enhance their effectiveness and satisfaction.

All colleges have cultures and climates. Student development professionals play a major role in how the parts function, how the pieces fit into a larger whole. How do the publications look? How well do bulletin boards provide information and market services? Does the layout of the place invite student interaction? Are the offices designed to invite students in? Are the policies, calendars, and directories "user friendly"? Are student success stories featured in area newspapers? Does the student newspaper inspire pride and keep the campus up to date? Are receptionists skilled at interacting with students? Have advisers been trained and supported in work with groups that need special help? Does the registration process convey chaos or orderly efficiency? The questions are endless, but it is obvious that students can be frustrated or supported by every part of the system. Using student development concepts to evaluate everything done outside the classroom can facilitate both large and small changes. Together, they add up to a lively, inviting, stimulating, friendly place that fosters student success.

Creating Educationally Powerful Environments

Hypothesis A: Educational environments that have powerful impacts on human development can be created.

Hypothesis B: We know enough about the key principles and ingredients for such environments to tackle that challenge.

Sound research, dating back to the 1920s and 1930s, indicates that educational environments that encourage key dimensions of human development can be created and sustained. That research also indicates some of the key principles and characteristics of such environments.

The most important principle recognizes that any environment is a system or a totality of interacting parts. An educationally powerful environment coordinates all elements—awareness of students' precollege characteristics and background, admission, orientation and advising, curriculum, teaching, and evaluation, cocurricular activities, norms concerning relationships among students and between students and faculty, facilities—so that they are internally consistent with regard to desired outcomes. In many institutions, different parts of the system conflict with other parts and thus neutralize potential sources of influence on students. So the starting point is to undertake an analysis that examines institutional policies and behaviors for their internal consistency with regard to objectives for student learning and development important to the institution.

The second principle is to examine existing assumptions. When Einstein was asked how he got started on his theory of relativity, he said, "I questioned an axiom." President Kennedy urged us to "forgo the comfort of opinion and bear the discomfort of thought" (Schlesinger, 1965, p. 238). Our own posture should be the same.

The other chapters in Part Two identify major sources of institutional impact on students and describe ways they can be shaped to maximize such impact. As our first "system" principle makes clear, these sources are highly interdependent. If no clearly agreed-on institutional objectives exist, there is no basis for examining and coordinating the system. If institutional size is such that students are redundant, all forces for change are minimized. If curriculum and teaching leave students as passive receptacles for predigested information and treat them all alike, then few students will be affected. If strong friendships and student communities are not created, those major opportunities for personal identification and involvement will be lost. If student programs and services do not have clearly defined educational purposes, their potential contributions will be diminished.

Three other principles must help shape these interdependent parts:

1. Integrate work and learning.

2. Recognize and respect individual differences.

3. Remember that significant learning and human development involve cycles of challenge and response, differentiation and integration, disequilibrium and regained equilibrium.

Creating and sustaining such an environment requires committed leadership and an appropriate organizational culture. Eight elements characterize high-quality institutions that are themselves "learning organizations." These organizations

1. Clearly define core values, mission, and vision.

2. Emphasize an ethic of quality.

3. Make people their prime resource.

4. Learn from the people they serve.

5. Emphasize autonomy and entrepreneurship.

6. Orient toward action.

7. Analyze strengths and weaknesses.

8. Invest in professional development.

These ingredients suggest the leadership and organizational culture we need in order to create and sustain educational environments that contribute powerfully to human development.

Identity Development in a Pluralistic Society

Harold E. Cheatham

The central thesis for this chapter is that the unique sociocultural and psychosocial experiences of ethnic minority persons are too little appreciated and thus have not been incorporated into collegiate programming that would serve these persons. There is a specific and unique history and set of attendant expectations that ethnic minority students bring to campus; these are rooted in the dynamics of the family and culture and in the repertoire which develops as a function of the complex interactions between family members and the external environment. Ethnic minority students' social and intellectual development will be better served when their distinct cultures and experiences have been identified and intentionally incorporated into campus life.

Many collegiate institutions have sought to increase enrollment of ethnic minority students, particularly of African Americans, but many external and internal barriers remain (Edwards, 1988; Gibbs, 1973; Madrazo-Peterson & Rodriquez, 1978; Wharton, 1986). Further, many institutions have attempted to educate ethnic minority, specifically African American, students while ignoring their sociocultural reality. Despite a near universal perception and expectation of education as the vehicle to upward mobility, African American students report that the climate for learning at predominantly White institutions (PWIs) operates against their academic success (Fleming, 1984; Gibbs, 1974; Hughes, 1987).

African American students in PWIs frequently have noted the scarcity of African American faculty, of appropriate and responsive support systems, and of curricular and cocurricular conventions that make collegiate environment "legible" (i.e., assist the student in translating and understanding institutional policies and procedures). Edwards (1979, 1988) concluded that much of the failure to provide equity resides in deficiencies in the environment, or in "structural discrimination," which Hill (1990, p. 91) defined as unintended, adverse consequences of societal trends. The outcomes related to functioning in such collegiate settings include higher sensitivity to discrimination, comparatively lower academic performance, and lower satisfaction with college.

African American students believe that White faculty are prejudiced toward them (Semmes, 1985), a perception that contributes both to lowered expectations of these students' academic performance and to low-quality faculty interaction with and responsiveness to African American students. Mingle (1978) reported that White faculty consciously interact less frequently with African American students than with White students and that these faculty also harbor the perception that the African American students have entered the institution under different standards. The persistence of indifference and hostility on PWI campuses was noted by Lunneborg and Lunneborg (1985), who reported that minority students feel isolated and ignored, that the university is "cold," and that they are subjected to racism, prejudice, and patronizing attitudes. In their look at the durability of normative systems on U.S. campuses, Loo and Rolison

(1986) reported greater sociocultural alienation for minority than for nonminority students, and that fewer minority students felt that the university reflects their values. Madrazo-Peterson and Rodriquez (1978) reported similar perceptions and adjustment issues for Hispanic students attending a PWI.

Those barriers to cultural pluralism that are reported to pervade PWIs, contravening minority students' sense of self, provide a stark contrast to African American students' reported experiences in historically Black colleges (HBCs). Researchers generally have concluded that the HBC provides a unique educational environment (Allen, 1986; Cheatham, Tomlinson, & Ward, 1990; Fleming, 1984; Hughes, 1987). These environs are supportive and better assist students' psychosocial adjustment and development of self-efficacy (Bandura, 1982,1986). Specifically, in regard to their adjustment and experiences, students at HBCs report comparatively less loneliness and isolation, and higher quantity and quality of interaction with peers and with faculty and staff. Further, Baratz and Ficklen (1983) reported that HBCs produce graduates with greater cultural awareness than their PWI counterparts, yet of equal competitiveness in the U.S. Labor market.

There is much that can and must be done to enable ethnic minority students'— and, indeed, all students'—optimal functioning at PWIs. Negative experiences notwithstanding, some African American and other ethnic minority students continue to achieve within PWIs and particularly in institutions where students experience higher levels of interaction with other African Americans. A heightened incidence of interaction with Whites is an apparent consequence of increased interaction with one's ethnic peer group members. In that regard, Smith and Allen (1984) reported a correlation between African American students' success and a characteristic within PWIs that they termed "institutional quality." Smith and Allen called upon undergraduate educators to observe the connection among the institution's agents and agencies, its operating procedures, and the resulting influence of these conventions on African American students' academic performances.

The point advanced in these observations is that depending upon institutional climate, with its historical, social and cultural antecedents, students' development is either enhanced or impeded.

Institutional Climate

Recent reports (see chapter 9 by Clay and Sherrill in this volume) herald the resurgence of racism and violence directed toward members of ethnic minority groups in the larger U.S. society and on U.S. campuses. These reports fly in the face of the position that openly espoused, ideological racism has all but disappeared. For all of its post-civil-rights-era adjustments, U.S. higher education has failed to meet the educational and developmental needs of ethnic minority Americans (Egerton, 1982; Nettles & Baratz, 1985; Wharton, 1986). Actually, there is some speculation as to whether U.S. higher education understands the needs of its consumers, in general (Katchadourian & Boli, 1986).

These citations of the disposition of ethnic minority students on PWIs do not imply universality. Numerous U. S. colleges and universities enjoy enviable success at recruiting and retaining ethnic minority students, notably African Americans; an even greater number boast of success within specific programs. The haunting question is, With the significant amount of human and capital resources and scores of programs directed to African American students attending PWIs during the last two decades, how can the record continue to be so uneven? A partial answer has been advanced in the charge that many institutions have continued business as usual after acting to relieve rather than excise the pain. If the purpose in attending to ethnic minorities' educational quest is to aid the individual goal of self-actualization, that is one thing. And perhaps that self-actualization can be achieved within the existing institutional structure once the normative, Eurocentric model of cultural intervention has been appropriately criticized and refined. If, however ethnic minority persons' quest extends beyond self-actualization and onward to education for social utility, the quest collides with traditional barriers. Education that liberates and promotes personal authenticity presumes systemic change and adaptation that do not depend upon initiatives of those to be served. Rather, collegiate institutions must make an unqualified commitment to developing enduring multicultural environs. The quality of the institutional climate is indispensable to the matriculation, development, and graduation of ethnic minority Americans.

From a review of two decades of research on African Americans in U.S. higher education, Sedlacek (1987) suggested that perhaps the noted success is attributable to a Hawthorne-like effect (cf. Lindzey & Aronson, 1969). He concluded that although researchers have provided contradictory conclusions, positive—even if inconsistent—efforts to serve the needs of African American students have contributed to retention. Academic persistence has been linked to the student's integration into and affiliation with the institution (Tinto, 1975; 1982), contact with faculty outside of the classroom (Braddock, 1981; Nettles, Thoeny, & Gosman, 1986), preventive or special counseling services (Carroll, 1987; Trippi & Cheatham, 1989; Trippi & Cheatham, 1991), institutional environment (Smith & Allen, 1984), and to the complex interaction of institutional characteristics and student characteristics (Spady, 1970).

Historical, Social, and Cultural Antecedents of the Black Self

African American/ethnic minority students have been variously characterized as "strange and formidable" (Calia, 1966, p. 100), guarded, diffuse, inhibited, aggressive, of high *and* low self-concept and self-esteem, optimistic, committed, and unrealistic (cf. Fleming, 1984; Gibbs, 1973; Gurin & Epps, 1975; Smith & Allen, 1984; Taylor, 1986). Efforts to identify commonality, let alone universality, among African Americans is indeed risky; the diversity implied by the preceding descriptors persuades that African Americans/ethnic minorities are not monolithic. Blackwell (1975) noted that except for the consequences of racism and the pervasiveness of color consciousness in America, there is no experience universal to African Americans.

African Americans and other ethnic minorities, in general, share related sociohistorical experiences that are based upon negative attributions to their ethnicity and color and, in the case of African Americans, upon the vestiges of the "peculiar institution" of slavery (Stampp, 1956). Mathis (1978) and Nobles (1974) contended that African Americans, in response to enforced isolation and disenfranchisement, evolved systems and relationships to meet their needs. Moreover, these scholars contend that these new forms or systems had their genesis in African form and tradition. Included among the transplanted African forms are family pattern, attitudes and behaviors, verbal expression, gender-related role expectations, and epicurean traditions (Blackwell, 1975). This conceptualization argues that the African American community contains elements similar to other social systems, including value consensus. Further, it argues that the African American community is a political, social, and economic entity with shared norms and expectations. African American families are characterized by (a) strong kinship bonds, (b) strong work orientation, (c) adaptability of family role, (d) high achievement orientation, and (e) a religious orientation (Hill, 1972).

In a meticulously documented account of slave community and its legacy to African Americans, Blassingame (1979) contended that the predominant view of the slave community denies that the slave had a meaningful and distinctive culture. That view further obscures the slave's inner life, thought, action, and sense of self. Blassingame demonstrated that the slave held fast to African culture and practiced and enhanced its meaning such that not only was the culture preserved but that it also added to American culture through merging and synthesizing those aspects that had shared similarity. Among those enduring forms exist religion, African linguistic style (i.e., Black English) or "Ebonics" (Asante, 1988), and art form. Particularly noted among art forms are music and folktale, the prototypes of which are regarded as most resistant to European forms (Blassingame, 1979).

For our purpose, the summary notion here is that in the exchange and adaptation process African slaves in America retained the African cultural determinants of their status (Blassingame, 1979; Herskovits, 1941). The demonstration of retained African form is basic to the preference here for the term *Afrocentric,* which suggests continuity, as opposed to *Afrocentric* suggesting instead a form that is a derivative of the African form. This sense of self-efficacy, together with the demonstrated resilience of African cultural forms that were merged with American forms, provides a different and more positive view of the slave's existence and hence of the legacy of African Americans.

Unlike the Western philosophic system, the African tradition has no heavy emphasis on the individual. Rather, the individual being is authenticated only in terms of others. (For a demonstration of the African sense of self, consider, for example, Nelson Mandela's personal triumph over apartheid and *his* triumphant 1990 tour of the United States. Then consider how Mr. Mandela takes no individual or personal credit but refers to self only in the plural form: "While *we* were in prison. . . .") Similarly, African American families generally stress affiliation, collectivity, interdependence, respect for elders, and obedience to authority as preferable to the Euro-American/ Eurocentric values of individuation, autonomy, and competition. There is a pervasive awareness of corporate responsibility and collective destiny as epitomized in the traditional African self-concept: "I am because we are; and because we are, therefore, I am" (Nobles, 1974). In this regard, Hughes (1987) noted that the relationship characteristic among African American family members suggests individuation patterns unique to African American students. Contrary to the interpretations and attributions made by those unknowledgeable of African American family form and function, these students do not perceive their familial relationships and reliance on friends as delaying their development of independence. Rather, African Americans' individuation patterns perpetuate the Afrocentric form that is termed "the extended family."

In sum, scholars have concluded that despite the intent to destroy community and values of African slaves in America, slavery inadvertently ensured that social organization as it existed in the souls of slaves was actualized in African Americans. Social organization—where norms, role ascription, ethical conduct, group solidarity and defense, cooperation, accommodation and conflict, and related sociologic concepts descriptive of peoples and cultures resided in the lives of slaves—forms the legacy of African Americans. This social organization, different from that of free peoples, provided for the traditional functions of group solidarity and family organization in the face of staggering odds.

Thus the truncated view of the culture of African Americans' forebears—and hence of African Americans—leads to unfounded conclusions. Further, for some, this view also justifies interventions that ignore the unique characteristics of the person being "treated." Simplistic interventions result from describing racial and ethnic minority persons n*ot as they are but as they are different* from the modal individual (McAdoo, 1981). In that comparative context, the emphasis remains on validating the majority experience as opposite to studying the ethnic minority experience. Mathis (1978) observed, "One's ability to understand [B]lack reality is limited if the interpretive framework is based on assumptions associated with non-[B]lack reality" (p. 676). Mathis' essential argument was also advanced by Merton (1968), who suggested that outsiders lack the intuitive sensibility for understanding the target group's culture. Again, it is noted that although this discussion is focused on the African American experience its essence is transportable to other ethnic peoples.

Those embracing intervention models that ignore the unique and vital heritage of ethnic minority persons and treat them rather as deficient Whites reveal an ethnocentric or, more specifically, Eurocentric bias. The conceptualization holding that because of their retention of African form and tradition African Americans ought to be thought of as African in *nature* and American in *nurture* (Nobles, 1978) is termed Africentric. An essential characteristic of Africentric theory or worldview is the belief in simultaneous and harmonious existence of all things.

The Africentric model is advanced here not as universally applicable but rather as a useful alternative to the predominant Euro-American or Eurocentric model, which does not fully accommodate the intellectual and social development of African Americans on White campuses. It is asserted as having validity for understanding the diversity and complexity of the heritage of African Americans. Further, it is presented as useful for fostering African American students' demonstrated strengths so as to enable them to function in the competitive, achievement-oriented environment of the U.S. campus while holding fast to their cultural heritage (see Figure 1). By

Figure 1

Heuristic Model for Factors Affecting African American Students' Academic Development

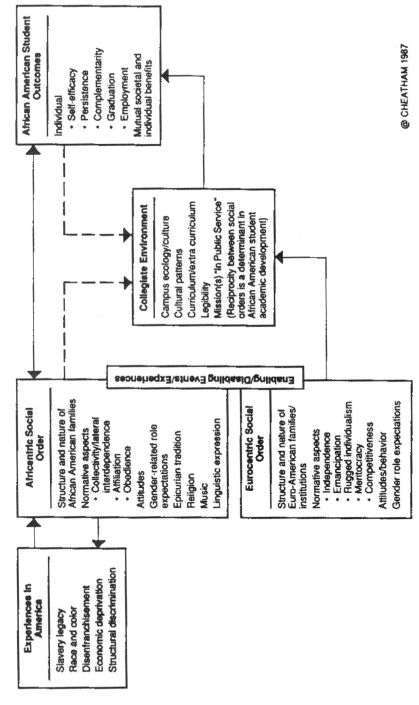

@ CHEATHAM 1987

transporting variables endemic to other cultures, one can extend the utility of this model (Cheatham, 1989).

Figure 1's heuristic model depicts aspects of the experience of African Americans in U.S. society as these are effected through synthesis and adaptation of elements from both the Africentric and Eurocentric social orders. Further, the model depicts the empirical evidence that suggests that individuals from each order embody behaviors and characteristics derived from their respective order as well as from the complementary order. The vertical bar connecting these social orders depicts individual options to synthesize, adapt, and even reject social order phenomena that are perceived or experienced as either enabling or disabling of one's functioning in this society. That the collegiate environment is more syntonic with the Eurocentric social order than with the Africentric is illustrated by the solid line from the former and the broken line (to suggest the tentativeness of its influence) from the latter. Some ethnic minority students certainly emerge from this depicted, impoverished environment personally integrated, strong and fully functional. The implication to be drawn from the model, however, is that creating more culturally syntonic collegiate environments (i.e., that reflect and respect ethnic minority cultures) is an appropriate and critical undertaking for societal institutions that proclaim human development among their goals.

The various ways African American students have been described suggests that most are somewhere between the constants depicted in the Africentric and Eurocentric models. The Eurocentric model may be more appropriate to the African American student whose precollege social experience was quite diverse (i.e., racially integrated, cosmopolitan). Just as social and cultural exchange, synthesis and adaptation has resulted in people who are similar in attitudes, beliefs, and values, the sociocultural experiences of some African American students may render them more or less amenable to Africentric-focused interventions. No application is automatic, however. Those committed to serving the needs of ethnic minority students and to hastening the arrival of cultural pluralism ought to be familiar with Africentric theory and models as well as with the various theories and models of identity development of other ethnic minority groups' members.

It seems redundant but necessary to suggest that to ignore the cultural specificity of the ethnic minority student while treating him or her as the idealized American is to continue to engender problematic situations on U.S. campuses. A growing body of research and literature substantiates sociocultural experiences and developmental differences distinguishing African American, Asian American, American Indian, and Latino students from their Caucasian American counterparts.

It seems equally redundant and necessary to petition that through observation of and "unconditional positive regard" for that specificity, there is much that many traditionally White collegiate institutions have done and that others can do to enable ethnic minority students to function optimally and emerge with an intact, validated self.

Student Development Theory

Student development theory is a specific psychology derived from theories of human development with a special focus on developmental changes occurring throughout the phase of the life cycle of one termed "student." Chickering (1981) proposed that student development is an *intentional* intervention that promotes such capacities as clear values, integrity, communication skills, critical thinking and synthesis, a sense of tolerance and interdependence, empathy, understanding and cooperation, and a capacity for intimacy that goes beyond mere competence and tolerance. In sum, he proposed the development of a basic sense of personal identity, neither superimposed nor mediated but conscientiously facilitated through appropriate programmatic interventions. He conceptualized collegiate institutions as developmental communities and recognized that students are not homogeneous but are instead developmentally different from one another. (Chickering's theory and schema is but one of several available postulations of student development. For a broader presentation of college student development theory and practice, see Creamer & Associates, 1990, and Knefelkamp, Widick, & Parker, 1978.) Chickering posed the question of the consequence of taking this human development as the unifying purpose of higher education as well as of the consequences that accrue to the individual and the society when there is greater awareness of the interactions between self and system.

Chickering's model is interactionist. It contains seven vectors: (a) developing competence, (b) managing emotions, (c) developing autonomy, (d) establishing identity, (e) freeing interpersonal relationships, (f) clarifying purpose, and (g) developing integrity. The collegiate environment then is postulated as providing the conditions that facilitate students' development along the vectors. Among the experiences postulated as focusing and nurturing behavior and, in turn, provoking introspection and growth are (a) clarity and consistency of objectives, (b) redundancy that occurs as a function of institutional size, (c) choice and flexibility in curriculum, teaching, and evaluation, (d) residence hall arrangements that foster interpersonal relationships, (e) positive faculty-student and student-administration interactions, and (f) a student culture that complements a positive academic environment (Knefelkamp et al., 1978). These experiences, it should be noted, are central to the themes of the chapters in this volume.

The Student Development Task and Lifestyle Inventory (SDTLI) (Winston, Miller, & Prince, 1987) and its predecessor, the 1979 Student Development Task Inventory based on Chickering's widely applied theory, assess college students' psychosocial development. Despite the ". . . considerable evidence to support the contention that college students as a *group* [italics added] share common challenges and that development is coherent and predictable" (Miller & Winston, 1990, p. 102), there exists little evidence that the identity development of African American and other ethnic minority students is accounted for in the aggregate data. In a study of student socialization, Nettles & Johnson (1987) found that African American students ranked higher than White students on peer group relations and lower on academic integration and satisfaction. They concluded that these two student cohorts have different developmental needs and that differential approaches are necessary in collegiate institutions addressing ethnic group members' socialization needs.

Developmental differences have been reported in two studies using the SDTLI to assess African American students. Both reported gender differences not shown in studies of White students.

In the first study, Jordan-Cox (1987), in a cross-sectional design study of African American students in three HBCs in the same city found African American women preceding their male counterparts in interpersonal relationships, autonomy, and life purpose. She suggested that these differences might be a function of the type of collegiate environment (i.e., one was historically a women's college). She also noted that first-year students differed on 9 of 12 variables whereas seniors differed from each other on only three variables—all three concentrated in the interpersonal relationships area. There is a hint in her conclusions that this diminishing of differences may have resulted as a function of the characteristics of the collegiate environs. This notion, moreover, is consistent with the nurturing experiences postulated by Chickering (cited in Knefelkamp et al., 1978).

In the second study, Cheatham, Slaney, and Coleman (1990), also using a cross-sectional design to study African American students in an HBC and a PWI in the same state, found seniors, regardless of institution, preceding other students in Educational Involvement, Career Planning, and Life Management. SDTLI results yielded three main effects for institution: PWI students reported greater incidence of Cultural Participation and posted higher scores than HBC students on Emotional Autonomy. The results of the Salubrious Lifestyle (i.e., sense of well-being) favored students at the HBC.

Although the role ethnic and cultural influences play in psychosocial development is not yet clear, it is certain that the characteristics that distinguish ethnic minority students from their counterparts must be taken into account in student development conceptualizations and programs. From the aggregate research it seems safe to conclude that identity development is a specific task faced by ethnic minority students and as such ought to be incorporated into stage development theory.

Several writers have provided evidence that African American students are responsive to a variety of interventions, particularly to those that authenticate the student's sense of self and that provide the students with a sense of genuine community on White campuses (c.f. Carroll, 1987;

Jackson, 1985; Jones, 1985; Locke & Zimmerman, 1987). Locke and Zimmerman reported that a program predicated on a theory of human development promoted significant growth in ego development in African American students. Those student volunteers trained as peer counselors registered positive gains in moral reasoning. Locke and Zimmerman noted that counseling about racial issues triggered more intense responses among peer counselors and resulted in less objective levels of reasoning. That effect noted, they concluded that psychological growth among African American students may be a key to enhancing these students' success on White campuses.

Trippi and Cheatham (1989) identified six areas of concern that dominate counseling interactions with an African American cohort of students served in an academic assistance program for differentially prepared students. They reported that 70% of 1,620 counseling contacts addressed academic concerns, academic skill deficiencies, course scheduling, financial need, introductory interviews, and legibility or understanding of institutional procedures and norms. They also found that African American freshmen for whom counselors unilaterally scheduled subsequent appointments were significantly less likely to persist to second-year status than were students who independently initiated follow-up appointments or with whom no specific follow-up appointments were scheduled. Using a cross-sectional design, they found that the number of in-person counseling contacts was the independent variable most related to persistence of African American first-year students. In a longitudinal study of this same cohort (Trippi & Cheatham, 1991), they reported legibility as the single most important variable in student persistence in college.

Summary and Conclusions

Certainly not all efforts to recruit and retain ethnic minority students have been poorly conceived nor met by dismal failure. What is evident is that after two recent decades of bold, new societal efforts for providing equity in U.S. higher education the retention and graduation results are uneven and unenviable. Most African American students are enrolled in PWIs and continue to be at some risk as casualties of these institutions (Wharton, 1986). Berrian (1982) contended that, contrary to lore, PWIs *once committed* succeed in developing ethnic minority students. Of critical importance in this observation is the institutional climate and the student's experience of that climate. There is evidence suggesting that although African American students express a preference for a counselor from their own ethnic group they rate the counselor's education, attitudes and values, age, and personality as being more important than similar ethnicity (Atkinson, Furlong, & Poston, 1986). Negative learning environments—aside from perpetrating a disturbing and disgraceful waste of psychic energy—totally contradict the purposes of education in a democratic society.

This appraisal ushers the conclusion that there is much that can and must be done to provide positive educational and developmental experiences for ethnic minority students on White campuses—and beyond that to hasten the day when equity and, even more critically, cultural pluralism is a reality in U.S. higher education and society. Collegiate officials cannot homogenize ethnic minority students amidst proclamations that color and ethnicity are of no consequence. Even in the optimal situation where the culture accepts unconditionally the members of its cocultures, to proclaim that ethnicity and sociocultural experience are inconsequential would be to impede the growth of ethnic minority persons. Color and ethnicity are critical dimensions of how one defines self and particularly so in a society that has placed such importance on color and "race." The critical prerequisite to serving fully the developmental needs of ethnic minority students is to reconceptualize development theory and models with ethnic minority identity development as a specific developmental task.

Investigations of factors affecting minority students' academic success have focused on the characteristics of the student, of the institution, and on the complex interaction of the two. The discussion of those factors in the preceding sections provides premises from which to suggest that notable success has been registered by some institutions, whereas others have yet to undertake modifications of institutional policies and practices. Unfortunately, some institutions' lack of progress is traceable to their investment in narcotizing rhetoric suggesting that without a cadre of committed ethnic minority professionals they cannot fashion an environment conducive to minority student development. Jones (1985), specifically addressing counseling service delivery but in a context relevant to our purposes, noted that no research to date demonstrates that all minority clients view all White counselors as inappropriate sources of help. It follows that although staffing that is representative of the institution's various ethnic groups is a desirable convention, institutional commitment should not await that event.

The thesis for this chapter is that the sociocultural or psychosocial experiences of African Americans, and indeed of all ethnic minority groups, are not adequately appreciated and accommodated in theoretical postulations and programmatic interventions designed to serve these groups' members. There is a specific and unique history and attendant set of expectations that the African American and the ethnic minority student, in general, bring to campus. These are rooted in the psychosocial dynamics of the family and in the repertoire that develops as a function of the complex interaction among the family's members and the external environment. Those who would be helpful to ethnic minority students on U.S. campuses must increase their knowledge and appreciation of these students' sociocultural and sociohistorical legacies.

There is no easy resolution of the complex task of how to ensure cultural pluralism on U.S. campuses. There is faith that the issue will yield to the concerted efforts of principled, committed educators—both those responsible for the curricula and those responsible for the cocurricula. There also is impressive evidence that many institutions have made significant inroads. Review of the relevant literature suggests, further, that not just the prestigious or quality institutions (i.e., those characterized by diverse curricula, resources and annual budget, and sometimes even by the date and place of founding) are reporting some success. Rather, impressive accomplishments are reported by diverse institutions that are attuned to the society's rapidly changing needs and are addressing with integrity the complementary mission of service to the nation. The characteristic common among these institutions is the will to challenge the normative system and its assumptions.

References

Allen, W. R. (1986). *Gender and campus race differences in Black student academic performance, racial attitudes, and college satisfaction.* Atlanta, GA: Southern Education Foundation.

Asante, M. K. (1988). *The Afrocentric idea.* Philadelphia, PA: Temple University Press. Atkinson, D. R., Furlong, M. J., & Poston, W. C. (1986). Afro-American preferences for counselor characteristics. *Journal of Counseling Psychology, 33,* 326–330.

Bandura, A. (1982). Self-efficacy mechanism in human agency. *American Psychologist, 37,* 122–147.

Bandura, A. (1986). Fearful expectations and avoidant actions as coefficients of perceived self-inefficacy. *American Psychologist, 41,* 1389–1391.

Baratz, J. S., & Ficklen, M. (1983). *Participation of recent Black graduates in the labor market and in graduate education.* Princeton, NJ: Educational Testing Service.

Berrian, A. H. (1982). Toward desegregation and enhancement. In R. Wilson (Ed.), *Race and equity in higher education* (pp. 137–153). Washington, DC: American Council on Education.

Blackwell, J. E. (1975). *The Black community: Diversity and unity.* New York: Harper & Row.

Blassingame, J. (1979). *The slave community: Plantation life in the antebellum South.* New York: Oxford.

Braddock, J. H., II. (1981). Desegregation and Black student attrition. *Urban Education, 36,* 15–23.

Calia, V. F. (1966). The culturally deprived client: A reformulation of the counselor's role. *Journal of Counseling Psychology, 11,* 100–105.

Carroll, J. (1988). Factors affecting academic success and dropout behavior among Black freshmen at a predominantly Black urban community college. *Journal of College Student Development, 29,* 52–59.

Cheatham, H. E. (1989). Reversing the decline of African American enrollment in U.S. higher education. *Southeastern Association of Educational Opportunity Program Personnel Journal, 8,* 14–22.

Cheatham, H. E., Slaney, R. B., & Coleman, N. (1990). Institutional effects on the psychosocial development of African American college students. *Journal of Counseling Psychology, 37,* 453–458.

Cheatham, H. E., Tomlinson, S. M., & Ward, T. J. (1990). The African self-consciousness construct and African American students. *Journal of College Student Development, 31,* 492–499.

Chickering, A. (1981). *The modern American college.* San Francisco: Jossey-Bass.

Creamer, D. G., & Associates (1990). *College student development: Theory and practice for the 1990s.* Washington, DC: American College Personnel Association.

Edwards, H. (1979). Sport within the veil: The triumphs, tragedies, and challenges of Afro-American involvement. *Annals of the American Academy of Political and Social Science, 445,* 116–127.

Edwards, H. (1988). The single-minded pursuit of sports fame and fortune is approaching an institutional tragedy in Black society. *Ebony, 43,* 138–140.

Egerton, J. (1982). Race and equity in higher education. In R. Wilson (Ed.), *Race and equity in higher education* (pp. 1–27). Washington, DC: American Council on Education.

Fleming, J. (1984). *Blacks in college.* San Francisco: Jossey-Bass.

Gibbs, J. T. (1973). Black students/White university, different expectations. *Personnel and Guidance Journal, 51,* 463–469.

Gibbs, J. T. (1974). Patterns of adaptation among Black students in a predominantly White university: Selected case studies. *American Journal of Orthopsychiatry, 44,* 728–740.

Gurin, P., & Epps, E. (1975). *Black consciousness, identity, and achievement: A study of students in historically Black colleges.* New York: Wiley.

Herskovits, M. (1941). *The myth of the Negro post.* New York: Harper.

Hill, R. B. (1972). *The strengths of Black families.* New York: Emerson Hall.

Hill, R. B. (1990). Economic forces, structural discrimination, and the Black family. In H. E. Cheatham & J. B. Stewart (Eds.), *Black families: Interdisciplinary perspectives* (pp. 87–105). New Brunswick, NJ: Transaction.

Hughes, M. S. (1987). Black students' participation in higher education. *Journal of College Student Personnel, 28,* 532–545.

Jackson, G. G. (1985). Cross-cultural counseling and the Afro-American. In P. Pedersen (Ed.), *Handbook of cross-cultural counseling and therapy* (pp. 231–237). Westport, CT: Greenwood Press.

Jones, E. (1985). Psychotherapy and counseling with Black clients. In P. Pedersen (Ed.), *Handbook of cross-cultural counseling and therapy* (pp. 173–179). Westport, CT: Greenwood Press.

Jordan-Cox, C. A. (1987). Psychosocial development of students in traditionally Black institutions. *Journal of College Student Personnel, 28,* 504–511.

Katchadourian, H., & Boli, J. (1986). *Careerism and intellectual change among college students.* San Francisco: Jossey-Bass.

Knefelkamp, L., Widick, C., & Parker, C. (1978). *Applying new developmental findings* (New Directions for Student Services, No. 4). San Francisco: Jossey-Bass.

Lindzey, G., & Aronson, E. (Eds.). (1969). *The handbook of social psychology* (Vol. 5, 2nd ed.). Reading, MA: Addison-Wesley.

Locke, D., & Zimmerman, N. A. (1987). The effects of peer counseling training on the psychological maturity of Black students. *Journal of College Student Personnel, 28,* 525–531.

Loo, C., & Rolison, G. (1986). Alienation among ethnic minority students at a predominantly White university. *Journal of Higher Education, 57,* 58–77.

Lunneborg, P. W., & Lunneborg, C. E. (1985). Student-centered versus university centered solutions to problems of minority students. *Journal of College Student Personnel, 26,* 224–228.

Madrazo-Peterson, R., & Rodriquez, M. (1978). Minority students: Perceptions of a university environment. *Journal of College Student Personnel, 19,* 259–263.

Mathis, A. (1978). Contrasting approaches to the study of Black families. *Journal of Marriage and the Family, 40,* 667–676.

McAdoo, H. P. (1981). *Black families.* Beverly Hills, CA: Sage.

Merton, R. (1968). *Social theory and social structure.* New York: Free Press.

Miller, T. K., & Winston, R. B., Jr. (1990). Assessing development from a psychosocial perspective. In D. G. Creamer & Associates, *College student development: Theory and practice for the 1990s* (pp. 99–126). Washington, DC: American College Personnel Association.

Mingle, J. (1978). Faculty and departmental response to increased Black student enrollment. *Journal of Higher Education, 49,* 201–217.

Nettles, M., & Baratz, J. C. (1985). Black colleges: Do we need them? *Change, 17* (2), 58–60.

Nettles, M., & Johnson, J. (1987) . Race, sex, and other factors as determinants of college students' socialization. *Journal of College Student Personnel, 28* (6), 512–524.

Nettles, M., Thoeny, A. R., & Gosman, E. J. (1986). Comparative and predictive analyses of Black and White students' college achievement. *Journal of Higher Education, 57,* 289–318.

Nobles, W. W. (1974). African root and American fruit: The Black family. *Journal of Social and Behavioral Sciences, 20,* 66–77.

Nobles, W. W. (1978). Toward an empirical and theoretical framework for defining Black families. *Journal of Marriage and the Family, 40,* 679–688.

Sedlacek, W. E. (1987). Black students on White campuses: 20 years of research. *Journal of College Student Personnel, 26,* 484–495.

Semmes, C. E. (1985). Minority status and the problem of legitimacy. *Journal of Black Studies, 15,* 259–275.

Smith, A. W., & Allen, W. R. (1984). Modeling Black student academic performance in higher education. *Research in Higher Education, 21,* 210–225.

Spady, W. (1970). Dropouts from higher education: An interdisciplinary review and synthesis. *Interchange, 1,* 64–85.

Stampp, K. M. (1956). *The peculiar institution: Slavery in the antebellum South.* New York: Vintage Books.

Taylor, C. A. (1986). Black students on predominantly White college campuses in the 1980s. *Journal of College Student Personnel, 24,* 196–202.

Tinto, V. (1982). *Defining dropout: A matter of perspective.* Washington, DC: Jossey-Bass.

Tinto, V. (1975). Dropout from higher education: A theoretical synthesis of recent research. *Review of Educational Research, 45,* 89–125.

Trippi, J., & Cheatham, H. E. (1989). Effects of a special counseling program for Black students on a predominantly White campus. *Journal of College Student Development, 30,* 35–40.

Trippi, J., & Cheatham, H. E. (1991). Counseling effects on African American college student graduation. *Journal of College Student Development, 32.*

Wharton, C. R., Jr. (1986, July). *Public higher education and the Black American: Today's crises, tomorrow's disaster?* Plenary address to the National Urban League Conference, San Francisco, CA.

Winston, R. B., Jr., Miller, T. K., & Prince, J. S. (1987). *Assessing student development: A preliminary manual for the Student Development Task Inventory (rev. 2nd ed.) and the Student Developmental Profile and Planning Record.* Athens, GA: Student Development Associates.

Incorporating the Development of African-American Students Into Psychosocial Theories of Student Development

Marylu K. McEwen, Larry D. Roper,
Deborah R. Bryant, and Miriam J. Langa

Nine dimensions that address the development of African-American students are proposed for inclusion in psychosocial theories of college student development.

Colleges and universities in the United States have a tradition and mission of transforming and enriching the lives of students (Boyer, 1987). This mission is consistent with the goals of preserving, enriching, and transmitting culture, as was identified by the Student Personnel Point of View (SPPV) (American Council on Education [ACE], 1937, 1949). The SPPV suggests that college personnel, especially student affairs professionals, should fulfill their mission by responding to the whole person, acknowledging individual differences, and meeting students at their level of development (Saddlemire & Rentz, 1986). In addition, college and university programs help students to make "significant life transitions" (National Association of Student Personnel Administrators [NASPA], 1987). Implied in all three of these statements (ACE, 1937, 1949; NASPA, 1987) is that student affairs professionals also have a responsibility of responding to all students, which includes both majority and racial and ethnic minority students.

For much of history, however, higher education in the United States was racially segregated. Beginning in the 1960s, large numbers of Black students began attending predominantly White institutions (Fleming, 1984). The sudden influx of Black students created an educational dilemma for college and university professionals—how could they respond to the educational needs of students for whom their institutions were not designed? Predominantly White institutions (PWIs) were founded for the intention of educating the White middle class (Kovel, 1970). These institutions, based on Anglo-Saxon, Euro-American values, are like all social institutions; they survive because they are symbolically related to the cultural values of the broader American society.

The cultural values of PWIs also influence how students are viewed and how education is approached. The cultural values of institutions affect what students are taught, how they are taught, and how student learning is evaluated. Most important, cultural values influence the direction that educators attempt to move students, how student behavior is evaluated, and what knowledge base is used to explain student (human) development. Because educators at PWIs have historically relied upon a body of knowledge that supports and reinforces Euro-American values, they often prove unsuccessful in responding to the educational and cultural needs of

African-American students (Bulhan, 1985). Black students at PWIs are taught and evaluated from an Anglo-Saxon perspective.

Those responsible for teaching and helping Black students must create models of human and student development that take into account the unique needs and experiences that Black students bring to the college campus. Issues specific to African-American students that are not accounted for in the traditional theories of human development are (a) the unique psychohistory of Blacks in this country and the adaptations that Blacks must make (Essien-Udom, 1971); (b) the "colonized" nature of Black existence in this country (Fanon, 1967); (c) the extended nature of the Black family and Black homelife (Willie, 1976); (d) the unique educational/socialization role of the Black family (Willie, 1976); (e) the oral tradition within the Black community (Hall & Freedle, 1975); (f) the impact of racial hostility and environmental press (Ogbu, 1981); (g) the unique character of Black Americans (Essien-Udom, 1971); (h) the psychological dynamics that accompany being "a caste-like minority" (Ogbu, 1981), representing a "rejected strain" in society (Cruse, 1967), being "codified" (Scruggs, 1971) and attempting to reconcile two identities (DuBois, 1953); and (i) the philosophical connections to African tradition, such as oral tradition, action/belief connection, elastic concept of time, kinship tradition/group consciousness, survival focus (collective versus individual), spiritual disposition, and view of people as an integrated whole (Baldwin, 1981; Nobles, 1980). Among other issues to be considered are the limitations of Euro-American definitions of normalcy (Bulhan, 1985) for African-American students.

Black scholars suggest that the Black experience in American society requires that Blacks interact with and participate in White institutions. This participation results in *oppression, dehumanization,* and *deracialization.* Deracialization occurs through a process by which people are required/forced to abandon "cultural forms, . . . [one's] language, . . . [one's] food habits, . . . [one's] sexual behavior, . . . [one's] way of sitting down, of resting, of laughing, of enjoying [oneself]" (Fanon, 1972, pp. 20–21). Student affairs professionals must concern themselves with whether or not, through the use of traditional theories and practices, they are participating in the dehumanization of African-American students. One way of responding is by expanding psychosocial theories of college student development to address the experience of African-American students.

Psychosocial theories, one of five clusters of student development theories (Knefelkamp, Widick, & Parker, 1978, p. xi), are those based directly or indirectly on Erikson's (1968) theory of human development. Examples of psychosocial theories/models include those of Chickering (1969), Sanford (1962), Keniston (1971), Coons (1970), and King (1973). Roy Heath's (1964) typology model and Douglas Heath's (1968) maturity model can also be included in the psychosocial framework.

The purpose of this discussion is to offer ways in which proponents of psychosocial theories of student development can incorporate more effectively the developmental issues of African-American students. A number of different dimensions must be added to extend the boundaries of student development theories. Nine such dimensions for inclusion in psychosocial theories are proposed below. These issues have been identified both through theoretical literature and essays on the Black experience and through quantitative and qualitative research conducted with African-American students in higher education.

Developmental Issues

Nine factors relate to developmental tasks of African-American students. These issues, which either have not been addressed adequately in the psychosocial theories or need to be considered in more complex ways for African-American students, include developing ethnic and racial identity, interacting with the dominant culture, developing cultural aesthetics and awareness, developing identity, developing interdependence, fulfilling affiliation needs, surviving intellectually, developing spiritually, and developing social responsibility.

Developing Ethnic and Racial Identity

A number of authors have cited the need to expand the notion of identity development to include attitudes about the race to which one belongs, that is, the role of racial or ethnic identity (Baldwin, 1981, 1984: Baldwin & Bell, 1985; Baldwin, Duncan, & Bell, 1987; Cross, 1971, 1978; Fleming, 1984; Helms, 1981; Parham, 1989; Parham & Helms, 1981, 1985a, 1985b; Pounds, 1987). Fleming (1984) indicated that Black students may hold doubts about their ethnic identity and that they must put psychological energy into protecting themselves against identity loss. Helms (1984) contrasted this issue for Black students with that of Whites, in which many Whites do not see themselves as White and thus may not hold a set of attitudes about the racial group to which they belong.

Cross (1971, 1978) offered a useful model from which to consider the development of racial identity. He proposed five stages, namely, (a) Preencounter, in which the Black student has not yet encountered the issue of one's own racial identity; (b) Encounter, in which one has a significant experience and begins to develop a Black identity; (c) Immersion-Emersion, in which one becomes intensely focused upon one's new Black identity; (d) Internalization, in which one resolves the conflicts between the old and new worldviews; and (e) Internalization-Commitment, encompassing the previous stage but adding commitment to resolution of problems shared by one's racial group. In discussing cycles of psychological Nigrescence, Parham (1989) suggested that the racial identity of a Black person is "potentially influenced by his or her life stage and the developmental tasks associated with that period of life" (p. 196). Parham (1989) also described "how the stages of racial identity may be manifested at three phases of life (late adolescence/early adulthood, middle adulthood, and late adulthood)" (p. 197).

Parham and Helms (1981, 1985a, 1985b) have extended Cross's (1971, 1978) model by developing the Racial Identity Attitude Scale (Parham & Helms, 1981) and by conducting research with Black college students on the relationship between racial identity and self-esteem (1985a), self-actualization (1985b), and counselor preference (1981). In Parham and Helms's study of counselor preference, pre-encounter attitudes were negatively related and encounter attitudes positively related to preference for Black counselors; furthermore, pre-encounter attitudes were positively related to preference for White counselors (Parham & Helms, 1981). Parham and Helms (1981) summarized that (a) the preencounter stage is characterized by pro-White-anti-Black counselor preferences, (b) the encounter stage is characterized by pro-Black-anti-White counselor preferences, and (c) the immersion-emersion and internalization stages are similar in pro-Black attitudes but are not as anti-White as is the encounter stage (p. 254). In two studies, Parham and Helms found that both preencounter and immersion attitudes were significantly related to low self-esteem (1985a) and less self-actualization (1985b), whereas encounter attitudes were associated with positive self-esteem and greater self-actualization .

In both cases, the variance explained by a combination of the racial identity attitudes was between 15% and 18%. Parham and Helms (1985b) concluded that (a) the racial identity process may be more complex than is expected, and (b) both professionals and Black students should be aware that some of the feelings associated with particular racial identity attitudes may be unpleasant and require resolution but may be a natural part of the Nigrescence process. Parham and Helms (1985a) also concluded that "self-concept may be governed by the way the student handles the conditions of the Black experience" (p. 145). In a later study, Carter and Helms (1988) found that socioeconomic status variables were not significant predictors of racial identity attitudes.

Baldwin (1981, 1984), Baldwin and Bell (1985), and Baldwin et al. (1987) discussed the concept of African self-consciousness as "central to normal and healthy Black personality functioning" (Baldwin et al., 1987, p. 28). According to their theory, African self-consciousness involves (a) the recognition of oneself as "African" and what being "African means," (b) the recognition of African survival and proactive development as one's first priority value, (c) respect for and active perpetuation of all things African, and (d) having a standard of conduct toward all things "non-African" and "anti-African" (Baldwin et al., 1987, p. 29). Baldwin and Bell (1985) have developed the African Self-Consciousness (ASC) Scale that measures competency in the four areas of African self-consciousness identified previously. In a study of the relationship of background characteristics and social cultural setting to African self-consciousness, Baldwin et al. (1987) found that Black students at a predominantly Black college had significantly higher ASC scale scores than did Black students attending a predominantly White institution.

They also found that older students and upperclass students had higher ASC scores than did younger students and underclass students, with the class difference being more pronounced for students in the predominantly Black college. Baldwin et al. (1987) concluded that a predominantly Black academic setting may have a more positive influence on the development of African self-consciousness than will a predominantly White academic setting.

Interacting with the Dominant Culture

Another aspect of culture is the role that assimilation and acculturation play in the development of racial and ethnic minority students. Because White students are part of the majority and dominant culture, this issue of assimilation/acculturation does not emerge for students of the dominant culture. For African-American students, however, the task of "adjusting to living/learning in a campus environment that varies from the accustomed cultural frame of reference" (Wright, 1987, p. 11) is a most important issue.

Gibbs (1974) cited numerous studies in which Black students suffer from a series of identity problems resulting from culture conflict. Through clinical experience with Black students experiencing ethnic or cultural conflicts, Gibbs identified four modes of adaptation to the college and university environment. These four modes are withdrawal, described as movement away from the dominant culture and characterized by apathy and depression; separation, described as movement against the dominant culture and characterized by anger, hostility, and conflicts with the dominant culture assimilation, described as movement toward the dominant culture and characterized by social anxiety and desire for acceptance; and affirmation, described as movement with the dominant culture and characterized by self-acceptance, high achievement, and a positive ethnic identity. Three of these modes of adaptation are similar to Pettigrew's (1964) three major modes of response to oppression. Among the 41 students in Gibbs's study, withdrawal was the most frequent response mode. Gibbs found that 70% of those students who described themselves as feeling adequate were in the affirmation category, and 61% of those who felt inadequate were in the withdrawal category.

In examining four different categories of socioeconomic class, class differences were found among three of the four response categories. For students of the two highest socioeconomic classes, affirmation and assimilation were the second and third most frequent response modes. There were no students in the separation category among the highest class, and none in the assimilation or affirmation categories among the lowest class. Among working-class students (third lowest class), there were "fewer in the affirmation category and more in the separation and assimilation categories" (p. 738) than there were students in the top two socioeconomic classes.

Developing Cultural Aesthetics and Awareness

Developing cultural aesthetics and awareness is an additional developmental issue for African-American students (Jones, 1987; Stikes, 1984; Wright, 1987). This relates to an appreciation of one's own culture and of other cultures, especially in addition to the dominant culture, and also developing ways in which African-American students can express and celebrate their own cultures.

Developing Identity

The general concept of identity must also be expanded and viewed from a different perspective for African-American students. Sedlacek (1987) addressed this in terms of the importance of self-concept and self-appraisal. Erikson (1968) noted the message of lost, confused, and "surrendered identity" contained in the writings of revolutionary Black authors. These same authors speak of inaudibility, namelessness, facelessness, and invisibility that Blacks have been made to experience. Knefelkamp and Golec (1985) echoed the invisibility that certain persons in American society have had to face. Others (Anson, 1987; DuBois, 1953; Wright, 1987) addressed the duality or even multiplicity with which Black students must struggle, an identity consideration not typically faced by majority students. As Wright (1987) indicated, many minority students live and learn in bicultural/biracial/bilingual environments, which are different from and frequently in conflict with those experienced at college. According to Bradley and Stewart (1982), Blacks experience depersonalization, which brings with it a loss of one's sense of identity, pride, and accomplishment. Cummins (1986) talked about bicultural ambivalence. Brown-Collins and Sussewell (1986) raised the issue of multiple self-referents for African-American students, especially Black women, and suggested at least three self-referents, that of the psychophysiological (Gilligan, 1982), the African American, and oneself (self-knowledge). All of these authors suggest the multiplicity of roles or identities, the implication of contextual identities for students of nondominant cultures, and the intense struggle for African-American students at PWIs to develop identity when the environment seems to work at cross-purposes to such development.

Furthermore, identity development, according to Erikson (1968), relates both to a developmental stage in the life of an individual and to a period in history. Thus, his statement provides strong support for DeVos's (1980) notion of the importance of considering the current social environment. Gurin and Epps (1975), in a series of studies conducted in several historically Black colleges between 1964 and 1970, found that the Black student's sense of identity involves both uniquely personal and collective elements that result from social interaction and group identifications and demonstrated that the students used being Black as the basis for collective elements of identity.

Developing Interdependence

For African-American students, developing independence and autonomy seems to occur within the context of interdependence and relationships, contrasted with the developmental issue of separating oneself from family and significant others as suggested by the literature (Chickering, 1969; Erikson, 1968). Hughes (1987), based on her qualitative research with 79 Black students, found patterns of individuation unique to Black students resulting from the close relationship that Black students maintain with their families. She highlighted the importance of interdependence in individuation and suggested that "it is likely that Black individuation helps to integrate Afrocentric cultural values, commonly referred to as the 'extended family'" (p. 540). Hughes's findings are supported by the literature on the extended nature of the Black family and Black homelife (Willie, 1976) and the unique educational/socialization role of the Black family (Willie, 1976). The roles of family and community are also strongly tied to philosophical connections with the African tradition, such as kinship tradition/group consciousness, survival focus (collective versus individual) and view of people as an integrated whole (Baldwin, 1981; Nobles, 1980).

Fulfilling Affiliation Needs

The role of affiliation needs is also highlighted by Hughes (1987). Affiliation opportunities play a significant role in the survival, success, and development of African-American students at PWIs. On predominantly White campuses, affiliations can counter the social isolation experienced by Black students. In Hughes's (1987) study, Black students' needs were fulfilled external to the university campus, through the Black community, Black churches, and the extended family. DeVos (1980) also addressed the importance of peers or a reference group in the development of Black students, especially in the development of ethnic identity.

Surviving Intellectually

The intellectual survival of African-American students on predominantly White campuses must also be addressed. Fleming (1984) eloquently discussed, based on her research, the impoverished environment for Black students in terms of their cognitive development and the intense struggle that many Black students face in developing the most basic intellectual competence, which is necessary for survival on the college campus. Others (DeVos, 1980; Hughes, 1987) also provide evidence in support of this issue. Hughes goes even further when she indicates that many Black students realize that development in other areas will be delayed or postponed because of their preoccupation with intellectual survival.

Developing Spiritually

The role of religion and spiritual development are two related dimensions that are frequently important to African-American students but that have not been accounted for adequately in most student development theories. Religion not only remains an important activity for African-American students throughout the college years (Wright, 1987), but the church is often an important support for African-American students (Erikson, 1968; Hughes, 1987). Similarly, spiritual development needs to be incorporated in student development theories for a better understanding of African-American students. An additional support reported by Black students in Hughes's (1987) study was reliance on spiritual strength, with spirituality being a deeply rooted aspect of Afrocentric culture (Hughes, 1987). Baldwin (1981) and Nobles (1980) also address the spiritual disposition of African Americans.

Developing Social Responsibility

Wright (1987) suggested that the development of social responsibility is a special psychosocial issue for racial and ethnic minority students. Because of their ethnic status and their exposure to real and perceived social injustice, African-American students frequently assume major responsibility for social advocacy roles on campus. Wright suggests that the greatest dilemma for racial/ethnic minority students in relation to social responsibility is not whether to assume it, but rather how it relates to other multiple responsibilities they hold.

Summary

The following recommendations are offered:

1. Student affairs professionals must develop out of the experiences of African Americans workable theories of student development. When traditional theories are used in working with Black students, conclusions are often reached that are not accurate. Traditional theories are based on the values, philosophical assumptions, and experiences of European Americans.

2. The philosophical connections to Africa have created a distinct African-American ethos. There are many additional factors that contribute to the unique experience and psychological disposition of African Americans. These issues must be taken into account if there is to be created an accurate working model to understand the attitudes, behaviors, feelings, and development of African-American students.

3. Because of the diversity in the Black community, there is no such thing as a "typical Black person." The shared experience of being Black in American society, however, provides a link in the experiences of all African Americans. The link consists of a core of behavioral/dispositional variables upon which theories of the development of African-American students may be developed.

4. Student affairs professionals can work with Black students neither meaningfully nor successfully without understanding their philosophical assumptions and their life experiences.

5. Black student development must not be viewed/approached as "deficit development." There are at least two approaches that may be taken to look at Black student

developmental issues. One approach focuses on the negative experiences that African Americans have in American society and at PWIs; the other approach focuses on the positive traits that connection to the African tradition brings to Black students and their efforts to succeed in an Anglo-Saxon social structure. Focus on the former causes a person to view the Black student from a deficit-deficiency perspective. By focusing on the latter, African-American students are approached based on the positive skills and personal characteristics that they bring to the campus community, and subsequent programs will build on those values, traditions, and attitudes.

6. One way of creating a workable theory of college student development is to incorporate the nine issues identified above into an existing psychosocial theory. Chickering's (1969) theory, as one of the most comprehensive of the psychosocial theories and also as one of the best known and most frequently applied theories, offers a good possibility. Some of the nine developmental issues discussed earlier, such as developing identity in multicultural environments, developing cultural aesthetics and awareness, and fulfilling affiliation needs, could be incorporated into a more comprehensive understanding of Chickering's seven vectors. One example would be expanding Chickering's conceptualization of developing identity with the notions of invisibility (Erikson, 1968; Knefelkamp & Golec, 1985), multiple identities (Anson, 1987; Cummins, 1986; DuBois, 1953; Wright, 1987), and African-American psychohistory (Essien-Udom, 1971). Other issues, such as developing racial and ethnic identity, interacting with the dominant culture, and developing spiritually, could become additional vectors in Chickering's theory. With such an approach, an empirical base would need to be developed to determine the appropriateness of such a rationally derived theory.

A real danger, however, is involved in taking an existing theory, such as Chickering's theory, which is based upon the values and philosophical assumptions of European Americans and upon research with predominantly Caucasian samples. The problem in revising an existing theory is making the assumption that the theory, such as Chickering's, is indeed appropriate for African-American students, although not sufficient. Straub and Rodgers (1986) and Taub (1989) have already raised questions about the applicability of the order of Chickering's vectors to female students. Taub (1989) also has reported findings that challenge the appropriateness of Chickering's theory for Black female students. Thus, as student affairs professionals attempt to make theories of human and student development more inclusive of other populations, it seems more important to create new theories rather than to modify or revise existing ones.

In conclusion, if colleges and universities are to achieve the lofty ideals that they have set forth in their various mission statements, they must begin to approach the education of African-American students in a more positive manner. This approach must include seeing the strengths that African-American students bring to the campus, understanding the influence of various life situations on the educational/developmental process, and treating the campus environment as the deficit in the deficit-deficiency model.

References

American Council on Education. (1937). *The student personnel point of view*. Washington, DC: Author.

American Council on Education. (1949). *The student personnel point of view* (rev. ed.). Washington, DC: Author.

Anson, R. S. (1987). *Best intentions: The education and killing of Edmund Perry*. New York: Vintage Books.

Baldwin, J. A. (1981). Notes on an Afrocentric theory of personality. *Western Journal of Black Studies, 5*, 172–179.

Baldwin, J. A. (1984). African self-consciousness and the mental health of African-Americans. *Journal of Black Studies, 15,* 174–194.

Baldwin, J. A., & Bell, Y. (1985). The African self-consciousness scale: An Afrocentric personality questionnaire. *Western Journal of Black Studies, 9,* 61–68.

Baldwin, J. A., Duncan, J. A., & Bell, Y. (1987). Assessment of African self-consciousness among Black students from two college environments. *Journal of Black Psychology, 13,* 27–41.

Boyer, E. L. (1987). *College: The undergraduate experience in America.* New York: Harper & Row.

Bradley, L. R., & Stewart, M. A. (1982). The relationship between self-concept and personality development in Black college students: A developmental approach. *Journal of Non-White Concerns, 10,* 114–125.

Brown-Collins, A. R., & Sussewell, D. R. (1986). The Afro-American woman's emerging selves. *The Journal of Black Psychology, 13,* 1–11

Bulhan, H. A. (1985). *Frantz Fanon and the psychology of oppression.* New York: Plenum Press.

Carter, R. T., & Helms, J. E. (1988). The relationship between racial identity attitudes and social class. *Journal of Negro Education, 57,* 22–30.

Chickering, A. W. (1969). *Education and identity.* San Francisco: Jossey-Bass.

Coons, F. (1970). The resolution of adolescence in college. *Personnel and Guidance Journal, 48,* 533–541.

Cross, W. E., Jr. (1971). The Negro-to-Black conversion experience: Toward a psychology of Black liberation. *Black World, 20*(9), 13–27.

Cross, W. E., Jr. (1978). The Thomas and Cross models of psychological Nigrescence: A review. *Journal of Black Psychology, 5,* 13–31.

Cruse, H. (1967). *The crisis of the Negro intellectual.* New York: Morrow.

Cummins, I. (1986). Empowering minority students: A framework for intervention. *Harvard Educational Review, 56,* 18–30.

DeVos, G . A. (1980). Ethnic adaptation and minority status. *Journal of Cross-Cultural Psychology, 11,* 101–124.

DuBois, W. E. B. (1953). *The souls of Black folks.* Greenwich, CT: Fawcett Publications, Inc.

Erikson, E. H. (1968). *Identity: Youth and crisis.* New York: Norton.

Essien-Udom, E. U. (1971). Black identity in the international context. In N. I. Huggins, M. Kilson, & D. M. Fox (Eds.), *Key issues in the Afro-American experience* (Volume 2, pp. 233–258). New York: Harcourt Brace Jovanovich.

Fanon, F. (1967). *Black skin, White masks* New York: Grove Press.

Fanon, F. (1972). Racism and culture. In W. King & E. Anthony (Eds.), *Black poets and prophets: The theory, practice and esthetics of the Pan-Africanist revolution* (pp. 13–25). New York: Mentor Books.

Fleming, J. (1984). *Blacks in college.* San Francisco: Jossey-Bass.

Gibbs, J. T. (1974). Patterns of adaptation among Black students at a predominantly white university: Selected case studies. *American Journal of Orthopsychiatry, 44,* 728–740.

Gilligan, C. (1982). *In a different voice.* Boston: Harvard University Press.

Gurin, P., & Epps, E. (1 975). *Black consciousness, identity and achievement.* New York: Wiley.

Hall, W. S., & Freedle, R. O. (1975). *Culture and language: The Black American experience.* Washington, DC: Hemisphere Publishing.

Heath, D. H. (1968). *Growing up in college: Liberal education and maturity.* San Francisco: Jossey-Bass.

Heath, R. (1964). *The reasonable adventurer.* Pittsburgh: University of Pittsburgh Press.

Helms, J. E. (1984). Toward a theoretical explanation of the effects of effects on counseling: A Black and White model. *Counseling Psychologist, 12*(4), 153–165.

Hughes, M. S. (1987). Black students' participation in higher education. *Journal of College Student Personnel, 28,* 532–545.

Jones, W. T. (1987). Enhancing minority-white peer interactions. In D. J. Wright (Ed.), *Responding to the needs of today's minority students* (pp. 81–94). San Francisco: Jossey-Bass.

Keniston, K. (1971). *Youth and dissent.* New York: Harcourt Brace Jovanovich.

King, S. H. (1973). *Five lives at Harvard: Personality change during college.* Cambridge: Harvard University Press

Knefelkamp, L. L., & Golec, R. R. (1985). *A workbook for using the P-T-P model.* College Park, MD: University Book Store.

Knefelkamp, L., Widick, C., & Parker, C. A. (Eds.). (1978). *Applying new developmental findings.* San Francisco: Jossey-Bass.

Kovel, J. (1970). *White racism: A psychohistory.* New York: Vintage Books.

National Association of Student Personnel Administrators. (1987). *Perspective on student affairs.* Washington, DC: Author.

Nobles, W. W. (1980). African philosophy: Foundations for Black psychology. In R. L. Jones (Ed.), *Black psychology* (pp. 23–36). New York: Harper & Row.

Ogbu, J.U. (1981) Black education. In H. P. McAdoo (Ed.), *Black families* (pp. 139–153). Beverly Hills: Sage.

Parham, T. A. (1989). Cycles of psychological Nigrescence. *Counseling Psychologist, 17,* 187–226.

Parham, T. A., & Helms, J. E. (1981). The influence of Black students' racial identity attitudes on preferences for counselor's race. *Journal of Counseling Psychology, 28,* 250–257.

Parham, T. A., & Helms, J. E. (1985a). Attitudes of racial identity and self-esteem of Black students: An exploratory investigation. *Journal of College Student Personnel, 26,* 143–147.

Parham, T. A., & Helms, J. E. (1985b). Relation of racial identity attitudes to self-actualization and affective states of Black students. *Journal of Counseling Psychology, 32,* 431–440.

Pettigrew, T. F. (1964). *A profile of the Negro American.* Princeton: Van Nostrand.

Pounds, A. W. (19S7). Black students' needs on predominantly white campuses. In D. J. Wright (Ed.), *Responding to the needs of today's minority students* (pp. 23–38) . San Francisco: Jossey-Bass.

Saddlemire, G. L., & Rentz, A. L. (Eds.). (1986). The student personnel point of view. In *Student affairs: A profession's heritage* (rev. ed., pp. 122–140). Alexandria. VA: American College Personnel Association.

Sanford, N. (1962). Developmental status of the entering freshman. In N. Sanford (Ed.), *The American college* (pp. 253–282). New York: Wiley.

Scruggs, O. M. (1971). The economic and racial components of Jim Crow. In N. I. Huggins, M. Kilson, & D. M. Fox (Eds.), *Key issues in the Afro-American experience* (Volume 2, pp. 70–87). New York: Harcourt Brace Jovanovich.

Sedlacek, W. E. (1987). Black students on White campuses: 20 years of research. *Journal of College Student Personnel, 28,* 484–495.

Stikes, C. S. (1984). *Black students in higher education.* Carbondale, IL: Southern Illinois University Press.

Straub, C., & Rodgers, R. F. (1986). An exploration of Chickering's theory and women's development. *Journal of College Student Personnel, 27,* 216–224.

Taub, D. G. (1989). The patterns of development of autonomy and mature interpersonal relationships in Black and White undergraduate women. Unpublished master's thesis, University of Maryland, College Park.

Willie, C. V. (1976). *A new look at Black families.* New York: General Hall Inc.

Wright, D. J. (1987). Minority students: Developmental beginnings. In D. J. Wright (Ed.), *Responding to the needs of today's minority students* (pp. 5–22). San Francisco: Jossey-Bass.

The Development of Gay, Lesbian, and Bisexual Identities

HEIDI LEVINE AND NANCY J. EVANS

To understand the issues faced by gay, lesbian, and bisexual people on college campuses, we must first examine the life experiences of these individuals. What it means to be gay, lesbian, or bisexual is unique to each person; but some commonalities exist as individuals become aware of their attraction to others of the same sex and integrate these feelings into other aspects of their identity.

The research that considers timing and age factors in the gay and lesbian identity development process suggests that many developmental issues occur during the traditional undergraduate years (Bell, Weinberg, & Hammersmith, 1981; McDonald, 1982). As student development professionals, we know that this is a key time for identity development in general (Chickering, 1969; Erikson, 1968; Moore & Upcraft, 1990). College and university students are faced with many areas in which they need to reconsider their self-perceptions, develop new skills, and master developmental tasks. The possibility or certainty that one is gay, lesbian, or bisexual complicates these developmental challenges and adds an additional set of complicated issues that must be resolved.

This chapter examines gay, lesbian, and bisexual identity development as it is experienced in Western society. In the next chapter, Wall and Evans more fully address the relevance of student development theory for gay, lesbian, and bisexual students and explore the wide range of developmental issues faced by gay, lesbian, and bisexual students.

Much confusion exists in the literature concerning the terms *homosexual, gay,* and *lesbian* as well as what the concepts of identity and identity development mean. This chapter thus begins by clarifying terms used in relation to the development of a gay, lesbian, or bisexual identity. Gay identity development models are then reviewed, with special attention given to the model proposed by Cass (1979). Distinctions are made between social and psychological models, and the advantages of Cass' psychosocial approach are noted.

Most models of development have failed to consider gender differences, and none has taken into account bisexuality. Therefore, unique aspects of lesbian identity development and special concerns of bisexual individuals are next considered to complement discussion of the major models of gay identity development. The chapter ends with a summary and critique of the work done to date related to gay, lesbian, and bisexual identity development.

Definitional Issues

Researchers and theorists have paid little attention to the factors involved in the development of a gay, lesbian, or bisexual identity. Richardson (1981b) suggested that the development of gay, lesbian, and bisexual identities has been neglected for three reasons: (a) the study of homosexuality has focused almost exclusively on determining its causes, (b) homosexuality has been defined in terms of sexual acts, and (c) homosexuality has been viewed as a pathological state.

Until as recently as the 1970s, the focus of all discussions of homosexuality was etiology. Various biological and psychological causes of homosexual behavior were hypothesized, investigated, and hotly debated. The assumption in this debate was that homosexuality is a universal experience and that homosexuals are a specific type of being who exhibit predictable behaviors (Browning, 1984; Plummer, 1981). More recent writers do not assume that an individual is born with a homosexual identity but rather suggest that such an identity is socially constructed and maintained through interaction with others (Richardson, 1981a).

A number of writers have noted that homosexual *identity* must be distinguished from homosexual *acts* because individuals frequently engage in homosexual behavior without identifying themselves as homosexual (Cass, 1983–1984; Marmor, 1980; Nungesser, 1983; Richardson & Hart, 1981; Weinberg, 1978). Often, same-sex sexual activity is a precursor to developing a gay identity (Cass, 1983–1984; Weinberg, 1978).

Few writers have taken the time to define clearly the concept of homosexual or gay identity. Cass (1983–1984) identified a number of conflicting definitions in her review of the literature, including "(1) defining oneself as gay, (2) a sense of self as gay, (3) image of self as homosexual, (4) the way a homosexual person is, and (5) consistent behavior in relation to homosexual-related activity" (p. 108). She pointed out that some of these definitions are interpersonally focused, others are intrapersonal, and occasionally still others are both. The lack of clarity and agreement, as well as the difficulty in operationalizing these potential definitions, is troublesome.

Homosexual identity must be recognized as only one aspect of the person's total identity. Troiden (1984) defined identity as "organized sets of characteristics an individual perceives as definitively representing the self in relation to a social situation" (p. 102). Homosexual identity, then, is "a perception of self as homosexual in relation to a social setting" (p. 103). Minton and McDonald (1984) saw identity as including "the ascribed, achieved, and adopted roles characteristically enacted by the individual" (p. 91); sexual identity is one of these roles. They went on to define homosexual identity formation as "a life-span, developmental process that is part of the general maturational process of achieving a coherent sense of personal identity" (p 91).

A distinction must be made between the terms *homosexual identity* and *gay identity*. Homosexual identity is a narrower term, referring to sexual behavior only, whereas gay identity suggests the total experience of being gay (Warren, 1974). The use of the term *homosexual identity* is often viewed negatively by the gay and lesbian community because it has been used as a diagnostic label by many clinicians and is often associated with a negative self-image. *Gay identity*, however, has a positive connotation within the gay and lesbian communities and is seen as encompassing emotional, lifestyle, and political aspects of life rather than being exclusively sexual (Beane, 1981).

Jandt and Darsey (1981) noted that all definitions of homosexual or gay identity have in common a shift in perception of self as a member of the majority to self as a member of the minority. Along with this change in perception comes adoption of a new set of values and a redefinition of acceptable behavior. As such, development of a gay, lesbian, or bisexual identity is mainly an internal, psychological process.

As various models of homosexual identity development are examined, the reader needs to note problems related to definition. Some theorists and researchers are careful to define their terms, others assume the reader will know what they mean. In addition, terms such as *homosexual* or *gay identity* and labels given to various stages of gay or lesbian identity development often have different connotations in various models of development.

Identity Development Models

Models addressing homosexual or gay identity development evolved throughout the 1970s and 1980s. During this period, research started to move from a focus of "becoming homosexual" to one of "developing a homosexual identity." A great deal of overlap is evident in this research, as is some ambivalence about what is being studied.

One issue to be aware of in reviewing these models is that, given their focus on gay men's development, they may not accurately reflect the perspectives of lesbian women. Similarly, there is little or no room in these models for the attainment of a healthy bisexual identity. Indeed, an inherent assumption of some is that a "healthy bisexual identity" would be a contradiction in terms! These issues are specifically addressed in later sections of this chapter.

Shively and deCecco's (1977) article on aspects of homosexual identity provided a good example of this early trend. They identified biological sex, gender identity, social sex role, and sexual orientation as the four components of sexual identity. Although the last component (orientation) encompasses physical and affectional preference, no mention is made of the establishment of identity as a gay or lesbian person.

At the same time, others were beginning to look at how a gay or lesbian identity is formed. Models based on developmental perspectives, and outlining a series of stages through which an individual moves in acquiring a homosexual identity, were proposed. These models fit loosely into two categories: those addressing social factors and those focusing on psychological changes. Many, however, encompass both areas. Those models that present specific stages of development (Lee, 1977; Coleman, 1981–1982; Plummer, 1975; Troiden, 1979; Minton & McDonald, 1984; Cass, 1979) are shown in the table.

Social Models

One of the first works to address the concept of gay identity was that of Dank (1971). In his study of men coming out within the gay community, Dank looked at the time lapse and (to a lesser extent) process involved in moving from first awareness of attraction to other men and then to self-labeling as homosexual. He suggested that identity development is based on the meanings that an individual ascribes to homosexuality and made clear that identification as gay and self-acceptance do not necessarily occur at the same time. Although a clear portrait of how movement

Table 1
Stage Models of Gay Identity Theory

State	Social Models			Psychological Models			Psychosocial Model
	Lee (1977)	Coleman (1981–1982)	Plummer (1975)	Troiden (1979)	Minton and McDonald (1984)		Cass (1979)
I. First Awareness	Signification	Pre-Coming Out			Symbiotic		
		Coming Out	Sensitization	Sensitization			Identity Confusion
				Dissociation and Signification	Egocentric		Identity Comparison
II. Self-Labeling							Identity Tolerance
III. Community Involvement and Disclosure	Coming Out	Exploration	Signfication				
				Coming Out	Coming Out	Sociocentric	Identity Acceptance
	Going Public	First Relationships					Identity Pride
IV. Identity Integration		Integration	Stabliization	Commitment	Universalistic		Identity Synthesis

through these levels occurs is not presented in this paradigm, it gave an early way to look at homosexual identity and its development.

The impact of the gay community and development of a social role have been the focus of several studies. As mentioned before, Warren (1974) was one of the first to make a distinction between homosexual and gay identities. She described gay identity as being based on the degree of affiliation that an individual has with the gay community. Generally this attachment follows engagement in homosexual (sexual) behavior and the development of a homosexual identity. In addition to the impact of the gay community, she described a "conversion effect" involved in the formation of gay identity. Through this process societal stigmas are converted into a positive identity as myths about homosexuality are encountered and challenged.

In a more radical exploration of gay identity, DuBay (1987) suggested that identity development is based on an interaction between social contacts and roles. He challenged the belief that there is an inherent, internal quality about an individual that leads to the development of a specific identity. Rather, he saw *identity* or *role* (terms that he used interchangeably) as being made up of a number of more distinct roles, which for gay and lesbian individuals serve the purpose of dealing with societal homophobia. He suggested that gay identity is made up of the merging of self-concept and sexuality, which becomes the central component in the individual's self-view. DuBay advocated dropping such roles, moving away from the concept of a gay identity, and, instead, looking at sexuality as one part of the person's total identity.

A number of writers who have approached gay identity from the social perspective focus on the coming out process. *Coming out* is an aspect of gay identity development that has been defined in various ways. In the 1960s, coming out was seen as a specific occasion—a person's initial acknowledgement of same-sex attraction to another person (Gramick, 1984). Now, writers stress the ongoing developmental nature of coming out, beginning when individuals start to question their sexual orientation and continuing through ongoing self-discovery and disclosure to others of their identity (Ponse, 1980; Richardson, 1981b).

Lee (1977) (see table 1) described coming out as one facet of a three-stage model of homosexual self-identity. His emphasis was on individuals' movement from privately recognizing themselves as homosexual to publicly sharing this identity. In the first stage, individuals self-label homosexual fantasies or experiences as deviant; then, in the second stage, they begin to enter the gay culture, selectively disclose their identity, and become involved in political and social organizations. The third stage clearly builds on stage two, with individuals becoming more public in their activities and willing to be spokespersons.

Another approach that has been taken to coming out is to frame it as a developmental process encompassing both social and psychological factors. Hencken and O'Dowd (1977) suggested that there are three levels to this process: (1) awareness, (2) behavioral acceptance, and (3) public identification. At each level an individual comes out in a key area (e.g., coming out of ignorance and into awareness of feelings in the first stage), building a framework for future growth.

A more fully conceptualized model of the coming out process was offered by Coleman (1981–1982). Coleman presented a five-stage developmental model of coming out (see table 1), with the establishment of a gay identity centering around interpersonal relationships. As individuals progress through the stages, developmental tasks are confronted, the resolution of which determines whether movement to a new level will occur. Although such social/relational issues as seeking validation through self-disclosure, exploring sexual relationships, and establishing emotional intimacy are primary areas of focus, attention is also paid to more psychological issues. Coleman discussed ways in which these developmental tasks have impact on self-esteem and self-view, and presented stage 5 (Integration) as the point at which individuals develop a sense of both personal and interpersonal wholeness.

Psychological Models

Another perspective for looking at the development of gay identity focuses on the psychological (rather than social) processes involved. One of the first such models to be proposed was that of Plummer (1975) (see table 1). He identified four stages of identity development, moving from early awareness to the attainment of an integrated and stable identity.

Building on Plummer's work, Troiden (1979) (see table 1) suggested that there are four stages of gay identity acquisition. As movement through the stages occurs, feelings that the individual experiences shift from being ego-dystonic (dissonant with self-perceptions) to positively integrated and ego-syntonic (consistent with self-perceptions). As is true of several of the models discussed above, Troiden distinguished between homosexual and gay identities, with the latter reflecting involvement in a committed relationship and commitment to this identity. This last point notwithstanding, he also stated that identity is fluid and is never completely acquired in all aspects of an individual's life.

Looking at homosexual identity formation as one aspect of a lifelong developmental process, Minton and McDonald (1984) had as their foundation a nonlinear ego development model (see table 1). Growth is based on the interaction between the individual and societal values and beliefs. The two primary developmental tasks involved in this process are (1) forming a homosexual self-image, which culminates in attaining a positive gay identity, and (2) identity management, choosing the extent to which this identity will be shared. The goal of this model is to achieve identity synthesis (versus having a fragmented personal identity), which requires integration of all aspects of personal identity.

Cass' Psychosocial Model of Sexual Identity Formation (SIF)

To varying extents, each of the social and psychological models discussed in the preceding sections addresses the variables that have an impact on how gay identity develops. This process is a complex one, with development being affected by such diverse factors as self-image, social support, and even geography. As Troiden (1979) pointed out, gay identity evolves slowly and with some struggle. The presence (or absence) of information, resources, and a supportive community, along with such factors as family attitudes and individual personality, help determine how much struggle any one individual faces in developing an identity as a gay, lesbian, or bisexual person.

Vivienne Cass (1984) has pointed out the need for integration of the social and psychological elements of identity development and for consideration of the changes involved at the cognitive, emotional, and behavioral levels. In her model of Sexual Identity Formation (SIF), Cass (1979) fully described each of the six stages into which she divides the identity development process (see table 1), specifying the challenges found at each stage. Cass' model provides an exceptionally comprehensive description of gay identity development. Cass has also conducted extensive research on her theory, something which is lacking with several of the other models.

Cass' SIF model is built upon a theoretical base that addresses the interaction between psychological and sociological factors. Progression from one stage to another is motivated by incongruities felt by the individual within what Cass described as the "intrapersonal matrix." The components that make up this matrix are individuals' self-perceptions, perceptions of their behavior, and perceptions of others' responses to them. At each stage, some conflict will be experienced, either within or between areas of the intrapersonal matrix. This conflict is resolved either through advancement to a new stage or identity foreclosure.

The first stage (Identity Confusion) is ushered in by a growing awareness of thoughts, feelings, or behaviors that may be homosexual in nature. These self-perceptions are incongruent with earlier assumptions of personal heterosexuality and constitute the first developmental conflict of the model. How individuals perceive these characteristics or behaviors will influence the way in which they seek to resolve the incongruence, either through repression (identity foreclosure) or by moving into the second stage.

Identity Comparison (stage 2) allows individuals to begin checking out those qualities first experienced in stage 1. As they begin to gather information and seek out contacts with gay others, there is increasing congruence between self-perceptions and behaviors but increased conflict with others. As this sense of conflict heightens, individuals may move into stage 3, Identity Tolerance. This stage is marked by increased contact with the gay community, leading to feelings of greater empowerment. At this point individuals hold an increasingly strong homosexual self-image but continue to present themselves (outside the community) as heterosexual.

Moving into stage 4, Identity Acceptance, the conflict between the self and nongay others' perceptions is at an intense level. This conflict may be resolved through either passing as "straight," limited contact with heterosexuals, or selectively disclosing to significant (heterosexual) others. Those who find that these strategies effectively manage the conflict may stay at this level comfortably; otherwise the continuing conflict pushes the individual into the fifth stage of Identity Pride. In this stage, the conflict is managed through fostering a dichotomized homosexual (valued) and heterosexual (devalued) world view. Stage 5 is marked not only by strong pride in the gay community and identity but also by intense anger directed toward and isolation from the heterosexual society.

How others, particularly those who are not gay, respond to the expression of these feelings influences whether individuals move into the final stage, Identity Synthesis. Movement into the sixth stage is most likely when individuals experience positive reactions from heterosexual others, creating new incongruence in their perceptions. Individuals in stage 6 perceive similarities and dissimilarities with both homosexuals and heterosexuals, and sexuality is seen as one part of their total identity. Although some conflict is always present, it is at the lowest and most manageable point in this stage.

To test her theory, Cass (1984) developed factors that describe elements of each of her six stages of homosexual identity formation. For each factor she identified the underlying cognitive, behavioral, and affective dimensions. These dimensions provided criteria for assigning individuals to one of the six stages of identity development. Cass compared participants' assignment to a specific stage according to these criteria with self-ratings on her Stage Allocation Measure (SAM). She found that individuals both matched the profile for the stage to which they had been assigned and could be placed into that same stage according to the SAM. Cass suggested these findings support the concept that individuals who perceive homosexuality to be relevant to them will have characteristics identified in her model.

Summary of Identity Development Models

The six models presented in the table approach the question of how individuals develop an identity as a gay or lesbian person from a fairly wide range of perspectives. Of these models, Lee's (1977) presentation of gay self-identification conceptualizes this process with the most narrowly social focus.

Although varying degrees of balance between personal and social factors are found across the theories, there is a general trend toward a more psychological perspective in the later models. Those theories developed earlier present coming out as a culminating event or marker, followed only by a stage of integration or further commitment. In contrast, the models of Coleman (1981–1982), Minton and McDonald (1984), and Cass (1979) place coming out very early in the process, and the latter two do not identify it as a separate stage at all.

These differences notwithstanding, there is a general pattern of developmental levels that emerges across the models We have identified four levels, which are used as a basis of comparison in table 1 (column 1). Although the models presented do not all fit into this conceptu-alization at exactly the same points, each passes through and refers to the tasks found in all four levels.

The level of First Awareness is a distinct component of all but one model (Minton & McDonald, 1984). At this first level, individuals are becoming conscious of homoerotic feelings and behaviors, generally with no sense of these feelings being "okay." Two models (Coleman, 1981–1982; Minton & McDonald, 1984) explicitly mentioned stages before this first level, and Cass (1984) discussed assumptions about individuals' beliefs prior to entering her first stage.

The second level that we have identified is Self-Labeling. This point centers around individuals beginning to identify themselves as being gay and having early contacts with the gay community. The main distinction between the second level and the third (Community Involvement and Disclosure) is in the growing sense of acceptance of a gay identity and increasing comfort with sharing this aspect of the self with nongay others. The fourth and final level is Identity Integration, which involves incorporating gay identity into individuals' total sense of self.

Lesbian Identity Development

Differences in Identity Development Between Gay Men and Lesbians

Largely because of differences in the way men and women are socialized in Western society, a number of variations are evident in the patterns of identity development and lifestyles of gay men and lesbians (Cass, 1979).

The timing of events associated with the process of developing a gay or lesbian identity is different for men and women. Lesbians exhibit more variation than gay men in age at which awareness of attraction to individuals of the same sex occurs (Moses & Hawkins 1986), and evidence suggests that gay men become aware of same-sex attractions, act on those attractions, and self-identify as gay at earlier ages than do lesbians. Men also disclose their homosexual identity earlier than women (DeMonteflores & Schultz, 1978, Sohier 1985–1986; Troiden, 1988). Henderson (1984) proposed two hypotheses in reference to these timing variations: (1) women's sexual orientation may be more variable than men's and more tied to particular relationships, or (2) women are more likely to be influenced by societal norms that expect everyone to be heterosexual and so adhere longer to heterosexual behavior patterns and a heterosexual identity. Gramick (1984) concurred with the latter point of view.

Lesbians tend to establish ongoing love relationships earlier than gay men (Troiden, 1988, and are more likely to commit to a homosexual identity within the context of an intense emotional relationship, whereas gay men do so within the context of their sexual experiences (Groves & Ventura, 1983; Sohier, 1985–1986; Troiden, 1988). In general, emotional attachment is the most significant aspect of relationship for lesbians, but sexual activity is most important for gay men (DeMonteflores & Schultz, 1978; Gramick, 1984). As a result, lesbians tend to look for and maintain more stable, long-term relationships than do gay men (Gramick, 1984).

Although this pattern may be changing because of concern arising from the spread of AIDS, historically, gay men have been involved with many more one-time-only sexual partners than have lesbians (Kimmel, 1978; Marmor, 1980). This pattern, again, can be related to differences in the manner in which men and women are socialized; men are expected to be interested in sex before love, whereas women look for love before sex (Henderson, 1984; Westfall, 1988). Men are also encouraged to experiment sexually more than women (Coleman, 1981–1982). As one might expect given these socialization patterns, "tricking" (picking up unknown individuals for brief sexual liaisons) has been much more common among gay men than among lesbians, who tend to meet others and interact in more intimate, private settings (Cronin, 1974; Gramick, 1984; Nuehring, Fein, & Tyler, 1974).

DeMonteflores and Schultz (1978) suggested that lesbians often use feelings to avoid thinking of themselves as homosexual, whereas men use denial of feelings as a way to avoid self-labeling as gay. Women use the rationale that they merely love one particular woman, but men view their homosexual activity as insignificant because they are not emotionally involved with their partners.

Some researchers (Bell & Weinberg, 1978; Sohier, 1985–1986) have suggested that acceptance of homosexuality is easier for women than for men since sexual relationships between women are less stigmatized than those between men (DeMonteflores & Schultz, 1978; Marmor, 1980; Paul, 1984). The women's movement may have assisted lesbians to come out; there has been no comparable movement for men (DeMonteflores & Schultz, 1978). Also, since many lesbians become aware of their identity at later ages, they may have resolved other identity issues and be more adept at handling the coming out process than gay men, who generally self-identify during their teens (Paul, 1984).

A number of writers have suggested that lesbians are more likely to view their sexuality as a choice, whereas gay men see it as a discovery (Henderson, 1984; Kimmel, 1978; Westfall, 1988). This distinction is particularly true for feminist lesbians. Feminist lesbians also identify more strongly with the political-philosophical aspects of their lifestyle, whereas gay men are more concerned with the physical-social aspects (Jandt & Darsey, 1981).

With regard to relationship development, lesbians more closely resemble other women than they do gay men (Marmor, 1980). Women, in general, are more concerned with the relational aspects of their attachments to other people and focus on establishing intimate, long-term relationships. Because they fear displeasing others, they may have difficulty breaking norms and acknowledging that they cannot accept the roles family, friends, and society have identified for them. Men, however, are taught to be independent, competitive, and autonomous. These factors appear to play an important role in the differences exhibited between lesbians and gay men.

Relational versus Political Lesbians

Great variation exists in the way lesbians describe themselves and how they come to identify themselves as lesbian (Miller & Fowlkes, 1980). And as Golden (1987) noted, feelings, behaviors, and self-identification do not always agree nor do they always remain the same over time. Two major philosophical approaches to lesbianism can be identified in the literature, however: a traditional relational viewpoint that focuses on emotional and sexual attraction to other women (Moses, 1978; Ponse, 1980) and a radical feminist perspective that views the lesbian lifestyle as a political statement (Faraday, 1981; Lewis, 1979).

A number of theorists note that a distinction must be made between women who view their lesbianism as beyond their control and those who see it as a choice (Golden, 1987; Richardson, 1981b). Generally, lesbian feminists adhere to the latter viewpoint, but relational lesbians take the former position (Richardson, 1981b; Sophie, 1987).

In a small study of 20 self-identified lesbians, Henderson (1979) distinguished three groups: (1) *ideological lesbians,* women who can be viewed as radical feminists for whom a lesbian lifestyle is politically correct; (2) *personal lesbians,* women concerned with establishing an independent identity who find homosexuality supportive of this goal and who view lesbianism as a choice; and (3) *interpersonal lesbians,* women who find themselves involved with another woman, often to their chagrin, and who experience their involvement as a discovery rather than a choice.

Development of a Lesbian Identity

Although a number of writers believe that sexual activity between women has become more acceptable as a result of the women's movement and the freeing of sexual norms (Blumstein & Schwartz, 1974; Henderson, 1979), the developmental process of identifying oneself as a lesbian is still difficult.

Many lesbians recall being "tomboys" as youngsters: a preference for "masculine" rather than "feminine" activities as a child is often the first indication that they do not fit the heterosexual pattern (Lewis, 1979). This awareness intensifies during puberty when the adolescent finds herself attracted to women rather than men. This discovery can lead to intense feelings of loneliness. Because of the difficulty young lesbians experience in finding a support group of other lesbians or identifying positive role models, this period is particularly difficult in the person's life (Sophie, 1982).

Most lesbians have a history of sexual involvement with men and, contrary to popular belief, become involved with women not because of unsatisfactory relationships with men but rather because they experience greater emotional and sexual satisfaction from women (Groves & Ventura, 1983). Indeed, women frequently identify themselves as bisexual prior to adopting a lesbian identity.

It needs to be noted that most lesbians go through a period during which they reject their identity because they are unable to deal with the stigma associated with the label *lesbian* (Groves & Ventura, 1983). Often they seek security and an escape from their feelings of isolation and anxiety in heterosexual activity or marriage (Lewis, 1979; Sophie, 1982).

Usually involvement in an intense, all-encompassing love relationship with another woman is the decisive factor in embracing a lesbian identity (Groves & Ventura, 1983; Lewis, 1979). Such an involvement often develops slowly, starting out as a friendship.

Sophie (1982) noted that it is difficult for lesbians to feel good about themselves until they reconceptualize the term *lesbian* into positive terms. This process rarely occurs in isolation. Interaction with other lesbians and other sources of information about positive aspects of a lesbian lifestyle are helpful.

Coming out, both to other lesbians and to accepting heterosexuals, is also supportive of establishment of a lesbian identity (Richardson, 1981b; Sophie, 1982). Often the individual decides to come out because it takes too much energy to maintain a heterosexual image. Usually the individual comes out first to close friends who appear trustworthy (Lewis, 1979). As the woman becomes involved in the lesbian community, pressure is often applied to come out publicly (Lewis, 1979). Doing so can be viewed as the final step in the solidification of a lesbian identity.

Identity Development Models

A number of theorists have proposed models of identity development specific for lesbians. Ponse (1980) noted three steps in lesbian identity development: becoming aware of feeling different because of sexual-emotional attraction to other women, becoming involved in a lesbian relationship, and seeking out other lesbians. This model differs from many of the gay male models in that a serious relationship is formed *before* the individual becomes involved in the lesbian community.

Gramick (1984) pointed out that in attempting to make meaning of their experiences, many lesbians reinterpret past events, feelings, and behaviors as sexual that were not perceived as such at the time they occurred. She suggested that the process of developing a lesbian identity first involves strong emotional attachment to other women, leading to a feeling of "differentness" within the context of the social environment but without a recognition that this difference might be labeled as lesbian. In adolescence, heterosexual socialization patterns strongly influence all young women and often delay development of homosexual identity. Meeting other lesbians and becoming emotionally and sexually involved with another woman are usually key events in confirming and accepting a lesbian identity. In Gramick's model, supportive others, as well as sexual involvements, play a crucial role in identity development.

Lewis (1979) identified five stages in the development of a lesbian identity and focused more on the political aspects of lesbianism. Her stages include (1) experience of discomfort with the heterosexual and patriarchal nature of socialization, (2) labeling self as different from other women, (3) becoming aware of lesbianism, (4) finding and becoming involved in a lesbian community, and (5) educating self about the lesbian lifestyle.

Also writing from a feminist perspective, Faderman (1984) questioned the appropriateness of Minton and McDonald's (1984) model of identity development for lesbian feminists. She suggested that the developmental progression for these women is roughly the opposite of the model they proposed. The first step for lesbian feminists, according to Faderman, involves rejection of societal norms concerning the role of women and acceptance of a lesbian identity. This step is followed by experiences of prejudice and discrimination, resulting in feelings of aloneness outside of the community of radical feminists and, finally, by sexual experiences with other women. Faderman suggested that because lesbian feminists are exposed to and accept the movement's political philosophy prior to their first homosexual experience, they may not experience the guilt and shame felt by other lesbians and gay men.

In line with the two philosophical perspectives evident within the lesbian community, Sophie (1982) identified two endpoints for lesbians who have achieved identity synthesis: *integration*, that is, living as an open lesbian in both the lesbian and nonlesbian communities; and *separation*, that is, limiting one's interactions to the lesbian community as much as possible.

Bisexual Identity

The gay rights movement has generally ignored bisexual men and women. Although Kinsey and his colleagues (Kinsey, Pomeroy, & Martin, 1948; Kinsey, Pomeroy, Martin, & Gebhard, 1953) discovered that more individuals are bisexual than strictly homosexual, later researchers and theorists have held to a rigid dichotomization of sexual behavior as either heterosexual or homosexual (Klein, Sepekoff, & Wolf, 1985). Acknowledging and attempting to understand the variation and fluidity of sexual attraction and behavior are important if we are to advance our knowledge of human sexuality and sexual identity development (Paul, 1985).

Bisexuality, particularly among women, seems to have increased in Western society, perhaps as a result of more relaxed sexual norms and the women's movement (MacDonald, 1981). A study based on a questionnaire published in *Forum* magazine found that male bisexuals outnumber female bisexuals, bisexual activity increases over the lifetime, and sexual preference changes over time (Klein, Sepekoff, & Wolf, 1985). The biased sample upon which this study was based (*Forum* readers who responded to a questionnaire) must be kept in mind, however.

Bisexuality comes in many forms. MacDonald (1982) identified four areas of variation: (1) individuals may have a preference for one gender over the other or may have no preference; (2) they may have partners of both sexes either simultaneously or sequentially; (3) they may be monogomous or have several partners; and (4) their bisexuality may be transitory, transitional, a basis for homosexual denial, or an enduring pattern. Zinik (1985) proposed the following criteria for assuming a bisexual identity: (1) being sexually aroused by both males and females, (2) desiring sexual activity with both, and (3) adopting bisexuality as a sexual identity label.

Two contrasting theories have been offered to account for bisexuality (Zinik, 1985): The conflict model suggests that bisexuality is associated with conflict, confusion, ambivalence, and an inability to determine one's sexual preference; the flexibility model hypothesizes that bisexuality is characterized by flexibility, personal growth, and fulfillment. The media tends to adhere to the former view, presenting bisexuality as a confused or conflicted lifestyle, as retarded sexual development, or as a denial of a true heterosexual or homosexual identity (Hansen & Evans, 1985).

Because the stigma attached to bisexuality is greater in many ways than that associated with homosexuality, many people who are bisexual in behavior do not identify themselves as such (Blumstein & Schwartz, 1974; Golden, 1987; Hansen & Evans, 1985; Paul, 1984; Zinik, 1985). Although some individuals are quite open about their identity, others hide it from both the heterosexual and the homosexual communities (Blumstein & Schwartz, 1977a). MacDonald (1981) suggested that bisexuals are less willing to disclose their identity than any other group because they believe that neither gays nor heterosexuals will accept them.

Bisexuals experience the same type of oppression as gay men and lesbians because society tends to group bisexuals with homosexuals. Heterosexuals assume that individuals are trying to excuse their homosexual inclinations by labeling themselves as bisexual (Blumstein & Schwartz, 1977a).

Because they do not conform to heterosexist culture, many bisexuals tend to align themselves with the gay and lesbian communities (Shuster, 1987). However, an individual's self-identification as bisexual is frequently met with skepticism in the homosexual community as well and viewed as an attempt to avoid the stigma of, or commitment to, a gay or lesbian lifestyle (Paul, 1984). The lesbian community, in particular, seems to have difficulty accepting bisexuality (Golden, 1987). Bisexuals are faced with considerable pressure to identify as homosexual and to behave in an exclusively homosexual manner (Blumstein & Schwartz, 1974; Hansen & Evans, 1985; Paul, 1985). Frequently, bisexuals respond to this pressure by pretending to be either exclusively homosexual or heterosexual depending on the social situation (Zinik, 1985).

Results of a study of 156 bisexuals conducted in the early 1970s (Blumstein & Schwartz, 1976, 1977a, 1977b) suggested that no identifiable bisexual life script exists and that identity and partner preferences change over the life course. Sexual experience and identity are not necessarily synonymous. The researchers identified several conditions that they saw as necessary for assumption of a bisexual identity: labeling, conflicting homosexual and heterosexual experiences, and contact with other bisexuals.

Zinik (1985) suggested that bisexual identity development may occur in stages similar to those proposed by Cass (1979) for homosexual identity formation. As with gay men and lesbians, the coming out process is one of both self-acknowledgment and disclosure to others (Shuster, 1987). Wide variation exists, however, in the timing and ordering of sexual experiences leading to a bisexual identification. In addition, because bisexuality lacks societal and scientific affirmation, acceptance of such an identity requires a high tolerance for ambiguity and is even harder than acceptance of a homosexual identity (MacDonald, 1981, Richardson & Hart, 1981). In most cases, bisexuals tend to identify in terms of particular relationships in which they are involved rather than with the abstract label bisexual (Shuster, 1987).

Although gay men and lesbians have formed support groups and political organizations, few such groups of bisexuals exist (Paul, 1985). As MacDonald (1981) noted, there is no "bisexual liberation movement" (p. 21). As a result, no clear bisexual identity exists, and little scientific research has examined the life experiences of bisexual men and women.

Critique and Summary

Over the past two decades, a number of theorists and researchers have addressed the question of how individuals develop identities as gay, lesbian, and bisexual men and women. The shift in focus from "why" or "how" individuals "become homosexual" to understanding the process whereby they develop a gay, lesbian, or bisexual identity speaks to a more positive and healthy perspective on homosexuality. There are, however, a number of areas that need to be addressed.

One area of concern involves the datedness of some of the models discussed in this chapter. The concept of a gay identity first began to be addressed in the early 1970s, the years immediately following the Stonewall riots. The focus on coming out as a discrete step and social statement in models such as those of Dank (1971) and Lee (1977) clearly reflected the mood of the early gay-rights era. Similarly, these models are based on a social culture that has changed significantly, due in large part to the impact of the AIDS crisis, and do not necessarily describe today's realities.

Many of the models of lesbian identity development also were shaped by the political and social forces of the 1970s. The early feminist movement had tremendous influence on many of these models, leading to conceptualizations of identity centered around breaking away from patriarchal and oppressive social norms (Browning, 1984; Faraday, 1981; Lewis, 1979).

The political climate today is much different than that of 15 or even 10 years ago. There is general consensus that a conservative backlash took place during the 1980s, but we have not looked at what impact this change has had on the development and maintenance of a gay or lesbian identity. Although many (or even most) aspects of identity development have probably remained relatively constant, these models need to be reconsidered in light of a new societal context.

A second area needing consideration deals with the problems inherent in working with stage models of development. By nature, these models break the process of development into discrete, stable, and clearly discernible levels. In reality, growth is rarely so clear cut.

McDonald (1982) suggested that linear developmental models do not account or leave room for individual differences and variations in development. He found that there are clearly milestone events in the coming out process for gay men, and that these events occur in a fairly stable pattern. There is sufficient variety in the timing and direction of these events, however, to justify moving away from a linear conceptualization of the process.

Another writer who has questioned the developmental stage concept is Troiden (1984). He suggested that rather than attaining one identity, individuals develop one self-concept (or self-image) and a variety of identities that are used to assist the individual specifically in social situations. Within this framework, homosexual identity presents a way of placing self in a defined social category. The interplay between self-concept and identities shifts over time, as social contexts change, thus creating a fluid sense of identity(ies).

In the only study that has focused on women in the process of developing a lesbian identity, Sophie (1985–1986) found extensive variety in the sequence and timing of significant events. She found that events such as self-definition, contact with other lesbians, and involvement in a significant same-sex relationship occur at different points in the identity development process for different women. She pointed out that looking at this process through a linear lens is difficult and becomes more problematic as the process advances and greater individual differences emerge.

In general, there is a great need for more research on the identity development process. For example, more research testing the models that have been (and are being) developed is needed.

One of the reasons Cass's (1979) model has found wide acceptance is that she has conducted fairly extensive testing of her theory (Cass, 1984). Rather than considering external criteria as a means of validating her model, Cass compared two techniques based on her own theory for estimating level of development. Studies that contrast models or determine and measure underlying factors will add to the creation of a strong research base in this area.

As has been pointed out throughout this chapter, an area that has been severely overlooked has been identity development among lesbian and bisexual persons. Sophie's (1985–1986) study is the only one to date that looked specifically at the development of a lesbian identity, and there are no models that describe the attainment of a bisexual identity. The little research that has been conducted with these two groups clearly shows that the male-oriented models that have been developed do not adequately describe their different experiences. We need to address and fill the gaps in our understanding of these processes.

A similar gap in the research involves identity development among college and university students. Working through questions about the relevance of homosexuality or bisexuality in one's own life while also dealing with the challenges of being a college or university student adds to the magnitude of transition and potential for experiencing periods of crisis. We need to conduct research that helps us to understand the interplay between student development and the acquisition of gay, lesbian, and bisexual identities.

One issue that is of concern in all research with gay, lesbian and bisexual people is that of obtaining truly random samples. This problem is most apparent with the *Forum* article (Klein, Sepekoff, & Wolf, 1985) mentioned earlier in this chapter. The issue of having a nonrandom sample is inherent, however, in any study that utilizes a group of individuals who self-identify as gay, lesbian, or bisexual.

The models and studies discussed in this chapter give us the foundations for this future work. We know much about college and university students and are learning about what it means to be a gay, lesbian, or bisexual person in our society. The framework is there, and our challenge is to move ahead toward expanding and bringing together these areas of understanding.

References

Beane, J. (1981). "I'd rather be dead than gay": Counseling gay men who are coming out. *Personnel and Guidance Journal, 60,* 222–226.

Bell, A. P., & Weinberg, M. S. (1978). *Homosexualities: A study of diversity among men and women.* New York: Simon and Schuster.

Bell, A. P., Weinberg, M. S., & Hammersmith, S. K. (1981). *Sexual preference: Its development in men and women.* Bloomington: Indiana University.

Blumstein, P. W., & Schwartz, P. (1974). Lesbianism and bisexuality. In E. Goode & R. R. Troiden (Eds.), *Sexual deviance and sexual deviants* (pp. 278–295). New York: Morrow.

Blumstein, P. W., & Schwartz, P. (1976). Bisexuality in women. *Archives of Sexual Behavior, 5,* 171–181.

Blumstein, P. W., & Schwartz, P. (1977a). Bisexuality in men. In C. A. B. Warren (Ed.), *Sexuality: Encounters, identities, and relationships* (pp. 79–98). Beverly Hills, CA: Sage.

Blumstein, P. W., & Schwartz, P. (1977b). Bisexuality: Some social psychological issues. *Journal of Social Issues, 33,* 30–45.

Browning, C. (1984). Changing theories of lesbianism: Challenging the stereotypes. In T. Darty & S. Potter (Eds.), *Women-identified women* (pp. 11–30). Palo Alto, CA: Mayfield.

Cass, V. C. (1979). Homosexual identity formation: A theoretical model. *Journal of Homosexuality, 4,* 219–235.

Cass, V. C. (1983–1984). Homosexual identity: A concept in need of definition. *Journal of Homosexuality, 9*(213), 105–126.

Cass, V. C. (1984). Homosexual identity formation: Testing a theoretical model. *Journal of Sex Research, 20,* 143–167.

Chickering, A. W. (1969). *Education and identity.* San Francisco: Jossey-Bass.

Coleman, E. (1981–1982). Developmental stages of the coming out process. *Journal of Homosexuality, 7,* 31–43.

Cronin, D. M. (1974). Coming out among lesbians. In E. Goode & R. R Troiden (Eds.), *Sexual deviance and sexual deviants* (pp. 268–277). New York: Morrow.

Dank, B. M. (1971). Coming out in the gay world. *Psychiatry, 34*(2), 180–197.

DeMonteflores, C., & Schultz, S. (1978). Coming out: Similarities and differences for lesbians and gay men. *Journal of Social Issues, 34*(3), 59–72.

DuBay, W. H. (1987). *Gay identity: The self under ban.* Jefferson, NC: McFarland.

Erikson, E. H. (1968). *Identity: Youth and crisis.* New York: Norton.

Faderman, L. (1984). The "new gay" lesbians. *Journal of Homosexuality, 10*(3/4), 85–95.

Faraday, A. (1981). Liberating lesbian research. In K. Plummer (Ed.), *The making of the modern homosexual* (pp. 112–129). Totowa, NJ: Barnes & Noble.

Golden, C. (1987). Diversity and variability in women's sexual identities. In Boston Lesbian Psychologies Collective (Eds.), *Lesbian psychologies: Explorations and challenges* (pp. 19–34). Urbana, IL: University of Illinois Press.

Gramick, J. (1984). Developing a lesbian identity. In T. Darty & S. Potter (Eds.), *Women-identified women.* (pp. 31–44). Palo Alto, CA: Mayfield.

Groves, P. A., & Ventura, L. A. (1983). The lesbian coming out process: Therapeutic considerations. *Personnel and Guidance Journal, 62,* 146–149.

Hansen, C. E., & Evans, A. (1985). Bisexuality reconsidered: An idea in pursuit of a definition. In F. Klein & T. J. Wolf (Eds.), *Bisexualities: Theory and research* (pp. 1–6). New York: Haworth.

Hencken, J . D., & O'Dowd, W. T. (1977). Coming out as an aspect of identity formation. *Gai Saber, 1* (1), 18–22.

Henderson, A. F. (1979). College age lesbianism as a developmental phenomenon. *Journal of American College Health, 28*(3), 176–178.

Henderson, A. F. (1984). Homosexuality in the college years: Development differences between men and women. *Journal of American College Health, 32,* 216–219.

Jandt, F. E., & Darsey, J. (1981). Coming out as a communicative process. In J. W. Chesebro (Ed.), *Gayspeak* (pp. 12–27). New York: Pilgrim.

Kimmel, D. C. (1978). Adult development and aging: A gay perspective. *Journal of Social Issues, 34,* 113–130.

Kinsey, A. C., Pomeroy, W. B., & Martin, C. E. (1948). *Sexual behavior in the human male.* Philadelphia: Saunders.

Kinsey, A. C., Pomeroy, W. B., Martin, C. E., & Gebhard, P. H. (1953). *Sexual behavior in the human female.* Philadelphia: Saunders.

Klein, F., Sepekoff, B., & Wolf, T. J. (1985). Sexual orientation: A multivariable dynamic process. In F. Klein & T. J. Wolf (Eds.), *Bisexualities: Theory and research* (pp. 35–49). New York: Haworth.

Lee, J. A. (1977). Going public: A study in the sociology of homosexual liberation. *Journal of Homosexuality, 3*(1), 49–78.

Lewis, S. G. (1979). *Sunday's women: A report on lesbian life today.* Boston: Beacon.

MacDonald, Jr., A. P. (1981). Bisexuality: Some comments on research and theory. *Journal of Homosexuality, 6* (3), 21–35.

MacDonald, Jr., A. P. (1982). Research on sexual orientation: A bridge that touches both shores but doesn't meet in the middle. *Journal of Sex Education and Therapy, 8,* 9–13.

Marmor, J. (1980). Overview: The multiple roots of homosexual behavior. In J. Marmor (Ed.), *Homosexual behavior: A modern reappraisal* (pp. 3–22). New York: Basic Books.

McDonald, G. J. (1982). Individual differences in the coming out process for gay men: Implications for theoretical models. *Journal of Homosexuality 8*(1), 47–90.

Miller, P. Y., & Fowlkes, M. R. (1980). Social and behavior constructions of female sexuality. *Signs, 5,* 783–800.

Minton, H. L., & McDonald, G. J. (1984). Homosexual identity formation as a developmental process. *Journal of Homosexuality, 9*(2/3), 91–104.

Moore, L. V., & Upcraft, M. L. (1990). Theory in student affairs: Evolving perspectives. In L. V. Moore (Ed.), *Evolving theoretical perspectives on students.* (pp. 3–23). *New Directions for Student Services,* No. 51. San Francisco: Jossey-Bass.

Moses, A. E. (1978). *Identity management in lesbian women.* New York: Praeger.

Moses, A. E., & Hawkins, R. O. (1986). *Counseling lesbian women and gay men: A life issues approach.* Columbus, OH: Merrill.

Nuehring, E., Fein, S. B., & Tyler, M. (1974). The gay college student: Perspectives for mental health professionals. *Counseling Psychologist, 4,* 64–72.

Nungesser, L. G. (1983). *Homosexual acts, actors, and identities.* New York: Praeger.

Paul, J. P. (1984). The bisexual identity: An idea without social recognition. In J. P. deCecco & M. G. Shively (Eds.), *Bisexual and homosexual identities: Critical theoretical issues* (pp. 45–631). New York: Haworth.

Paul, J. (1985). Bisexuality: Reassessing our paradigms of sexuality. In F. Klein & T. J. Wolf (Eds.), *Bisexualities: Theory and research* (pp. 21–34). New York: Haworth.

Plummer, K. (1975). *Sexual stigma: An interactionist account.* London: Routledge & Kegan Paul.

Plummer, K. (1981). Going gay: Identities, life cycles, and lifestyles in the male gay world. In J. Hart & D. Richardson (Eds.), *The theory and practice of homosexuality* (pp. 93–110). London: Routledge & Kegan Paul.

Ponse, B. (1980). Lesbians and their worlds. In J. Marmor (Ed.), *Homosexual behavior: A modern reappraisal.* (pp. 157–175). New York: Basic Books.

Richardson, D. (1981a). Theoretical perspectives on homosexuality. In J. Hart & D. Richardson (Eds.), *The theory and practice of homosexuality* (pp. 5–37). London: Routledge & Kegan Paul.

Richardson, D. (1981b). Lesbian identities. In J. Hart & D. Richardson (Eds.), *The theory and practice of homosexuality* (pp. 111–124). London: Routledge & Kegan Paul.

Richardson, D., & Hart, J. (1981). The development and maintenance of a homosexual identity. In J. Hart & D. Richardson (Eds.), *The theory and practice of homosexuality* (pp. 73–92) London: Routledge & Kegan Paul.

Shively, M. G., & deCecco, J. P. (1977). Components of sexual identity. *Journal of Homosexuality, 3,* 41–48.

Shuster, R. (1987). Sexuality as a continuum: The bisexual identity. In Boston Lesbian Psychologies Collective (Eds.), *Lesbian psychologies: Explorations and challenges* (pp. 56–71). Urbana, IL: University of Illinois Press.

Sohier, R. (1985–1986). Homosexual mutuality: Variation on a theme by E. Erikson. *Journal of Homosexuality, 12*(2), 25–38.

Sophie, J. (1982). Counseling lesbians. *Personnel and Guidance Journal, 60*(6), 341-344.

Sophie, J. (1985-1986). A critical examination of stage theories of lesbian identity development. *Journal of Homosexuality, 12*(2), 39–51.

Sophie, J. (1987). Internalized homophobia and lesbian identity. *Journal of Homosexuality, 14*, 53–65.

Troiden, R. R. (1979). Becoming homosexual: A model of gay identity acquisition. *Psychiatry, 42,* 362–373.

Troiden, R. R. (1984). Self, self-concept, identity, and homosexual identity: Constructs in need of definition and differentiation. *Journal of Homosexuality, 10*(314), 97–109.

Troiden, R. R. (1988). Homosexual identity development. *Journal of Adolescent Health Care, 9* (2), 105–113.

Warren, C. A. B. 1974). *Identity and community in the gay world.* New York: Wiley.

Weinberg, T. S. (1978). On "doing" and "being" gay: Sexual behavior and homosexual male self-identity. *Journal of Homosexuality, 4*(2), 143–156.

Westfall, S. B. (1988). Gay and lesbian college students: Identity issues and student affairs. *Journal of the Indiana University Student Personnel Association,* 1–6.

Zinik, G. (1985). Identity conflict or adaptive flexibility? Bisexuality reconsidered. In F. Klein & T. J. Wolf (Eds.), *Bisexualities: Theory and research* (pp. 7–19). New York: Haworth

PART IV
SUMMARY AND REFLECTIONS

Introduction

We have included Pascarella and Terenzini's chapter, "How College Makes a Difference: A Summary," for two reasons. First, the authors synthesize the research reviewed on (1) student changes during college (2) college's unique or "net" impact on students (3) the long-term effects of college and (4) the influences on different types of students (conditional effects). As such, the chapter provides a concise, comprehensive description of our current knowledge of college students

In "College Outcomes and Student Development: Filling the Gaps," Stage summarizes the 'state of the art.' She reminds us that our knowledge base on college students comes from sociological and psychological literatures and that those studying students from one perspective tend to ignore the other. She also reminds us that the bulk of the literature on college students is 'monocultural' and that we are in dire need of process models, so that practitioners might translate what we 'know' into their own work with college students.

Finally, Tierney presents us with an essay that should stimulate discussion about "some of the most commonly held perceptions we currently have about college life, about students, and about how we think about cultural difference." He intends that this examination and subsequent discussions will facilitate the development of "more culturally responsive ways to engage" all students in our learning process.

How College Makes a Difference: A Summary

E. T. Pascarella and P. T. Terenzini

How *does* college affect students? In responding to this question, we are reminded of a wonderful story told about Bernard Berelson (Menges, 1988). Berelson had published (with Gary Steiner) *Human Behavior: An Inventory of Scientific Findings* (1964), in which they synthesized over a thousand "verified generalizations" about human behavior. In reflecting on his work, Berelson is said to have offered three general conclusions (Menges suggests these were Berelson's "meta-findings"). Our conclusions about how college students change are the same as Berelson's about human change: "(1) some do, some don't; (2) the differences aren't very great; and (3) it's more complicated than that" (Menges, 1988, p. 259).

In the preceding ten chapters, we have reviewed the evidence on a wide range of specific college outcomes. This chapter is our summary or, if you will, our own "meta-findings." It attempts a comprehensive synthesis of what we know about the impact of college on students; in short, it seeks to provide a general answer to this question: In what areas and through what kinds of conditions, activities, and experiences does college affect students?

In shaping this global synthesis, we employ a somewhat different organizational framework than that used in chapters three through twelve. In each of those chapters, the evidence pertaining to a specific category of outcome (for example, learning, moral development, psychosocial development) was, where appropriate, summarized across six fundamental questions: (1) Do students change during the college years, and if so, how much and in what directions? (this is the "change" question); (2) To what extent are these changes attributable to college attendance as distinct from other sources, such as normal maturation or noncollege experiences? (the "net effects" question); (3) Are these changes differentially related to the kind of institution attended? (the "between-college effects" question); (4) Are these changes related to differences in students' experiences on any given campus? (the "within-college effects" question); (5) Are these changes differentially related to students' characteristics? (the "conditional effects" question); and (6) Is college's influence durable? (the "long-term effects" question).

In the present chapter, this organizational framework is inverted. Here we synthesize the evidence that addresses each of the six fundamental questions posed by the book across the various outcome categories. This will provide a somewhat different perspective than preceding chapters have given, in that the focal emphasis will be on the various impacts of college on a broad spectrum of outcomes rather than on how a specific category of outcome may be influenced by various elements of the college experience.

In addition to the main objective of providing a comprehensive summary of major conclusions, this chapter also does some other things. First, it attempts, where possible, to draw comparisons between our conclusions and the major conclusions of previous comprehensive syntheses of the impact of college on students, primarily the work of Feldman and Newcomb

(1969) and Bowen (1977). Second, where possible, it tries to articulate the extent to which the evidence is supportive of the major theses or models of student development and the impact of college. Finally, the chapter suggests important areas for future research and comments on methods of inquiry that may be most useful in increasing our understanding of the impact of college.

Change During College

Consistent with the composite findings of Feldman and Newcomb (1969) and Bowen (1977), our synthesis of the evidence indicates that the college years are a time of student change on a broad front. A number of the shifts we observed appear to be fairly substantial in magnitude. Indeed, the changes that occur during college from freshman to senior year are generally the largest "effects" we noted in our synthesis. It is the breadth of change and development, however, that is perhaps the most striking characteristic of the evidence. Students not only make statistically significant gains in factual knowledge and in a range of general cognitive and intellectual skills; they also change on a broad array of value, attitudinal, psychosocial, and moral dimensions. There is some modest tendency for changes in intellectual skills to be larger in magnitude than changes in other areas, but the evidence is quite consistent in indicating that the changes coincident with the college years extend substantially beyond cognitive growth. Thus, the change that occurs during the college years does not appear to be concentrated in a few isolated areas. Rather, the research portrays the college student as changing in an integrated way, with change in any one area appearing to be part of a mutually reinforcing network or pattern of change in other areas. Such a tendency in the evidence is generally consistent with the theoretical models of Chickering (1969) and Heath (1968), both of whom envision maturation during college as holistic in nature and embracing many facets of individual change.

There are some very clear directions to this overall pattern of change in college. The nature of the changes that occur and our best estimates of their average magnitude are shown in Tables 1 through 4. We turn now to a brief summary of those changes.

Learning and Cognitive Change

As shown in Table 1, students make gains from freshman to senior year on a variety of different dimensions of learning and cognition. Modest advances are evidenced in general verbal and quantitative skills, and fairly substantial advances are demonstrated in knowledge of the specific subject matter related to one's major field of study. These conclusions, particularly the latter, are not very surprising. Indeed, more surprising would be the discovery that such changes did not occur during college. Less intuitively obvious, perhaps, are the gains that students make on a range of general intellectual competencies and skills that may be less directly or explicitly tied to a college's formal academic program. Compared to freshmen, seniors are not only more effective speakers and writers, they are also more intellectually advanced. This intellectual change includes an improved ability to reason abstractly or symbolically and to solve problems or puzzles within a scientific paradigm, an enhanced skill in using reason and evidence to address issues and problems for which there are no verifiably correct answers, an increased intellectual flexibility that permits one to see both the strengths and weaknesses in different sides of a complex issue, and an increased capacity for cognitively organizing and manipulating conceptual complexity.

It is likely that gains in college on such dimensions as abstract reasoning, critical thinking, reflective judgment, and intellectual and conceptual complexity also make the student more functionally adaptive. That is, other things being equal, this enhanced repertoire of intellectual resources permits the individual to adapt more rapidly and efficiently to changing cognitive and noncognitive environments. Put another way, the individual becomes a better learner. It is in this area, we believe, that the intellectual development coincident with college has its most important and enduring implications for the student's postcollege life.

Table 1
Summary of Estimated Freshman-to-Senior *Changes: Learning and Cognitive Development*

Outcome	Estimated Magnitude of Change	
	Effect Size[a]	Percentile Point Difference[b]
General verbal skills	.56	21
General quantitative skills	.24	10
Specific subject matter knowledge	.84	31
Oral communication skills	.60	22
Written communication skills	.50	19
Piagetian (formal) reasoning	.33	13
Critical thinking	1.00	34
Use of reason and evidence to address ill-structured problems (reflective judgment, informal reasoning)	1.00	34
Ability to deal with conceptual complexity	1.20	38

[a]Effect size = (senior mean minus freshman mean) divided by freshman standard deviation.
[b]Effect size converted to the equivalent percentile point under the normal curve. This is the percentile point difference between the freshman- and senior-year means when the freshman means is set at the 50th percentile.

Attitudes and Values

Table 2 shows our estimates of the typical freshman-to-senior changes during college in the general area of values and attitudes. A number of these changes are quite consistent with the changes noted in the area of learning and cognitive development. Students not only become more cognitively advanced and resourceful, but they also make gains in their aesthetic, cultural, and intellectual sophistication, gains that are complemented by increased interests and activities in such areas as art, classical music, reading, and creative writing; discussion of philosophical and historical issues; and the humanities and performing arts. Similarly, there are clear gains in the importance students attach to liberal education and exposure to new ideas. In short, the enhancement of cognitive skills during college appears to be concurrent with an increased valuing of and interest in art, culture, and ideas.

If one theme underlying changes in values and attitudes during college is that they tend to be supportive of or at least consistent with observed changes in cognitive growth, a second theme is that the changes also coalesce around a general trend toward liberalization. Considering consistent changes in the areas of sociopolitical, religious, and gender role attitudes and values, it would appear that there are unmistakable and sometimes substantial freshman-to-senior shifts toward openness and a tolerance for diversity, a stronger "other-person orientation," and concern for individual rights and human welfare. These shifts are combined with an increase in liberal political and social values and a decline in both doctrinaire religious beliefs and traditional attitudes about gender roles. The clear movement in this liberalization of attitudes and values is away from a personal perspective characterized by constraint, narrowness, exclusiveness, simplicity, and intolerance and toward a perspective with an emphasis on greater individual freedom, breadth, inclusiveness, complexity, and tolerance.

A third unifying thread that characterizes attitude and values change during college is a shift away from the instrumental or extrinsic values of education and occupation toward a higher valuing of intrinsic rewards. Compared to freshmen, seniors attach greater importance to the value of a liberal education and less importance to the value of a college education as vocational preparation. Consistently, seniors (as compared to freshmen) also place greater value on the intrinsic characteristics of a job (intellectual challenge, autonomy, and so forth) and less value on extrinsic rewards (salary, job security, and the like).

Table 2
Summary of Estimated Freshman-to-Senior *Changes: Attitudes and Values*

Outcome	Estimated Magnitude of Change		
	Effect Size[a]	Percentile Point Difference[b]	Percentage Point Difference Between Freshmen & Seniors[c]
Aesthetic, cultural, and intellectual values	.25–.40	10–15	
Value placed on liberal education			+20 to +30%
Value placed on education as vocational preparation			−10 to −30%
Value placed on intrinsic occupational rewards			+12%
Value placed on extrinsic occupational reward			−.10 to −.15%
Altruism, social and civic conscience, humanitarianism	.10–.50	4–19	+ 2 to + 8%
Political and social liberalism	.20	8	+15 to +25%
Civil rights and liberties + 5 to +25%			
Religiosity, religious affiliation	−.49	19 (in religiosity)	Up to −11% in conventional religious preferences
Traditional views of gender roles			−10 to −25%

[a]Effect size = (senior mean minus freshman mean) divided by freshman standard deviation.
[b]Effect size converted to the equivalent percentile point under the normal curve. This is the percentile point difference between the freshman- and senior-year means when the freshman mean is set at the 50th percentile.
[c]Percentage point increase or decrease of seniors (versus freshmen) holding a particular view or position.

At first glance, such changes may seem inconsistent with what was clearly an increasing trend between 1970 and 1985 toward vocationalism or materialism in the reasons underlying an individual's decision to attend college (Astin, Green, & Korn, 1987). The motivation for attending college and the changes that occur during college, however, may be largely independent of each other. Thus, even if succeeding cohorts of recent freshmen have increasingly chosen to attend college for its instrumental or extrinsic returns, it would still appear that the freshman-to-senior changes that occur during college lead to an increased value being placed on the nonvocational aspects of one's educational experience and the intrinsic rewards of one's prospective work.

Psychosocial Changes

The motif noted earlier of the interrelatedness of student change during the college years is apparent in the several areas of student psychosocial change summarized in Table 3. While the changes in these areas are, on the whole, more modest than those relating to learning and cognitive development, they are approximately the same size as the shifts in attitudes and values. Moreover, their general character and direction are clearly consistent with those of the other two areas. Gains in various kinds of substantive knowledge and in cognitive competence may provide both a basis and the intellectual tools for students to examine their own identities, self-concepts, and the nature of their interactions with their external world.

Thus, perhaps as a partial consequence of their cognitive gains, students appear to move toward greater self-understanding, self-definition, and personal commitment, as well as toward more refined ego functioning. Similarly, students' academic and social self-images, as well as their self-esteem, while perhaps somewhat bruised initially, not only recover but become more positive over the college years.

Table 3
Summary of Estimated Freshman-to-Senior
Changes: Self and Relational Systems in Psychosocial Development

Outcome	Estimated Magnitude of Change		
	Effect Size[a]	Percentile Point Difference[b]	Percentage Point Difference Between Freshmen & Seniors[c]
Self Systems			
Identity status			+15 to +25% (in reaching identity achievement status)
Ego development	.50	19	
Self-concept			
Academic			+4 to +14% (rating self "above avg.")
Social			+7% (rating self "above avg.")
Self-esteem	.60	23	
Relational Systems			
Autonomy, independence, and locus of control	.36	14	
Authoritarianism	−.81	29	
Ethnocentrism	−.45	17	
Intellectual orientation	.30	12	
Interpersonal relations	.16	6	
Personal adjustment and psychological well-being	.40	16	
Maturity and general personal development	Not available		

[a]Effect size = (senior mean minus freshman mean) divided by freshman standard deviation.
[b]Effect size converted to the equivalent percentile point under the normal curve. This is the percentile point difference between the freshman- and senior-year means when the freshman mean is set at the 50th percentile.
[c]Percentage point increase or decrease of seniors (versus freshmen) holding a particular view or position.

The psychosocial changes experienced during the college years extend beyond the inner world of the self to include the relational aspects of students' lives: the manner in which they engage and respond to other people and to other aspects of their external world. As students become better learners, they also appear to become increasingly independent of parents (but not necessarily of peers), gain in their sense that they are in control of their world and what happens to them, and become somewhat more mature in their interpersonal relations, both in general and in their intimate relations with others, whether of the same or opposite sex. They also show modest gains in their general personal adjustment, sense of psychological well-being, and general personal development and maturity. Moreover, consistent with the observed shifts toward greater openness in attitudes and values, the evidence quite consistently indicates that students gain in their general intellectual disposition or orientation toward their world, their willingness to challenge authority, their tolerance of other people and their views, their openness to new ideas, and their ability to think in nonstereotypic ways about others who are socially, culturally, racially, or ethnically different from them.

Moral Development

As suggested in Table 4, there is clear and consistent evidence that students make statistically significant gains during college in the use of principled reasoning to judge moral issues. This finding holds across different measurement instruments and even different cultures. The absence of descriptive statistics in much of the evidence, however, makes it difficult if not impossible to

Table 4
Summary of Estimated Freshman-to-Senior *Changes: Moral Development*

Outcome	Estimated Magnitude of Change		
	Effect Size[a]	Percentile Point Difference[b]	Percentage Point Difference Between Freshmen & Seniors[c]
Use of principled reasoning in judging moral issues	Difficult to estimate magnitude of effect, but major change during college is from the use of "conventional" to "postconventional" or "principled" reasoning		

[a]Effect size = (senior mean minus freshman mean) divided by freshman standard deviation.
[b]Effect size converted to the equivalent percentile point under the normal curve. This is the percentile point difference between the freshman- and senior-year means when the freshman mean is set at the 50th percentile.
[c]Percentage point increase or decrease of seniors (versus freshmen) holding a particular view or position.

estimate with confidence the magnitude of the freshman-to-senior change in the same way that we have done for other outcomes. As we have stressed in Chapter Eight on moral development, the magnitude of the freshman-to-senior gain may not be as important as the fact that the major shift during college is from conventional to postconventional or principled judgment. (The former is based strongly on morality as obedience to rules and meeting the expectations of those in authority, while the latter is based strongly on a view of morality as a set of universal principles of social justice existing independently of societal codification.) This shift in and of itself represents a major event in moral development.

The freshman-to-senior changes in moral judgment noted in our synthesis are perhaps another example of how change during college on one dimension is typically consistent with change in other areas. Measures of moral reasoning are themselves positively correlated not only with areas of general cognitive development that increase during college (such as abstract reasoning, critical thinking, and reflective judgment) but also with the general liberalization of personality and value structures coinciding with college attendance (for example, decreases in authoritarianism or dogmatism; increases in autonomy, tolerance, and interpersonal sensitivity; increased concern for the rights and welfare of others). Thus, the enhancement of principled moral judgment during college is embedded within an interconnected and perhaps mutually reinforcing network of cognitive, value, and psychosocial changes that occur at approximately the same time.

Some Final Thoughts on Change During College

Our conclusions about the changes that occur during college differ in only minor ways from those of Feldman and Newcomb (1969) and Bowen (1977). Indeed, taken as a total body of evidence, all three syntheses suggest that a reasonably consistent set of cognitive, attitudinal, value, and psychosocial changes have occurred among college students over the last four or five decades. Students learn to think in more abstract, critical, complex, and reflective ways; there is a general liberalization of values and attitudes combined with an increase in cultural and artistic interests and activities; progress is made toward the development of personal identities and more positive self-concepts; and there is an expansion and extension of interpersonal horizons, intellectual interests, individual autonomy, and general psychological maturity and well-being. Thus, it can be said that the nature and direction of freshman-to-senior changes appear to be reasonably stable and to some extent predictable.

In some instances our estimate of the magnitude of freshman-to-senior changes differs from estimates of previous syntheses, particularly Bowen's (1977). Since the differences are quite modest, however, we are inclined to attribute them to chance variations in the bodies of literature reviewed and perhaps even different typologies or operational definitions of outcomes. At any rate, it would seem that the consistency in the nature and direction of changes across syntheses is a much more salient and noteworthy characteristic of the evidence than are small differences in estimates of the magnitude of the changes across the same syntheses.

It may also be the case that the absolute magnitude of freshman-to-senior changes is not as educationally important as either the qualitative nature or the breadth and scope of the changes. One danger in focusing on quantitative estimates of change such as effect size is that one tends to consider change as happening on a continuum where all change is smoothly continuous and equally important. Many developmental theorists would argue that development does not always happen in such even and equivalent fashion (for example, Kitchener & King, 1990; Kohlberg, 1969; Perry, 1970; Rest, 1986b). Moreover, not all changes are equivalent in size or importance: Some shifts are particularly critical to development irrespective of whether or not they are reflected in a large quantitative change on some continuous scale. For example, the qualitative shift during college from a style of reasoning based on beliefs to one relying on evidence in making judgments represents a key prerequisite to rational problem solving. Similarly, the shift from conventional to principled reasoning during college represents a major qualitative advance in moral development. On both of these dimensions of development, the qualitative nature of the change is likely to be of greater consequence than the magnitude of the change.

We would also suggest that the magnitude of change on any particular dimension or set of dimensions during college may not be as significant as the pronounced breadth of interconnected changes we noted in our synthesis. As posited by major models of student development (for example, Chickering, 1969; Heath, 1968), the evidence indicates not only that individuals change on a broad developmental front during college but also that the changes are of a mutually consistent and supporting nature. Although there may be insufficient empirical grounds to speak of changes in one area causing or permitting changes in other areas, it is clear from the body of evidence we reviewed that the changes coincident with college attendance involve the whole person and proceed in a largely integrated manner. Certainly the notion of broad-based integrative change during college is not a new finding, but the evidence we reviewed was sufficiently compelling to warrant its reaffirmation.

There are, of course, at least three nontrivial problems endemic to the study of freshman-to-senior change. The first stems from the fact. that the evidence is based largely on studies measuring typical or average change in some sample (longitudinal studies) or typical or average differences between samples (cross-sectional studies). By focusing on average group shifts or differences, the findings of such studies tend to mask individual differences in patterns of change. Some students may change substantially during college, some may change little or not at all, and some may actually shift in a direction counter to the typical movement of the group. Moreover, some students may change in one way on certain variables and in opposite ways on other variables. Thus, although the average change may be our best estimate of the dominant shift or development occurring in a group, it is not without limitations.

A second problem, one that we have emphasized throughout the book, is that freshman-to-senior change during college does not necessarily reflect the impact of college. Many of the dimensions on which change occurs during college may have a developmental base. If so, this means that individuals tend to exhibit more sophisticated levels of development through the process of maturation or simply growing older. Consequently, similar individuals not attending college might well change in essentially the same ways as college students over the same time period. In the absence of a control group of noncollege attenders (a typical weakness in most studies of change during college), it is essentially impossible to separate the changes due to college attendance from those attributable to natural maturation.

The focus on change during college as an indication of college impact can also be misleading in another way. Just as the presence of change does not necessarily indicate the impact of college, so too the absence of change does not necessarily indicate the absence of college impact. One important consequence of college attendance may be to fix development at a certain level and prevent reversion or regression (Feldman & Newcomb, 1969). If such were the case on a specific trait, little or no freshman-to-senior change would be noted. Those not attending college, however, might well regress or change in a negative direction. We will see an example of this as we turn to a summary of the net effects of college.

Finally, it is important to differentiate change from development. Whereas *change* simply means that some fact or condition at Time$_2$ is different from what it was at Time$_1$, *development* implies ordered, predictable, even hierarchical shifts or evolution have taken place in fundamental, intra-individual structures or processes. In many areas of observed change during college, it is tempting simply to conclude that observed change reflects some form of internal growth or development in the individual, that an inner restructuring has taken place, and that the senior is functioning with an advanced set of inner rules or perspectives not present in the typical freshman. This is a particular temptation when the changes that occur are consistent with those posited by developmental models or theories. The danger inherent in this assumption is that what we commonly refer to as development may in large measure be the result of an individual's response to the anticipated norms of new social settings or social roles. Different categories of people may be socialized to think and behave differently in society, and a substantial part of this categorization may have its basis in educational level. Thus, for example, college-educated men and women may have certain psychosocial traits and values and may think about controversial issues in certain ways not necessarily because of some inner developmental restructuring but because they have been socialized to behave and think in ways consistent with dominant cultural norms for educated adults.

This is not to say that the changes that occur during college merely represent the learning of social or cultural norms instead of important developmental steps. Rather, it is to suggest that we need to be wary of the tendency to equate the learning of social or cultural norms with development. It behooves us to bear in mind that change during the college years is produced by multiple influences, some internal (and perhaps ontogenetic) and others external to the individual. Theories can overly restrict as well as focus vision.

Net Effects of College

Because self-selection, as opposed to random assignment, determines who attends and who does not attend college, studies that seek to estimate the unique or net impact of college (as distinct from normal maturation, mere aging, or other noncollege sources of change) employ some rather creative research designs or, more typically, statistical controls. Although the causal inferences one can make from such studies are not of the same order of certitude as those made from randomized experiments, we can nevertheless arrive at a reasonably valid set of tentative conclusions about the changes or outcomes observed that are attributable to college attendance and not to rival explanations. It is worth recalling, however, that change during the college years involves a complex, weblike network. Change in one area may cause or be accompanied by change in other areas as well. Given this interrelatedness, estimates of change and of college's net effect in each discrete area no doubt understate college's overall, cumulative impact.

Tables 5 through 8 array those dimensions on which the weight of evidence offers support for claims about college's unique or net impact. (When we use the term *unclear* in the column reporting the magnitude of net effects in this and all subsequent tables in the chapter, we are acknowledging that the studies do not allow such estimates or that the evidence, though generally consistent, is still sufficiently complex to make an estimate of effect size hazardous.) As Tables 5 through 8 show, we judge the evidence on net impact to be more compelling for some outcomes than for others. Specifically, there is more extensive and consistent evidence to support the net impact of college on learning and cognition, moral reasoning, and career and economic returns than in the areas of attitudes, values, and psychosocial characteristics. This does not necessarily mean that college has a stronger impact on the former outcomes than on the latter ones. Indeed, we had a difficult time estimating the magnitude of the net impact of college in nearly all areas of our synthesis. Some of these differences could be more a reflection of variations in the extent and quality of the available evidence across different areas of inquiry than of major differences in the actual impact of college. More likely, they are real. It would probably be unreasonable to expect uniform changes across substantive areas. Students vary considerably in the characteristics they bring with them to college, not only in a wide variety of personal, educational, and family background traits but also in their readiness and capacity for change. Moreover, higher educational institutions do not invest their energies and resources equally across areas of change.

Learning and Cognitive Changes

Table 5 shows those learning and cognitive development outcomes that the weight of evidence suggests are significantly influenced by college attendance. Perhaps the clearest generalization to be made from this evidence is that on nearly all of the dimensions on which we find freshman-to-senior change, a statistically significant part of that change is attributable to college attendance, not to rival explanations. College not only appears to enhance general verbal and quantitative skills as well as oral and written communication, but it also has a statistically significant positive net effect on general intellectual and analytical skills, critical thinking, the use of reason and evidence in addressing ill-structured problems, and intellectual flexibility. These effects cannot be explained away by maturation or differences between those who attend and those who do not attend college in intelligence, academic ability, or other precollege characteristics.

These conclusions about the net effects of college on learning and cognitive development are limited by those dimensions that individual scholars have chosen to investigate. It is perhaps useful to think of these dimensions of net college effects as analogous to geological probes designed to define the nature and extent of mineral or oil deposits. They sample and begin to define the boundaries, but they may not capture the fullness of the phenomenon being measured. From this perspective, it is reasonable to conclude that college attendance positively influences a wide range of cognitive skills and intellectual functioning. The existing research, however, probably provides only a rough outline of the types of learning and cognitive development enhanced by college without necessarily tapping the full range or richness of effects.

As briefly alluded to in the previous section on change during college, research on college's net effects illustrates the potentially misleading nature of change. The net positive effect of college on general quantitative skills, for example, occurred not because students who attended college made greater gains than those who did not attend. Instead, the effect was largely attributable to the fact that college attendance tended to anchor quantitative skills at precollege levels while those not attending college actually regressed. Thus, an important net effect of college may be to stabilize an individual's development on certain dimensions and to prevent the regressions that might occur in the absence of college attendance.

Attitudes and Values

Evidence concerning the net impact of college on attitudes and values is summarized in Table 6. Although the weight of this evidence is not totally consistent and certainly not without rival explanations, it nevertheless suggests that a statistically significant, if modest, part of the broadbased attitudinal and value changes that occur during college can be attributed to the college experience. Perhaps of equal importance, the net effects of college, particularly in the areas of social, political, and sex role values, appear not to be simple reflections of trends in the larger society across the last two decades. Rather, college attendance seems to have an impact on attitudes and values in these areas, an impact that is generally consistent both within and across age cohorts.

This is not to say that what occurs during college happens in total isolation from cultural and social forces. Clearly, student values are significantly affected by those dominant in society, and general societal changes make unambiguous attributions of change to college more difficult. Nevertheless, college attendance would appear to influence political, social, and gender role attitudes and values in consistent ways regardless of cultural and societal trends.

A note of caution needs to be made with respect to this conclusion, because there is some evidence to suggest that recent college effects on social and political values may be less pronounced than earlier studies have indicated. Whether this is a chance fluctuation or the precursor of an important generational effect, however, awaits replication of the findings on future samples.

Table 5

Summary of Estimated *Net* Effects of College: *Learning and Cognitive Development*

Outcome	Strength of Evidence	Direction of Effect	Major Rival Explanations Controlled	Magnitude of Net Effect
General verbal skills	Strong	Positive	Precollege verbal skills, race, socioeconomic status	.26 to .32 SD (10 to 13 percentile point advantage)
General quantitative skills	Strong	Positive	Precollege quantitative skills, race, socioeconomic status	.29 to .32 SD (11 to 13 percentile point advantage)
Oral communication skills	Moderate	Positive	Age, academic ability	Unclear[a]
Written communication skills	Moderate	Positive	Age, academic ability	Unclear
General intellectual and analytical skill development	Moderate	Positive	Age, verbal ability, quantitative ability	Community college graduates higher than incoming freshmen; magnitude of effect unclear
Critical thinking	Strong	Positive	Precollege critical thinking, academic aptitude, socioeconomic status, educational aspirations	Freshman-year net effect, .44 SD (17 percentile point advantage); magnitude of net four-year effect unclear
Use of reason and evidence to address ill-structured problems (reflective judgment, informal reasoning)	Moderate to strong	Positive	Age, academic ability	Unclear
Intellectual flexibility	Moderate to strong	Positive	Age, intelligence, academic aptitude	Unclear

[a]"Unclear," as used in this table, means we are acknowledging that the studies do not allow such estimates or that the evidence, though generally consistent, is still sufficiently complex to make an estimate of effect size hazardous.

Table 6
Summary of Estimated *Net* Effects of College: *Attitudes and Values*

Outcome	Strength of Evidence	Direction of Effect	Major Rival Explanations Controlled	Magnitude of Net Effect
Aesthetic, cultural, and intellectual values	Moderate	Positive	Age, gender, religion, socioeconomic status, residential origin	Unclear[a]
Value placed on liberal education	Strong	Positive	Aptitude, race, gender, family socio-economic status, precollege values	Graduates two to three times more likely to value education than are people with less education
Value placed on education as vocational preparation	Moderate	Negative	Aptitude, occupation, interaction thereof	Unclear
Value placed on intrinsic occupational rewards	Strong	Positive	Gender, race, socioeconomic status, job characteristics	Unclear, probably small
Value placed on extrinsic occupational rewards	Strong	Negative	Gender, race, socioeconomic status, job characteristics	Small
Social liberalism	Weak	Positive	Gender, race, age, religion, socioeconomic status, residential origin, cohort, aging and period effects	Unclear
Political liberalism	Strong	Positive	Gender, race, age, religion, socioeconomic status, residential origin, cohort, aging and period effects	Unclear
Civil rights and liberties	Mixed	Positive	Age, income, socioeconomic status, religion	Unclear, probably small
Secularism	Weak	Positive	Gender, race, initial religious attitudes	Unclear
Gender roles (toward the "modern")	Strong	Positive	Initial gender role values, gender, age, race, income, religion, marital status, work history, number of children, period and cohorts effects	Unclear

[a]"Unclear," as used in this table, means we are acknowledging that the studies do not allow such estimates or that the evidence, though generally consistent, is still sufficiently complex to make an estimate of effect size hazardous.

Psychosocial Changes

Table 7 summarizes the evidence relating to college's psychosocial net effects. As can be seen there, virtually nothing can be said with confidence about the net effects of college on changes in students' identity statuses or their stages of ego development. The research literature simply does not deal with the effects of college in these areas in any methodologically rigorous or generalizable way. The vast majority of studies are concerned with structural rather than process questions, with whether hypothesized statuses or stages exist and the characteristics of the individuals at any given stage rather than with the variables (including education) that influence status or stage change. Where change is examined, educational and age or maturational effects remain confounded.

Persuasive evidence exists to indicate that college attendance is reliably and positively related to increases in students' academic and social self-concepts, as well as their self-esteem. After holding constant a variety of relevant precollege characteristics, educational attainment is consistently and positively related to increases in students' perceptions of themselves relative to their peers in both academic areas (for example, writing and mathematical abilities, general academic abilities, intellectual self-confidence) and social areas (leadership abilities, popularity in general and with the opposite sex, general social self-confidence, and the like). Net college effects are also apparent in the increases students experience in their self-esteem: the general regard in which they hold themselves and their abilities, the extent to which they consider themselves to be capable, significant, worthy, or of value. After precollege self-concepts or self-esteem and other background characteristics have been controlled, however, college's effects in each of these areas appear to be small. Moreover, college's influence on students' self-concepts appears to be indirect rather than direct, being mediated through certain characteristics students bring with them to college and through the kinds of academic and interpersonal experiences they have once on campus.

The net effects of college on changes in the ways students relate to people, institutions, and conditions in their external world are somewhat less limited. Consistent with the net gains made in cognitive areas, we can attribute to college (with moderate to considerable confidence) declines in authoritarianism and dogmatism and increases in students' internal sense (locus) of control, intellectual orientation, personal adjustment, and general psychological well-being. College's contributions to the declines in authoritarianism and dogmatism appear to be strong, but its effects in the other areas are much more modest, even small. Because of methodological limitations, however, few claims (if any) can be made with confidence about college's net effects on changes in students' levels of autonomy or independence, the maturity of their interpersonal relations, or their overall maturity and personal development.

Moral Development

Table 8 reveals that college has a net positive effect on the use of principled reasoning in judging moral issues. This effect holds even when controls are made for maturation and for differences between those who attend and those who do not attend college in level of precollege moral reasoning, intelligence, and socioeconomic status. The net impact of college on actual moral behavior is less clear. On the basis of a synthesis of two separate bodies of research, however, we hypothesize a positive indirect effect. College enhances the use of principled moral reasoning, which in turn is positively linked to a variety of principled actions. These include resistance to cheating, social activism, keeping contractual promises, and helping behavior. The acceptance of this hypothesis is tentative, however, and awaits fuller empirical support.

Long-Term Effects of College

Nearly all of the considerable body of research on the long-term effects of college is concerned with estimating the enduring impact of attending versus not attending college. Consequently, it has much in common, both conceptually and methodologically, with research that attempts to

Table 7
Summary of Estimated *Net Effects* of College: *Psychosocial Development*

Outcome	Strength of Evidence	Direction of Effect	Major Rival Explanations Controlled	Magnitude of Net Effect
Identity and ego development	Very weak	Positive	Few	Unknown
Self-concept: Academic	Strong	Positive	Gender, race, prior achievement, socioeconomic status, degree aspirations	Small, indirect
Self-concept: Social	Strong	Positive	Gender, race, prior achievement, socioeconomic status, degree aspirations	Small, indirect
Self-concept: Self-esteem	Strong	Positive	Ability, achievement, socioeconomic status, race, precollege self-esteem	Small
Autonomy, independence, and internal locus of control	Weak to moderate (strong for locus of control)	Positive	Ability, socioeconomic status, precollege locus of control	Unclear[a] (small for locus of control)
Authoritarianism, dogmatism, and ethnocentrism	Moderate	Negative	Gender, ability, socioeconomic status	Unclear
Intellectual orientation	Moderate	Positive	Gender, ability, socioeconomic status	Unclear
Interpersonal relations	Weak	Mixed	None	Unclear
Personal adjustment and psychological well-being	Strong	Positive	Socioeconomic status, family situation, religiosity	Small
Maturity and general personal development	No evidence	Unknown	None	Unclear

a"Unclear," as used in this table, means we are acknowledging that the studies do not allow such estimates or that the evidence, though generally consistent, is still sufficiently complex to make an estimate of effect size hazardous.

Table 8
Summary of Estimated *Net Effects* of College: *Moral Development*

Outcome	Strength of Evidence	Direction of Effect	Major Rival Explanations Controlled	Magnitude of Net Effect
Use of principled reasoning in judging moral issues	Strong	Positive	Age, precollege differences in moral reasoning, intelligence, socioeconomic status	Unclear[a]
Principled behavior or action	Weak	Positive	Socioeconomic status	Hypothesized effect is indirect and probably small

a"Unclear," as used in this table, means we are acknowledging that the studies do not allow such estimates or that the evidence, though generally consistent, is still sufficiently complex to make an estimate of effect size hazardous.

estimate the net effects of college. Indeed, one could reasonably regard evidence on the enduring impact of college attendance essentially as an estimate of the net effects of college extended over time. For this reason we depart from the typical pattern of most chapters and summarize the evidence on the long-term effects of college here rather than near the end of this chapter.

Our synthesis of the evidence suggests that college has a rather broad range of enduring or long-term impacts. These include not only the more obvious impacts on occupation and earnings but also influences on cognitive, moral, and psychosocial characteristics, as well as on values and attitudes and various quality of life indexes (for example, family, marriage, consumer behavior). Moreover, it would also appear that the impacts extend beyond the individuals who attend college to the kinds of lives their sons and daughters can expect.

It is clear that part of the long-term impact of college (for example, on job status and income) can be traced directly back to college attendance or degree attainment. Another part of this impact, however, may be an indirect result of the socioeconomic positioning and kinds of life interests, experiences, and opportunities made more likely by being a college graduate. As suggested by Withey (1971) and Bowen (1977), part of the impact of college arises out of the distinctive kinds of lives led by the people who attend and graduate from college. Such indirect routes of influence are a major consideration in understanding the long-term and full impact of college. In short, our conclusion about the nature of the long-term effects of college is generally consistent with that of Feldman and Newcomb (1969). The distinctive effects of college tend to persist in large measure as a result of living in postcollege environments that support those effects.

Socioeconomic Outcomes

The impact of college on socioeconomic outcomes (occupation and earnings) is a function not only of what happens during college but also of how college graduates are themselves regarded by employers. It is difficult to separate these two influences, but it is quite clear that obtaining a bachelor's degree has a strong net influence on one's socioeconomic attainments. We should perhaps avoid the temptation to make too much of these influences. Most prediction models of status attainment explain somewhat less than 50 percent of the individual differences in occupational status or earnings. Nevertheless, as summarized in Table 9, the evidence we reviewed is consistent in indicating that a bachelor's degree remains a major, if not *the* major, prerequisite for entrée into relatively high-status and high-paying technical, managerial, and professional jobs.

The socioeconomic impact of being a college graduate is not realized exclusively at the early stages in one's career, however. A college degree continues to provide advantages throughout one's working life. These are manifest as enhanced earnings, an increased likelihood of stable employment, and generally higher levels of career mobility and attainment. Moreover, despite periodic fluctuations, the private economic rate of return on investment in a bachelor's degree compares favorably to benchmark rates for alternative ways of investing one's money. In short, our reading of the body of evidence is quite consistent with that of Bowen (1977): A bachelor's degree continues to be a primary vehicle by means of which one gains an advantaged socioeconomic position in American society.

With respect to the importance of college graduation on other major indexes of socioeconomic attainment, such as occupational status and income, two additional observations are relevant. First, there is replicated evidence to suggest that in terms of the relative incremental advantage it confers, a bachelor's degree is typically the single most important educational rung on the socioeconomic attainment ladder. Second, although there are discernible between- and within-college effects, the occupational and economic impacts of completing one's bachelor's degree are typically more pronounced than the impacts due either to where one completes it or to the nature of one's educational experiences while doing so (for example, major field of study, academic achievement, extracurricular involvement).

The way in which a bachelor's degree positions one occupationally and economically represents an important long-term impact of college in and of itself. But this socioeconomic positioning effect has additional implications for other long-term impacts. One stems from the simple fact that the jobs that college graduates typically hold are characterized by a relatively high level of earnings. This permits the acquisition of a variety of material and nonmaterial resources and opportunities (including books, travel, cultural experiences, household maintenance, medical care, and additional education) that have potential impact on other long-term outcomes. A second implication stems from the fact that college graduates tend to be employed in jobs characterized by relatively high levels of social interaction and self-direction. Such job traits may provide an important continuing influence on trends in cognitive and psychosocial changes partially shaped during the college experience.

Learning and Cognitive Development

As indicated in Table 10, the body of evidence on the long-term impact of college on indexes of learning and cognitive characteristics is not without methodological problems. Nevertheless, there is clear evidence from extensive national samples to indicate that college graduates have a substantially larger general knowledge base across a wide range of topics than do individuals whose education ends with high school. Similarly, in an impressive set of national surveys, alumni were consistent in reporting that college had a major positive influence both on their specific and their general knowledge base and on their ability to think critically, analytically, and clearly.

As suggested by the retrospective perceptions of graduates, part of this enduring impact can probably be traced directly to what transpires in college. A substantial amount of factual learning and general intellectual development obviously occurs during that time. Yet it is likely that what happens during college represents only part of the story. Another part is probably the result of differences in the kinds of posteducation lives that college and high school graduates lead. The former are more likely to engage in intellectually challenging activities (serious reading, attending cultural events, participating in continuing education, and the like), and to be employed in the kinds of intellectually challenging jobs that further enlarge their knowledge base and continue to enhance their intellectual development. Moreover, even if college crystallizes one's interest in lifelong learning, the economic advantages linked to a college degree contribute in part by increasing one's ability to purchase the goods and services required. It is probably this complex interplay of mutually supporting direct and indirect influences (that is, what happens during college, postcollege experiences, and the ability to acquire material and nonmaterial opportunities) that most fully accounts for the long-term impact of college on knowledge acquisition and more general cognitive advances.

Attitudes and Values

The most notable conclusion from the body of research on the long-term effects of college on attitudes and values, summarized in Table 11, is that nearly all of the trends that occur during college tend either to persist or to stabilize in the years following college. Certainly there are exceptions to this conclusion. Intervening experiences in such areas as work, marriage and family, military service, and graduate education are potentially profound influences on one's attitudes and values. Nevertheless, for college students as a group, the intellectual, aesthetic, social, political, religious, educational, and occupational attitudes and values one holds as a graduating senior appear to be an important determinant of the attitudes and values one holds throughout the adult years.

Part of this long-term impact may be directly traceable to the college experience. College may, in fact, function to influence a broad range of attitudes and values in directions that may be relatively impervious to subsequent influence and thus tend to persist throughout adult life. It is unlikely, however, that the total enduring impact of college on attitudes or values is confined to the college years. Perhaps more important is the fact that college tends to channel graduates into postcollege lives that often reinforce trends shaped by the college experience. This indirect impact on attitudes and values may manifest itself in a variety of ways. For example, one's attitudes and values may be influenced by the type of job one holds; by the attitudes and values of a spouse,

Table 9
Summary of Estimated *Long-Term* Effects of College: *Socioeconomic Outcomes*

Outcome	Strength of Evidence	Direction of Effect	Major Rival Explanations Controlled	Magnitude of Net Effect
Occupational status	Strong	Positive	Socioeconomic status, aspirations, intelligence	Bachelor's degree confers 1 SD (34 percentile point) advantage over high school diploma
Stability of employment	Moderate	Positive	Socioeconomic status	Unclear,[a] probably large
Career mobility and attainment	Strong	Positive	Initial job level	Unclear
Earnings	Strong	Positive	Socioeconomic status, aspirations, occupational status, intelligence, work experience	Bachelor's degree confers 20 to 40 percentage point advantage over high school diploma
Private rate of return	Strong	Positive	Intelligence, costs of education, foregone earnings	Bachelor's degree confers 9.3 to 11% return on investment

[a]"Unclear," as used in this table, means we are acknowledging that the studies do not allow such estimates or that the evidence, though generally consistent, is still sufficiently complex to make an estimate of effect size hazardous.

Table 10
Summary of Estimated *Long-Term* Effects of College: *Learning and Cognitive Development*

Outcome	Strength of Evidence	Direction of Effect	Major Rival Explanations Controlled	Magnitude of Net Effect
General knowledge	Moderate	Positive	Race, gender, age, initial socioeconomic status, current socioeconomic status, religion, geographical origin	Unclear[a]
General cognitive competencies and skills (e.g., critical thinking and analytical skills, ability to think clearly, oral communication skills)	Moderate	Positive	Age	Unclear

[a]"Unclear," as used in this table, means we are acknowledging that the studies do not allow such estimates or that the evidence, though generally consistent, is still sufficiently complex to make an estimate of effect size hazardous.

professional acquaintances, and friends with a similar level of education; or by the nature of one's leisure-time interests and activities (cultural opportunities, travel, civic involvement, reading, and so on), which is often shaped by interests and available financial resources. In short, the kinds of postcollege lives college graduates lead may transmit an important indirect long-term impact of college on attitudes and values.

The long-term effect of college on attitudes and values may also involve an intergenerational legacy; the attitudes and values that students develop at least partially as a consequence of their college experiences are passed on to their children. For example, a small body of evidence has found a positive link between a mother's education and nontraditional gender role attitudes in children, particularly daughters. This may be a less obvious part of the indirect impact of a mother's education on her daughter's conceptions of herself and on the likelihood of her entering a traditionally male-dominated occupation.

Psychosocial Changes

The nature and extent of college's long-term effects on students' psychosocial characteristics are summarized in Table 12. As can be seen there, the research literature is silent on the extent to which college has any identifiable long-term effect on identity status or ego stage development. While there is ample evidence that identity and ego development do not end with the college years, education's role in those changes remains virtually unexamined and thus unknown. Even though the research base is small, however, it is methodologically strong and consistent in indicating that college does have a positive and unique effect on students' academic and social concepts, as well as on their self-esteem. These effects are discernible up to a decade after matriculation, although they appear to be small and largely indirect, mediated through the higher-status jobs college graduates tend to obtain compared to those held by people with less education. Moreover, college's long-term effects on self-concepts appear to be greater among white students than among black students. Nine years after entry, college attendance appears to have no measurable effects—positive or negative, direct or indirect—on the self-concepts of black males.

With a few exceptions, the research base exploring long-term changes in the several facets of students' relational systems is severely constrained either by idiosyncratic samples or by designs that do not control plausible rival hypotheses (sometimes by both). Limited but sound nationally based evidence indicates that educational attainment is positively related to increases in individuals' internal locus of control seven and nine years after high school graduation, but occupational effects were left uncontrolled, leaving claims of college's long-term effects open to challenge. The evidence in the other areas of relational change is explored by single-institution studies with only marginal generalizability. What evidence exists suggests little postcollege change in level of authoritarianism or in intellectual orientation, slight declines in anxiety and the willingness to express impulses, and gains in personal integration, psychological well-being, and general maturity. Thus, although the evidence is limited, there is some basis for believing that education at least has no deleterious effects on overall psychosocial status and probably has some decidedly beneficial ones, even though they may be slight and indirect.

Moral Development

As indicated in Table 13, there is strong evidence for an enduring impact of college on the use of principled moral reasoning, at least through the first six years after graduation. Students attending college not only make greater gains in the use of principled reasoning during college than individuals whose formal education ends with high school, but the gap between the two groups continues to widen in the years subsequent to college. These different patterns of change cannot be accounted for by initial differences in moral development or differential regression effects. Again, we see evidence that part of this long-term impact is directly attributable to trends shaped by the college experience. Another part, however, is indirectly attributable to college through differences between high school and college graduates in posteducational environments, particu-

Table 11
Summary of Estimated *Long-Term* Effects of College: *Attitudes and Values*

Outcome	Strength of Evidence	Direction of Effect	Major Rival Explanations Controlled	Magnitude of Net Effect[a]
Aesthetic, cultural, and intellectual values	Moderate	Stable over time	Gender, race, religion, socioeconomic status	Unclear
Value placed on liberal education	Moderate	Positive	Aptitude, employment situation	Unclear
Value placed on education as vocational preparation	Moderate	Negative	Aptitude, employment situation	Unclear
Value placed on intrinsic occupational rewards	Strong	Positive	Gender, race, socioeconomic status, precollege values, college GPA	Unclear
Value placed on extrinsic occupational rewards	Strong	Negative	Gender, race, socioeconomic status, precollege values, college GPA	Unclear
Political and social attitudes	Moderate	Stable over time	Aptitude, age, race, gender, religion, socioeconomic status, region, historical period	Unclear; part of effect probably indirect through employment situation
Secularism	Weak	Stable over time	None	Unclear
Gender roles (toward the "modern")	Weak	Positive	Initial attitudes, various background characteristics, occupational experience	Unclear

[a]"Unclear," as used in this table, means we are acknowledging that the studies do not allow such estimates or that the evidence, though generally consistent, is still sufficiently complex to make an estimate of effect size hazardous.

Table 12
Summary of Estimated *Long-Term* Effects of College: *Psychosocial Changes*

Outcome	Strength of Evidence	Direction of Effect	Major Rival Explanations Controlled	Magnitude of Net Effect
Identity and ego development	Virtually no evidence			
Self-concept: Academic	Strong	Positive	Gender, race, precollege self-concept, achievement, socioeconomic status, degree aspirations, occupational status	Small; stronger among whites than among blacks
Self-concept: Social	Strong	Positive	Gender, race, precollege self-concept, achievement, socioeconomic status degree aspirations, occupational status	Small; stronger among whites than among blacks
Self-concept: Self-esteem	Strong	Positive	Race, gender, socioeconomic status, ability, precollege self-esteem	Small
Autonomy, independence, and internal locus of control	Moderate	Positive	Gender, race, socioeconomic status, aptitude, precollege locus of control	Unclear,[a] but probably small and perhaps indirect
Authoritarianism, dogmatism, and ethnocentrism	Weak	Stable over time	None	Unclear
Intellectual orientation	Weak	Stable over time; some declines possible	None	Unclear
Interpersonal relations	Weak	Positive	None	Unclear
Personal adjustment and psychosocial well-being	Moderate	Positive	Income, occupational status	Unclear
Maturity and general personal development	Weak	Positive	Unclear	Unclear

[a]"Unclear," as used in this table, means we are acknowledging that the studies do not allow such estimates or that the evidence, though generally consistent, is still sufficiently complex to make an estimate of effect size hazardous.

larly in the area of continuing intellectual stimulation (reading, cultural events, travel, job demands, and so on). There is clear evidence that the level of continuing intellectual stimulation in one's posteducational life has a strong positive impact on further advances in principled moral reasoning.

Quality of Life Indexes

Problems in research design and the inability to control important confounding influences make causal attributions about the long-term impact of college on various quality of life indexes somewhat tenuous. As shown in Table 14, the overall quality of evidence is not particularly strong. Consequently, we consider the findings as more suggestive than conclusive.

Having said this, it nevertheless remains true that college-educated individuals consistently rank higher than those with less education on a clear majority of the quality of life indexes considered. Compared to those with less education, the college educated tend to have better overall health and a lower mortality rate, have smaller families and be more successful in achieving desired family size through informed and effective use of contraceptive devices, and spend a greater portion of time in child care, particularly in activities of a developmentally enriching nature (such as teaching, reading, and talking). They also tend to be more efficient in making consumer choices, save a greater percentage of their income, make more effective long-term investment of discretionary resources, and spend a greater proportion of discretionary resources and leisure time on developmentally enriching activities (reading, participation in arts and cultural events, involvement in civic affairs, and so forth).

It is likely that at least part of the impact of college on these indexes of life quality is indirect, being mediated through the socioeconomic advantages that tend to accrue to the college educated. Having the economic resources to pay for desired goods and services is not without important consequences for the quality of one's life. At the same time, the positive link between educational level and many quality of life indexes remains even after economic resources are held constant. This suggests the possibility at least that college may also have a direct impact on quality of life by enhancing such characteristics as the ability to acquire new information and process it effectively, the ability to evaluate new ideas and technologies, the capacity to plan rationally and with a long-term perspective, the willingness to accept reasonable risk, and the developmental and cultural level of one's leisure interests and tastes. It should be pointed out, however, that with some exceptions, such as health status, the absence of controls for initial traits makes it difficult to separate the direct impact of college from the confounding influence of preexisting differences between those who attend and those who do not attend college.

It is interesting that even though college-educated individuals clearly rank higher on a broad array of quality of life indicators, they do not, on the average, express appreciably greater satisfaction with their lives than do those with less education. We would suggest that this does not signify the absence of impact but rather reflects the fact that the impact of college has dimensions that function both to increase and to diminish expressions of satisfaction with one's life. On the one hand, the clear job status and economic returns to college are likely to have a positive impact on some dimensions of life satisfaction, particularly the intrinsic (for example, autonomy, challenge) and extrinsic (for example, earnings) aspects of one's work. This probably explains a major part of the modest direct impact of college on job satisfaction. On the other hand, one probable impact of college is that it tends to foster a more critical perspective in individuals. Consequently, as compared to those with less education, college-educated men and women may be more sophisticated, skeptical, analytical, and critical in their judgments of some facets of job satisfaction, marital satisfaction, and overall sense of well-being.

Intergenerational Effects

An often overlooked element of the long-term impact of college is the intergenerational transmission of benefits. Indeed, there is evidence to support the expectation that the net benefits of a college education are not restricted to the individual who receives them but are passed along to

Table 13
Summary of Estimated *Long-Term* Effects of College: *Moral Development*

Outcome	Strength of Evidence	Direction of Effect	Major Rival Explanations Controlled	Magnitude of Net Effect
Use of principled reasoning in judging moral issues	Strong	Positive	Precollege level of principled reasoning, regression artifacts	Unclear[a]

[a]"Unclear," as used in this table, means we are acknowledging that the studies do not allow such estimates or that the evidence, though generally consistent, is still sufficiently complex to make an estimate of effect size hazardous.

Table 14
Summary of Estimated *Long-Term* Effects of College: *Quality of Life Indexes*

Outcome	Strength of Evidence	Direction of Effect	Major Rival Explanations Controlled	Magnitude of Net Effect
Health status	Moderate	Positive	Income, age, prior health status, socioeconomic status	College graduates have 4% advantage in health status and 1.6% advantage in mortality rate over high school graduates[a]
Marital stability	Weak	Positive	Age, age at marriage, job prestige, number of children, income	Probably indirect and small
Family size	Moderate	Positive	Income, family demographic traits	Unclear[b]
Nurturance of children	Weak	Positive	Mother employed	Unclear
Consumer behavior or efficiency	Moderate	Positive	Income	Unclear
Savings and investment efficiency	Moderate	Positive	Age, income, family size, occupation	Unclear
Cultured leisure	Weak	Positive	Income	Unclear
Job satisfaction	Weak	Positive	Age, religious preference	Unclear, but probably small
Marital satisfaction	Moderate	Mixed	Age, age at first marriage, employment outside home, job status	Very small
Subjective well-being (life satisfaction)	Moderate	Mixed	Age, income, job status, socioeconomic status origins	Very small

[a]These estimates were obtained by multiplying by four the advantage attributable to each year of college completed.
[b]"Unclear," as used in this table, means we are acknowledging that the studies do not allow such estimates or that the evidence, though generally consistent, is still sufficiently complex to make an estimate of effect size hazardous.

his or her sons and daughters. Most of the evidence on intergenerational effects concerns the socioeconomic achievements of offspring. These are summarized in Table 15. Having college-educated parents modestly enhances one's educational attainment, job status, early career earnings, and, if one is a woman, the likelihood of entering a male-dominated occupation. The last of these has consequences for gender equality in the work force in that male-dominated occupations are traditionally linked with relatively high status and earnings.

What is perhaps most notable about these intergenerational impacts, however, is that with the possible exception of offsprings' educational attainment, they manifest themselves essentially through indirect routes. Having college-educated parents positively affects the socioeconomic achievement of sons and daughters largely by influencing important intervening variables in the status attainment process. Such variables include family income, career aspirations, the type of college attended, and in, some instances educational attainment. Through this complex matrix of indirect influences, a college education is likely to make nontrivial contributions to the socioeconomic positioning of one's children.

Although the causal linkage is less clearly established, it is also likely that having college-educated parents may enhance the cognitive development of young children through the indirect route of the home environment. Compared to those with less education, college-educated parents, particularly mothers, spend more time with their children in developmentally enriching activities such as reading and teaching. Differences in such home activities may at least partially account for the positive link found between parental and, in particular, mother's education and the cognitive development of preschool children.

There is also reason to believe that the long-term effects of college via the intergenerational legacy also extend to the attitudes and values parents pass along to their children. Ample evidence indicates that successive generations and cohorts of students are increasingly more liberal in their social, political, religious, and sexual attitudes and values. These generational shifts are, of course, highly correlated with increases in average educational attainment levels over the past half-century. Thus, it would appear that as children are raised by successively better-educated generations of parents who have themselves increased to varying degrees in social and political tolerance, humanitarianism, and sense of civic responsibility, the children's attendance at college leads to even greater differences relative to grandparents and great-grandparents. The long-term trend of these intergenerational legacies appears to be not only toward greater socioeconomic security and well-being but also toward greater cognitive growth and openness, tolerance, and concern for human rights and liberties.

. . .

Conditional Effects of College

Despite many undoubtedly sincere statements in the postsecondary education literature about the need to respect individual student differences, relatively little attention has been paid to the assessment of conditional effects—changes that are differentially related to the interaction of students' characteristics and either the duration or nature of the collegiate experience. To be sure, there are isolated exceptions to this conclusion, for example, in research on instructional methods. By and large, however, the research has been more interested in assessing the average impact of various college experiences on all students than in determining whether different college environments or experiences have different effects on different kinds of students.

The presence of conditional effects is most pronounced in two areas of research on college impact: learning and cognitive development and the socioeconomic outcomes of college. (See Table 30.) In the area of learning and cognitive development there is reasonably strong evidence that certain kinds of students benefit more from one instructional approach than another. For example, instructional approach may interact with student personality traits. Students high in need for independent achievement or internal locus of control appear to learn more when instruction stresses independence, self-direction, and participation. Conversely, students high in the need for conforming or dependent achievement or external locus of control appear to benefit more from more highly structured, teacher-directed instructional formats.

Table 15
Summary of Estimated *Long-Term* Effects of College: *Intergenerational Effects*

Outcome	Strength of Evidence	Direction of Effect	Major Rival Explanations Controlled	Magnitude of Net Effect
Educational attainment of children	Strong	Positive	Family income, intelligence, aspirations, race, gender	Unclear[a] effect may be both direct and indirect and is probably small
Occupational status	Moderate	Positive	Family income, intelligence, aspirations, race, gender	Unclear; effect is probably indirect and small
Daughters entering male-dominated occupations	Moderate	Positive	Family income, academic achievement, aspirations, race	Unclear; effect is probably indirect and small
Earnings of children	Moderate	Positive	Family income, academic achievement, aspirations, race, gender	Unclear; direct effects mixed; effect is probably indirect and small

[a]"Unclear," as used in this table, means we are acknowledging that the studies do not allow such estimates or that the evidence, though generally consistent, is still sufficiently complex to make an estimate of effect size hazardous.

It seems reasonable that other types of instruction may also interact with individual student personality traits. Here the emerging work of Perry and colleagues with remedial instructional interventions, such as attributional retraining, shows considerable promise (Perry & Dickens, 1984; Perry & Magnusson, 1987; Perry & Penner, 1984; Perry & Tunna, 1988).

There is additional evidence to suggest that instruction interacts not only with personality but also with the student's level of cognitive development. For example, instruction stressing inductive learning based on concrete activities (learning-cycle or inquiry approach) appears to have its most pronounced benefits on the development of abstract reasoning for students functioning at initially lower (concrete) levels of reasoning.

What may be most important is not the findings we have to date but rather what they suggest. We should fully expect that individual student differences will moderate the effects of college instruction. Not all students will benefit equally from the same classroom settings and instructional approaches. A more comprehensive mapping of these interactions between student traits and the instructional process may allow for a more precise and effective application of different instructional approaches.

In terms of socioeconomic outcomes, perhaps the clearest set of conditional effects concerns race. Unfortunately, the analyses are largely limited to male samples, but it would appear that in terms of occupational status, nonwhite or black men derive somewhat greater relative benefits from a bachelor's degree than do white men. The evidence on earnings is less consistent but suggests that since about 1970 nonwhite or black men may also be receiving somewhat greater relative benefits from a bachelor's degree than are their white counterparts.

Gender effects are less clear and for private economic rate of return may depend on race. Of all groups, nonwhite women appear to receive the greatest economic return on investment from a bachelor's degree. In terms of incremental effects on earnings, a bachelor's degree is probably more valuable to a woman than to a man. What men and women major in during college can also have a differential impact on early occupational status. For example, women are less likely than men to major in the natural sciences or technical fields (for example, engineering), but they receive incrementally greater occupational status benefits from doing so than do their male counterparts.

What is perhaps most seductive about the conditional effects of college based on race and gender is that college appears to function in a compensatory manner. That is, it confers incrementally different socioeconomic benefits in a manner that should produce greater racial and gender equality. What should be kept in mind, however, is that the groups who would benefit most from obtaining a bachelor's degree (racial and ethnic minorities) or from majoring in scientific or technical fields (women) are at a distinct disadvantage when it comes to doing either. Thus, while the benefits may be greater, the chances of obtaining them are smaller.

A note of caution is in order here. As indicated by the above conclusions, our reading of the evidence suggests that replicable conditional effects involving gender and race are largely limited to socioeconomic outcomes. This in no way precludes the possibility, even the likelihood, that there may be significant gender or racial differences in the processes of intellectual and personal maturation. Our synthesis, however, was concerned with a different question: specifically, whether or not the magnitude of the impact of college on intellectual and personal maturation varies for gender or racial groups. We found little in the way of replicable evidence to indicate that this is the case.

A final set of conditional effects concerns the influence of college selectivity on various indexes of career attainment. Although the general effect of college selectivity on occupational status is quite small and perhaps trivial, there is reasonably consistent evidence that selectivity matters for occupational status in professional careers but may be of questionable value for business or managerial careers. Consistent with this evidence is the finding that good undergraduate grades have a more positive impact on entry into professional careers (for example, medicine and law) if they were earned at selective rather than at less selective institutions. Thus, part of the explanation for why college selectivity has trivial or at best small effects on overall occupational prestige and career mobility is that its impact is of greater consequence in some career paths than in others.

A similar conditional effect is that the positive net impact of college selectivity on earnings is stronger for men from relatively high family socioeconomic backgrounds (managerial, profes-

Table 30
Summary of Estimated *Conditional* College Effects

Outcome	Strength of Evidence	Direction of Effect	Major Rival Explanations Controlled	Magnitude of Net Effect
Effects Conditional on Student Characteristics				
Learning	Moderate	Students high in need for independent achievement or internal locus of control do better in courses stressing self direction and independent learning; students with high need for conforming or dependent achievement or external locus of control do better in structured, teacher-directed courses	Results based on randomized experiments	Moderate
Cognitive development (formal reasoning)	Weak	Less-advanced reasoners benefit more from learning-cycle or inquiry approach to instruction; students advance most via instuctional methods matched to their reasoning level	Initial level of formal reasoning	Unclear[a]
Occupational status	Strong	Nonwhite males derive greater benefits than whites from a bachelor's degree; women derive greater benefits than men from majoring in natural science and technical fields	Socioeconomic status, intelligence, educational aspirations, grades, occupational aspirations	Unclear
Earnings	Strong	Since about 1970, black and other nonwhite men have derived greater relative earnings benefits from a bachelor's degree than have white men; women derive greater relative earnings benefits than men from each year of college completed and from a bachelor's degree	Socioeconomic status, academic ability, place of residence, years of work experience	Moderate to substantial
Private rate of return	Moderate	White men enjoy somewhat higher private economic rate of return on a bachelor's degree than do nonwhite (primarily black) men, but this gap may be closing; black and other nonwhite women have a higher rate of return on a bachelor's degree than do white women	Unclear	Moderate
Effects Conditional on Institutional Characteristics				
Occupational status	Moderate	College selectivity may have stronger positive impact or occupational status in professional careers than in nonprofessional careers	Socioeconomic status, secondary school achievement, occupational aspirations, race	Small; effect may be both direct and indirect through educational attainment
Earnings	Moderate	College selectivity may have stronger positive impact on earnings for men from relatively high family socioeconomic backgrounds than for men from relatively low family socioeconomic backgrounds	Socioeconomic status, educational attainment, occupational status, race	Small

[a]"Unclear," as used in this table, means we are acknowledging that the studies do not allow such estimates or that the evidence, though generally consistent, is still sufficiently complex to make an estimate of effect size hazardous.

sional) than for men from lower socioeconomic origins (blue-collar). Such a finding suggests that attendance at a selective college may be part of the process of cumulative advantage in American society. Students from advantaged social backgrounds are not only more likely to attend elite undergraduate colleges than their counterparts from less advantaged social origins; they may also be more likely to convert the status conferred by such an institution into greater economic success.

Some Final Thoughts

When asked why he robbed banks, Willie Sutton, the notorious bank robber, is. reputed to have replied: "Because that's where the money is." In developing this synthesis we have gone "where the evidence is," and that evidence is not without some bias. It is based almost exclusively on samples of traditional college students who are age eighteen to twenty-two, who attend four-year institutions fulltime, and who live on campus. It has also tended to focus on nonminority students, although there have been some recent major exceptions to this. The research methodologies have almost exclusively been quantitative and positivistic in their orientation.

If there is a major future direction for research on the impact of college, it will be to focus on that growing proportion of students whom we have typically classified as nontraditional, although they are rapidly becoming the majority participants in the American postsecondary system. These include minority and older students, those who commute to college and quite likely work part- or fulltime, and those who attend college part time. Some of our most cherished notions about the determinants of impact may have little relevance to these students. Indeed, we may need to revise our traditional ideas about what the impact of college really means for nontraditional students. Specifying the effects of college for the vast numbers of nontraditional students who now populate American postsecondary education may be the single most important area of research on college impacts in the next decade. In mounting such a research effort, it may be necessary to be particularly sensitive to the impressive diversity of students classified as nontraditional. For example, in a national study of older students, Lenning and Hanson (1977) found that the category "older student" masks great variability in many individual traits and motivations that might well determine in what ways and to what extent postsecondary education will exert an influence on these students. Failure to take such diversity into account when studying the impact of college on nontraditional students could easily produce trivial or inconsistent general effects that mask important conditional effects.

The positivistic, quantitative paradigm has served us well. The vast preponderance of what we know about the impact of college has been learned from this approach to inquiry. Yet although the broad framework is in place, there is still much important fine-grained work to be done. We suspect that the most informative future research on the impact of college must take a number of directions.

First, greater attention needs to be given to the rigorous examination of net college effects. The drop in the volume of relevant research when one moves from studies of change *during* college to studies of change *due to* college is striking and a source of some concern. Current claims about the benefits of college attendance frequently extend well beyond the empirical evidence to support them. Controlling the numerous alternative, noncollege sources of influence can be a daunting undertaking. It will require greater use of noncollege control groups, more specific theories, and more extensive use of relevant theories in the design of studies. Such careful theoretical preparation and grounding is not one of the distinctive characteristics of most of the research done over the past two decades, but higher education as a field of inquiry has clearly started down that road, and we wish to encourage its continuation. Theory-based research will not only be more sharply focused and parsimonious but is also likely to reflect more fully the complexity of college impacts.

Second and relatedly, researchers need to make greater efforts to estimate the *magnitudes* of college's net effects. While it may be meaningful to report simply whether an independent variable is related to a dependent variable at some level of statistical significance, it is much more meaningful, as well as theoretically and practically more informative, also to estimate the strength of that relation. Many of the studies we reviewed failed to report even the most basic information (for example, means *and* standard deviations) that might be used to estimate effect sizes. Reporting estimated effect size can reasonably be expected to lead to theories that are more parsimonious and better reflect the reality of college impact, and to substantially improve the effective allocation of scarce resources to programs intended to enhance desired institutional impacts on student outcomes.

Third, greater attention in the preparation of research studies needs to be given to bodies of theory and evidence in fields not always reflected in past and present studies. This need is particularly acute in studies of students' noncognitive, psychosocial changes. Psychological paradigms have dominated this area of study over the past twenty years, although important inroads and contributions have been made by scholars trained as sociologists and anthropologists. An alarming number of studies reflect little familiarity with the knowledge base outside the author's main disciplinary paradigm. Whether many of the observed changes are due to developmental, psychosocial restructuring within students or to the learning, through the socialization process, of competencies, attitudes, values, and behaviors valued by important others remains very much an open and vital question.

Fourth, future theory-based research should consider indirect as well as direct effects. As much of the evidence we have reviewed suggests, it is entirely possible that we may be underestimating or even misrepresenting the impact of many college influences by failing to consider their indirect effects. Because some source of influence in the causal chain is one step removed from having a direct effect on a given outcome makes it no less theoretically or practically important. Indeed, its consideration may add substantially to our knowledge of educational effects. Of course, any consideration of indirect effects means that one must typically conceptualize research questions in terms of theoretical models; but such a process is likely to reflect the complexity of college impacts more fully.

A fifth direction for future research is to focus on conditional effects. We found few replicable conditional effects in the body of evidence. This is probably because such effects have not been assessed either routinely or consistently rather than because they do not exist. We still strongly suspect that students' individual characteristics frequently mediate the impact of college; not all students benefit equally from the same experience. If certain experiences are indeed shown to be especially beneficial for particular kinds of students, it may be possible to craft more developmentally specific and effective programs and policies.

Sixth, more attention needs to be given to the analysis of the *timing* of change during the college experience. Most studies of change focus on the freshman year or on freshman-senior differences. Only a handful of studies have monitored change on an annual, sequential basis. Thus, we know little about whether change is mostly linear and monotonic or primarily episodic and discontinuous over the college years. Moreover, it seems reasonable to suggest (and there is some basis for believing) that the pacing of change varies across outcomes areas. Designing maximally effective educational interventions requires knowing *when* an intervention will make a difference and when it will not.

A seventh important direction of future research on college impact should be a greater dependence on naturalistic and qualitative methodologies. When employed judiciously, such approaches are capable of providing greater sensitivity to many of the subtle and fine-grained complexities of college impact than more traditional quantitative approaches. Naturalistic inquiries may be particularly sensitive to the detection of the kinds of indirect and conditional effects just discussed. We anticipate that in the next decade important contributions to our understanding of college impact will be yielded by naturalistic investigations.

While there are a number of topics on which important research remains to be done, one in particular stands out as a significant focus for future inquiry. This is the impact of the academic program and the teaching-learning process. How do different teaching and instructional approaches influence not only how much content is learned but also what higher-order thinking skills are developed? How and in what ways does the academic program influence values and personal change? Are there particular teaching or instructional approaches that are differentially effective for different kinds of students? What is the connection between the intellectual competencies acquired through the academic experience and those required in one's career? Answers to these and similar questions would constitute a major contribution to our understanding of the impact of college.

College Outcomes and Student Development: Filling the Gaps

FRANCES K. STAGE

Dr. Russell, a newly hired assistant professor, is asked to develop a course on student development theory and research. The course should contain a segment on special student populations. In addition, because the class will be mostly masters' students, it should touch on practical application. Her most recent administrative position was associate dean for academic affairs at a university of 18,000 students, where her primary responsibility was to research student admissions and retention, track students within college, and follow the graduates. It has been six years since Russell earned her doctorate, and she does not want to rely on the syllabus from the class she took eight years ago.

Her colleague passes along a syllabus from a course on "The College Student" being taught in a similar program. Flipping to the bibliography, Russell is surprised to recognize few authors. From the list of Gilligan, Perry, King, Kitchener, Kegan, Astin, and Chickering, only a few seem familiar. The names she expects—Tinto, Pascarella, Cross, Bean, Pace are not there.

Realizing that the literature in which she has immersed herself for the past several years might have been "incomplete," she begins to reeducate herself. Again she is dismayed to discover that only a few of the readings mention the special populations whose problems she is to address in her class. She searches for more but finds only scattered articles, for the most part descriptive.

Finally, although Russell finds a few examples of a particular theory being implemented in very specific settings, she finds few "process models" to help her use a particular theory in more general circumstances.

In the past two decades, a great deal of research has focused on the college student. A shift from atheoretical to theoretical studies of college outcomes (satisfaction, progress, persistence, etc.) and the subsequent testing of those theories have spurred research on the topics. Additionally, a change of focus in the student affairs profession has sparked research on the nature of students and how they develop in college. However, I find gaps between these two bodies of research; if filled, they could provide broader insights into the college student experience.

Since the early seventies, colleges have gradually relinquished the *in loco parentis* role. Professionals have become less concerned with controlling and limiting student behavior and more concerned with enabling and fostering student development. This shift has led to further exploration of college student development. Additionally, institutional concerns with enrollment and retention have inspired research on student progress and satisfaction.

These relatively recent shifts in focus have yielded seemingly endless knowledge about the college student and the college process. With so much information on the topic, constructing a curriculum to inform practitioners might seem easy. However, closer examination of this literature brings some troublesome observations:

1. There are actually two separate literatures on the college student (sociological and psychological) and few clear links to meaningfully synthesize both the outcomes and the development literature.

2. Much college-student literature is monocultural, focusing on white upper- and middle-class students at large residential research universities. Such research does little to inform us about students at nontraditional institutions or about the multicultural populations on most campuses.

3. Too few process models tie directly to specific theory and can be used to guide practice on college campuses.

I will discuss each of these observations in turn and offer some recommendations for researchers and those attempting to incorporate theory in practice.

Two Separate Literatures

Most research on college students is based either on sociology or on psychology. In general, those of us who study student outcomes view the college-going process at the macro level and tend to take a sociological approach in our research. We study students in large aggregates and place them in broad demographic classifications. We assess how these broadly defined groups of students react to their environment and attempt to determine how these variables relate to such outcomes as academic achievement, satisfaction, and persistence.

On the other hand, those of us who study the development of college students view the college-going process at more of a micro level and tend to take more of a psychological approach in our research. We may use one of many student development theories to identify developmental levels or tasks of the students being studied. Usually, as researchers, we seek to link the theoretical development of students to specific kinds of campus experiences or activities.

Unfortunately, there is little current overlap in these two literatures. The research on student outcomes seeks to determine which aspects of college life can have positive influences on satisfaction, career choice, persistence, and grade point average. On the other hand, the student development research focuses on the students' development as college students and on what can be done to foster further development.

A few early, ambitious, and well-known studies conceptually and methodologically linked student psychological characteristics with sociological experiences and outcomes (Astin 1968; Feldman and Newcomb 1973). However, since the development of causal models in the study of college students, possible connections between these two bodies of literature have been weak and, for the most part, remain unexplored (Stage 1988).

Student Development Research

Theories and research that focus on student development are, for the most part, psychologically based and provide a rich body of information for faculty as well as student affairs practitioners. The most widely used student development theories can be classified into three major families: cognitive theory, psychosocial theory, and typology theory.

Cognitive development theorists like Kohlberg, Gilligan, Perry, King, Kitchener, and Kegan focus on how students reason when faced with decisions (e.g., what thoughts guide a decision about career choice?). Generally, these theories delineate stages in a hierarchy of reasoning with higher levels representing broader, more sophisticated ways of making meaning of the world. Researchers exploring these theories tend to focus on classifying individuals into stages and determining what causes movement from one stage to another.

The psychosocial theorists include Chickering, Heath, Levinson, and Sheehy. They are more interested in the content or the developmental tasks with which students are dealing (e.g., is the student working on establishing autonomy or on establishing identity?). Researchers operating within these frameworks attempt to identify issues and to explain how such issues are resolved.

Both cognitive development theorists and psychosocial theorists believe that development results from an "optimal mismatch." That is, if a student feels challenged by a situation but also receives sufficient support to meet that challenge, he or she will likely develop. If the challenge is too great, if there is insufficient support, or if there is no challenge, development is unlikely.

Finally, typology theorists include Clark-Trow, Astin, Pace, Holland, and Myers-Briggs. These theorists focus on characteristics of the individual and of the environment, and the fit or lack of fit (interaction) between these two constructs (e.g., is the student an academic type or more of a social type?). Researchers using these theoretical frameworks may use physical, sociological, or perceptual measures of the campus environment. They contrast these measures with measures of a student's needs, personality, or sociological type, or perception of the ideal campus environment to identify discrepancies. These discrepancies then may explain lack of performance, dissatisfaction, or attrition.

As these theories became widely tested, replicated, and understood, researchers as well as college administrators began to recognize and appreciate their value in studying and dealing with college students. Currently these theories form the basis for most research on the development of the college student.

The Student Outcomes Research

During the past fifty years, much of the research in higher education focused on the study of such student outcomes as grade point average (GPA), persistence, intellectual achievement, change of major, and satisfaction with many aspects of the college environment (Ewell 1985; Pace 1984). The field of outcomes research, though not new, has changed radically in the last decade. Before the 1970s, researchers had explored the relationship of many individual variables (gender, socioeconomic status, religion, etc.) to any given outcome (grades, satisfaction, persistence, etc.). Only a few researchers attempted to tie characteristics, attitudes, experiences, and achievements together conceptually (Astin 1968; Feldman and Newcomb 1973). More recently, theorists developed models which provided structure and direction to subsequent research (Bean 1980; Ethington and Wolfle 1986; Pascarella and Staver 1985; Tinto 1975).

Theorists no longer view achievement and satisfaction as simple phenomena that can be predicted from a few easily gathered variables (Pace 1984). Rather, they now view these outcomes as constellations of characteristics, attitudes, experiences, and subsequent changes in attitudes which can be depicted graphically. Studies conducted within the scope of the new theoretical frameworks have been replicated and modified so that we can now speak with greater confidence about a few consistent positive influences on persistence, grades, and satisfaction. Important environmental and experiential influences include the residence of the student, the perceived intellectual atmosphere of the campus, contacts with faculty members, perceived value of their education, and academic satisfaction (Tinto 1987). Student aspirations and attitudes about the importance of the college experience also help shape positive college outcomes (Astin 1985).

Despite the general coalescence of knowledge on the topic, a satisfactory explanation of outcomes eludes researchers. They cannot predict with assurance the success or failure, satisfaction or dissatisfaction, persistence or attrition of a student with certain background characteristics and attitudes, studying in a certain environment, and participating at a particular level of campus experiences. Researchers can advise administrators on strategies to promote positive outcomes, but large segments of the population go unaided by such recommendations. Outcomes phenomena seem to be complex webs of interaction that differ from student to student.

Any practitioner attempting to use these two bodies of research to incorporate theory in practice would find little guidance. Marcia Mentkowski and Arthur Chickering (1988) describe several possibilities for such study, but to date only a few recent researchers have begun to explore such links empirically (Pascarella 1987; Stage in press). In contrast, most of us seem to assume that students at widely differing levels of intellectual development will respond similarly to influences of the campus environment. Or we assume that students of widely differing psychosocial types are influenced positively or negatively by similar experiences. So rather than attempting to use developmental or psychosocial types to categorize students for analysis, we use only easily obtained demographic indicators. This method directly contradicts research based on student development theory, which tells us that students of differing psychological makeup respond in various ways to the same environmental stimulations.

A Monocultural Literature

Typically, research conducted on college students focuses on the majority, middle- to upper-middle-class students attending a residential university. However, large segments of the population are not majority, and increasing numbers of students commute to and from home. Some work has been done to let us know who these students are, and strategies have been developed to help them negotiate a college campus that may seem alien to them.

Unfortunately, most of the psychologically based student development theory is founded in studies of the mainstream college student. Little research has focused on the development of students outside the mainstream culture, although these are frequently the students who need the most help in negotiating a culturally different environment (Manning and Stage 1988).

Fortunately, the sociologically based outcomes research has begun to focus on some of these special populations (Fox 1986; Healy, Mitchell, and Mourton 1987; Pascarella, Smart, and Nettles 1987; Richardson and Bender 1987; Wolfle 1985). As positive as these nascent efforts are, some populations of students (e.g., the learning disabled, homosexuals, native Americans) are not easily identified nor numerous enough to be included in research currently being conducted. For these particular populations, qualitative approaches are probably needed.

Process Models for Practice

Identifying process models to help apply theory to research can prove frustrating. Only a few good process models link research and practice. Donald Blocher (1987) describes three basic types of conceptual frameworks in the counseling profession. First are the basic philosophical assumptions derived from global and abstract representations of human experience. They are empirically untestable but help professionals clarify their values. Second are the scientific theories focusing on and guiding empirical inquiry. And third are the process models, which serve as a guide for those attempting to implement theory.

Blocher described process models as cognitive maps that provide a direct and immediate guide for implementation and specify appropriate action in a given situation. Such models should be evaluated in terms of outcomes. Also important, they should be constantly polished and modified as experience provides more knowledge about their practical usefulness.

Several multidimensional process models are useful to guide the development of the college student. The COSPA II cube focuses on differing clientele, roles, and competencies. Similarly, the Colorado State University cube focuses on target, purpose, and method of intervention (see Rodgers 1980). An administrator attempting to solve a campus problem may refer to the Kuh (1984) cube, which requires the identification of disciplinary perspective, intervention theory, and student affairs function. The behavior engineering model (Gilbert 1978) focuses on the interplay between environmental supports and an individual's behavior in three categories: information, instrumentation, and motivation.

These models have provided rich fodder for those who study student development and student affairs organizations. They have also guided many administrators who are informed and sophisticated enough to choose a theory to fit their particular issue. Unfortunately, many of those who work with college students have just begun to explore student development and outcomes. Models with a wide range of possible options might not provide enough guidance for those with limited experience and insight.

At the other extreme, the literature is replete with idiosyncratic articles that discuss implementation of a particular theory at a particular institution with a particular set of problems. Such articles are too specific and do not help identify and match implementation strategies to wider environmental and institutional conditions.

Less-experienced practitioners may need process models as defined by Donald Blocher (1987) that outline in a general way how to implement a specific theory and include guides for appraisal, action, and evaluation. Carole Widick and Deborah Simpson (1978) provide an excellent example of the Perry model applied to the college classroom. Similar models focusing on other aspects of the college experience would be useful.

Recommendations

In the midst of these discoveries and complex conditions, Professor Russell, who had thought she would be spending most of her first semester exploring and developing new research ideas, found herself spending more time than she wanted developing her course. Fortunately, her efforts provided several options toward which to direct energy and research.

For each of the three problem areas, Professor Russell identified a solution to the short-term problem (information for the class) as well as the long-term problem (focus of research).

Two Separate Literatures

She drew from both bodies of literature in her course on development of the college student. College students generally do not develop where there are no positive outcomes. Those who work with students need to learn which aspects of the campus environment have positive effects on achievement, persistence, and satisfaction. Russell made sure her class read both bodies of research, drew parallels between them, and identified gaps in information.

As a researcher, Russell began to fill in the gap between the two literatures. For example, using student development theory to inform outcomes research, she studied predictors of changes in majors according to John Holland's (1985) framework. She hypothesized that satisfactory campus experiences might be rooted in different activities for an artistic type than for a social type.

Similarly, outcomes research guided a study of student development; possibly studies of developmental growth of students underestimated the importance of peer influences. Russell designed a study to explore the effects of peer pressure on cognitive development of college students.

The Monocultural Literature

To find readings for the class on students outside the mainstream culture, Russell supplemented higher education readings with those from other disciplines. Since the middle seventies, much counseling literature has focused on the problems counseling professionals have in dealing with those who are culturally different from themselves. Those cross-cultural perspectives provided rich resources to better understand students. Psychology, anthropology, and political science also provided insight into the difficulties inherent in negotiating a culturally foreign system and the effects those adjustments might have on student satisfaction and motivation.

Another possibility for Russell was research on the development of particular student populations. Because there were too few nonmajority students to conduct the quantitative multivariable research traditionally used to predict outcomes, Russell had to shift her research style and "tool up" for a naturalistic study.

Process Models

Russell required students to read the "how we do it" articles as well as the broader, less directive process models. With a firm knowledge of a specific development theory, the class developed its own process models. Linking "scientific theory" to actual practice provided students with a sense of satisfaction and professionalism as well as a more thorough knowledge of the theory being studied.

This third problem presented Russell with a third possibility for research. She began to develop and polish a process model for her "favorite" student development theory. She designed the model to provide more direction for new professionals as well as for older professionals who had trouble applying theory in their daily practice.

Conclusion

We can learn from Russell's experiences. First, we can pay more attention to one another as researchers. It is tempting to focus our attention on those who are testing similar frameworks, operating within the same paradigm, and speaking our language. Unfortunately, this limited focus stifles creativity and reinforces narrow notions of research rather than encouraging us to explore new directions.

Second, research and researchers must be flexible. It is easier to use the same populations, types of variables, and modes of analysis than it is to expand our repertoires. Unfortunately, these self-limiting practices do little to enlarge our knowledge of the development and outcomes we study. To accommodate the nonmainstream students' experiences, which presumably differ from the majority students', we must use more open-ended ways of collecting information. Researchers may need to adopt more of a cultural perspective and focus at first on small numbers of students. Considering a broader range of situations and experiences may lead to new models of development and satisfaction.

Finally, we must work to develop process models with tangible links to practice. These models will enable professionals to use the knowledge that researchers are generating.

Bibliography

Astin, Alexander. *Achieving Educational Excellence.* San Francisco: Jossey-Bass, 1985.

_____. *The College Environment.* Washington, D.C.: American Council on Education, 1968.

Bean, John. "Dropouts and Turnover: The Synthesis and Test of a Causal Model of Student Attrition." *Research in Higher Education* 12, no. 2 (1980): 155–87.

Blocher, Donald. "On the Uses and Misuses of the Term 'Theory.'" *Journal of Counseling and Development* 66 (October 1987): 67–68.

Ethington, Corinna, and Lee Wolfle. "A Structural Model of Mathematics Achievement for Men and Women." *American Educational Research Journal* 23 (Spring 1986): 69–75.

Ewell, Peter, ed. *Assessing Educational Outcomes.* New Directions for Institutional Research, No. 47. San Francisco: Jossey-Bass, 1985.

Feldman, Kenneth, and Theodore Newcomb. *The Impact of College on Students.* San Francisco: Jossey-Bass, 1973.

Fox, Richard. "Application of a Conceptual Model of College Withdrawal to Disadvantaged Students." *American Educational Research Journal* 23 (Fall 1986): 415–24.

Gilbert, Thomas. *Human Competence: Engineering Worthy Performance.* New York: McGraw-Hill, 1978.

Healy, Charles, Judith Mitchell, and Don Mourton. "Age and Grade Differences in Career Development among Community College Students." *Review of Higher Education* 10 (Spring 1987): 247-58.

Holland, John. *Making Vocational Choices: A Theory of Vocational Personalities and Work Environments.* Englewood Cliffs, N.J.: Prentice-Hall, 1986.

Kuh, George. "A Framework for Understanding Student Affairs Work." *Journal of College Student Personnel* 25 (January 1984): 25–38.

Manning, Kathleen, and Frances K. Stage. "Personalizing the College Context from a Cultural Perspective." Paper presented at the Annual Meeting of the National Association of Student Personnel Administrators, St. Louis, Missouri, March 1988. Copy in my possession.

Mentkowski, Marcia, and Arthur Chickering. "Linking Educators and Researchers in Setting a Research Agenda for Undergraduate Education." *Review of Higher Education* 1 (Winter 1987): 137–40.

Pace, Robert. "Historical Perspectives on Student Outcomes: Assessment with Implications for the Future." *NASPA Journal* 22 (Fall 1984): 10–18.

Pascarella, Ernest. "The Development of Critical Thinking: Does College Make a Difference?" *Journal of College Student Development* 30, no. 1 (January 1989): 19–26.

Pascarella, Ernest, John Smart, and Michael Nettles. "The Influence of College on Self-concept: A Consideration of Race and Gender Differences." *American Educational Research Journal* 24 (Spring 1987): 49–77.

Pascarella, Ernest, and J. R. Staver. "The Influence of On-campus Work in Science on Science Career Choice in College: A Causal Modeling Approach." *Review of Higher Education* 8 (Spring 1985): 229–45.

Richardson, Richard, and Louis Bender. *Fostering Minority Access and Achievement in Higher Education.* San Francisco: Jossey-Bass, 1987.

Rodgers, Robert. "Theories Underlying Student Development. In *Student Development in Higher Education,* edited by Don Creamer. Cincinnati: ACPA Media, 1980.

Stage, Frances K. "Motivation, Academic and Social Integration, and the Early Dropout." *American Educational Research Journal,* in press.

_____. "Student Typologies and the Study of College Outcomes." *Review of Higher Education* 11 (Spring 1988): 247–57.

Tinto, Vincent. "Dropout from Higher Education: A Theoretical Synthesis of Recent Research." *Review of Educational Research* 45 (Winter 1975): 89–125.

_____. *Leaving College: Rethinking the Causes and Cures of Student Attrition.* Chicago: University of Chicago Press, 1987.

Widick, Carole, and Deborah Simpson. "Developmental Concepts in College Instruction." In *Encouraging Development in College Students,* edited by Clyde Parker. Minneapolis: University of Minnesota Press, 1978.

Wolfle, Lee. "Postsecondary Educational Attainment among Whites and Blacks." *American Educational Research Journal* 22 (Winter 1985): 501–25.

An Anthropological Analysis of Student Participation in College

William G. Tierney

The fundamental factor that keeps Indians and non-Indians from communicating is that they are speaking about two entirely different perceptions of the world.

Vine Deloria, Jr., *The Metaphysics of Modem Existence*

In this article I take issue with Tinto's widely accepted theoretical model that views college participation as if it were a "rite of passage" where academic and social integration is essential for student persistence. First, I argue that Tinto has misinterpreted the anthropological notions of ritual, and in doing so he has created a theoretical construct with practical implications that hold potentially harmful consequences for racial and ethnic minorities. I critique the epistemological argument Tinto has articulated—that of social integration—from a cultural perspective informed by critical theory [11, 12, 13, 14, 36]. That is, I take a social constructionist view of reality and I operate from the perspective that the purpose of our theoretical models is not merely to describe the world, but to change it.

I then highlight the practical or "real world" implications of a social integrationist stance by deconstructing the discourse of two college administrators who were part of a two year investigation pertaining to the college-going patterns of American Indian college students [36]. The administrators describe how they perceived Native American students' attendance at their institutions. The assumption here is that the ideas and discourse that speakers utilize influence the actions that occur on their campuses. And in large part, those actions and policies have been ineffectual in stemming the tide of minority student departure in general, and Native American leave-taking, in particular. I conclude by suggesting that rather than think about student participation from a social integrationist perspective, an alternative model is to conceive of universities as multicultural entities where difference is highlighted and celebrated. Accordingly, if we want our colleges and universities to be multicultural we need theoretical models different from those of the social integrationists, which in turn will call for different assumptions about reality and what must be done to engage college students.

A caveat is in order. This is an essay in the root sense of the word—a trial of some ideas. By taking issue with a theorist's notions or deconstructing the words of an individual one runs the risk of painting heroes and villains, of encasing one theory as morally wrong and another as politically correct. The argument here, however, is neither to canonize one discourse over another nor to accentuate the foibles of any administrator. Rather, the article seeks to provoke dialogue by taking issue with some of the most commonly held perceptions we currently have about college life, about students, and about how we think about cultural difference in order to develop more culturally responsive ways to engage minority students.

Perspectives on College Participation: Theory

Tinto's model and rituals of integration. Over the last twenty years a variety of researchers have sought to understand why some students leave college and others remain [1, 4, 28]. Indeed, one could argue that student departure has been the central focus of higher education research. In general, much of this research has tried to delineate different causal variables that might plausibly lead to the retention of students. The search for an understanding about why students leave college is not merely of theoretical interest; if a model may be built that explains student departure then it may be possible for colleges to retain students. The successful retention of students offers at least three benefits: the student will be able to reap the rewards that a college degree affords, the college or university will be able to maintain the income that derives from the student's attendance, and society will be able to utilize the skills of students in becoming more productive. Clearly, it is to everyone's benefit to come to terms with why students leave college.

Such a concern is particularly germane in a discussion about minority student achievement. Researchers have long documented the underrepresentation of racial and ethnic minorities in academe. For the purpose of this article we may add that American Indian involvement in postsecondary institutions is of particular concern. Although researchers differ about the precise percentages of Native Americans who attend college, everyone is in agreement about gross averages, and those averages highlight problems throughout the academic pipeline. If one hundred students are in ninth grade, about sixty of them will graduate from high school, and about twenty will enter academe. Of those twenty students only about three will eventually receive a four-year degree [36].

Researchers have been able to discover that certain characteristics in a student's background help or deflect one's persistence in college. For example, we have learned that if a student's parents have gone to college, the student is more likely to attend and to graduate from college than a student whose parents did not go to a postsecondary institution. We know that an individual whose brothers or sisters have attended college is more likely to persist in college than the young man or woman whose siblings have not participated in college. We know that someone who has had an academic track in high school is more likely to attend a four-year college than someone who has pursued a vocational track.

We also have learned a great deal about gross characteristics that pertain to race and class. As noted, an individual who is white is more likely to go to college than someone who is African American or Native American. Someone whose parents earn over $40,000 a year is more likely to attend a four-year institution than someone whose parents are on welfare. Although each of these pieces of information may have helped researchers in predicting the success of students, such individualistic characteristics have stymied researchers in their search for a general causal model of student participation. In turn, minority student participation in academe has remained problematic.

Vincent Tinto has developed a theoretical model that takes into account the individualistic pieces of information such as those reported above but he has done so in a manner that is comprehensive rather than particularistic [38, 39, 40]. That is, Tinto has sought to explain why students leave college by calling upon a framework that incorporates factors such as family income or student background. He has utilized such information not as ends in themselves but to develop a general theory of student participation as opposed to an individualistic analysis of why one or another student is likely to attend and eventually graduate.

In doing so, Tinto has worked in the tradition of other researchers, such as Spady [28, 29], by asking two central questions: (1) what are those bonding mechanisms that integrate students into the life of the institution, and (2) how might postsecondary institutions and students be theoretically conceived? A significant number of researchers have accepted Tinto's basic formula and have returned to testing specific variables to see whether the model holds up under scrutiny when different characteristics are analyzed. As Stage has noted, "Today few would question that students' commitment, academic integration, and social integration are crucial to their academic success" [32, p. 250].

Following Spady, Tinto developed his model by calling upon the work of two prominent social theorists of the early twentieth century— Emile Durkheim and Arnold Van Gennep. Durkheim, considered by many to be the father of modern sociology, posited that the degree to which an individual was integrated into the fabric of societal institutions lessened the likelihood that someone experienced anomie. In turn, the less one experienced anomie the less likely it was that the individual would commit suicide. Thus, by manipulating a variety of characteristics drawn from data about European countries, Durkheim showed how married Italian Catholics in tightly knit families in small towns, for example, were less likely to commit suicide than unmarried urban Protestant Englishmen [10].

Van Gennep was an anthropologist who studied tribal societies; in particular he investigated "rites de passage" [42]. Rites of passage in a particular culture were rituals designed to move individuals from one developmental stage to another. These rituals took place throughout an individual's life. The most obvious rites of passage in tribal societies occurred for young men and women when they were to assume the mantle of adulthood. Although the actual rituals differed dramatically from culture to culture both in act and duration, Van Gennep argued that all cultures had rituals that functioned in similar fashion. In effect, as a functionalist, Van Gennep believed that rituals were a crucial mechanism necessary to every tribal society. Without such rituals the developmental patterns necessary for society's maintenance would be destroyed and the culture would not survive.

Tinto has suggested that we ought to think of colleges in light of Durkheim's and Van Gennep's work. Following Durkheim, Tinto argues that to the degree participants are integrated into the institution's fabric, the greater likelihood exists that the individual will not develop a sense of anomie, and will not commit "suicide" by leaving the institution. In effect, a college is an institution designed as a rite of passage that functions in much the same manner as ritualized institutions in other societies. Postsecondary institutions serve as functional vehicles for incorporating the young into society by way of their integration into the college or university.

Tinto is the first to acknowledge that his model is not perfect. Adult students, for example, may not necessarily fit the schema that he has outlined. Tinto also has been most vocal about redirecting how researchers think of college departure so that we no longer conceive of student leave-taking by using a pejorative term such as "dropping out," because the student may well return at another point in time. Nevertheless, Tinto's model also holds up well when one thinks of different populations. Traditionally aged students are more likely to graduate than contraditionally aged populations. A residential institution that has an active social life is more likely to have a higher retention rate than urban commuter institutions. Full-time students have a greater likelihood of graduating from a four-year institution than do part-time students. On one level each of these facts gives credence to Tinto's formula: to the extent that institutions function as societal rites of passage and to the degree that individuals are bonded and integrated into the life of the institution, the more likely it is that students will persist and graduate.

Presently, most work has been in a similar vein; as noted, researchers have utilized different variables to test whether Tinto's model holds [7, 20]. Unfortunately, those individuals who have undertaken such studies implicitly have agreed with the epistemological foundations from which Tinto has worked. To his considerable credit, Tinto has developed a conceptual model that calls for investigation and analysis at the foundational level rather than simply at the causal level. Instead of merely accepting the scaffolding upon which he has built his theory, researchers need to interrogate the assumptions of that scaffolding. I turn now to one such possible interpretation and interrogation. A discussion of the foundations of social integration will highlight some essential dilemmas when considered from an anthropological perspective.

An anthropological analysis of Tinto's *model.* As I discuss Tinto's model, it is helpful to keep in mind racial and ethnic minorities such as American Indians who attend mainstream institutions. Social integrationists assert that all individuals—regardless of race, class or gender—must undergo a "rite of passage" in order to achieve full development in society. The assumption is that a uniform set of values and attitudes remain in an institution and that it is the individual's task to adapt to the system. The problems with such a view, however, are fourfold. Two problems pertain to (a) a misinterpretation of the cultural definition of ritual, and two problems concern (b) an overreliance on an integrative framework.

Culture and rituals. Consider the differences between Van Gennep's and Tinto's use of the term "ritual." When Van Gennep wrote about rites of passage he spoke of rituals within a specific culture. The Maori of New Zealand or the Arunta of Australia had rituals that initiated the young into society. The Ndembu of Africa had puberty rites for girls and rituals of manhood for boys [A1]. The same point, however, cannot be made of Tinto's rituals that occur in American colleges and universities. An American Indian who sets foot on a mainstream campus undergoes a disruptive cultural experience not because college is a rite of passage, but because the institution is culturally distinct from the Indian youth's own culture. When Van Gennep developed his functionalist theory, he never anticipated that it would be used to explain one culture's ritual to initiate a member of another culture.

The first problem, then, with social integrationist theory is that it borrows an anthropological term—ritual—yet extracts the term from its cultural foundations. One cannot speak of ritual without first considering the cultural contexts in which that ritual is embedded. In the case of American higher education we find that colleges and universities reflect the culture of the dominant society. In America, that dominant culture is white.

To be sure, organizations such as traditionally black institutions or tribally controlled colleges exist in the United States, but of necessity these institutions also incorporate the dominant mores of American society simply by having to meet accreditation requirements, utilizing faculty who come from mainstream institutions and the like [36]. Institutions such as tribal colleges are under perhaps the greatest pressure to conform, given the serious financial constraints in which they must operate; these institutions garner most of their income from a federal law which stipulates that they meet specified standards [21, 22]. To assume that colleges and universities do not reflect the culture of mainstream society is to overlook the crucial importance of the sociocultural contexts surrounding postsecondary organizations. Simply stated, higher education's institutions have histories and current contexts that help determine their ideology and culture. Up until very recently in American higher education colleges and universities were designed to educate a clientele that was overwhelmingly composed of white males who came from the middle and upper classes.

Although critics may certainly argue with a cultural analysis of postsecondary institutions, one is hard pressed to do so while at the same time utilizing as a central concept the cultural idea of a rite of passage. In short, if social integrationists are to employ an anthropological term, such as a ritual, then of necessity they must take into account the cultures in which those rituals exist. If one does so with regard to Tinto's model, one finds that he has developed an analytic tool that is dysfunctional: individuals from one culture, such as Apache, are to undergo a ritual in another culture, such as Anglo.

A second conceptual problem with the utilization of a ritual in academe pertains to the assumption of one's leave-taking from such a ritual. In traditional cultures rites of passage do not have notions such as "departure," "failure," or "dropout." Choice does not exist about whether to undergo the ritual; one simply partakes of it. As noted, Tinto has accurately pointed out that the use of a term such as "dropout" has negative connotations, and he has argued that one should instead use the term "departure" because it is value-neutral. He has assumed, however, that departure is normal. "It seems unlikely that we will be able to greatly reduce dropouts," he has noted [39, p. 695]. Along a similar line, he added:

> There is much to be said for a system of education that serves to distinguish between those with the competence or interest, motivation, and drive to finish given courses of study, and those who, for a variety of reasons do not or simply will not seek to complete their programs [39, p. 695].

Although a term such as "departure" may well appear to be value-neutral to those who use the term, what social integrationists overlook is that concepts such as "departure" "dropout" or "failure" are all cultural constructs. Tinto assumes that for one reason or another some students will choose not to participate in a rite of passage and other students will not complete the ritual.

Yet when one considers rituals in traditional cultures we find that an initiate neither chooses to participate nor to leave the ritual. The anthropologists, George and Louise Spindler, are helpful in explaining how the Arunta of Australia conceive of initiation rituals:

> Despite the onerous nature of the initiation, . . . all of the young initiates survive the ordeal and are dedicated to seeing that the next class of initiates gets the same treatment. All of the initiates succeed, none fail. . . . To fail would mean at least that one could not be an Arunta, and usually this must mean death as well, but not death at the hands of another, but social death. . . . The whole operation of the initiation school is managed to produce success. To fail to initiate the young successfully is unthinkable. The continuity of culture would be broken and the society would disintegrate. There are no dropouts [30, p. 10].

Nor are there "departers." To be sure, someone may die in a "rite of passage," but the essential point here is that in traditional societies individuals do not have the option to leave their group as students do who attend a college or university. What Tinto again has failed to do is to investigate the cultural context of the anthropological term "ritual ' and in turn, how the language of student participation is a cultural construction. He has assumed that student departure is a universal concept rather than a cultural category developed by the society that utilizes the ritual. Dropouts exist in modern American schools and colleges; the term is absent from Arunta vocabulary as well as any number of other tribal societies. The language used to think and talk about students is a cultural construct. Failure exists in postsecondary institutions before students are admitted, enrolled, or take classes. Failure, or leave-taking, or departure, does not come in the door when students enter. Human discourse and action are cultural categories; to come to terms with these categories one must investigate the categories themselves rather than assume that actions such as leaving college are natural and universal.

Individuals and integration. The third and fourth anthropological problems with Tinto's model pertain to the Durkheimian reliance on individuals and integration. Tinto has conceptualized college-going at the individualist level rather than a collective one. From a social integrationist perspective individuals attend college, become integrated or not, graduate or depart. Conformity is the norm and it is the responsibility of the individual. Absent from this analysis is any discussion about the cultural formations of groups. Social integrationists assume that culture exists at a meta level—all cultures are similar and the institution merely reflects the culture of society. Indeed, Tinto's book *Leaving College* emphasizes the "roots of individual departure" and a "theory of individual departure." From an anthropological standpoint to emphasize "individual" at the expense of the "group" or the "culture" is backwards. Indeed, Native American authors such as Badwound [3], Benally [5], McNeley [19], Padilla* and Pavel [24] and Wright and Tierney* [44] have effectively argued that the importance of tribal culture is crucial when thinking about the roots of student departure. Olneck has argued how critical this issue is with regard to minorities in general: "[We] must recognize the identities and claims of groups *as groups* and must facilitate, or at least symbolically represent and legitimate collective identity" [23, p. 148]. Again, what is particularly odd with regard to Tinto's analysis is that he utilizes anthropological terms in an individualist manner.

Furthermore, Tinto never takes into account, or at least never explains to readers, that he is a "native" studying "native rituals." As a faculty member at a mainstream university he describes processes in which he partakes. The point is not that a native observer's analysis is useless. To the contrary. Native perceptions of the world are essential to understanding that world, but one must necessarily accept that those under standings are provisional, subjective, and never complete. As Edmund Leach has observed, "to understand the word ritual we must take note of the user's background and prejudices" [17, p. 521]. Indeed, in our field of study Attinasi similarly has commented, "What are needed are naturalistic, descriptive studies guided by research perspectives that emphasize the insider's point of view" [2, p. 250].

The need to understand the user's "background and prejudices" reflects the anthropological belief that reality is socially constructed. Individuals and groups do not perceive reality in the same fashion. The researcher must come to terms not only with his or her own preconceived notions of reality and the phenomenon under study but also with those of the individuals who partake in the ritual. Yet Tinto works from a positivist framework where law-like generalizations are possible and the implicit assumptions and beliefs of both the researcher and the researched are irrelevant. Again, one may reject a cultural model that assumes reality is socially constructed, but that cannot be done while at the same time one employs analytical tools that derive from those same cultural models.

Thus, an anthropological analysis of Tinto's model has two overarching concerns. On the one hand, rituals of transition have never been conceptualized as movements from one culture to another. Van Gennep never assumed that a Sioux youth underwent an initiation ritual in Navajo society. Yet Tinto's model assumes that same Sioux youth will undergo a rite of passage in Anglo society. On the other hand, a model of integration that never questions who is to be integrated and how it is to be done assumes an individualist stance of human nature and rejects differences based on categories such as class, race, and gender.

Such concerns bring into question Tinto's overall model; however, this discourse of integration is of particular importance when we consider college participation of underrepresented racial and ethnic groups. As Olneck has observed, the language of integration is, "the voice of white middle-class education professionals speaking about 'problem' groups and about the solutions to the problems posed by diversity" [23, p. 163]. Although Tinto and other like-minded researchers should be applauded for their attempt to shift the burden of blame for dropouts away from the victims, essentially models of integration have the effect of merely inserting minorities into a dominant cultural frame of reference that is transmitted within dominant cultural forms, leaving invisible cultural hierarchies intact [8].

I now turn to an example of how such implicit assumptions get played out at mainstream universities. The data derive from a two-year investigation of Native Americans on college campuses [36]. I undertook case studies at ten campuses and conducted slightly over two hundred interviews. The point of the following section is to analyze the discourse of two individuals in order to underscore how social integrationist notions get enacted.

Perspectives on College Participation: Practice

Defining the problem. At one university the president commented on the problems Native Americans have in college by pointing out: "They have a terrible problem with acculturation. They grow up without competition and when they come here to a university whose ethic is achievement and competition, it's tough." At a second institution a top administrator added, "The major problem is that they have a foot in each culture that draws them back to their roots. They are drawn back to their own culture and it's a difficult transition to make. It's a real problem that's not easy for us to solve."

I offer these comments for two reasons. First, they are commonplace. I consistently heard similar kinds of observations from other individuals. Second, these comments logically accompany the social integrationist position. Following the recent deconstructionist work of Rhoades [25], Rhoades and Slaughter [26], Slaughter [271], and the content analysis of Bensimon [6], Goffman [15], Tannen [33] and Tierney [34], I will attempt here to deconstruct what these individuals have said by breaking apart their sentence structure so that we might contextualize more fully what the comments suggest. How one defines deconstructionism is notoriously contested; for the purposes of this analysis I call upon the work of Johnathan Culler. Culler notes, "Deconstruction emphasizes that discourse, meaning, and reading are historical through and through, produced in processes of contextualization, decontextualization, and recontextualization" [9, p. 129]. Essentially, following Derrida, Culler argues that one comes to "meaning" by interpreting the context in which statements are said, deconstructing those contexts and statements, and then "reconstructing" them. In doing so, a deconstructionist assumes that (I) final interpretation is never achieved, and (2) that reinterpretation is always necessary. Accordingly, I offer one possible interpretation of the speakers' comments.

The first speaker noted:

"They have a terrible problem with acculturation."

The statement defined how the speaker perceived the situation. The group that has the "problem" are American Indians. The problem is acculturation and it is not minor; it is a major problem which the speaker defined as "terrible."

The speaker made this point when asked a "grand tour" open-ended interview question [31], "Tell me about Native American participation on this campus." The speaker's comment presumably points out knowledge he had with regard to Native American recruitment and retention to postsecondary education in general, and to his campus, in particular. Over ninety percent of those American Indian students who enter his university will not receive a degree from the institution. The nature of the problem, then, is that Native Americans need to become acculturated to the university in order to persist. Acculturation to the university presumably implies that the Indian student must learn the ways of the white world.

> "They grow up without competition, and when they come here to a university whose ethic is achievement and competition, it's tough."

The speaker followed his first comment with a consistent line of reasoning. He offered a comparison; Native Americans do not compete and the university is founded on competition. Indeed, a core "ethic" of the university appears to be "competition."

"Achievement" is in some way related to "competition." That is, the assumption of the speaker was that to achieve one must necessarily compete. What one achieves, presumably, is a college degree. Again, drawing upon general and specific data, the speaker knew that Native Americans are not successful; they do not "achieve." The speaker also empathized with American Indians. He recognized the problems they face and pointed out that "it's tough." The speaker, then, assumed that he understood the problems the students face and that these problems are difficult.

The second speaker added:

> "The major problem is that they have a foot in each culture that draws them back to their roots."

This speaker also pointed out that those who have the "problem" are Native Americans, and he believed the same problem existed as the first speaker pointed out. American Indians do not have both feet firmly I planted in the university's soil. Their "roots" are in another culture. The problem, then, is that Native Americans have extensive roots and until they cut those roots, they will not be successful. The speaker also thought that Indian students are involved in two cultures—an Indian culture and an Anglo culture, as experienced at the institution.

> "They are drawn back to their own culture and it s a difficult transition to make."

The individual reiterated his first comment. The Indian culture has a serious pull; it "draws" students "back" rather than pushes them forward. To move from one's own culture to a mainstream university was seen as a "transition" and again, it is a "difficult" or terrible transition to make. To attend a mainstream institution requires that an individual move from one world to another—move from the Native American culture to the Anglo culture. Presumably, such movement propels students forward.

> "It's a real problem that's not easy for us to solve."

The speaker concluded by objectifying American Indian students— they have become the problem—and the realization that the problem is a difficult one. The problem is also "real"; unlike some problems that mask other concerns, the speaker implied that he has been able to define the problem precisely. However, the problem is like a puzzle; the solution will not be easy.

The individuals who will solve the problem were identified as "us." Insofar as the speaker was a senior white male administrator at a mainstream university we can reasonably presume that the problem's solution lies in the hands of similar, white male administrators. At a minimum, the answers will be found by "us"—university administrators—and not "them"—American Indian students.

Analyzing the discourse. The comments of both speakers reinforce the theoretical argument of the social integrationists. As Tinto has pointed out, college is a transition where a student leaves his or her past community. He stated:

> College students are, after all, moving from one community or set of communities, most typically those of the family and local high school, to another, that of the college. Like other persons in the wider society, they too must separate themselves, to some degree, from past associations in order to make the transition to eventual incorporation in the life of the college [38 p. 94].

Thus, social integrationists have hypothesized that success in college is contingent upon an individual's ability to become academically and socially integrated into the life of the institution, a process that in part is predicated on the individual's ability to separate from previous communities. To utilize Tinto's Durkheimian formulation, the implicit assumption is that Native Americans will need to undergo a cultural suicide of sorts to avoid an intellectual suicide.

Because discourse is never fixed and determined, a number of alternative possibilities exists with regard to how one might see minority participation in academe. For example, rather than defining Native Americans as the ones who have the "problem" we might think of the institutions as having the "problem." Indeed, the "problem" might be defined not as a group's lack of "acculturation" but as an institution's inability to operate in a multicultural world. From a Native American perspective a "problem" might be defined as the university's "ethic of achievement and competition" as opposed to an ethic of cooperation and willingness to work together.

Instead of implying that being "drawn back" to one's own culture is a shortcoming, one might accentuate that ripping one away from his or her native culture is detrimental and harmful. Rather than think of college as an abrupt transition from one world to another, we might try to conceptualize college life as reinforcing and incorporating what one has learned from one's extended family.

And, of course, regardless of how one defines a problem, it is possible to think of the "solution" lying not in the hands of the powerful, but in the hands of those who are most centrally involved in the issue. Rather than objectify Native Americans as the problem, one might point out that institutional racism and the mindset of the powerful is the "real problem."

Discussion

My point in this article has been to highlight the conceptual inadequacy of current theories of student participation. I have concentrated on Tinto's research primarily because his work is the most widely accepted and sophisticated analysis we currently have. And as the statements from the college officials highlight, the theoretical formulations of social integrationists do get enacted in the words and actions of college administrators. My assumption here is that theory does inform practice and that many of the recent attempts by college officials pertaining to minority recruitment and retention have utilized researchers' findings in order to solve the "problem." However, the solutions have been inadequate precisely because we are asking the wrong questions.

From the argument advanced in this article, the challenge for researchers is twofold. First, we need to utilize different theoretical models rather than those that insist upon an integrative framework that assume an individualist stance. In effect, Tinto's use of culture as a framework has moved us in the right direction, but he has not gone far enough. Critical and feminist theories are but two examples of the kinds of models we might find useful as we reconceptualize student participation in academe. The recent work of Holland and Eisenhart [16], and others [35, 36, 43] are examples of how such theories may be usefully employed to analyze academe.

The second challenge relates to how decision makers might be able to utilize these more recent theoretical developments. The changes required are not just theoretical; as the examples from the administrators demonstrate, theoretical reconceptualizations also need to influence how individuals act. As McLaughlin has argued, "Many times, critical theorists' calls for transformative leadership and transformative intellectualism amount to obfuscating rhetoric which, in over intellectualizing what is wrong with mainstream school practices without identifying what actually teachers and school administrators can do, simply add to the problem" [18]. Thus, we need to go further by not only delineating the scaffolding for critical or feminist theories and the like but also by suggesting how we might employ such theoretical orientations in the daily operations of our institutions. We need to consider how institutionally sponsored interventions function within the variety of different contexts that exist for different issues such as minority student retention.

I am arguing, then, for a radical reorientation of how we conceptualize and, hence, act in the organizational worlds of academe. The task of conceiving different theoretical horizons will enable us not only to offer alternative strategies for developing multicultural environments, but such horizons also will enable us to reconfigure the social conditions of power that give voice to some and silence others. In doing so, we will be moving away from a model of social integration and assimilation and toward a framework of emancipation and empowerment.

Note

*Not Native American.

References

1. Astin, A. *Four Critical Years: Effects of College on Beliefs, Altitudes, and Knowledge.* San Francisco: Jossey-Bass, 1977.

2. Attinasi, L. C., Jr. "Getting In: Mexican Americans' Perceptions of University Attendance and the Implications for Freshman Year Persistence." *Journal of Higher Education,* 60 (May/June 1989), 247–77.

3. Badwound, E. *Leadership and American Indian Values: The Tribal College Dilemma.* Ph.D. dissertation, The Pennsylvania State University, University Park, 1990.

4. Bean, J. P., and B. S. Metzner. *"A Conceptual Model of Nontraditional Student Attrition.* Paper presented at the annual meeting of the Association for the Study of Higher Education, Chicago, March 1985.

5. Benally, H. "Dine Philosophy of Learning." *Journal of Navajo Education,* 6 (1988), 10–13.

6. Bensimon, E. M. "A Feminist Reinterpretation of Presidents' Definitions of Leadership." *Peabody Journal of Education,* 66 (1989), 143–56.

7. Cabrera, A. F., O. J. Stampen, and W. L. Hansen. "Explaining the Effects of Ability to Pay on Persistence in College." *Review of Higher Education,* 13 (1990), 303-36.

8. Colon, A. "Race Relations on Campus: An Administrative Perspective. *The Racial Crisis in American Higher Education,* edited by P. G. Altbach and K. Lomotey. Albany, N.Y.: State University of New York Press, *1991.*

9. Culler, J. *On Deconstruction: Theory and Criticism after Structuralism.* Ithaca, N.Y.: Cornell University Press, 1982.

10. Durkheim, E. *Suicide.* Trans. J. A. Spaulding and G. Simpson, Glencoe, N.J.: The Free Press, 1951.

11. Fay, B. *Critical Social Science.* Ithaca, N.Y.: Cornell University Press, 1987.

12. Foster, W. "The Administrator as a Transformative Intellectual." *Peabody Journal of Education,* 66 (1989), 5–18.

13. Giroux, H. "Border Pedagogy in the Age of Postmodernism." *Journal of Education,* 170(1988), 162–81.

14. _____. The Politics of Postmodernism." *Journal of Urban and Cultural Studies*, 1 (1990), 5–38.

15. Goffman, E. *Frame Analysis.* New York: Harper and Row, 1974.

16. Holland D. C., and M. A. Eisenhart. *Educated in Romance: Women, Achievement, and College Culture.* Chicago, 111.: The University of Chicago Press, 1990.

17. Leach. E. *International Encyclopedia of the Social Sciences* (vols. 13–14). New York: Macmillan, 1968.

18. McLaughlin, D. "Power and the Politics of Knowledge: Transformative Leadership and Curriculum Development for Minority Language Learners." *Peabody Journal of Education,* 66 (1989), 41–60.

19. McNeley, J. P. "A Navajo Curriculum in the National Context." *Journal of Navajo Life*(1988), 125-36.

20. Nora, A., L. C. Attinasi, Jr., and A. Matonak. Testing Qualitative Indicators of Precollege Factors in Tinto's Attrition Model: A Community College Student Population. *Review of Higher Education,* 13 (1990), 337–55.

21. Olivas, M. A. "Indian, Chicano, and Puerto Rican Colleges: Status and Issues." *Bilingual Review,* 9 (1982) 36–58.

22. _____. "The Tribally Controlled Community College Assistance Act of *1978:* The Failure of Federal Indian Higher Education Policy." *American Indian Law Review,* 9 (1983), 219–51.

23. Olneck, M. R. "The Recurring Dream: Symbolism and Ideology in Intercultural and Multicultural Education. *American Journal of Education,* 98 (1990), 147–74.

24. Padilla, R. V., and M. Pavel. "The Role of Student Advising in Academic Integration." Paper presented at the annual meeting of the American Educational Research Association, San Francisco, March 1989.

25. Rhoades, G. "Calling on the Past: The Quest for the Collegiate Model." *Journal of Higher Education,* 61 (September/ October 1990), 512–34.

26. Rhoades, G., and S. Slaughter. "The Public Interest and Professional Labor: Research Universities." In *Culture and Ideology in Higher Education: Advancing a Critical Agenda,* edited by W. G. Tierney, pp. 187–212. New York: Praeger, 1991.

27. Slaughter, S. "The 'Official' Ideology of Higher Education: Ironies and Inconsistencies." In *Culture and Ideology in Higher Education: Advancing a Critical Agenda,* edited by W. G. Tierney, pp. 59–86. New York: Praeger, 1991.

28. Spady, W. "Dropouts from Higher Education: An Interdisciplinary Review and Synthesis." *Interchange,* 1 (1970), 64–85.

29. _____. "Dropouts from Higher Education: Toward an Empirical Model. *Interchange,* 2 (1971), 38–62.

30. Spindler, G., and L. Spindler. "There Are No Dropouts among the Arunta and Hutterites." In *What do Anthropologists Have to Say about Dropouts?,* edited by H. T. Trueba, G. Spindler, and L. Spindler, pp. 7–15. New York: The Falmer Press, 1989.

31. Spradley, J. P. *The Ethnographic Interview.* New York: Holt, Rinehart, and Winston, 1979.

32. Stage, F. K. Research on College Students: Commonality, Difference and Direction. *Review of Higher Education,* 13 (1990), 249–58.

33. Tannen, D. *You Jutr Don't Understand.* New York: Morrow and Co., 1990.

34. Tierney, W. G. "Governance by Conversation: An Essay on the Structure, Function, and Communicative Codes of a Faculty Senate." *Human Organization,* 42 (1983), 172–77.

35. _____. *Curricular Landscapes, Democratic Vistas: Transformative Leadership in* Higher Education. New York: Praeger, 1989.

36. _____. *Official Encouragement, Institutional Discouragement: Minorities in Academe—The Native American Experience.* Norwood, N.J.: Ablex, 1992.

37. _____. "The College Experience of Native Americans: A Critical Analysis. In *Beyond Silenced Voices: Class, Race and Gender in United States Schools,* edited by L. Weis and M. Fine. Ithaca, N.Y.: SUNY Press, in press.

38. Tinto, V. "Dropout from Higher Education: A Theoretical Synthesis of Recent Research. *Review of Educational Research,* 45 (1975), 89–125.

39. _____. "Limits of Theory and Practice in Student Attrition." *Journal of Higher Education,* 53 (November/December 1982), 687–700.

40. _____ . *Leaving College: Rethinking the Causes and Cures of Student Attrition.* Chicago: The University of Chicago Press, 1987.

41. Turner, V. *The Ritual Process: Structure and Anti-Structure.* Ithaca, N.Y.: Cornell University Press, 1977.

42. Van Gennep, A. *The Rites of Passage.* Trans. M. Vizedon and G. Caffee, Chicago: University of Chicago Press, 1960.

43. Weis, L. *Between Two Worlds.* Boston: Routledge and Kegan Paul, 1985.

44. Wright, B., and W. G. Tierney. "American Indians in Higher Education: A History of Cultural Conflict." *Change,* 23 (March/ April 1991), 11–18.

Additional Readings

As with all such projects, we wished to include articles and chapters that would have taken the book beyond reasonable limitations of length and cost. Instead, we offer a selection of articles that readers might find helpful in their attempts to learn more about the college student experience.

Allen, W. R., & Haniff, N. Z. (1991). Race, gender, and academic performance in U.S. higher education. In W. R. Allen, E. G. Epps, & N. Z. Haniff (Eds.), *College in black and white* (pp. 95–109. Albany, NY: SUNY Press.

Armstrong-West, S., & de la Teja, M. H. (1988). Social and psychological factors affecting the retention of minority students. In M. C. Terrell & D. J. Wright, *From survival to success: Promoting minority student retention* (pp. 25–53). Washington, D.C.: National Association of Student Personnel Administrators.

Astin, A. W. (1993). Effects of involvement. In *What matters in college: Four critical years revisited* (pp. 365–395. San Francisco: Jossey-Bass.

Astin, A. W. (1993). Implications for Education Theory and Practice. In *What matters in college: Four critical years revisited* (pp. 396–437). San Francisco: Jossey-Bass.

Baxter Magolda, M. B. (1990). The impact of the freshman year on epistemological development: Gender differences. *The Review of Higher Education, 13*(3), 259–284.

Dannefer, D. (1984). Adult development and social theory: A paradigmatic reappraisal. *American Sociological Review, 49* (February), 100–116.

Feldman, K. (1994). Introduction to the Transaction edition. In K. A. Feldman & T. M. Newcomb, *The Impact of College on Students.* New Brunswick, NJ: Transaction.

Gilligan, C. (1982). Woman's place in man's life cycle. In *In a different voice: Psychological theory and women's development* (pp. 5–23). Cambridge, MA: Harvard University Press.

Hearn, J. C. (1991). Academic and nonacademic influence on the college destinations of 1980 high school graduates. *Sociology of Education, 64* (July: 158–171).

Jones, W. T. (1990). Perspectives on ethnicity. In L. V. Moore (Ed.), *Evolving theoretical perspectives on students* (New Directions for Student Services, No. 51), (pp. 59–71). San Francisco: Jossey-Bass.

Moore, L. V., & Upcraft, M. L. (1990). Theory in student affairs: Evolving perspectives. In L. Moore (Ed.), *Evolving theoretical perspectives on students* (New Directions in Student Services, No. 51). San Francisco: Jossey-Bass.

Rodgers, R. F. (1990). Recent theories and research underlying student development. In D. C. Creamer & Associates, *College student development: Theory and practice for the 1990s.* Alexandria, VA: American College Personnel Association.

Sedlacek, W. E. (1987). Black students on white campuses: 20 years of research. *Journal of College Student Personnel, 28*(6) 484–495.

Terrell, M. C. (1992). *Diversity, disunity, and campus community.* Washington, DC: National Association of Student Personnel Administrators.

Weidman, J. C. (1989). Undergraduate socialization: A conceptual approach. In J. C. Smart (Ed.), *Higher education: Handbook of theory and research, Vol. 5.* New York: Agathon.